TREASURY OF GREAT
DOG STORIES

EDITED WITH AN INTRODUCTION BY ROGER CARAS

A COLLECTION OF TALES THAT CELEBRATES
MAN'S BEST FRIEND

BRISTOL PARK BOOKS / NEW YORK

Copyright © 1999 by Roger Caras and Martin H. Greenberg

All rights reserved. No part of this work may be reproduced
or transmitted in any form or by any means, electronic or mechanical,
including photocopying, recording, or any information storage and retrieval
system without permission in writing from BBS Publishing Corporation,
252 W. 38th Street, New York, NY 10018

First Bristol Park Books edition published by BBS Publishing Corporation
in 1999.

This edition distributed by:
Bristol Park Books
252 W. 38th Street
NYC, NY 10018

Bristol Park Books is a registered trademark of
Bristol Park Books, Inc.

Library of Congress Catalog Number: 98-73943

ISBN 10: 0-88486-416-2
ISBN 13: 978-0-88486-416-5

Printed in the United States of America

CONTENTS

Contents

CONTENTS

v

Contents

ACKNOWLEDGMENTS

Grateful acknowledgment is made to the following for permission to reprint copyright material:

"Like Cats and Dogs" by Roger Caras. Copyright © 1994 by Roger Caras. Reprinted from *The Cats of Thistle Hill*. Reprinted by permission of the author.

"A Contest Fit for a Queen" by Susan Dunlap. Copyright © 1995 by Susan Dunlap. Reprinted from *Crimes of the Heart*. Reprinted by permission of the author.

"Coyote and Quarter Moon" by Bill Pronzini and Jeffrey Wallmann. Copyright © 1979 by Renown Publications, Inc. First published in *Mike Shayne's Mystery Magazine*. Reprinted by permission of the authors.

"Deaths of Distant Friends" by John Updike. Copyright © 1987 by John Updike. Reprinted from *Trust Me* by John Updike. Reprinted by permission of Alfred A. Knopf, Inc.

"Dispatching Bootsie" by Joyce Harrington. Copyright © 1980 by Joyce Harrington. First published in *Ellery Queen's Mystery Magazine*. Reprinted by permission of the author.

"Dogs" by Ring Lardner. Reprinted with the permission of Scribner, a Division of Simon & Schuster from *First and Last* by Ring Lardner. Copyright © 1934 by Ellis A. Lardner; copyright renewed © 1962 by Ring Lardner, Jr.

"Dogs' Lives" by Michael Bishop. Copyright © 1984 by Michael Bishop. Reprinted from *Close Encounters with the Deity*. Reprinted by permission of the author. First published by *The Missouri Review*.

Acknowledgments

"Good Boy" by Jane M. Lindskold. Copyright © 1993 by Jane M. Lindskold. Reprinted from *Journeys to the Twilight Zone.* Reprinted by permission of the author.

"The Great Escape" by James Herriot. Copyright © 1986 by James Herriot. From *James Herriot's Dog Stories* by James Herriot. Reprinted by permission of St. Martin's Press, Incorporated, and David Higham Associates.

"In the Doghouse" by Orson Scott Card with Jay A. Parry. Copyright © 1990 by Orson Scott Card with Jay A. Parry. Reprinted by permission of the authors.

"Josephine Has Her Day" by James Thurber. Copyright © 1955 by James Thurber. Copyright © renewed 1983 by Helen Thurber and Rosemary A. Thurber. Reprinted by permission of Rosemary A. Thurber and the Barbara Hogensen Agency.

"The Last Dog" by Mike Resnick. Copyright © 1977 by Mike Resnick. Reprinted by permission of the author.

"The Last of the Winnebagos" by Connie Willis. Copyright © 1988 by Connie Willis. First appeared in *Asimov's Science Fiction 1988.* Reprinted by permission of the author.

"Lucifer and Hey-You" by James Michener. From *Creatures of the Kingdom* by James Michener. Copyright © 1993 by James Michener. Reprinted by permission of Random House, Inc.

"A Mess of Skunks" by Farley Mowat. From *The Dog Who Wouldn't Be* by Farley Mowat. Copyright © 1957 by Curtis Publishing Group; Copyright © 1957 by Farley Mowat Ltd. Reprinted by permission of Little, Brown and Company and McClelland & Stewart, Inc. *The Canadian Publishers.*

ACKNOWLEDGMENTS

"Pelt" by Carol Emshwiller. Copyright © 1991 by Carol Emshwiller. Reprinted by permission of the author and Mercury House, San Francisco, CA.

"Penny and Willie" by Bette Pesetsky. Copyright © 1989 by Bette Pesetsky. Reprinted from *Confessions of a Bad Girl and Other Stories.* Reprinted by permission of the author and her agents, Goodman Associates Literary Agency.

"Shaggy Dog" by Margaret Maron. Copyright © 1997 by Margaret Maron. Reprinted from *Funny Bones,* edited by Joan Hess. Reprinted by permission of the author.

"Strange Meets Matilda Jean" by Patrick F. McManus. Copyright © 1991 by Patrick F. McManus. Reprinted from *Real Ponies Don't Go Oink!.* Reprinted by permission of Henry Holt and Company, Inc.

"Winter Dog" by Alistair MacLeod. Copyright © 1986 by Alistair MacLeod. Reprinted from *As Birds Bring Forth the Sun.* Reprinted by permission of McClelland & Stewart, Inc. *The Canadian Publishers.*

"Yellow Journalism" by Dave Barry. Copyright © 1991 by Dave Barry. From *Dave Barry Talks Back* by Dave Barry. Reprinted by permission of Crown Publishers, Inc.

INTRODUCTION

What is it about dogs that inspires the likes of G.K. Chesterton, Rudyard Kipling, Mark Twain, Edith Wharton, and Arthur Conan Doyle to write about them? Add to that notable roster John Updike, James Michener, Ring Lardner, Jack London, and James Thurber, and the mystery deepens. Those are industrial-strength literary talents, and they had the whole wide, wonderful world to attract their pens, but they chose from time to time to wonder about our companion canines.

We are vastly more intelligent than even our smartest dogs yet we share very similar social senses and drives. Our ability to communicate with each other is far more complex than the "language" our dogs can call up from their reserves. Yet we share common needs for affection and all manner of social bonding. Those needs, by the way, involve dogs with dogs, people with people and dogs and people. It is very complex. Somehow, it is profound.

The writers referred to all appear in this book along with a good many others. Writers by definition articulate what their fellow human beings are thinking about. That is what writers do with their art. It is fair to surmise that much of the human race has for the last 150 to 200 centuries wondered about the dogs they had extracted from the genes of the wolf. These writers wrote about what all of these centuries of people pondered. Scientists, artists, and writers have wondered about dogs, as have common men, too.

For it all we don't know how dogs think or what they think. We don't know what they feel although we are now certain that they do both think and feel. A very short time ago, a span measured in only decades, we were certain that they did neither. We know now that they really do have emotions, again something until recently we denied them. There is a problem here, however. We have to borrow words that were created to describe human activities, for we have none custom-made for animal attributes. Is it the same thing when we say our dogs love us, the same as when we say we love each other or we love our dogs? We simply don't know.

One thing is very clear in all of this. We need our dogs, at least most of us do, and our dogs need us. Those of us who don't believe they need dogs are missing the point. They do, but they just don't know it. They have higher blood pressure than they should, and they are running a far higher risk of a heart attack or a stroke than need be the case. The therapy of the canine companion is so well known now that insurance companies are offering, or at least pondering, lower premiums for policy holders with pets. It is all that real.

This collection is about dogs in the minds of some of the most creative writers of recent times. It is about the wonder and the mystery inherent in the fact that two very different species were made for each other and came together between fifteen and twenty thousand years ago and have stayed together through all of that vast time. It is a wonderful series of events held intact with profoundly complicated social glue. Read on and discover this for yourself.

Jane M. Lindskold

GOOD BOY

Running. Eyes on the spinning thing above, hard to keep track of in the growing twilight. Joy in muscles bunching for the leap and snap. Leaping, ground gone from under pads before I hear the approaching car and the boy's shrill cry, "Rover!"

As my teeth close on the plastic, I feel a thud and something breaking in me as a beef bone does in my teeth. There is pain and falling. Then there is nothing.

Next knowing comes slow and hurting. I am on my side; beneath is hard. Sharp bitter scents sting my nose, almost masking the Joey scent, the Mom scent, and one other. The pain and stink helps me to know this one—the hurting man. I try to raise my head to run, but it is too heavy.

I settle for opening my eyes and hear Joey's voice and my name. His voice is happy, but when he comes near I can smell that he has been crying. I want to lick at the tears, but I cannot make my head go up. I whimper instead, and Joey pats me, gently, not touching the side that hurts so much.

"Good boy," he says, over and over. "Good Rover."

There are more words, fast, to the Mom, but I cannot follow. I manage to lick the boy's hand when it comes close and taste salt.

The hurting man pushes the table then and it moves. Scared, I whimper again, louder when the Mom pats me and then takes Joey away. The place the table stops in is brighter and the acrid scent is stronger.

I am not awake, not asleep, but somewhere in both—I smell soap and hear voices, all unfamiliar except for the hurting man's. I feel pressing on my broken side but cannot growl to warn them away. They say the words that Joey says, but not the same.

I tremble. Then a young man comes into this place, holding something carefully. He smells of blood—dog or human? In this place I cannot tell. The hurting man touches me with his thorn hand. I feel the sharp puncture. Then I sleep.

When slow waking comes, I smell dogs and much sickness. Sharp barks and whimpers, some close, some muffled by distance, fill my ears. I don't move for a long time. Then I smell water and am thirsty. More awake, I realize that I am not at home, not in the kitchen on my rug or on Joey's floor. But there is water, tasting of metal from the bowl. I drink.

Looking about, I see bigger and smaller kennels, and in them more dogs than even in the Park on a warm day. Next to me, in one of the big kennels, is a heavily built dog with thick, dark fur. His eyes are light and watch me. I stare back, my hackles rising as I scent him. His scent is wrong, not dog—something like dog but wilder, rougher, dangerous to me. Wolf. And mingled in with the wolf scent is that of a human.

I find that I can roll without so much hurt, so turn to watch this dangerous one, my head resting on my paws. Other of the dogs watch him too, I see, but he watches only me. Much time passes and sleep takes me again.

Waking, I find a man outside of my kennel. The wolf's kennel is empty and the man has light eyes and smells of wolf. I growl and he laughs, an unfriendly sound.

"Good boy. Good Rover."

Then he turns and goes out a door. Behind him, all the dogs join me in furious barking.

People come in time, but none is Joey or the Mom or the Dad. I eat and drink. Stiffly, I go outside and smell many dogs, but no wolf.

I remember sleeping times when I caught the squirrel before it reached the tree and Joey and I ate hot squirrel together. Perhaps the wolf is like the caught squirrel. Unreal.

I forget it all when Joey comes with the Mom. I try to wriggle and romp, but I am yet too stiff and the pain bites sharp. I still my body and bark loudly in greeting instead.

I am too long in the kennel, the lair of the hurting man, before I am free to go home with Joey. The pain is less now, too, so I am happy. At home, the Mom and Dad let me sleep in Joey's room instead of in the kitchen. We are both happy. My rug is on the floor, but when the door is closed, Joey lets me on the bed.

Pain is nearly a memory when cold wakes me one night. I try to curl my tail around my nose and paws, but it does not listen. My belly fur is also not there when I try to nestle my nose into its warmth. Sleepily, I thump at one ear with my hind foot and kick myself hard with a knee into my nose.

My nose? Knee? I awake and try to shake and find myself sitting upright on the foot of Joey's bed. A full moon shines through the window and I am cold because a boy doesn't have any fur.

I want to hide under the bed like I do when the crashing rain gets too loud, but my legs are hinged wrong and I tumble down in a heap and Joey wakes up.

"Rover?"

His voice sounds a bit different, but it is his. I try to wag my tail, but there is not a tail. The moonlight is enough, though, for Joey to see that I am different.

He asks something. Frustrated because I do not know the words, I lie there and hope that he will help me. He says something else. The inflection is curious, not angry or afraid. When he turns on the bedside light, I blink and then I shriek and my voice is a boy's, but I cover my eyes with my hands, instinctive action coming easily. I must guard from the too many colors that the light has revealed. Something in me recognizes them as normal, but I am afraid.

Joey speaks and I hear two words I know, "Rover's collar." It seems to be a question and I hear my tags jingle and feel the warmth of Joey near. His hand is on my shoulder, then on my head fur.

"This is Rover's collar," he says, his voice quiet like he speaks when he does not want the Mom to hear. "Where is Rover?"

I know this phrase, from a game, and I peep out from under my hands. These human eyes sort the colors into shapes and I can see Joey is crouched next to me on the bed. He is looking at my side where, without fur, the fresh scars from my accident are easy to see—pink and red against pale flesh. His face is wrinkled with concern.

"Where is Rover?" he repeats.

I look at him and try to yap, like I would in the game. It comes out funny, but he understands.

"Rover?"

I yap and try to smile; the tongue won't loll out right, but he smiles hesitantly back.

"Rover?"

He says too many words, too fast; all I know is "boy." He waits, when I cannot answer, he sighs and says "Good boy" and awkwardly pats me.

I cannot tell if he is afraid—this human nose is dead to all but heavy scents, but he does not run. Instead he reaches for the cloth he keeps with his slippers. He fits my paws through the cloth and ties it around me. I am almost as warm as if I had fur and when he comes close, I lick his face. He giggles and puts the slippers on my feet.

"Good boy," he says, "Slippers. Robe. Collar."

I know most of the words and am content.

He gets up, "Stay, boy. Stay, Rover."

4

He leaves the room, carefully closing the door. I stay and look about. I find that, as with color, if I let my human senses work I am less afraid. I can see and even hear fairly well. Smell is gone, but there is color.

My nose itches and my hand moves to scratch it. The motion reveals my fingers to me and I play with them—absorbed in discovering how they move, picking up and dropping one of the slippers, wishing I did not have to "Stay" because I wanted my ball.

Joey comes back when the moon has moved only a little. He carries a paper bag which is bulging full. Happy, I leap off of the bed, stumbling only a little.

"Stay, boy," he cautions softly and I freeze, glad for the moment to test my balance and new orientation.

Joey closes the door and pushes his desk chair against it. When he walks over to me, I realize that we are nearly the same height, though he is still the taller. I look into his light eyes and tremble when I remember the wolf, but Joey comforts me.

"Good Rover. Sit."

I try, and manage to lower myself halfway. Joey laughs softly and untangles my legs so that I am comfortable.

"I said 'sit,' not hunker," he chuckles.

I don't know all the words, but his tone is comforting. Since I can't thump my tail on the floor, I try smiling again. It works easier without the tongue and Joey smiles back.

Joey digs into his bag, pulling out many things. Most are people things, but he has brought my ball and something that even the human nose can tell is roast beef.

I whine.

"Quiet, boy," Joey orders. Then he places the ball in my hand and holds out a slice of roast beef.

I have trouble snatching the treat, but he feeds it to me.

"Stay, Rover. Sit. Quiet."

I sit and play with the ball. Fingers are better than mouth for this—boy mouth won't open enough and the head is too high.

Joey plays with the things from his bag. One thing flashes and makes a noise. Another leaves my finger pads dirty. Joey puts soap and water on them. He looks out the window at the moon a lot and says some words that I don't know.

We eat roast beef.

Joey is excited. I realize this from the noises that he makes, but it is night and finally he gets sleepy. The moon is almost gone when he buries his toys in the bag and buries the bag under the bed.

Then he takes away the slippers and the "robe" and puts the leash on my collar.

"Up, boy," he says, pointing to the bed and I jump clumsily up, "Good boy. Stay."

He puts a blanket on me and I am warm and tired. Joey yawns and, still holding the leash, gets under his blankets and turns out the lights.

"Good night, Rover."

I can't thump my tail, so I smile. Before I fall asleep I think I see pale eyes at the window, but I am too tired and too full of roast beef to care. Besides, Joey is there and already asleep.

When morning comes, I am a dog and I shake happily. Joey wakes up, too. Sometimes he goes away all day, but since it got warm he hasn't. Now that it is warm, we go to the Park or for Walks. I like this.

The Mom and the Dad leave and the Mrs. Peters comes soon. She guards the house and moves things. Joey likes her so I do, too, even if her voice is high and she talks to me in a different voice than she uses for anyone else.

While Joey eats, I go outside. Running in the yard on legs that work, I suddenly catch a scent that makes my hackles rise. The man/wolf scent. It starts by the gate from the alley and goes to Joey's window. I growl and pee all over the scent, scratching dirt to make it go away.

Mrs. Peters shrieks at me, scolding, so Joey takes me to the Park. I chase a stick and swim in the Pond, almost forgetting the night before. Joey plays with me. He calls me "boy" a lot and laughs.

A few times, I smell the man/wolf scent and stop to destroy it, leaving my mark over the stranger's.

Days pass and get warmer. I remain a dog. Joey teaches me to find things when he hides them: ball, stick, slippers, robe, shoe, bone, newspaper. I can remember many things, so he teaches me the names of hiding

6

places: closet, garage, Joey's room, kitchen. The Mom, the Dad, the Mrs. Peters are very pleased. They call me "good boy" and "clever dog."

The moon gets fuller in the sky. In my sleep I chase gray squirrels under green trees and swim with Joey in blue water. Sometimes I am a dog. Sometimes I am a boy. Sometimes a wolf with yellow eyes watches me. Sometimes it is a man with yellow eyes who watches. Always when I see him, I am afraid.

As the moon gets fuller, Joey gets more excited. When it is full, I can feel it below the horizon even when the day is still bright and hot. Joey knows, too—he is wise. He is yawning before full dark comes, but he does not smell tired. The Mom and the Dad smile at us when we go to Joey's room and Joey makes noises as if he is going to sleep.

They smell tired and something else—I do not think that they will leave their room tonight. I feel relieved, as if I had dug a hole and Mrs. Peters did not find it. Becoming a boy may be worse than digging a hole. I don't know.

Joey has buried many things in his room. He takes them out and lines them up. We get sleepy and I think we must sleep because when I next notice I am a boy, the same as before I think when I raise my hand and sniff it. Joey's blue eyes are wide and he laughs with excitement—reaching out and touching my collar.

"Oh, Rover!" He hugs me, "Oh, boy!"

I shiver and try to bark, but it doesn't work well. Joey lets me go.

"Quiet, boy," he warns. Then he gets the robe and the slippers and helps me put them on, "Here, boy."

I come when he calls and go to where he stands in front of a dresser. The colors make people who move on the wall. Two boys. One is Joey—light golden hair tumbling into blue eyes. One has the robe and my collar; his hair is brown, so are his eyes. I shake and the boy shakes and the tags on my collar jingle.

Confused, I whine and Joey pats me. He goes to the bed and climbs on.

"Here, Rover," he says, "Up!"

I try, but the bed is unsteady and I fall. Joey laughs, not unkindly.

"Easy, boy. Sit."

I do. It is easier this time. I remember how it is done. I smile. We eat ham and Joey shows me things and says the words. Some I know. Others are new. But I remember easier—color helps and boy seems to do this like dog makes history from smells.

Some things I do not like and will not touch. These are metal and their shine seems like a menacing scent. Joey calls them "silver." I want to bury them.

We play this way until I get tired. Then Joey shows me more about fingers and feet. We are playing catch with something like a ball that Joey calls a "nerf" when a tap startles us both.

Joey darts to the door, but I have heard better and growl as I look at the window where two pairs of yellow eyes reflect back the light.

Joey turns at my growl and sees the eyes and I do not need scent to know that he is afraid. My guard dog soul sparks and I get between Joey and the strangers, my growls roughing my throat.

I cannot smell man/wolf, but the hands that remove the screen and then push up the window are not human like Joey's and mine. They are covered with fur and the fingers end in heavy claws. As soon as the window is open a bit, a gray and black wolf leaps in, more easily than I could, even as a dog.

I start to lunge forward, but Joey's hand grabs my collar. I feel him trembling, but his grip is strong.

"No, boy. Stay." The rest of his words mean nothing to me, but his tone is firm.

The window opens enough to let in a man. Or is it a wolf? I am confused. He walks almost like a man, but he has heavy fur and his teeth are fangs. His eyes are the yellow of a wolf.

Joey has let go of my collar and now he runs to his toys. He picks up a silver knife—I had not liked it before—and holds it before him.

"Stay," he tells the wolf and the man/wolf. There are more words. I only know "silver" and "knife," but I can hear the threat in his tone even though he keeps his voice low. I growl.

The intruders sit and stay.

I am proud of Joey. For lack of a tail I smile, but I do not stop growling, though my boy throat hurts. I move to stand in front of Joey—away from the silver.

Man Wolf speaks to Joey. I know "boy," "dog," "silver," "Rover." Joey answers. I understand "Joey," "knife," "silver." There are many words I do not know. They talk for a long time. I glare at the wolf who stretches lazily on Joey's floor. His pose is not one of threat. In fact, I detect only alertness and amusement.

The talking stops and Joey says, motioning to his right side, "Rover, sit."

I am hesitant, but he sits on the floor, putting the knife in front of him. Man Wolf sits, too.

"Sit, Rover," Joey repeats.

Reluctantly, I obey. Then Man Wolf extends one of his hairy hands toward Joey who takes it in his left, his right hand hovering over the knife.

Man Wolf holds his other hand to me and says, "Shake, Rover."

Almost by reflex, I obey, resting my boy's hand in his rough-furred grasp.

"Good boy," Joey says, and I hear the words twice, once with my ears and once, somehow, through Man Wolf's hand.

I growl and would fold my ears back, but they do not fold. Man Wolf tightens his grip on my hand and speaks and, though my ears know only a few of the words, what comes through his hand is as clear as the scent of a squirrel run across wet grass or bat song at twilight. I stiffen and listen.

"Good, Rover. You obey Joey wonderfully."

I growl softly and Joey laughs happily.

"I understood that, Rover. Obedience and agreement aren't the same things. Still, I think you need to hear what Mr. Lobo has to say."

Man Wolf—or Mr. Lobo—smiles, his fangs shiny in the moonlight, "Briefly, then, Rover, when the car hit you you were bleeding inside. The doctors at the ASPCA emergency clinic needed a source of fresh blood to keep you alive while you were made well."

"A transfusion," Joey says, nodding.

"Yes, but keep the words simple, Joey. I'm afraid telepathic translation works best with basic concepts."

"Sorry." Joey sounds shamed and I growl.

"Yes, Rover, I understand. I won't hurt Joey. Now, as I was saying, because German shepherds (like you are most of the time) are big dogs, they need lots of blood. The easiest dog available was a big mix-breed (or so they thought) who had just been brought in and was still in a squeeze cage for his routine medical exam. Unfortunately, the dog was actually my friend, Clyde, over there—who has a rampant case of lycanthropy."

"Clyde?" Joey giggles and the wolf growls, thumping his tail playfully to take the edge off his ire.

Mr. Lobo shakes his head ruefully, the emotion translated through his hold on my hand, "Yes, Clyde. Well, as I've already told Joey, the lycanthropy made you, Rover, into a boy."

"Why not a wolf?" I wonder, wishing that I had the words, but Mr. Lobo understands.

"Because a dog, especially a German shepherd, is still awfully close to a wolf, I'd guess. But, honestly, I don't know. How old are you, Rover?"

I blink, puzzled, but Joey knows the answer.

"He's about eighteen months."

"Then that's why he's a boy, not a man, like Clyde is when he's not a wolf. I had wondered how the virus designed the human form. An eighteen-month-old dog is about equal to an eight- or nine-year-old boy."

"I though it was seven years to one," Joey comments, "Wouldn't that make him closer to ten?"

"That formula is a bit outdated, especially with modern canine health care. If Rover gets a balanced diet and his shots regularly, you'll extend this vital period. Still, you're, what, fourteen?"

"In October," Joey agrees.

"Before Rover is three his human form will be older than yours."

"Oh," Joey becomes thoughtful.

I am rapidly discovering that translation doesn't help much, but since Joey doesn't seem scared I mentally thump my tail and wait for them to make sense.

"Well, you know the story now, Joey. Your dog will turn into a human, once, sometimes twice a month. As you may have discovered, his lycanthropy will make him brighter than normal—and as long as you are patient this will be a bonus. But if you're not, he'll have a greater tendency toward boredom. He may even become aggressive because of it."

Joey waits, sensing more is coming. I wait, too, suddenly apprehensive again.

Mr. Lobo sighs, "You've kept Rover's lycanthropy hidden so far, but it will get more difficult. What if he changes on a winter night when the moon may be visible for twelve or more hours? How do you conceal that? What if your parents walk in and find a man sleeping buff naked on the foot of your bed? Or if the neighbors are watching the dog while your family is away?"

His words come as pictures to me and I begin to shiver. Joey pats my leg with his free hand.

"Easy, boy. Good dog." His words are soft, but his blue eyes stay on Mr. Lobo, "What do you want?"

"Give us Rover, Joey. Clyde and I are both respectable businessmen with country houses. I was born with lycanthropy. (That's why I can manage a halfway shape and a couple of other tricks. They come with practice.) We'll understand and protect Rover, even when you can't. And you can visit him, of course."

I stiffen, a whine escaping. Absently, Joey pats me, but I can feel his thoughts are on Mr. Lobo's promises of safe, green pastures.

"Like I told you before, Mr. Lobo, I sort of guessed what must have happened the first time. I've seen horror films and, I mean, Occam's Razor and all. This kid had to be Rover; he couldn't be anyone else. But to check, I took pictures and showed them around. Nobody had ever seen that kid. I can see what he's going to face, so if he wants to go—I'll let him. Okay, boy?"

He looks at me, "You understand, Rover. These people can keep you safe in a place with lots of squirrels to chase. If you stay here with me, honest, I don't know what Mom and Dad will say if they learn. So, you do what you want and I'll come and see you. Okay, good boy?"

I can see the options, feel Joey's emotions bittersweet, but there is no real choice.

My lips shape their first words, "Rover, stay."

Joey throws his arms around me, sobbing with joy, squashing my tags into my soft boy's chest. Mr. Lobo and Clyde stand.

"I'll get in touch when the moon has waned a bit," Mr. Lobo promises, while Clyde wags his tail, "You're going to need help—but hopefully this'll be a unique situation."

Then the lycanthropes leave by the window, stopping to wave as they open the gate and step out into the shadows.

Joey hugs me again, "Oh, good boy. Such a good dog."

Clumsily, I hug him back and then, dissatisfied, lick him sloppily across one salty cheek.

G. K. Chesterton

THE ORACLE
OF THE DOG

"Yes," said Father Brown, "I always like a dog so long as he isn't spelt backwards."

Those who are quick in talking are not always quick in listening. Sometimes even their brilliancy produces a sort of stupidity. Father Brown's friend and companion was a young man with a stream of ideas and stories, an enthusiastic young man named Fiennes, with eager blue eyes and blond hair that seemed to be brushed back, not merely with a hairbrush, but with the wind of the world as he rushed through it. But he stopped in the torrent of his talk in a momentary bewilderment before he saw the priest's very simple meaning.

"You mean that people make too much of them?" he said. "Well, I don't know. They're marvellous creatures. Sometimes I think they know a lot more than we do."

Father Brown said nothing, but continued to stroke the head of the big retriever in a half-abstracted but apparently soothing fashion.

"Why," said Fiennes, warming again to his monologue, "there was a dog in the case I've come to see you about; what they call the 'Invisible Murder Case,' you know. It's a strange story, but from my point of view the dog is about the strangest thing in it. Of course, there's the mystery of the crime itself, and how old Druce can have been killed by somebody else when he was all alone in the summer house—"

The hand stroking the dog stopped for a moment in its rhythmic movement; and Father Brown said calmly, "Oh, it was a summer house, was it?"

"I thought you'd read all about it in the papers," answered Fiennes. "Stop a minute; I believe I've got a cutting that will give you all the particulars." He produced a strip of newspaper from his pocket and handed it to the priest, who began to read it, holding it close to his blinking eyes with one hand while the other continued its half-conscious caress of the dog. It looked like the parable of a man not letting his right hand know what his left hand did.

Many mystery stories, about men murdered behind locked doors and windows, and murderers escaping without means of entrance and exit, have come true in the course of the extraordinary events at Cranston on the coast of Yorkshire, where Colonel Druce was found stabbed from behind by a dagger that has entirely disappeared from the scene, and apparently even from the neighbourhood.

The summer house in which he died was indeed accessible at one entrance, the ordinary doorway which looked down the central walk of the garden towards the house. But by a combination of events almost to be called a coincidence, it appears that both the path and the entrance were watched during the crucial time, and there is a chain of witnesses who confirm each other. The summer house stands at the extreme end of the garden, where there is no exit or entrance of any kind. The central garden path is a lane between two ranks of tall delphiniums, planted so close that any stray step off the path would leave its traces; and both path and plants run right up to the very mouth of the summer house, so that no straying from the straight path could fail to be observed, and no other mode of entrance can be imagined.

Patrick Floyd, secretary of the murdered man, testified that he had been in a position to overlook the whole garden from the time when Colonel Druce last appeared alive in the doorway to the time when he was found dead; as he, Floyd, had been on the top of a stepladder clipping the garden hedge. Janet Druce, the dead man's daughter, confirmed this, saying that she had sat on the terrace of the house throughout that time and had seen Floyd at his work. Touching some part of the time, this is again supported by Donald Druce, her brother, who overlooked the garden standing at his bedroom window in his dressing gown, for he had risen late. Lastly the account is consistent with that given by Dr. Valentine, a neighbour, who called for a time to talk with Miss Druce on the terrace, and by the colonel's solicitor, Mr. Aubrey Traill, who was apparently the last to see the murdered man alive—presumably with the exception of the murderer.

All are agreed that the course of events was as follows: about half past three in the afternoon, Miss Druce went down the path to ask her father when he would like tea; but he said he did not want any and was waiting to see Traill, his lawyer, who was to be sent to him in the summer house. The girl then came away and met Traill coming down the path; she directed him to her father and he went in as directed. About half an hour afterwards he came out again, the colonel coming with him to the door and showing himself to all appearance in health and even high spirits. He had been somewhat annoyed earlier in the day by his son's irregular hours, but seemed to recover his temper in a perfectly normal fashion, and had been rather markedly genial in receiving other visitors, including two of his nephews who came over for the day. But as these were out walking during the whole period of the tragedy, they had no evidence to give. It is said, indeed, that the colonel was not on very good terms with Dr. Valentine, but that gentleman only had a brief interview with the daughter of the house, to whom he is supposed to be paying serious attentions.

Traill, the solicitor, says he left the colonel entirely alone in the summer house, and this is confirmed by Floyd's bird's-eye view of the garden, which showed nobody else passing the only entrance. Ten minutes later Miss Druce again went down the garden and had not reached the end of the path when she saw her father, who was conspicuous by his white linen coat, lying in a heap on the floor. She uttered a scream which brought others to the spot, and on entering the place they found the colonel lying dead beside his basket-chair, which was also upset. Dr. Valentine, who was still in the immediate neighbourhood, testified that the wound was made by some sort of stiletto, entering under the shoulder blade and piercing the heart. The police have searched the neighbourhood for such a weapon, but no trace of it can be found.

"So Colonel Druce wore a white coat, did he?" said Father Brown as he put down the paper.

"Trick he learnt in the tropics," replied Fiennes with some wonder. "He'd had some queer adventures there, by his own account; and I fancy his dislike of Valentine was connected with the doctor coming from the tropics too. But it's all an infernal puzzle. The account there is pretty accurate; I didn't see the tragedy, in the sense of the discovery; I was out walking with the young nephews and the dog—the dog I wanted to tell you about. But I saw the stage set for it as described: the straight lane between the blue flowers right up to the dark entrance, and the lawyer going down it in his blacks and his silk hat, and the red head of the secretary showing high above the green hedge as he worked on it with his shears. Nobody could have mistaken that red head at any distance; and if people say they saw it there all the time, you may be sure they did. This red-haired secretary Floyd is quite a character: breathless, bounding sort of fellow, always doing everybody's work as he was doing the gardener's. I think he is an American; he's certainly got the American way of life; what they call the viewpoint, bless 'em."

"What about the lawyer?" asked Father Brown.

There was a silence and then Fiennes spoke quite slowly for him. "Traill struck me as a singular man. In his fine black clothes he was almost foppish, yet you can hardly call him fashionable. For he wore a pair of long, luxuriant black whiskers such as haven't been seen since Victorian times. He had rather a fine grave face and a fine grave manner, but every now and then he seemed to remember to smile. And when he showed his white teeth he seemed to lose a little of his dignity and there was something faintly fawning about him. It may have been only embarrassment, for he would also fidget with his cravat and his tiepin, which were at once handsome and unusual, like himself. If I could think of anybody—but what's the good, when the whole thing's impossible? Nobody knows who did it. Nobody knows how it could be done. At least there's only one exception I'd make, and that's why I really mentioned the whole thing. The dog knows."

Father Brown sighed and then said absently, "You were there as a friend of young Donald, weren't you? He didn't go on your walk with you?"

"No," replied Fiennes, smiling. "The young scoundrel had gone to bed that morning and got up that afternoon. I went with his cousins, two young officers from India, and our conversation was trivial enough. I remember the elder, whose name I think is Herbert Druce and who is an authority on horse breeding, talked about nothing but a mare he had bought and the moral character of the man who sold her; while his brother Harry seemed to be brooding on his bad luck at Monte Carlo. I only mention it to show you, in the light of what happened on our walk, that there was nothing psychic about us. The dog was the only mystic in our company."

"What sort of a dog was he?" asked the priest.

"Same breed as that one," answered Fiennes. "That's what started me off on the story, your saying you didn't believe in believing in a dog. He's a big black retriever named Nox, and a suggestive name too; for I think what he did a darker mystery than the murder. You know Druce's house and garden are by the sea; we walked about a mile from it along the sands and then turned back, going the other way. We passed a rather curious rock called the Rock of Fortune, famous in the neighbourhood because it's one of those examples of one stone barely balanced on another, so that a touch would knock it over. It is not really very high, but the hanging outline of it makes it look a little wild and sinister; at least it made it look so to me, for I don't imagine my jolly young companions were afflicted with the picturesque. But it may be that I was beginning to feel an atmosphere; for just then the question arose of whether it was time to go back to tea, and even then I think I had a premonition that time counted for a good deal in the business. Neither Herbert Druce nor I had a watch, so we called out to his brother, who was some paces behind, having stopped to light his pipe under the hedge. Hence it happened that he shouted out the hour, which was twenty past four, in his big voice through the growing twilight; and somehow the loudness of it made it sound like the proclamation of something tremendous. His unconsciousness seemed to make it all the more so; but that was always the way with omens; and particular ticks of the clock were really very ominous things that afternoon. According to Dr. Valentine's testimony, poor Druce had actually died just about half past four.

"Well, they said we needn't go home for ten minutes and we walked a little farther along the sands, doing nothing in particular—throwing stones for the dog and throwing sticks into the sea for him to swim after. But to me the twilight seemed to grow oddly oppressive and the very shadow of the top-heavy Rock of Fortune lay on me like a load. And then the curious thing happened. Nox had just brought back Herbert's walking stick out of the sea and his brother had thrown his in also. The dog swam out again, but just about what must have been the stroke of the half hour, he stopped swimming. He came back again on to the shore and stood in front of us. Then he suddenly threw up his head and sent up a howl or wail of woe, if ever I heard one in the world.

"What the devil's the matter with the dog?" asked Herbert; but none of us could answer. There was a long silence after the brute's wailing and whining died away on the desolate shore; and then the silence was broken. As I live, it was broken by a faint and far-off shriek, like the shriek of a woman from beyond the hedges inland. We didn't know what it was then; but we knew afterwards. It was the cry the girl gave when she first saw the body of her father."

"You went back, I suppose," said Father Brown patiently. "What happened then?"

"I'll tell you what happened then," said Fiennes with a grim emphasis. "When we got back into that garden the first thing we saw was Traill the lawyer; I can see him now with his black hat and black whiskers relieved against the perspective of the blue flowers stretching down to the summer house, with the sunset and the strange outline of the Rock of Fortune in the distance. His face and figure were in shadow against the sunset; but I swear the white teeth were showing in his head and he was smiling.

"The moment Nox saw that man, the dog dashed forward and stood in the middle of the path barking at him madly, murderously, volleying out curses that were almost verbal in their dreadful distinctness of hatred. And the man doubled up and fled along the path between the flowers."

Father Brown sprang to his feet with a startling impatience.

"So the dog denounced him, did he?" he cried. "The oracle of the dog condemned him. Did you see what birds were flying, and are you sure whether they were on the right hand or the left? Did you consult the augers about the sacrifices? Surely you didn't omit to cut open the dog and examine his entrails. That is the sort of scientific test you heathen humanitarians seem to trust, when you are thinking of taking away the life and honour of a man."

Fiennes sat gaping for an instant before he found breath to say, "Why, what's the matter with you? What have I done now?"

A sort of anxiety came back into the priest's eyes—the anxiety of a man who has run against a post in the dark and wonders for a moment whether he has hurt it.

"I'm most awfully sorry," he said with sincere distress. "I beg your pardon for being so rude; pray forgive me."

Fiennes looked at him curiously. "I sometimes think you are more of a mystery than any of the mysteries," he said. "But anyhow, if you don't believe in the mystery of the dog, at least you can't get over the mystery of the man. You can't deny that at the very moment when the beast came back from the sea and bellowed, his master's soul was driven out of his body by the blow of some unseen power that no mortal man can trace or even imagine. And as for the lawyer, I don't go only by the dog; there are other curious details too. He struck me as a smooth, smiling, equivocal sort of person; and one of his tricks seemed like a sort of hint. You know the doctor and the police were on the spot very quickly; Valentine was brought back when walking away from the house, and he telephoned instantly. That, with the secluded house, small numbers, and enclosed space, made it pretty possible to search everybody who could have been near; and everybody was thoroughly searched—for a weapon. The whole house, garden, and shore were combed for a weapon. The disappearance of the dagger is almost as crazy as the disappearance of the man."

"The disappearance of the dagger," said Father Brown, nodding. He seemed to have become suddenly attentive.

"Well," continued Fiennes, "I told you that man Traill had a trick of fidgeting with his tie and tiepin—especially his tiepin. His pin, like himself, was at once showy and old-fashioned. It had one of those stones with concentric coloured rings that look like an eye; and his own concentration on it got on my nerves, as if he had been a Cyclops with one eye in the middle of his body. But the pin was not only large but long; and it occurred to me that his anxiety about its adjustment was because it was even longer than it looked; as long as a stiletto in fact."

Father Brown nodded thoughtfully. "Was any other instrument ever suggested?" he asked.

"There was another suggestion," answered Fiennes, "from one of the young Druces—the cousins, I mean. Neither Herbert nor Harry Druce would have struck one at first as likely to be of assistance in scientific detection; but while Herbert was really the traditional type of heavy dragoon, caring for nothing but horses and being an ornament to the Horse Guards, his younger brother Harry had been in the Indian Police and knew something about such things. Indeed in his own way he was quite clever; and I rather fancy he had been too clever; I mean he had left the police through breaking some red-tape regulations and taking some sort of risk and responsibility of his own. Anyhow, he was in some sense a detective out of work, and threw himself in this business with more than the ardour of an amateur. And it was with him that I had an argument about the weapon—an argument that led to something new. It began by his countering my description of the dog barking at Traill; and he said that a dog at his worst didn't bark, but growled."

"He was quite right there," observed the priest.

"This young fellow went on to say that, if it came to that, he'd heard Nox growling at other people before then; and among others at

Floyd the secretary. I retorted that his own argument answered itself; for the crime couldn't be brought home to two or three people, and least of all to Floyd, who was as innocent as a harum-scarum schoolboy, and had been seen by everybody all the time perched above the garden hedge with his fan of red hair as conspicuous as a scarlet cockatoo. 'I know there's difficulties anyhow,' said my colleague, 'but I wish you'd come with me down the garden a minute. I want to show you something I don't think anyone else has seen.' This was on the very day of the discovery, and the garden was just as it had been: the stepladder was still standing by the hedge, and just under the hedge my guide stooped and disentangled something from the deep grass. It was the shears used for clipping the hedge, and on the point of one of them was a smear of blood."

There was a short silence, and then Father Brown said suddenly, "What was the lawyer there for?"

"He told us the colonel sent for him to alter his will," answered Fiennes. "And, by the way, there was another thing about the business of the will that I ought to mention. You see, the will wasn't actually signed in the summer house that afternoon."

"I suppose not," said Father Brown; "there would have to be two witnesses."

"The lawyer actually came down the day before and it was signed then; but he was sent for again next day because the old man had a doubt about one of the witnesses and had to be reassured."

"Who were the witnesses?" asked Father Brown.

"That's just the point," replied his informant eagerly, "the witnesses were Floyd the secretary and this Dr. Valentine, the foreign sort of surgeon or whatever he is; and the two had a quarrel. Now I'm bound to say that the secretary is something of a busybody. He's one of those hot and headlong people whose warmth of temperament has unfortunately turned mostly to pugnacity and bristling suspicion; to distrusting people instead of to trusting them. That sort of red-haired red-hot fellow is always either universally credulous or universally incredulous; and sometimes both. He was not only a jack-of-all-trades, but he knew better than all tradesmen. He not only knew everything, but he warned everybody against everybody. All that must be taken into account in his suspicions about Valentine; but in that particular case there seems to have been something behind it. He said the name of Valentine was not really Valentine. He said he had seen him elsewhere known by the name of De Villon. He said it would invalidate the will; of course he was kind enough to explain to the lawyer what the law was on that point. They were both in a frightful wax."

Father Brown laughed. "People often are when they are to witness a will," he said. "For one thing it means that they can't have any legacy under it. But what did Dr. Valentine say? No doubt the universal secretary knew more about the doctor's name than the doctor did. But even the doctor might have some information about his own name."

Fiennes paused a moment before he replied.

"Dr. Valentine took it in a curious way. Dr. Valentine is a curious man. His appearance is rather striking but very foreign. He is young but wears a beard cut square; and his face is very pale and dreadfully serious. His eyes have a sort of ache in them, as if he ought to wear glasses or had given himself a headache thinking; but he is quite handsome and always very formally dressed, with a top hat and dark coat and a little red rosette. His manner is rather cold and haughty, and he has a way of staring at you which is very disconcerting. When thus charged with having changed his name, he merely stared like a sphinx and then said with a little laugh that he supposed Americans had no names to change. At that I think the colonel also got into a fuss and said all sorts of angry things to the doctor; all the more angry because of the doctor's pretensions to a future place in his family. But I shouldn't have thought much of that but for a few words that I happened to hear later, early in the afternoon of the tragedy. I don't want to make a lot of them, for they weren't the sort of words on which one would like, in the ordinary way, to play the eavesdropper. As I was passing out towards the front gate with my two companions and the dog, I heard voices which told me that Dr. Valentine and Miss Druce had withdrawn for a moment into the shadow of the house, in an angle behind a row of flowering plants, and were talking to each other in passionate whisperings—sometimes almost like hissings; for it was something of a lovers' quarrel as well as a lovers' tryst. Nobody repeats the sorts of things they said for the most part; but in an unfortunate business like this I'm bound to say that there was repeated more than once a phrase about killing somebody. In fact, the girl seemed to be begging him not to kill somebody, or saying that no provocation could justify killing anybody; which seems an unusual sort of talk to address to a gentleman who has dropped in to tea."

"Do you know," asked the priest, "whether Dr. Valentine seemed to be very angry after the scene with the secretary and the colonel—I mean about witnessing the will?"

"By all accounts," replied the other, "he wasn't half so angry as the secretary was. It was the secretary who went away raging after witnessing the will."

"And now," said Father Brown, "what about the will itself?"

"The colonel was a very wealthy man, and his will was important. Traill wouldn't tell us the alternation at that stage, but I have since heard, only this morning in fact, that most of the money was transferred from the son to the daughter. I told you that Druce was wild with my friend Donald over his dissipated hours."

"The question of motive has been rather overshadowed by the question of method," observed Father Brown thoughtfully. "At that moment, apparently, Miss Druce was the immediate gainer by the death."

"Good God! What a cold-blooded way of talking," cried Fiennes, staring at him. "You don't really mean to hint that she—"

"Is she going to marry that Dr. Valentine?" asked the other.

"Some people are against it," answered his friend. "But he is liked and respected in the place and is a skilled and devoted surgeon."

"So devoted a surgeon," said Father Brown, "that he had surgical instruments with him when he went to call on the young lady at teatime. For he must have used a lancet or something, and he never seems to have gone home."

Fiennes sprang to his feet and looked at him in a heat of inquiry. "You suggest he might have used the very same lancet—"

Father Brown shook his head. "All these suggestions are fancies just now," he said. "The problem is not who did it or what did it, but how it was done. We might find many men and even many tools—pins and shears and lancets. But how did a man get into the room? How did even a pin get into it?"

He was staring reflectively at the ceiling as he spoke, but as he said the last words his eye cocked in an alert fashion as if he had suddenly seen a curious fly on the ceiling.

"Well, what would you do about it?" asked the young man. "You have a lot of experience; what would you advise now?"

"I'm afraid I'm not much use," said Father Brown with a sigh. "I can't suggest very much without having ever been near the place or the people. For the moment you can only go on with local inquiries. I gather that your friend from the Indian Police is more or less in charge of your inquiry down there. I should run down and see how he is getting on. See what he's been doing in the way of amateur detection. There may be news already."

As his guests, the biped and the quadruped, disappeared, Father Brown took up his pen and went back to his interrupted occupation of planning a course of lectures on the encyclical *Rerum Novarum*. The subject was a large one and he had to recast it more than once, so that he was somewhat similarly employed some two days later when the big black dog again came bounding into the room and sprawled all over him with enthusiasm and excitement. The master who followed the dog shared the excitement if not the enthusiasm. He had been excited in a less pleasant fashion, for his blue eyes seemed to start from his head and his eager face was even a little pale.

"You told me," he said abruptly and without preface, "to find out what Harry Druce was doing. Do you know what he's done?"

The priest did not reply, and the young man went on in jerky tones: "I'll tell you what's he's done. He's killed himself."

Father Brown's lips moved only faintly, and there was nothing practical about what he was saying—nothing that has anything to do with this story or this world.

"You give me the creeps sometimes," said Fiennes. "Did you—expect this?"

"I thought it possible," said Father Brown; "that was why I asked you to go and see what he was doing. I hoped you might not be too late."

"It was I who found him," said Fiennes rather huskily. "It was the ugliest and most uncanny thing I ever knew. I went down that old garden again and I knew there was something new and unnatural about it besides the murder. The flowers still tossed about in blue masses on each side of the black entrance into the old grey summer house; but to me the blue flowers looked like devils dancing before some dark cavern of the underworld. I looked all round; everything seemed to be in its ordinary place. But the queer notion grew on me that there was something wrong with the very shape of the sky. And then I saw what it was. The Rock of Fortune always rose in the background beyond the garden hedge and against the sea. And the Rock of Fortune was gone."

Father Brown had lifted his head and was listening intently.

"It was as if a mountain had walked away out of a landscape or a moon fallen from the sky; though I knew, of course, that a touch at any time would have tipped the thing over. Something possessed me and I rushed down that garden path like the wind and went crashing through that hedge as if it were a spider's web. It was a thin hedge really, though its undisturbed trimness had made it serve all the purposes of a wall. On the shore I found the loose rock fallen from its pedestal; and poor Harry Druce lay like a wreck underneath it. One arm was thrown round it in a sort of embrace as if he had pulled it down on himself; and on the broad brown sands beside it, in large crazy lettering, he had sprawled the words 'The Rock of Fortune falls on the Fool.'"

"It was the Colonel's will that did that," observed Father Brown. "The young man had staked everything on profiting himself by Donald's disgrace, especially when his uncle sent for him on the same day as the lawyer, and welcomed him with so much warmth. Otherwise he was done; he'd lost his police job; he was beggared at Monte Carlo. And he killed himself when he found he'd killed his kinsman for nothing."

"Here, stop a minute!" cried the staring Fiennes. "You're going too fast for me."

"Talking about the will, by the way," continued Father Brown calmly, "before I forget it, or we go on to bigger things, there was a simple explanation, I think, of all that business about the doctor's name. I rather fancy I have heard both names before somewhere. The doctor is really a French nobleman with the title of the Marquis de Villon. But he is also an ardent Republican and has abandoned his title and fallen back on the forgotten family surname. 'With your Citizen Requetti you have puzzled Europe for ten days.' "

"What is that?" asked the young man blankly.

"Never mind," said the priest. "Nine times out of ten it is a rascally thing to change one's name; but this was a piece of fine fanaticism. That's the point of his sarcasm about Americans having no names—that is, no titles. Now in England the Marquis of Hartington is never called Mr. Hartington; but in France the Marquis de Villon is called Monsieur de Villon. So it might well look like a change of names. As for the talk about killing, I fancy that also was a point of French etiquette. The doctor was talking about challenging Floyd to a duel, and the girl was trying to dissuade him."

"Oh, I *see*," cried Fiennes slowly. "Now I understand what she meant."

"And what is that about?" asked his companion, smiling.

"Well," said the young man, "it was something that happened to me just before I found that poor fellow's body; only the catastrophe drove it out of my head. I suppose it's hard to remember a little romantic idyll when you've just come on top of a tragedy. But as I went down the lanes leading to the colonel's old place, I met his daughter walking with Dr. Valentine. She was in mourning of course, and he always wore black as if he were going to a funeral; but I can't say that their faces were very funereal. Never have I seen two people looking in their way more respectably radiant and cheerful. They stopped and saluted me and then she told me they were married and living in a little house on the outskirts of the town, where the doctor was continuing his practice. This rather surprised me, because I knew that her old father's will had left her his property; and I hinted at it delicately by saying I was going along to her father's old place and had half expected to meet her there. But she only laughed and said, 'Oh, we've given up all that. My husband doesn't like heiresses.' And I discovered with some astonishment that they really had insisted on restoring the property to poor Donald; so I hope he's had a healthy shock and will treat it sensibly. There was never much really the matter with him; he was very young and his father was not very wise. But it was in connection with that that she said something I didn't understand at the time; but now I'm sure it must be as you say. She said with a sort of sudden and splendid arrogance that was entirely altruistic, "I hope it'll stop that red-haired fool from fussing any more about the will. Does he think my husband, who has given up a crest and a coronet as old as the Crusades for his principles, would kill an old man in a summer house for a legacy like that?' Then she laughed again and said, 'My husband isn't killing anybody except in the way of business. Why, he didn't even ask his friends to call on the secretary.' Now, of course, I see what she meant."

"I see part of what she meant, of course," said Father Brown. "What did she mean exactly by the secretary fussing about the will?"

Fiennes smiled as he answered, "I wish you knew the secretary, Father Brown. It would be a joy to you to watch him make things hum, as he calls it. He made the house of mourning hum. He filled the funeral with all the snap and zip of the brightest sporting event. There was no holding him, after something had really happened. I've told you how he used to oversee the gardener as he did the garden, and how he instructed the lawyer in the law. Needless to say, he also instructed the surgeon in the practice of surgery; and as the surgeon was Dr. Valentine, you may be sure it ended in accusing him of something worse than bad surgery. The secretary got it fixed in his red head that the doctor had committed the crime; and when the police arrived he was perfectly sublime. Need I say that he became on the spot the greatest of all amateur detectives? Sherlock Holmes never towered over Scotland Yard with more titanic intellectual pride and scorn than Colonel Druce's private secretary over the police investigating Colonel Druce's death. I tell you it was a joy to see him. He strode about with an abstracted air, tossing his scarlet crest of hair and giving curt impatient replies. Of course it was his demeanour during these days that made Druce's daughter so wild with him. Of course he had a theory. It's just the sort of theory a man would have in a book; and Floyd is the sort of man who ought to be in a book. He'd be better fun and less bother in a book."

"What was his theory?" asked the other.

27

"Oh, it was full of pep," replied Fiennes gloomily. "It would have been glorious copy if it could have held together for ten minutes longer. He said the colonel was still alive when they found him in the summer house and the doctor killed him with the surgical instrument on pretence of cutting the clothes."

"I see," said the priest. "I suppose he was lying flat on his face on the mud floor as a form of siesta."

"It's wonderful what hustle will do," continued his informant. "I believe Floyd would have got his great theory into the papers at any rate, and perhaps had the doctor arrested, when all these things were blown sky high as if by dynamite by the discovery of that dead body lying under the Rock of Fortune. And that's what we come back to after all. I suppose the suicide is almost a confession. But nobody will ever know the whole story."

There was a silence, and then the priest said modestly, "I rather think I know the whole story."

Fiennes stared. "But look here," he cried, "How do you come to know the whole story, or to be sure it's the true story? You've been sitting here a hundred miles away writing a sermon; do you mean to tell me you really know what happened already? If you've really come to the end, where in the world do you begin? What started you off with your own story?"

Father Brown jumped up with a very unusual excitement and his first exclamation was like an explosion.

"The dog!" he cried. "The dog, of course! You had the whole story in your hands in the business of the dog on the beach, if you'd only noticed the dog properly."

Fiennes stared still more. "But you told me just now that my feelings about the dog were all nonsense, and the dog had nothing to do with it."

"The dog had everything to do with it," said Father Brown, "as you'd have found out, if you'd only treated the dog as a dog and not as God Almighty, judging the souls of men."

He paused in an embarrassed way for a moment, and then said, with a rather pathetic air of apology:

"The truth is, I happen to be awfully fond of dogs. And it seemed to me that in all this lurid halo of dog superstitions nobody was really thinking about the poor dog at all. To begin with a small point, about barking at the lawyer or growling at the secretary. You asked how I guess things a hundred miles away; but honestly it's mostly to your credit, for you described people so well that I know the types. A man like Traill who frowns usually and smiles suddenly, a man who fiddles with things, especially at his throat, is a nervous, easily embarrassed man. I shouldn't wonder if Floyd, the efficient secretary, is nervy and jumpy too; those Yankee hustlers often are. Otherwise he wouldn't have cut his fingers on the shears and dropped them when he heard Janet Druce scream.

"Now dogs hate nervous people. I don't know whether they make the dog nervous too; or whether, being after all a brute, he is a bit of a bully; or whether his canine vanity (which is colossal) is simply offended at not being liked. But anyhow there was nothing in poor Nox protesting against those people except that he disliked them for being afraid of him. Now I know you're awfully clever, and nobody of sense sneers at cleverness. But I sometimes fancy, for instance, that you are too clever to understand animals. Sometimes you are too clever to understand men, especially when they act almost as simply as animals. Animals are very literal; they live in a world of truisms. Take this case; a dog barks at a man and a man runs away from a dog. Now you do not seem to be quite simple enough to see the fact; that the dog barked because he disliked the man and the man fled because he was frightened of the dog. They had no other motives and they needed none. But you must read psychological mysteries into it and suppose the dog had supernormal vision, and was a mysterious mouthpiece of doom. You must suppose the man was running away, not from the dog, but from the hangman. And yet, if you come to think of it, all this deeper psychology is exceedingly improbable. If the dog really could completely and consciously realize the murderer of his master, he wouldn't stand yapping as he might at a curate at a tea party; he's much more likely to fly at his throat. And on the other hand, do you really think a man who had hardened his heart to murder an old friend and then walk about smiling at the old friend's family, under the eyes of his old friend's daughter and post mortem doctor—do you think a man

29

like that could be doubled up by mere remorse because a dog barked? He might feel the tragic irony of it; it might shake his soul, like any other tragic trifle. But he wouldn't rush madly the length of a garden to escape from the only witness whom he knew to be unable to talk. People have a panic like that when they are frightened, not of tragic ironies, but of teeth. The whole thing is simpler than you can understand. But when we come to that business by the seashore, things are much more interesting. As you stated them, they were much more puzzling. I didn't understand that tale of the dog going in and out of the water; it didn't seem to me a doggy thing to do. If Nox had been very much upset about something else, he might possibly have refused to go after the stick at all. He'd probably go off nosing in whatever direction he suspected the mischief. But when once a dog is actually chasing a thing, a stone or a stick or a rabbit, my experience is that he won't stop for anything but the most peremptory command, and not always for that. That he should turn because his mood changed seems to me unthinkable."

"But he did turn round," insisted Fiennes, "and came back without the stick."

"He came back without the stick for the best reason in the world," replied the priest. "He came back because he couldn't find it. He whined because he couldn't find it. That's the sort of thing a dog really does whine about. A dog is a devil of a ritualist. He is as particular about the precise routine of a game as a child about the precise repetition of a fairy tale. In this case something had gone wrong with the game. He came back to complain seriously of the conduct of the stick. Never had such a thing happened before. Never had an eminent and distinguished dog been so treated by a rotten old walking stick."

"Why, what had the walking stick done?" inquired the young man.

"It had sunk," said Father Brown.

Fiennes said nothing, but continued to stare, and it was the priest who continued:

"It had sunk because it was not really a stick, but a rod of steel with a very thin shell of cane and a sharp point. In other words, it was a sword stick. I suppose a murderer never got rid of a bloody weapon so oddly and yet so naturally as by throwing it into the sea for a retriever."

"I begin to see what you mean," admitted Fiennes; "but even if a sword stick was used, I have no guess of how it was used."

"I had a sort of guess," said Father Brown, "right at the beginning when you said the words 'summer house.' And another when you said that Druce wore a white coat. As long as everybody was looking for a short dagger, nobody thought of it; but if we admit a rather long blade like a rapier, it's not so impossible."

He was leaning back, looking at the ceiling, and began like one going back to his own first thoughts and fundamentals.

"All that discussion about detective stories like the Yellow Room, about a man found dead in sealed chambers which no one could enter, does not apply to the present case, because it is a summer house. When we talk of a Yellow Room, or any room, we imply walls that are really homogeneous and impenetrable. But a summer house is not made like that; it is often made, as it was in this case, of closely interlaced but still separate boughs and strips of wood, in which there are chinks here and there. There was one of them just behind Druce's back as he sat in his chair up against the wall. But just as the room was a summer house, so the chair was a basketchair. That also was a lattice of loopholes. Lastly, the summer house was close up under the hedge; and you have just told me that it was really a thin hedge. A man standing outside it could easily see, amid a network of twigs and branches and canes, one white spot of the colonel's coat as plain as the white of a target.

"Now, you left the geography a little vague; but it was possible to put two and two together. You said the Rock of Fortune was not really high; but you said it could be seen dominating the garden like a mountain peak. In other words, it was very near the end of the garden, though your walk had taken you a long way round to it. Also, it isn't likely the young lady really howled so as to be heard half a mile. She gave an ordinary involuntary cry and yet you heard it on the shore. And among other interesting things that you told me, may I remind you that you said Harry Druce had fallen behind to light his pipe under a hedge."

Fiennes shuddered slightly. "You mean he drew his blade there and sent it through the hedge at the white spot. But surely it was a very odd chance and a very sudden choice. Besides, he couldn't be certain the old man's money had passed to him, and as a fact it hadn't."

Father Brown's face animated.

"You misunderstand the man's character," he said, as if he himself had known the man all his life. "A curious but not unknown type of character. If he had really *known* the money would come to him, I seriously believe he wouldn't have done it. He would have seen it as the dirty thing it was."

"Isn't that rather paradoxical?" asked the other.

"This man was a gambler," said the priest, "and a man in disgrace for having taken risks and anticipated orders. It was probably for something pretty unscrupulous, for every imperial police is more like a Russian secret police than we like to think. But he had gone beyond the line and failed. Now, the temptation of that type of man is to do a mad thing precisely because the risk will be wonderful in retrospect. He wants to say, 'Nobody but I could have seized that chance or seen that it was then or never. What a wild and wonderful guess it was, when I put all those things together: Donald in disgrace; and the lawyer being sent for; and Herbert and I sent for at the same time—and then nothing more but the way the old man grinned at me and shook hands. Anybody would say I was mad to risk it; but that is how fortunes are made, by the man mad enough to have a little foresight.' In short, it is the vanity of guessing. It is the megalomania of the gambler. The more incongruous the coincidence, the more instantaneous the decision, the more likely he is to snatch the chance. The accident, the very triviality, of the white speck and the hole in the hedge intoxicated him like a vision of the world's desire. Nobody clever enough to see such a combination of accidents could be cowardly enough not to use them! That is how the devil talks to the gambler. But the devil himself would hardly have induced that unhappy man to go down in a dull, deliberate way and kill an old uncle from whom he'd always had expectations. It would be too respectable."

He paused a moment; and then went on with a certain quiet emphasis.

"And now try to call up the scene, even as you saw it yourself. As he stood there, dizzy with his diabolical opportunity, he looked up and saw that strange outline that might have been the image of his own tottering soul—the one great crag poised perilously on the other like a pyramid on its point—and remembered that it was called the Rock of Fortune. Can you guess how such a man at such a moment would read such a signal? I think it strung him up to action and even to vigilance. He who would be a tower must not fear to be a toppling tower. Anyhow he acted; his next difficulty was to cover his tracks. To be found with a sword stick, let alone a blood-stained sword stick, would be fatal in the search that was certain to follow. If he left it anywhere, it would be found and probably traced. Even if he threw it into the sea the action might be noticed, and thought noticeable—unless indeed he could think of some more natural way of covering the action. As you know, he did think of one, and a very good one. Being the only one of you with a watch, he told you it was not yet time to return, strolled a little farther, and started the game of throwing in sticks for the retriever. But how his eyes must have rolled darkly over all that desolate seashore before they alighted on the dog!"

Fiennes nodded, gazing thoughtfully into space. His mind seemed to have drifted back to a less practical part of the narrative.

"It's queer," he said, "that the dog really was in the story after all."

"The dog could almost have told you the story, if he could talk," said the priest. "All I complain of is that because he couldn't talk, you made up his story for him, and made him talk with the tongues of men and angels. It's part of something I've noticed more and more in the modern world, appearing in all sorts of newspaper rumours and conversational catchwords; something that's arbitrary without being authoritative. People readily swallow the untested claims of this, that, or the other. It's drowning all your old rationalism and scepticism, it's coming in like a sea; and the name of it is superstition." He stood up abruptly, his face heavy with a sort of frown, and went on talking almost as if he were alone. "It's the first effect of not believing in God that you lose your common sense, and can't see things as they are. Anything that anybody talks about, and says there's a good deal in it, extends itself indefinitely like a vista in a nightmare. And a dog is an omen and a cat is a mystery and a pig is a mascot and a beetle is a scarab, calling up all the menagerie of polytheism from Egypt and old India; Dog Anubis and great green-eyed Pasht and all the holy howling Bulls of Bashan; reeling back to the bestial gods of the beginning, escaping into elephants and snakes and crocodiles; and all because you are frightened of four words: 'He was made Man.' "

The young man got up with a little embarrassment, almost as if he had overheard a soliloquy. He called to the dog and left the room with vague but breezy farewells. But he had to call the dog twice, for the dog had remained behind quite motionless for a moment, looking up steadily at Father Brown as the wolf looked at Saint Francis.

Rudyard Kipling

RED DOG

For our white and our excellent nights—for the nights of swift running!
  Fair ranging, far-seeing, good hunting, sure cunning!
For the smells of the dawning, untainted ere dew has departed!
For the rush through the mist, and the quarry blend-started!
For the cry of our mates when the sambhur *has wheeled and is standing at*
    bay,
      For the risk and the riot of night!
      For the sleep at the lair-mouth by day—
        It is met, and we go to the fight.
        Bay! O Bay!

It was after the letting in of the Jungle that the pleasant part of Mowgli's life began. He had the good conscience that comes from paying a just debt; and all the Jungle was his friend, for all the Jungle was afraid of him. The things that he did and saw and heard when he was wandering from one people to another, with or without his four companions, would make many, many stories, each as long as this one. So you will never be told how he met and escaped from the Mad Elephant of Mandla, who killed two-and-twenty bullocks drawing eleven carts of coined silver to the Government Treasury, and scattered the shiny rupees in the dust; how he fought Jacala, the Crocodile, all one long night in the Marshes of the North, and broke his skinning knife on the brute's back-plates; how he found a new and longer knife round the neck of a man who had been killed by a wild boar, and how he tracked that boar and killed him as a fair price for the knife; how he was caught up in the Great Famine by the moving of the deer, and nearly crushed to death in the swaying hot herds; how he saved Hathi the Silent from being caught in a pit with a stake at the bottom, and how next day he himself fell into a very cunning leopard-trap, and how Hathi broke the thick wooden bars to pieces about him; how he milked the wild buffaloes in the swamp, and how—

But we must tell one tale at a time. Father and Mother Wolf died, and Mowgli rolled a big boulder against the mouth of the cave and cried the Death Song over them, and Baloo grew very old and stiff, and even Bagheera, whose nerves were steel and whose muscles were iron, seemed slower at the kill. Akela turned from gray to milky white with pure age; his ribs stuck out, and he walked as though he had been made of wood, and Mowgli killed for him. But the young wolves, the children of the disbanded Seeonee Pack, throve and increased, and when there were some forty of them, masterless, clean-footed five-year-olds, Akela told them that they ought to gather themselves together and follow the Law, and run under one head, as befitted the Free People.

This was not a matter in which Mowgli gave advice, for, as he said, he had eaten sour fruit, and he knew the tree it hung from; but when Phao, son of Phaona (his father was the Gray Tracker in the days of Akela's headship), fought his way to the leadership of the Pack according to the Jungle Law, and when the old calls and the old songs began to ring under the stars once more, Mowgli came to the Council Rock for memory's sake. If he chose to speak the Pack waited till he had finished, and he sat at Akela's side on the rock above Phao. Those were the days of good hunting and good sleeping. No stranger cared to break into the jungles that belonged to Mowgli's people, as they called the Pack, and the young wolves grew fat and strong, and there were many cubs to bring to the Looking-over. Mowgli always attended a Looking-over, for he remembered the night when a black panther brought a naked brown baby into the pack, and the long call, "Look, look well, O Wolves," made his heart flutter with strange feelings. Otherwise, he would be far away in the jungle; tasting, touching, seeing, and feeling new things.

One twilight when he was trotting leisurely across the ranges to give Akela the half of a buck that he had killed, while his four wolves were jogging behind him, sparring a little and tumbling one over another for joy of being alive, he heard a cry that he had not heard since the bad days of Shere Khan. It was what they call in the Jungle the *Pheeal,* a kind of shriek that the jackal gives when he is hunting behind a tiger, or when there is some big killing afoot. If you can imagine a mixture of hate, triumph, fear, and despair, with a kind of leer running through it, you will get some notion of the *Pheeal* that rose and sank and wavered and quivered far away across the Waingunga. The Four began to bristle and growl. Mowgli's hand went to his knife and he too checked as though he had been turned into stone.

"There is no Striped One would dare kill here," he said, at last.

"That is not the cry of the Forerunner," said Gray Brother. "It is some great killing. Listen!"

It broke out again, half sobbing and half chuckling, just as though the jackal had soft human lips. Then Mowgli drew deep breath, and ran to the Council Rock, overtaking on his way hurrying wolves of the Pack. Phao and Akela were on the Rock together, and below them, every nerve strained, sat the others. The mothers and the cubs were cantering to their lairs; for when the *Pheeal* cries is no time for weak things to be abroad.

They could hear nothing except the Waingunga gurgling in the dark and the evening winds among the tree-tops, till suddenly across the river a wolf called. It was no wolf of the Pack, for those were all at the Rock. The note changed to a long despairing bay; and "Dhole!" it said, "Dhole! Dhole! Dhole!" In a few minutes they heard tired feet on the rocks, and a gaunt, dripping wolf, streaked with red on his flanks, his right fore-paw useless, and his jaws white with foam, flung himself into the circle and lay gasping at Mowgli's feet.

"Good hunting? Under whose headship?" said Phao gravely.

"Good hunting! Won-tolla am I," was the answer. He meant that he was a solitary wolf, fending for himself, his mate, and his cubs in some lonely lair. Won-tolla means an outlier—one who lies out from any pack.

When he panted they could see his heart shake him backwards and forwards.

"What moves?" said Phao, for that is the question all the Jungle asks after the *Pheeal.*

"The dhole, the dhole of the Dekkan—Red Dog, the Killer! They came north from the south saying the Dekkan was empty and killing out by the way. When this moon was new there were four to me—my mate and three cubs. She would teach them to kill on the grass plains, hiding to drive the buck, as we do who are of the open. At midnight I heard them together full tongue on the trail. At the dawn-wind I found them stiff in the grass—four, Free People, four when this moon was new! Then sought I my Blood-Right and found the dhole."

"How many?" said Mowgli; the Pack growled deep in their throats.

"I do not know. Three of them will kill no more, but at the last they drove me like the buck; on three legs they drove me. Look, Free People!"

He thrust out his mangled fore-foot, all dark with dried blood. There were cruel bites low down on his side, and his throat was torn and worried.

"Eat," said Akela, rising up from the meat Mowgli had brought him; the outlier flung himself on it famishing.

"This shall be no loss," he said humbly when he had taken off the edge of his hunger. "Give me a little strength, Free People, and I also will kill! My lair is empty that was full when this moon was new, and the Blood Debt is not all paid."

Phao heard his teeth crack on a haunch-bone and grunted approvingly.

"We shall need those jaws," said he. "Were their cubs with the dhole?"

"Nay, nay. Red hunters all: grown dogs of their pack, heavy and strong."

That meant that the dhole, the red hunting-dog of the Dekkan, was moving to fight, and the wolves knew well that even the tiger will surrender a new kill to the dhole. They drive straight through the Jungle, and what they meet they pull down and tear to pieces. Though they are not as big nor half as cunning as the wolf, they are very strong and very numerous. The dhole, for instance, do not begin to call themselves a pack till they are a hundred strong, whereas forty wolves make a very fair pack. Mowgli's wanderings had taken him to the edge of the high grassy downs of the Dekkan, and he had often seen the fearless dholes sleeping and playing and scratching themselves among the little hollows and tussocks that they use for lairs. He despised and hated them because they did not smell like the Free People, because they did not live in caves, and above all, because they had hair between their toes while he and his friends were clean-footed. But he knew, for Hathi had told him, what a terrible thing a dhole hunting-pack was. Hathi himself moves aside from their line, and until they are all killed, or till game is scarce, they go forward killing as they go.

Akela knew something of the dholes, too; he said to Mowgli quietly: "It is better to die in the Full Pack than leaderless and alone. It is good hunting, and—my last. But, as men live, thou hast very many more nights and days, Little Brother. Go north and lie down, and if any wolf live after the dhole has gone by he shall bring thee word of the fight."

"Ah," said Mowgli, quite gravely, "must I go to the marshes and catch little fish and sleep in a tree, or must I ask help of the *bandar-log* and eat nuts while the Pack fights below?"

"It is to the death," said Akela. "Thou hast never met the dhole— the Red Killer. Even the Striped One—"

"Aowa! Aowa!" said Mowgli pettingly. "I have killed one striped ape. Listen now: There was a wolf, my father, and there was a wolf, my mother, and there was an old gray wolf (not to wise: he is white now) was my father and my mother. Therefore I—" he raised his voice, "I say that when the dhole come, and if the dhole come, Mowgli and the Free People are of one skin for that hunting; and I say, by the Bull that bought me, by the bull Bagheera paid for me in the old days which ye of the Pack do not remember, *I say,* that the Trees and the River may hear and hold fast if I forget; *I* say that this my knife shall be as a tooth to the Pack—and I do not think it is so blunt. This is my Word which has gone from me."

"Thou dost not know the dhole, man with a wolf's tongue," Wontolla cried. "I look only to clear my Blood Debt against them ere they have me in many pieces. They move slowly, killing out as they go, but in two days a little strength will come back to me and I turn again for my Blood Debt. But for *ye*, Free People, my counsel is that ye go north and eat but little for a while till the dhole are gone. There is no sleep in this hunting."

"Hear the Outlier!" said Mowgli with a laugh. "Free People, we must go north and eat lizards and rats from the bank, lest by any chance we meet the dhole. He must kill out our hunting grounds while we lie hid in the north till it please him to give us our own again. He is a dog—and the pup of a dog—red, yellow-bellied, lairless, and haired between every toe! He counts his cubs six and eight at the litter, as though he were Chikai, the little leaping rat. Surely we must run away, Free People, and beg leave of the peoples of the north for the offal of dead cattle! Ye know the saying: North are the vermin; South are the lice. *We* are the Jungle. Choose ye. O choose. It is good hunting! For the Pack—for the Full Pack—for the lair and the litter; for the in-kill and the out-kill; for the mate that drives the doe and the little, little cub within the cave, it is met—it is met—it is met!"

The Pack answered with one deep crashing bark that sounded in the night like a tree falling. "It is met," they cried.

"Stay with these," said Mowgli to his Four. "We shall need every tooth. Phao and Akela must make ready the battle. I go to count the dogs."

"It is death!" Won-tolla cried, half rising. "What can such a hairless one do against the Red Dog? Even the Striped One, remember—"

"Thou art indeed an outlier," Mowgli called back, "but we will speak when the dholes are dead. Good hunting all!"

He hurried off into the darkness wild with excitement, hardly looking where he set foot, and the natural consequence was that he tripped full length over Kaa's great coils where the python lay watching a deer-path near the river.

"Kssha!" said Kaa angrily. "Is this jungle work to stamp and ramp and undo a night's hunting—when the game are moving so well, too?"

"The fault was mine," said Mowgli, picking himself up. "Indeed I was seeking thee, Flathead, but each time we meet thou art longer and broader by the length of my arm. There is none like thee in the Jungle, wise, old, strong, and most beautiful Kaa."

"Now whither does *this* trail lead?" Kaa's voice was gentler. "Not a moon since there was a Manling with a knife threw stones at my head and called me bad little tree-cat names because I lay asleep in the open."

"Ay, and turned every driven deer to all the winds, and Mowgli was hunting, and this same Flathead was too deaf to hear his whistle and leave the deer-roads free," Mowgli answered composedly, sitting down among the painted coils.

"Now this same Manling comes with soft, tickling words to this same Flathead, telling him that he is wise, and strong, and beautiful, and this same old Flathead believes and coils a place, thus, for this same stone-throwing Manling and . . . Art thou at ease now? Could Bagheera give thee so good a resting-place?"

Kaa had, as usual, made a sort of soft half-hammock of himself under Mowgli's weight. The boy reached out in the darkness and gathered in the supple cable-like neck till Kaa's head rested on his shoulder, and then he told him all that had happened in the jungle that night.

"Wise I may be," said Kaa at the end, "but deaf I surely am. Else I should have heard the *Pheeal*. Small wonder the eaters-of-grass are uneasy. How many be the dhole?"

"I have not seen yet. I came hot foot to thee. Thou art older than Hathi. But, oh, Kaa,"—here Mowgli wriggled with joy, "it will be good hunting! Few of us will see another moon."

"Dost *thou* strike in this? Remember thou art a man; and remember what pack cast thee out. Let the wolf look to the dog. *Thou* art a man."

"Last year's nuts are this year's black earth," said Mowgli. "It is true that I am a man, but it is in my stomach that this night I have said that I am a wolf. I called the River and the Trees to remember. I am of the Free People, Kaa, till the dhole has gone by."

"Free People," Kaa grunted. "Free thieves! And thou hast tied thyself into the Death-knot for the sake of the memory of dead wolves! This is no good hunting."

"It is my Word which I have spoken. The Trees know, the River knows. Till the dhole have gone by my Word comes not back to me."

"Ngssh! That changes all trails. I had thought to take thee away with me to the northern marshes, but the Word—even the Word of a little, naked, hairless Manling—is the Word. Now I Kaa, say—"

"Think well, Flathead, lest thou tie thyself into the Death-knot also. I need no word from thee, for well I know—"

"Be it so, then," said Kaa. "I will give no Word; but what is in thy stomach to do when the dhole come?"

"They must swim the Waingunga. I thought to meet them with my knife in the shallows, the Pack behind me; and so stabbing and thrusting we might turn them down stream, or cool their throats a little."

"The dhole do not turn and their throats are hot," said Kaa. "There will be neither Manling nor wolf-cub when that hunting is done, but only dry bones."

"Alala! If we die we die. It will be most good hunting. But my stomach is young, and I have not seen many Rains. I am not wise nor strong. Hast thou a better plan, Kaa?"

"I have seen a hundred and a hundred Rains. Ere Hathi cast his milk-tushes my trail was big in the dust. By the First Egg I am older than many trees, and I have seen all that the Jungle has done."

"But *this* is new hunting," said Mowgli. "Never before has the dhole crossed our trail."

"What is has been. What will be is no more than a forgotten year striking backwards. Be still while I count those my years."

For a long hour Mowgli lay back among the coils, playing with his knife, while Kaa, his head motionless on the ground, thought of all that he had seen and known since the day he came from the egg. The light seemed to go out of his eyes and leave them like stale opals, and now and again he made little stiff passes with his head to right and left, as though he were hunting in his sleep. Mowgli dozed quietly, for he knew that there is nothing like sleep before hunting, and he was trained to take it at any hour of the day or night.

Then he felt Kaa grow bigger and broader below him as the huge python puffed himself out, hissing with the noise of a sword drawn from a steel scabbard.

"I have seen all the dead seasons," Kaa said at last, "and the great trees and the old elephants and the rocks that were bare and sharp-pointed ere the moss grew. Art *thou* still alive, Manling?"

"It is only a little after moonrise," said Mowgli. "I do not understand—"

"Hssh! I am again Kaa. I knew it was but a little time. Now we will go to the river, and I will show thee what is to be done against the dhole."

He turned, straight as an arrow, for the main stream of the Waingunga, plunging in a little above the pool that hid the Peace Rock, Mowgli at his side.

"Nay, do not swim. I go swiftly. My back, Little Brother."

Mowgli tucked his left arm round Kaa's neck, dropped his right close to his body and straightened his feet. Then Kaa breasted the current as he alone could, and the ripple of the checked water stood up in a frill round Mowgli's neck and his feet were waved to and fro in the eddy under the python's lashing sides. A mile or so above the Peace Rock the Waingunga narrows between a gorge of marble rocks from eighty to a hundred feet high, and the current runs like a mill-race between and over all manner of ugly stones. But Mowgli did not trouble his head about the water: no water in the world could have given him a moment's fear. He was looking at the gorge on either side and sniffing uneasily, for there was a sweetish-sourish smell in the air, very like the smell of a big anthill on a hot day. Instinctively he lowered himself in the water, only raising his head to breathe, and Kaa came to anchor with a double twist of his tail round a sunken rock, holding Mowgli in the hollow of a coil, while the water raced by.

"This is the Place of Death," said the boy. "Why do we come here?"

"They sleep," said Kaa. "Hathi will not turn aside for the Striped One. Yet Hathi and the Striped One together turn aside for the dhole, and the dhole they say turns aside for nothing. And yet for whom do the Little People of the Rocks turn aside? Tell me, Master of the Jungle, who is the Master of the Jungle?"

"These," Mowgli whispered. "It is the Place of Death. Let us go."

"Nay, look well, for they are asleep. It is as it was when I was not the length of thy arm."

The split and weather-worn rocks of the gorge of the Waingunga had been used since the beginning of the Jungle by the Little People of the Rocks—the busy, furious, black, wild bees of India; and, as Mowgli knew well, all trails turned off half a mile away from their country. For centuries the Little People had hived and swarmed from cleft to cleft and swarmed again, staining the white marble with stale honey, and made their combs tall and deep and black in the dark of the inner caves, and neither man nor beast nor fire nor water had ever touched them. The length of the gorge on both sides was hung as it were with black shimmery velvet curtains, and Mowgli sank as he looked, for those were the clotted millions of the sleeping bees. There were other lumps and festoons and things like decayed tree-trunks studded on the face of the rock—the old combs of past years, or new cities built in the shadow of the windless gorge—and huge masses of spongy, rotten trash had rolled down and stuck among the trees and creepers that clung to the rock-face. As he listened he heard more than once the rustle and slide of a honey-loaded comb turning over or falling away somewhere in the dark galleries; then a booming of angry wings and the sullen drip, drip, drip, of the wasted honey, guttering along till it lipped over some ledge in the open and sluggishly trickled down on the twigs. There was a tiny little beach, not five feet broad, on one side of the river, that was piled high with the rubbish of uncounted years. There lay dead bees, drones, sweepings, stale combs, and wings of marauding moths and beetles that had strayed in after honey, all tumbled in smooth piles of the finest black dust. The mere sharp smell of it was enough to frighten anything that had no wings, and knew what the Little People were.

Kaa moved up stream again till he came to a sandy bar at the head of the gorge.

"Here is this season's kill," said he. "Look!"

On the bank lay the skeletons of a couple of young deer and a buffalo. Mowgli could see that no wolf nor jackal had touched the bones, which were laid out naturally.

"They came beyond the line, they did not know," murmured Mowgli, "and the Little People killed them. Let us go ere they awake."

"They do not wake till the dawn," said Kaa. "Now I will tell thee. A hunted buck from the south, many, many Rains ago, came hither from the south, not knowing the Jungle, a pack on his trail. Being made blind by fear he leaped from above, the pack running by sight, for they were hot and blind on the trail. The sun was high, and the Little People were many and very angry. Many, too, were those of the pack who leaped into the Waingunga, but they were dead ere they took water. Those who did not leap died also in the rocks above. But the buck lived."

"How?"

"Because he came first, running for his life, leaping ere the Little People were aware, and was in the river when they gathered to kill. The pack, following, was altogether lost under the weight of the Little People, who had been roused by the feet of that buck."

"The buck lived?" Mowgli repeated slowly.

"At least he did not die *then,* though none waited his coming down with a strong body to hold him safe against the water, as a certain old fat, deaf, yellow Flathead would wait for a Manling—yea, though there were all the dholes of the Dekkan on his trail. What is in thy stomach?"

Kaa's head lay on Mowgli's wet shoulder, and his tongue quivered by the boy's ear. There was a long silence before Mowgli whispered:—

"It is to pull the very whiskers of Death, but—Kaa, thou art, indeed the wisest of all the Jungle."

"So many have said. Look now, if the dholes follow thee—"

"As surely they will follow. Ho! ho! I have many little thorns under my tongue to prick into their hides."

"If they follow thee hot and blind, looking only at thy shoulders, those who do not die up above will take water either here or lower down, for the Little People will rise up and cover them. Now the Waingunga is hungry water, and they will have no Kaa to hold them, but will go down, such as live, to the shallows by the Seeonee lairs, and there thy Pack may meet them by the throat."

"Ahai! Eowawa! Better could not be till the Rains fall in the dry season. There is now only the little matter of the run and the leap. I will make me known to the dholes, so that they shall follow me very closely."

"Hast thou seen the rocks above thee? From the landward side?"

"Indeed no. That I had forgotten."

"Go look. It is all rotten ground, cut and full of holes. One of thy clumsy feet set down without seeing would end the hunt. See, I leave thee here, and for thy sake only I will carry word to the Pack that they may know where to look for the dhole. For myself, I am not of one skin with *any* wolf."

When Kaa disliked an acquaintance he could be more unpleasant than any of the Jungle people, except perhaps Bagheera. He swam down stream, and opposite the Rock he came on Phao and Akela listening to the night noises.

"Hssh! dogs," he said cheerfully. "The dhole will come down stream. If ye be not afraid ye can kill them in the shallows."

"When come they?" said Phao. "And where is my Man-cub?" said Akela.

"They come when they come," said Kaa. "Wait and see. As for *thy* Man-cub, from whom thou hast taken his Word and so laid him open to Death, *thy* Man-cub is with *me,* and if he be not already dead the fault is none of thine, bleached dog! Wait here for the dhole, and be glad that the Man-cub and I strike on thy side."

Kaa flashed up stream again and moored himself in the middle of the gorge, looking upwards at the line of the cliff. Presently he saw Mowgli's head move against the stars: then there was a whizz in the air, the keen clean *schloop* of a body falling feet first; next minute the body was at rest again in the loop of Kaa's body.

"It is no leap by night," said Mowgli quietly. "I have jumped twice as far for sport; but that is an evil place above—low bushes and gullies that go down deep—all full of the Little People. I have put big stones one above the other by the side of three gullies. These I shall throw down with my feet in running, and the Little People will rise up behind me angry."

"That is man's cunning," said Kaa. "Thou art wise, but the Little People are always angry."

"Nay, at twilight all wings near and far rest for awhile. I will play with the dhole at twilight, for the dhole hunts best by day. He follows now Won-tolla's blood-trail."

"Chil does not leave a dead ox, nor the dhole a blood-trail," said Kaa.

"Then I will make him a new blood-trail—of his own blood if I can, and give him dirt to eat. Thou wilt stay here, Kaa, till I come with my dholes?"

"Ay, but what if they kill thee in the Jungle, or the Little People kill thee before thou canst leap down to the river?"

"When to-morrow comes we will kill to-morrow," said Mowgli, quoting a Jungle saying; and again, "When I am dead it is time to sing the Death Song. Good hunting, Kaa."

He loosed his arm from the python's neck and went down the gorge like a log in a freshet, paddling towards the far bank, where he found slack water, and laughing aloud from sheer happiness. There was nothing Mowgli liked better than, as he himself said, "to pull the whiskers of Death" and make the Jungle feel that he was their overlord. He had often, with Baloo's help, robbed bees' nests in single trees, and he knew that the Little People disliked the smell of wild garlic. So he gathered a small bundle of it, tied it up with a bark string, and then followed Won-tolla's blood-trail as it ran southerly from the lairs, for some five miles, looking at the trees with his head on one side and chuckling as he looked.

"Mowgli the Frog have I been," said he to himself, "Mowgli the Wolf have I said that I am. Now Mowgli the Ape must I be before I am Mowgli the Buck. At the end I shall be Mowgli the Man. Ho!" and he slid his thumb along the eighteen-inch blade of his knife.

Won-tolla's trail, all rank with dark blood-spots, ran under a forest of thick trees that grew close together and stretched away north-eastward, gradually growing thinner and thinner to within two miles of the Bee Rocks. From the last tree to the low scrub of the Bee Rocks was open country, where there was hardly cover enough to hide a wolf. Mowgli trotted along under the trees, judging distances between branch and branch, occasionally climbing up a trunk and taking a trial leap from one tree to another, till he came to the open ground, which he studied very carefully for an hour. Then he turned, picked up Won-tolla's trail where he had left it, settled himself in a tree with an outrunning branch some eight feet from the ground, hung his bunch of garlic in a safe crotch, and sat still sharpening his knife on the sole of his foot.

A little before midday when the sun was very warm, he heard the patter of feet and smelt the abominable smell of the dhole pack as they trotted steadily and pitilessly along Won-tolla's trail. Seen from above the red dhole does not look half the size of a wolf, but Mowgli knew how strong his feet and jaws were. He watched the sharp bay head of the leader snuffing along the trail and gave him "Good hunting!"

The brute looked up and his companions halted behind him, scores and scores of red dogs with low-hung tails, heavy shoulders, weak quarters, and bloody mouths. The dholes are a very silent people as a rule, and they have no manners even in their own Dekkan. Fully two hundred must have gathered below him, but he could see that the leaders sniffed hungrily on Won-tolla's trail, and tried to drag the pack forward. That would never do, or they would be at the lairs in broad daylight, and Mowgli meant to hold them under his tree till twilight.

"By whose leave do ye come here?" said Mowgli.

"All jungles are our jungle," was the reply, and the dhole that gave it bared his white teeth. Mowgli looked down with a smile and imitated perfectly the sharp chitter-chatter of Chikai, the leaping rat of the Dekkan, meaning the dholes to understand that he considered them no better than Chikai. The pack closed up round the tree trunk and the leader bayed savagely, calling Mowgli a tree-ape. For an answer Mowgli stretched down one naked leg and wriggled his bare toes just above the leader's head. That was enough, and more than enough to wake the pack to stupid rage. Those who have hair between their toes do not care to be

48

reminded of it. Mowgli caught his foot away as the leader leaped and said sweetly: "Dog, red dog! Go back to the Dekkan and eat lizards. Go to Chikai thy brother, dog, dog, red, red dog! There is hair between every toe!" He twiddled his toes a second time.

"Come down ere we starve thee out, hairless ape," yelled the pack, and this was exactly what Mowgli wanted. He laid himself down along the branch, his cheek to the bark, his right arm free, and for some five minutes he told the pack what he thought and knew about them, their manners, their customs, their mates, and their puppies. There is no speech in the world so rancorous and so stinging as the language the Jungle People use to show scorn and contempt. When you come to think of it you will see how this must be so. As Mowgli told Kaa, he had many little thorns under his tongue, and slowly and deliberately he drove the dholes from silence to growls, from growls to yells, and from yells to hoarse slavery ravings. They tried to answer his taunts, but a cub might as well have tried to answer Kaa in a rage, and all the while Mowgli's right hand lay crooked at his side, ready for action, his feet locked round the branch. The big bay leader had leaped many times into the air, but Mowgli dared not risk a false blow. At last, made furious beyond his natural strength, he bounded up seven or eight feet clear of the ground. Then Mowgli's hand shot out like the head of a tree-snake, and gripped him by the scruff of his neck, and the branch shook with the jar as his weight fell back, and Mowgli was almost wrenched on to the ground. But he never loosed his grip, and inch by inch he hauled the beast, hanging like a drowned jackal, up on the branch. With his left hand he reached for his knife and cut off the red, bushy tail, flinging the dhole back to earth again. That was all he needed. The dhole would not go forward on Wontolla's trail now till they had killed Mowgli, or Mowgli had killed them. He saw them settle down in circles with a quiver of the haunches that meant revenge to the death, and so he climbed to a higher crotch, settled his back comfortably and went to sleep.

After three or four hours he waked and counted the pack. They were all there, silent, husky, and dry, with eyes of steel. The sun was beginning to sink. In half an hour the Little People of the Rocks would be ending their labours, and, as you know, the dhole does not fight well in the twilight.

"I did not need such faithful watchers," he said, standing up on a branch, "but I will remember this. Ye be true dholes, but to my thinking too much of one kind. For that reason I do not give the big lizard-eater his tail again. Art thou not pleased, Red Dog?"

"I myself will tear out thy stomach," yelled the leader, biting the foot of the tree.

"Nay, but consider, wise rat of Dekkan. There will now be many litters of little tailless red dogs, yea, with raw red stumps that sting when the sand is hot. Go home, Red Dog, and cry that an ape has done this. Ye will not go? Come then with me, and I will make ye very wise."

He moved monkey-fashion into the next tree, and so on and the next and the next, the pack following with lifted hungry heads. Now and then he would pretend to fall, and the pack would tumble one over the other in their haste to be in at the death. It was a curious sight—the boy with the knife that shone in the low sunlight as it sifted through the upper branches, and the silent pack with their red coats all aflame huddling and following below. When he came to the last tree he took the garlic and rubbed himself all over carefully, and the dholes yelled with scorn. "Ape with a wolf's tongue, dost thou think to cover thy scent?" they said. "We will follow to the death."

"Take thy tail," said Mowgli, flinging it back along the course he had taken. The pack naturally rushed back a little when they smelt the blood. "And follow now—to the death!"

He had slipped down the tree trunk, and headed like the wind in bare feet for the Bee Rocks, before the dholes saw what he would do.

They gave one deep howl and settled down to the long lobbing canter that can, at the last, run down anything that lives. Mowgli knew their pack pace to be much slower than that of the wolves, or he would never have risked a two-mile run in full sight. They were sure that the boy was theirs at last, and he was sure that he had them to play with as he pleased. All his trouble was to keep them sufficiently hot behind him to prevent them turning off too soon. He ran cleanly, evenly, and springily;

the tailless leader not five yards behind him; and the pack stringing out over perhaps a quarter of a mile of ground, crazy and blind with the rage of slaughter. So he kept his distance by ear, reserving his last effort for the rush across the Bee Rocks.

The Little People had gone to sleep in the early twilight, for it was not the season of late blossoming flowers; but as Mowgli's first footfalls rang hollow on the hollow ground he heard a sound as though all the earth were humming. Then he ran as he had never run in his life before, spurned aside one—two—three of the piles of stones into the dark sweet-smelling gullies; heard a roar like the roar of the sea in a cave, saw with the tail of his eye the air grow dark behind him, saw the current of the Waingunga far below, and a flat, diamond-shaped head in the water; leaped outward with all his strength, the tailless dhole snapping at his shoulder in mid-air, and dropped feet first to the safety of the river, breathless and triumphant. There was not a sting on his body, for the smell of the garlic had checked the Little People for just the few seconds that carried him across the rocks. When he rose Kaa's coils were steady-ing him and things were bounding over the edge of the cliff—great lumps it seemed, of clustered bees falling like plummets; and as each lump touched water the bees flew upward and the body of a dhole whirled down stream. Overhead they could hear furious short yells that were drowned in a roar like thunder—the roar of the wings of the Little People of the Rocks. Some of the dholes, too, had fallen into the gullies that communicated with the underground caves, and there choked, and fought, and snapped among the tumbled honeycombs, and at last, borne up dead on the heaving waves of bees beneath them, shot out of some hole in the river face, to roll over on the black rubbish heaps. There were dholes who had leaped short into the trees on the cliffs, and the bees blotted out their shapes; but the greater number of them, maddened by the stings, had flung themselves into the river; and, as Kaa said, the Waingunga was hungry water.

Kaa held Mowgli fast till the boy had recovered his breath.

"We may not stay here," he said. "The Little People are roused indeed. Come!"

Swimming low and diving as often as he could, Mowgli went down the river with the knife in his hand.

"Slowly, slowly!" said Kaa. "One tooth does not kill a hundred unless it be a cobra's, and many of the dholes took water swiftly when they saw the Little People rise. *They* are unhurt."

"The more work for my knife, then. Phai! How the Little People follow." Mowgli sank again. The face of the water was blanketed with wild bees buzzing sullenly and stinging all they found.

"Nothing was ever yet lost by silence," said Kaa—no sting could penetrate his scales—"and thou hast all the long night for the hunting. Hear them howl!"

Nearly half the pack had seen the trap their fellows rushed into, and, turning sharp aside, had flung themselves into the water where the gorge broke down in steep banks. Their cries of rage and their threats against the "tree-ape" who had brought them to their shame mixed with the yells and growls of those who had been punished by the Little People. To remain ashore was death, and every dhole knew it. The pack was swept along the current, down and down to the rocks of the Peace Pool, but even there the angry Little People followed and forced them to the water again. Mowgli could hear the voice of the tailless leader bidding his people hold on and kill out every wolf in Seeonee. But he did not waste his time in listening.

"One kills in the dark behind us!" snapped a dhole. "Here is tainted water!"

Mowgli had dived forward like an otter, twitched a struggling dhole under water before he could open his mouth, and dark, oily rings rose in the Peace Pool as the body plopped up, turning on its side. The dholes tried to turn, but the current forced them by, and the Little People darted at their heads and ears, and they could hear the challenge of the Seeonee Pack growing louder and deeper in the gathering darkness ahead. Again Mowgli dived, and again a dhole went under and rose dead, and again the clamour broke out at the rear of the pack, some howling that it was best to go ashore, others calling on their leader to lead them back to the Dekkan, and others bidding Mowgli show himself and be killed.

"They come to the fight with two stomachs and many voices," said Kaa. "The rest is with thy brethren below yonder. The Little People go back to sleep, and I will turn also. I do not help wolves."

A wolf came running along the bank on three legs, leaping up and down, laying his head sideways close to the ground, hunching his back, and breaking a couple of feet into the air, as though he were playing with his cubs. It was Won-tolla, the Outlier, and he said never a word, but continued his horrible sport beside the dholes. They had been long in the water now, and were swimming laboriously, their coats drenched and heavy, and their bushy tails dragging like sponges, so tired and shaken that they, too, were silent, watching the pair of blazing eyes that moved abreast of them.

"This is no good hunting," said one at last.

"Good hunting!" said Mowgli as he rose boldly at the brute's side and sent the long knife home behind the shoulder, pushing hard to avoid the dying snap.

"Art thou there, Man-cub?" said Won-tolla, from the bank.

"Ask of the dead, Outlier," Mowgli replied. "Have none come down stream? I have filled these dogs' mouths with dirt; I have tricked them in the broad daylight, and their leader lacks his tail, but here be some few for thee still. Whither shall I drive them?"

"I will wait," said Won-tolla. "The long night is before me, and I shall see well."

Nearer and nearer came the bay of the Seeonee wolves. "For the Pack, for the Full Pack it is met!" and a bend in the river drove the dholes forward among the sands and shoals opposite the Seeonee lairs.

Then they saw their mistake. They should have landed half a mile higher up and rushed the wolves on dry ground. Now it was too late. The bank was lined with burning eyes, and except for the horrible *Pheeal* cry that had never stopped since sundown there was no sound in the jungle. It seemed as though Won-tolla was fawning on them to come ashore; and "Turn and take hold!" said the leader of the dholes. The entire pack flung themselves at the shore, threshing and squattering through the shoal water till the face of the Waingunga was all white and torn, and the great ripples went from side to side like bow-waves from a boat. Mowgli followed the rush, stabbing and slicing as the dholes, huddled together, rushed up the river-beach in a wave.

Then the long fight began, heaving and straining and splitting and scattering and narrowing and broadening along the red wet sands, and over and between the tangled tree-roots, and through and among the bushes, and in and out of the grass clumps, for even now the dholes were two to one. But they met wolves fighting for all that made the Pack, and not only the short, deep-chested white-tusked hunters of the Pack, but the wild-eyed lahinis—the she-wolves of the lair, as the saying is—fighting for their litters, with here and there a yearling wolf, his first coat still half woolly, tugging and grappling by their sides. A wolf, you must know, flies at the throat or snaps at the flank, while a dhole by preference bites low, so when the dholes were struggling out of the water and had to raise their heads the odds were with the wolves; on dry land the wolves suffered, but in the water or on land Mowgli's knife came and went the same. The Four had worked their way to his aid. Gray Brother, crouched between the boy's knees, protected his stomach, while the others guarded his back and either side, or stood over him when the shock of a leaping, yelling dhole who had thrown himself on the steady blade bore him down. For the rest, it was one tangled confusion—a locked and swaying mob that moved from right to left and from left to right along the bank, and also ground round and round slowly on its own centre. Here would be a heaving mound, like a water-blister in a whirlpool, which would break like a water-blister, and throw up four or five mangled dogs, each striving to get back to the centre; here would be a single wolf borne down by two or three dholes dragging him forward, and sinking the while; here a yearling cub would be held up by the pressure round him, though he had been killed early in the fight, while his mother, crazed with dumb rage, rolled over snapping and passing on; and in the middle of the thickest fight, perhaps, one wolf and one dhole, forgetting everything else, would be manoeuvring for first hold till they were swept away by a rush of yelling fighters. Once Mowgli passed Akela, a dhole on either flank, and his all but toothless jaws closed over the loins of a third; and once he saw Phao, his teeth set in the throat of a dhole, tugging the unwilling beast forward till the yearlings could finish him. But the bulk of the fight was blind flurry and smother in the dark; hit, trip, and tumble, yelp, groan and worry-worry-worry round him and behind him and above him.

As the night wore on the quick giddy-go-round motion increased. The dholes were wearied and afraid to attack the stronger wolves, though they did not yet dare to run away; but Mowgli felt that the end was coming soon, and contented himself with striking to cripple. The yearlings were growing bolder; there was time to breathe; and now the mere flicker of the knife would sometimes turn a dhole aside.

"The meat is very near the bone," Gray Brother gasped. He was bleeding from a score of flesh-wounds.

"But the bone is yet to be cracked," said Mowgli. "Aowawa! *Thus* do we do in the Jungle!" The red blade ran like a flame along the side of a dhole whose hind-quarters were hidden by the weight of a clinging wolf.

"My kill!" snorted the wolf through his wrinkled nostrils. "Leave him to me!"

"Is thy stomach *still* empty, Outlier?" said Mowgli. Won-tolla was fearfully punished, but his grip had paralysed the dhole, who could not turn round and reach him.

"By the Bull that bought me," Mowgli cried, with a bitter laugh, "it is the tailless one!" And indeed it was the big bay-coloured leader.

"It is not wise to kill cubs and lahinis," Mowgli went on philosophically, wiping the blood out of his eyes, "unless one also kills the lair-father, and it is in my stomach that this lair-father kills thee."

A dhole leaped to his leader's aid, but before his teeth had found Won-tolla's flank, Mowgli's knife was in his chest, and Gray Brother took what was left.

"And thus do we do in the Jungle," said Mowgli.

Won-tolla said not a word, only his jaws were closing and closing on the backbone as life ebbed. The dhole shuddered, his head dropped and he lay still, and Won-tolla dropped above him.

"Huh! The Blood Debt is paid," said Mowgli. "Sing the song, Won-tolla."

"He hunts no more," said Gray Brother, "and Akela too is silent, this long time."

"The bone is cracked!" thundered Phao, son of Phaona. "They go! Kill, kill out, O hunters of the Free People!"

Dhole after dhole was slinking away from those dark and bloody sands to the river, to the thick jungle, up stream or down stream as he saw the road clear.

"The debt! The debt!" shouted Mowgli. "Pay the debt! They have slain the Lone Wolf! Let not a dog go!"

He was flying to the river, knife in hand, to check any dhole who dared to take water, when, from under a mound of nine dead, rose Akela's head and fore-quarters, and Mowgli dropped on his knees beside the Lone Wolf.

"Said I not it would be my last fight?" Akela gasped. "It is good hunting. And thou, Little Brother?"

"I live, having killed many."

"Even so. I die, and I would—I would die by thee, Little Brother."

Mowgli took the terrible scarred head on his knees, and put his arms round the torn neck.

"It is long since the old days of Shere Khan and a Man-cub that rolled naked in the dust," coughed Akela.

"Nay, nay, I am a wolf. I am of one skin with the Free People," Mowgli cried. "It is no will of mine that I am a man."

"Thou art a man, Little Brother, wolfling of my watching. Thou art all a man, or else the Pack had fled before the dhole. My life I owe to thee, and to-day thou hast saved the Pack even as once I saved thee. Hast thou forgotten? All debts are paid now. Go to thine own people. I tell thee again, eye of my eye, this hunting is ended. Go to thine own people."

"I will never go. I will hunt alone in the Jungle. I have said it."

"After the summer come the rains, and after the rains come the spring. Go back before thou art driven."

"Who will drive me?"

"Mowgli will drive Mowgli. Go back to thy people. Go to Man."

"When Mowgli drives Mowgli I will go," Mowgli answered.

"There is no more for thee," said Akela. "Now I would speak to my kind. Little Brother, canst thou raise me to my feet? I also am a leader of the Free People."

Very carefully and gently Mowgli raised Akela to his feet, both arms round him, and the Lone Wolf drew a deep breath and began the Death Song that a leader of the Pack should sing when he dies. It gathered strength as he went on, lifting and lifting and ringing far across the river, till it came to the last "Good hunting!" and Akela shook himself clear of Mowgli for an instant, and leaping into the air, fell backwards dead upon his last and most terrible kill.

Mowgli sat with his head on his knees, careless of anything else, while the last of the dying dholes were being overtaken and run down by the merciless lahinis. Little by little the cries died away, and the wolves came back limping as their wounds stiffened to take stock of the dead. Fifteen of the pack, as well as half a dozen lahinis, were dead by the river, and of the others not one was unmarked. Mowgli sat through it all till the cold daybreak, when Phao's wet red muzzle was dropped in his hand, and Mowgli drew back to show the gaunt body of Akela.

"Good hunting!" said Phao, as though Akela were still alive, and then over his bitten shoulder to the others: "Howl, dogs! A wolf has died tonight!"

But of all the pack of two hundred fighting dholes, Red Dogs of the Dekkan, whose boast is that no living thing in the Jungle dare stand before them, not one returned to the Dekkan to carry that news.

Carol Emshwiller

PELT

She was a white dog with a wide face and eager eyes, and this was the planet Jaxa, in winter.

She trotted well ahead of the master, sometimes nose to ground, sometimes sniffing the air, and she didn't care if they were being watched or not. She knew that strange things skulked behind iced trees, but strangeness was her job. She had been trained for it, and crisp, glittering Jaxa was, she felt, exactly what she had been trained for, *born* for.

I love it, I love it . . . that was in her pointing ears, her waving tail . . . I *love* this place.

It was a world of ice, a world with the sound of breaking goblets. Each time the wind blew they came shattering down by the trayful, and each time one branch brushed against another it was, "Skoal," "Down the hatch," "The Queen" . . . tink, tink, tink. And the sun was reflected as if from a million cut-glass punch bowls under a million crystal chandeliers.

She wore four little black boots, and each step she took sounded like two or three more goblets gone, but the sound was lost in the other tinkling, snapping, cracklings of the silver, frozen forest about her.

She had figured out at last what that hovering scent was. It had been there from the beginning, the landing two days ago, mingling with Jaxa's bitter air and seeming to be just a part of the smell of the place; she found it in criss-crossing trails about the squatting ship, and hanging, heavy and recent, in hollows behind flat-branched, piney-smelling bushes. She thought of honey, and fat men, and dry fur when she smelled it.

There was something big out there, and more than one of them, more than two. She wasn't sure how many. She had a feeling this was something to tell the master, but what was the signal, the agreed-upon noise for: We are being watched? There was a whisper of sound, short and quick, for: Sighted close, come and shoot. And there was a noise for danger (all these through her throat mike to the receiver at the master's ear), a special, howly bark: Awful, awful—there is something awful going to happen. There was even a noise, a low rumble of sound for: Wonderful, wonderful fur—drop everything and come after *this* one. (And she knew a good fur when she saw one. She had been trained to know.) But there was no sign for: We are being watched.

She'd whined and barked when she was sure about it, but that had got her a pat on the head and a rumpling of the neck fur. "You're doing fine, Baby. This world is all ours. All we got to do is pick up the pearls. This is what we've been waiting for." And Jaxa was, so she did her work and didn't try to tell him any more, for what was one more strange thing in one more strange world?

She was on the trail of something now, and the master was behind her, out of sight. He'd better hurry. He'd better hurry or there'll be waiting to do, watching the thing, whatever it is, steady on until he comes, holding tight back, and that will be hard. Hurry, hurry.

60

She could hear the whispered whistle of a tune through the receiver at her ear and she knew he was not hurrying but just being happy. She ran on, eager, curious. She did not give the signal for hurry, but she made a hurry sound of her own, and she heard him stop whistling and whisper back into the mike, "So, so, Queen of Venus. The furs are waiting to be picked. No hurry, Baby." But morning was to her for hurry. There was time later to be tired and slow.

That fat-man honeyish smell was about, closer and strong. Her curiosity became two-pronged—this smell or that? What *is* the big thing that watches? She kept to the trail she was on, though. Better to be sure, and this thing was not so elusive, not twisting and doubling back, but up ahead and going where it was going.

She topped a rise and half slid, on thick furred rump, down the other side, splattering ice. She snuffled at the bottom to be sure of the smell again, and then, nose to ground, trotted past a thick and tangled hedgerow.

She was thinking through her nose, now. The world was all smell, crisp air, and sour ice, and turpentine pine . . . and this animal, a urine and brown grass thing . . . and then, strong in front of her, honey-furry-fat man.

She felt it looming before she raised her head to look, and there it was, the smell in person, some taller than the master and twice as wide. Counting his doubled suit and all, twice as wide.

This was a fur! Wonderful, wonderful. But she just stood, looking up, mouth open and lips pulled back, the fur on the back of her neck rising more from the suddenness than from fear.

It was silver and black, a tiger-striped thing, and the whitish parts glistened and caught the light as the ice of Jaxa did, and sparkled and dazzled in the same way. And there, in the center of the face, was a large and terrible orange eye, rimmed in black with black radiating lines cross-ing the forehead and rounding the head. That spot of orange dominated the whole figure, but it was a flat, blind eye, unreal, grown out of fur. At first she saw only that spot of color, but then she noticed under it two small, red glinting eyes and they were kind, not terrible.

This was the time for the call: Come, come and get the great fur, for the richest lady on earth to wear and be dazzling in and, most of all, to pay for. But there was something about the flat, black nose and the tender, bow-shaped lips, and those kind eyes that stopped her from calling. Something masterly. She was full of wondering and indecision and she made no sound at all.

The thing spoke to her then, and its voice was a deep lullaby sound of buzzing cellos. It gestured with a thick, fur-backed hand. It promised, offered, and asked; and she listened, knowing and not knowing.

The words came slowly.

This . . . is . . . world.

Here is the sky, the earth, the ice. The heavy arms moved. The hands pointed.

We have watched you, little slave. What have you done that is free today? Take the liberty. Here is the earth for your four-shoed feet, the sky of stars, the ice to drink. Do something free today. Do, do.

Nice voice, she thought, nice thing. It gives and gives . . . something.

Her ears pointed forward, then to the side, one and then the other, and then forward again. She cocked her head, but the real meaning would not come clear. She poked at the air with her nose.

Say that again, her whole body said. I almost have it. I *feel* it. Say it once more and maybe then the sense of it will come.

But the creature turned and started away quickly, very quickly for such a big thing. It seemed to shimmer itself away until the glitter was only the glitter of the ice and the black was only the thick, flat branches.

The master was close. She could hear his crackling steps coming up behind her.

She whined softly, more to herself than to him.

"Ho, Queenie. Have you lost it?" She sniffed the ground again. The honey-furry smell was strong. She sniffed beyond, zigzagging. The trail was there. "Go to it, Baby." She loped off to a sound like Chinese wind chimes, businesslike again. Her tail hung guiltily, though, and she kept her head low. She had missed an important signal. She'd waited until it was too late. But was the thing a master? Or a fur? She wanted to do the right thing. She always tried and tried for that, but now she was confused.

She was getting close to whatever it was she trailed, but the hovering smell was still there too, though not close. She thought of gifts. She knew that much from the slow, lullaby words, and gifts made her think of bones and meat, not the dry fishy biscuit she always got on trips like this. A trickle of drool flowed from the side of her mouth and froze in a silver thread across her shoulder.

She slowed. The thing she trailed must be *there,* just behind the next row of trees. She made a sound in her throat . . . ready, steady . . . and she advanced until she was sure. She sensed the shape. She didn't really see it . . . mostly it was the smell and something more in the tinkling glassware noises. She gave the signal and stood still, a furry, square imitation of a pointer. Come, hurry. This waiting is the hardest part.

He followed, beamed to her radio. "Steady, Baby. Hold that pose. Good girl, good girl!" There was only the slightest twitch of her tail as she wagged it, answering him in her mind.

He came up behind her and then passed, crouched, holding the rifle-rod before him, elbows bent. He knelt then, and waited as if at a point of his own, rod to shoulder. Slowly he turned with the moving shadow of the beast, and shot, twice in quick succession.

They ran forward then, together, and it was what she had expected—a deerlike thing, dainty hoofs, proud head, and spotted in three colors, large gray-green rounds on tawny yellow, with tufts of that same glittering silver scattered over.

The master took out a flat-bladed knife. He began to whistle out loud as he cut off the handsome head. His face was flushed.

She sat down nearby, mouth open in a kind of smile, and she watched his face as he worked. The warm smell made the drool come at the sides of her mouth and drip out to freeze on the ice and on her paws, but she sat quietly, only watching.

Between the whistlings he grunted, and swore, and talked to himself, and finally he had the skin and the head in a tight inside-out bundle.

Then he came to her and patted her sides with a flat, slap sound, and he scratched behind her ears and held a biscuit for her on his thick-gloved palm. She swallowed it whole and then watched him as he squatted on his heels and ate one almost like it.

Then he got up and slung the bundle of skin and head across his back. "I'll take this one, Baby. Come on, let's get one more something before lunch." He waved her to the right. "We'll make a big circle," he said.

She trotted out, glad she was not carrying anything. She found a strong smell at a patch of discolored ice and urinated on it. She sniffed and growled at a furry, mammal-smelling bird that landed in the trees above her and sent a shower of ice slivers down on her head. She zig-zagged and then turned and bit, lips drawn back in mock rage, at a branch that scraped her side.

She followed for a while the chattery sound of water streaming along under the ice, and left it where an oily, lambish smell crossed. Almost immediately she came upon them—six small, greenish balls of wool with floppy, woolly feet. The honey-fat man smell was strong here too, but she signaled for the lambs, the "Come and shoot" sound, and she stood again waiting for the master.

"*Good* girl!" His voice has special praise. "By God, this place is a gold mine. Hold it, Queen of Venus. Whatever it is, don't let go."

There was a fifty-yard clear view here and she stood in plain sight of the little creatures, but they didn't notice. The master came slowly and cautiously, and knelt beside her. Just as he did, there appeared at the far end of the clearing a glittering silver and black tiger-striped creature.

She heard the sharp inward breath of the master and she felt the tenseness come to him. There was a new, faint whiff of sour sweat, and a special way of breathing. What she felt from him made the fur rise along her back with a mixture of excitement and fear.

The tiger thing held a small packet in one hand and was peering into it and pulling at the opening in it with a blunt finger. Suddenly there was a sweep of motion beside her and five fast, frantic pops sounded sharp in her ear. Two came after the honey-fat man had already fallen and lay like a huge, decorated sack.

64

The master ran forward and she came at his heels. They both stopped, not too close, and she watched the master looking at the big, dead, tiger head with the terrible eye. The master was breathing hard. His face was red and puffy. He didn't whistle or talk. After a time he took out his knife. He tested the blade, making a small, bloody thread of a mark on his left thumb. Then he walked closer, and she stood, and watched him, and whispered a questioning whine.

He stooped by the honey-fat master and it was that small, partly opened packet that he cut viciously through the center. Small round chunks fell out, bite-sized chunks of dried meat, and a cheesy substance, and some broken bits of clear, bluish ice.

The master kicked at them. His face was not red anymore, but pale. His mouth was open in a grin that was not a grin.

He went about the skinning then.

He did not keep the flat-faced, heavy head nor the blunt-fingered hands.

The master had to make a sliding thing of two of the widest kind of flat branches to carry the new heavy fur, as well as the head and the skin of the deer. Then he started directly for the ship.

It was past eating time but she looked at his restless eyes and did not ask about it. She walked in front of him, staying close. She looked back often, watching him pull the sled by the string across his shoulder and she knew, by the way he held the rod before him in both hands, that she should be wary.

Sometimes the damp-looking, inside-out bundle hooked on things, and the master would curse in a whisper and pull at it. She could see the bundle made him tired, and she wished he would stop for a rest and food as they usually did long before this time.

They went slowly, and the smell of honey-fat master hovered as it had from the beginning. They crossed the trails of many animals. They even saw another deer run off, but she knew that it was not a time for chasing.

Then another big silver and black tiger stood exactly before them. It appeared suddenly, as if actually it had been standing there all the time, and they had not been near enough to pick it out from its glistening background.

It just stood and looked and dared, and the master held his rifle rod with both hands and looked too, and she stood between them glancing from one face to the other. She knew, after a moment, that the master would not shoot, and it seemed the tiger thing knew too, for it turned to look at her and it raised its arms and spread its fingers as if grasping at the forest on each side. It swayed a bit, like bigness off balance, and then it spoke in its tight-strung, cello tones. The words and the tone seemed the same as before.

Little slave, what have you done that is free today? Remember this is world. Do something free today. Do, do.

She knew that what it said was important to it, something she should understand, a giving and a taking away. It watched her, and she looked back with wide eyes, wanting to do the right thing, but not knowing what.

The tiger-fat master turned then, this time slowly, and left a wide back for the master and her to see, and then it half turned, throwing a quick glance at the two of them over the heavy humped shoulder. Then it moved slowly away into the trees and ice, and the master still held the rifle rod with two hands and did not move.

The evening wind began to blow, and there sounded about them that sound of a million chandeliers tinkling like gigantic wind chimes. A furry bird, the size of a shrew and as fast, flew by between them with a miniature shriek.

She watched the master's face and, when he was ready, she went along beside him. The soft sounds the honey-fat master had made echoed in her mind but had no meaning.

That night the master stretched the big skin on a frame and afterward he watched the dazzle of it. He didn't talk to her. She watched him a while and then she turned around three times on her rug and lay down.

The next morning the master was slow, reluctant to go out. He studied charts of other places, round or hourglass-shaped maps with yellow dots and labels, and he drank his coffee standing up looking at them. But finally they did go out, squinting into the ringing air.

It was her world. More each day, right feel, right temperature, lovely smells. She darted on ahead as usual, yet not too far today, and sometimes she stopped and waited and looked at the master's face as he came up. And sometimes she would whine a question before she went on . . . Why don't you walk brisk, brisk, and call me Queen of Venus, or Bitch of Betelgeuse? Why don't you sniff like I do? Sniff, and you will be happy . . . And she would run on again.

Trails were easy to find, and once more she found the oily lamb smell, and once more came upon them quickly. The master strode up beside her and raised his rifle rod . . . but a moment later he turned, carelessly, letting himself make a loud noise, and the lambs ran. He made a face, and spat upon the ice. "Come on Queenie. Let's get out of here. I'm sick of this place."

He turned and made the signal to go back, pointing with his thumb above his head in two jerks of motion.

But why, why? This is morning now and our world. She wagged her tail and gave a short bark, and looked at him, dancing a little on her back paws, begging with her whole body.

"Come on," he said.

She turned then, and took her place at his heel, head low, but eyes looking up at him, wondering if she had done something wrong, and wanting to be right, and noticed, and loved because he was troubled and preoccupied.

They'd gone only a few minutes on the way back when he stopped suddenly in the middle of a step, slowly put both feet flat upon the ground and stood like a soldier at a stiff, off-balance attention. There, lying in the way before them, was the huge, orange-eyed head and in front of it, as if at the end of outstretched arms, lay two leathery hands, the hairless palms up.

She made a growl deep in her throat and the master made a noise almost exactly like hers. She waited for him, standing as he stood, not moving, feeling his tenseness coming in to her. Yet it was just a head and two hands of no value, old ones they had had before and thrown away.

He turned and she saw a wild look in his eyes. He walked with deliberate steps, and she followed, in a wide circle about the spot. When they had skirted the place, he began to walk very fast.

They were not far from the ship. She could see its flat blackness as they drew nearer to the clearing, the burned, iceless pit of spewed and blackened earth. And then she saw that the silver tiger masters were there, nine of them in a wide circle, each with the honey-damp fur smell, but each with a separate particular sweetness.

The master was still walking very fast, eyes down to watch his footing, and he did not see them until he was in the circle before them all, as they stood there like nine upright bears in tiger suits.

He stopped and made a whisper of a groan, and he let the rifle rod fall low in one hand so that it hung loose with the end almost touching the ground. He looked from one to the other and she looked at him, watching his pale eyes move along the circle.

"Stay," he said, and then he began to go toward the ship at an awkward limp, running and walking at the same time, banging the rifle rod handle against the air lock as he entered.

He had said, "Stay." She sat watching the ship door and moving her front paws up and down because she wanted to be walking after him. He was gone only a minute, though, and when he came back it was without the rod and he was holding the great fur with cut pieces of thongs dangling like ribbons along its edges where it had been tied to the stretching frame. He went at that same run-walk, unbalanced by the heavy bundle, to one of them along the circle. Three gathered together before him and refused to take it back. They pushed it, bunched loosely, back across his arms and to it they added another large and heavy package in a parchment bag, and the master stood, with his legs wide to hold it all.

Then one honey-fat master motioned with a fur-backed hand to the ship and the bundles, and then to the ship and the master, and then to the sky. He made two sharp sounds once, and then again. And another made two different sounds, and she felt the feeling of them . . . Take your things and go home. Take them, these and these, and go.

They turned to her then and one spoke and made a wide gesture. *This is world. The sky, the earth, the ice.*

They wanted her to stay. They gave her . . . was it their world? But what good was a world?

She wagged her tail hesitantly, lowered her head, and looked up at them . . . I do want to do right, to please everybody, everybody, but . . . Then she followed the master into the ship.

The locks rumbled shut. She took her place, flat on her side, take-off position. The master snapped the flat plastic sheet over her, covering head and all and, in a few minutes, they roared off.

Afterward he opened the parchment bag. She knew what was in it. She knew he knew too, but she knew by the smell. He opened it and dumped out the head and the hands.

She saw him almost put the big head out the waste chute, but he didn't. He took it into the place where he kept good heads and some odd paws or hoofs, and he put it by the others there.

Even she knew this head was different. The others were slantbrowed like she was and most had jutting snouts. This one was bigger even than the big ones, with its heavy, ruffed fur and huge eye staring, and more grand than any of them, more terrible . . . and yet a flat face, with a delicate black nose and tender lips. The tenderest lips of all.

Mark Twain

THE DACHSHUND

In the train, during a part of the return journey from Baroda, we had the company of a gentleman who had with him a remarkable-looking dog. I had not seen one of its kind before, as far as I could remember; though of course I might have seen one and not noticed it, for I am not acquainted with dogs, but only with cats. This dog's coat was smooth and shiny and black, and I think it had tan trimmings around the edges of the dog, and perhaps underneath. It was a long, low dog, with very short, strange legs—legs that curved inboard, something like parentheses turned the wrong way (. Indeed, it was made on the plan of a bench for length and lowness. It seemed to be satisfied, but I thought the plan poor, and structurally weak, on account of the distance between the forward supports and those abaft. With age the dog's back was likely to sag; and it seemed to me that it would have been a stronger and more practicable dog if it had had some more legs. It had not begun to sag yet, but the shape of the legs showed that the undue weight imposed upon them was beginning to tell. It had a long nose, and floppy ears that hung down, and a resigned expression of countenance. I did not like to ask what kind of a dog it was, or how it came to be deformed, for it was plain that the gentleman was very fond of it, and naturally he could be sensitive about it. From delicacy I thought it best not to seem to notice it too much. No doubt a man with a dog like that feels just as a person does who has a child that is out of true. The gentleman was not merely fond of the dog, he was also proud of it—just the same, again, as a mother feels about her child when it is an idiot. I could see that he was proud of it, notwithstanding it was such a long dog and looked so resigned and pious. It had been all over the world with him, and had been pilgriming like that for years and years. It had traveled fifty thousand miles by sea and rail, and had ridden in front of him on his horse eight thousand. It had a silver medal from the Geographical Society of Great Britain for its travels, and I saw it. It had won prizes in dog-shows, both in India and in England—I saw them.

He said its pedigree was on record in the Kennel Club, and that it was a well-known dog. He said a great many people in London could recognize it the moment they saw it. I did not say anything, but I did not think it anything strange; I should know that dog again, myself, yet I am not careful about noticing dogs. He said that when he walked along in London, people often stopped and looked at the dog. Of course I did not say anything, for I did not want to hurt his feelings, but I could have explained to him that if you take a great long low dog like that and waddle it along the street anywhere in the world and not charge anything, people will stop and look. He was gratified because the dog took prizes. But that was nothing; if I were built like that I could take prizes myself. I wished I knew what kind of a dog it was, and what it was for, but I could not very well ask, for that would show that I did not know. Not that I want a dog like that, but only to know the secret of its birth.

I think he was going to hunt elephants with it, because I know, from remarks dropped by him, that he has hunted large game in India and Africa, and likes it. But I think that if he tries to hunt elephants with it, he is going to be disappointed. I do not believe that it is suited for elephants. It lacks energy, it lacks force of character, it lacks bitterness. These things all show in the meekness and resignation of its expression. It would not attack an elephant, I am sure of it. It might not run if it saw one coming, but it looked to me like a dog that would sit down and pray.

Edith Wharton

KERFOL

"You ought to buy it," said my host; "it's just the place for a solitary-minded devil like you. And it would be rather worth-while to own the most romantic house in Brittany. The present people are dead broke, and it's going for a song—you ought to buy it."

It was not with the least idea of living up to the character my friend Lanrivain ascribed to me (as a matter of fact, under my unsociable exterior I have always had secret yearnings for domesticity) that I took his hint one autumn afternoon and went to Kerfol. My friend was motoring over to Quimper on business: he dropped me on the way, at a crossroad on a heath, and said: "First turn to the right and second to the left. Then straight ahead till you see an avenue. If you meet any peasants, don't ask your way. They don't understand French, and they would pretend they did and mix you up. I'll be back for you here by sunset—and don't forget the tombs in the chapel."

I followed Lanrivain's directions with the hesitation occasioned by the usual difficulty of remembering whether he had said the first turn to the right and second to the left, or the contrary. If I had met a peasant I should certainly have asked, and probably been sent astray; but I had the desert landscape to myself, and so stumbled on the right turn and walked across the heath till I came to an avenue. It was so unlike any other avenue I have ever seen that I instantly knew it must be *the* avenue. The grey-trunked trees sprang up straight to a great height and then inter-wove their pale grey branches in a long tunnel through which the autumn light fell faintly. I know most trees by name, but I haven't to this day been able to decide what those trees were. They had the tall curve of elms, the tenuity of poplars, the ashen color of olives under a rainy sky; and they stretched ahead of me for half a mile or more without a break in their arch. If ever I saw an avenue that unmistakably led to something, it was the avenue at Kerfol. My heart beat a little as I began to walk down it.

Presently the trees ended and I came to a fortified gate in a long wall. Between me and the wall was an open space of grass, with other grey avenues radiating from it. Behind the wall were tall slate roofs mossed with silver, a chapel belfry, the top of a keep. A moat filled with wild shrubs and brambles surrounded the place; the drawbridge had been replaced by a stone arch, and the portcullis by an iron gate. I stood for a long time on the hither side of the moat, gazing about me, and letting the influence of the place sink in. I said to myself: "If I wait long enough, the guardian will turn up and show me the tombs—" and I rather hoped he wouldn't turn up too soon.

I sat down on a stone and lit a cigarette. As soon as I had done it, it struck me as a puerile and portentous thing to do, with that great blind house looking down at me, and all the empty avenues converging on me. It may have been the depth of the silence that made me so conscious of my gesture. The squeak of my match sounded as loud as the scraping of a brake, and I almost fancied I heard it fall when I tossed it onto the grass. But there was more than that: a sense of irrelevance, of littleness, of futile bravado, in sitting there puffing my cigarette smoke into the face of such a past.

I knew nothing of the history of Kerfol—I was new to Brittany, and Lanrivain had never mentioned the name to me till the day before—but one couldn't as much as glance at that pile without feeling in it a long accumulation of history. What kind of history I was not prepared to guess: perhaps only that sheer weight of many associated lives and deaths which gives a majesty to all old houses. But the aspect of Kerfol suggested something more—a perspective of stern and cruel memories stretching away, like its own grey avenues, into a blur of darkness.

Certainly no house had ever more completely and finally broken with the present. As it stood there, lifting its proud roofs and gables to the sky, it might have been its own funeral monument. "Tombs in the chapel? The whole place is a tomb!" I reflected. I hoped more and more that the guardian would not come. The details of the place, however striking, would seem trivial compared with its collective impressiveness; and I wanted only to sit there and be penetrated by the weight of its silence.

"It's the very place for you!" Lanrivain had said; and I was overcome by the almost blasphemous frivolity of suggesting to any living being that Kerfol was the place for him. "Is it possible that anyone could *not* see—?" I wondered. I did not finish the thought: what I meant was undefinable. I stood up and wandered toward the gate. I was beginning to want to know more; not to *see* more—I was by now so sure it was not a question of seeing—but to feel more: feel all the place had to communicate. "But to get in one will have to rout out the keeper," I thought reluctantly, and hesitated. Finally I crossed the bridge and tried the iron gate. It yielded, and I walked through the tunnel formed by the thickness of the *chemin de ronde.* At the farther end, a wooden barricade had been laid across the entrance, and beyond it was a court enclosed in noble architecture. The main building faced me; and I now saw that one-half was a mere ruined front, with gaping windows through which the wild growths of the moat and the trees of the park were visible. The rest of the house was still in its robust beauty. One end abutted on the round tower, the other on the small traceried chapel, and in an angle of the building stood a graceful well-head crowned with mossy urns. A few roses grew against the walls, and on an upper windowsill I remember noticing a pot of fuchsias.

My sense of the pressure of the invisible began to yield to my architectural interest. The building was so fine that I felt a desire to explore it for its own sake. I looked about the court, wondering in which corner the guardian lodged. Then I pushed open the barrier and went in. As I did so, a dog barred my way. He was such a remarkably beautiful little dog that for a moment he made me forget the splendid place he was defending. I was not sure of his breed at the time, but have since learned that it was Chinese, and that he was of a rare variety called the "Sleeve-dog." He was very small and golden brown, with large brown eyes and a ruffled throat: he looked like a large tawny chrysanthemum. I said to myself: "These little beasts always snap and scream, and somebody will be out in a minute."

The little animal stood before me, forbidding, almost menacing: there was anger in his large brown eyes. But he made no sound, he came no nearer. Instead, as I advanced, he gradually fell back, and I noticed that another dog, a vague rough brindled thing, had limped up on a lame leg. "There'll be a hubbub now," I thought; for at the same moment a third dog, a long-haired white mongrel, slipped out of a doorway and joined the others. All three stood looking at me with grave eyes; but not a sound came from them. As I advanced they continued to fall back on muffled paws, still watching me. "At a given point, they'll all charge at my ankles: it's one of the jokes that dogs who live together put up on one," I thought. I was not alarmed, for they were neither large nor formidable. But they let me wander about the court as I pleased, follow-ing me at a little distance—always the same distance—and always keep-ing their eyes on me. Presently I looked across at the ruined facade, and saw that in one of its empty window frames another dog stood: a white pointer with one brown ear. He was an old grave dog, much more experi-enced than the others; and he seemed to be observing me with a deeper intentness.

"I'll hear from *him,*" I said to myself; but he stood in the window frame, against the trees of the park, and continued to watch me without moving. I stared back at him for a time, to see if the sense that he was being watched would not rouse him. Half the width of the court lay between us, and we gazed at each other silently across it. But he did not stir, and at last I turned away. Behind me I found the rest of the pack, with a newcomer added: a small black greyhound with pale agate-colored eyes. He was shivering a little, and his expression was more timid than that of the others. I noticed that he kept a little behind them. And still there was not a sound.

I stood there for fully five minutes, the circle about me—waiting, as they seemed to be waiting. At last I went up to the little golden brown dog and stooped to pat him. As I did so, I heard myself give a nervous laugh. The little dog did not start, or growl, or take his eyes from me— he simple slipped back about a yard, and then paused and continued to look at me. "Oh, hang it!" I exclaimed, and walked across the court toward the well.

As I advanced, the dogs separated and slid away into different corners of the court. I examined the urns on the well, tried a locked door or two, and looked up and down the dumb facade; then I faced about toward the chapel. When I turned I perceived that all the dogs had disappeared except the old pointer, who still watched me from the window. It was rather a relief to be rid of that cloud of witnesses; and I began to look about me for a way to the back of the house. "Perhaps there'll be somebody in the garden," I thought. I found a way across the moat, scrambled over a wall smothered in brambles, and got into the garden. A few lean hydrangeas and geraniums pined in the flower beds, and the ancient house looked down on them indifferently. Its garden side was plainer and severer than the other: the long granite front, with its few windows and steep roof, looked like a fortress prison. I walked around the farther wing, went up some disjoined steps, and entered the deep twilight of a narrow and incredibly old box walk. The walk was just wide enough for one person to slip through, and its branches met overhead. It was like the ghost of a box walk, its lustrous green all turning to the shadowy greyness of the avenues. I walked on and on, the branches hitting me in the face and springing back with a dry rattle; and at length I came out on the grassy top of the *chemin de ronde*. I walked along it to the gate tower, looking down into the court, which was just below me. Not a human being was in sight; and neither were the dogs. I found a flight of steps in the thickness of the wall and went down them; and when I emerged again into the court, there stood the circle of dogs, the golden brown one a little ahead of the others, the black greyhound shivering in the rear.

"Oh, hang it—you uncomfortable beasts, you!" I exclaimed, my voice startling me with a sudden echo. The dogs stood motionless, watching me. I knew by this time that they would not try to prevent my approaching the house, and the knowledge left me free to examine them. I had a feeling that they must be horribly cowed to be so silent and inert. Yet they did not look hungry or ill-treated. Their coats were smooth and they were not thin, except the shivering greyhound. It was more as if they had lived a long time with people who never spoke to them or looked at them: as though the silence of the place had gradually benumbed their busy inquisitive natures. And this strange passivity, this almost human lassitude, seemed to me sadder than the misery of starved and beaten animals. I should have liked to rouse them for a minute, to coax them into a game or a scamper; but the longer I looked into their fixed and weary eyes the more preposterous the idea became. With the windows of that house looking down on us, how could I have imagined such a thing? The dogs knew better: *they* knew what the house would tolerate and what it would not. I even fancied that they knew what was passing through my mind, and pitied me for my frivolity. But even that feeling probably reached them through a thick fog of listlessness. I had an idea that their distance from me was as nothing to my remoteness from them. The impression they produced was that of having in common one memory so deep and dark that nothing that had happened since was worth either a growl or a wag.

"I say," I broke out abruptly, addressing myself to the dumb circle, "do you know what you look like, the whole lot of you? You look as if you'd seen a ghost—that's how you look! I wonder if there *is* a ghost here, and nobody but you left for it to appear to?" The dogs continued to gaze at me without moving. . . .

It was dark when I saw Lanrivain's motor lamps at the crossroads—and I wasn't exactly sorry to see them. I had the sense of having escaped from the loneliest place in the whole world, and of not liking loneliness—to that degree—as much as I had imagined I should. My friend had brought his solicitor back from Quimper for the night, and seated beside a fat and affable stranger I felt no inclination to talk of Kerfol. . . .

But that evening, when Lanrivain and the solicitor were closeted in the study, Madame de Lanrivain began to question me in the drawing room.

"Well—are you going to buy Kerfol?" she asked, tilting up her gay chin from her embroidery.

"I haven't decided yet. The fact is, I couldn't get into the house," I said, as if I had simply postponed my decision, and meant to go back for another look.

"You couldn't get in? Why, what happened? The family are mad to sell the place, and the old guardian has orders—"

"Very likely. But the old guardian wasn't there."

"What a pity! He must have gone to market. But his daughter—?"

"There was nobody about. At least I saw no one."

"How extraordinary! Literally nobody?"

"Nobody but a lot of dogs—a whole pack of them—who seemed to have the place to themselves."

Madame de Lanrivain let the embroidery slip to her knee and folded her hands on it. For several minutes she looked at me thoughtfully.

"A pack of dogs—you *saw* them?"

"Saw them? I saw nothing else!"

"How many?" She dropped her voice a little. "I've always wondered—"

I looked at her with surprise: I had supposed the place to be familiar to her. "Have you never been to Kerfol?" I asked.

"Oh, yes: often. But never on that day."

"What day?"

"I'd quite forgotten—and so had Hervé, I'm sure. If we'd remembered, we never should have sent you today—but then, after all, one doesn't half believe that sort of thing, does one?"

"What sort of thing?" I asked, involuntarily sinking my voice to the level of hers. Inwardly I was thinking: "I *knew* there was something. . . ."

Madame de Lanrivain cleared her throat and produced a reassuring smile. "Didn't Hervé tell you the story of Kerfol? An ancestor of his was mixed up in it. You know every Breton house has its ghost story; and some of them are rather unpleasant."

"Yes—but those dogs?"

"Well, those dogs are the ghosts of Kerfol. At least, the peasants say there's one day in the year when a lot of dogs appear there; and that day the keeper and his daughter go off to Morlaix and get drunk. The women in Brittany drink dreadfully." She stooped to match a silk; then she lifted her charming inquisitive Parisian face. "Did you *really* see a lot of dogs? There isn't one at Kerfol," she said.

2

Lanrivain, the next day, hunted out a shabby calf volume from the back of an upper shelf of his library.

"Yes—here it is. What does it call itself? *A History of the Assizes of the Duchy of Brittany. Quimper, 1702.* The book was written about a hundred years later than the Kerfol affair; but I believe the account is transcribed pretty literally from the judicial records. Anyhow, it's queer reading. And there's a Hervé de Lanrivain mixed up in it—not exactly *my* style, as you'll see. But then he's only a collateral. Here, take the book up to bed with you. I don't exactly remember the details; but after you've read it I'll bet anything you'll leave your light burning all night!"

I left my light burning all night, as he had predicted; but it was chiefly because, till near dawn, I was absorbed in my reading. The account of the trial of Anne de Cornault, wife of the lord of Kerfol, was long and closely printed. It was, as my friend had said, probably an almost literal transcription of what took place in the courtroom; and the trial lasted nearly a month. Besides, the type of the book was very bad. . . .

At first I thought of translating the old record. But it is full of wearisome repetitions, and the main lines of the story are forever straying off into side issues. So I have tried to disentangle it, and give it here in a simpler form. At times, however, I have reverted to the text because no other words could have conveyed so exactly the sense of what I felt at Kerfol; and nowhere have I added anything of my own.

3

It was in the year 16— that Yves de Cornault, lord of the domain of Kerfol, went to the *pardon* of Locronan to perform his religious duties. He was a rich and powerful noble, then in his sixty-second year, but hale and sturdy, a great horseman and hunter and a pious man. So all his neighbors attested. In appearance he was short and broad, with a swarthy face, legs slightly bowed from the saddle, a hanging nose and broad hands with black hairs on them. He had married young and lost his wife and son soon after, and since then had lived alone at Kerfol. Twice a year he went to Morlaix, where he had a handsome house by the river, and spent a week or ten days there; and occasionally he rode to Rennes on business. Witnesses were found to declare that during these absences he led a life different from the one he was known to lead at Kerfol, where he busied himself with his estate, attended mass daily, and found his only amusement in hunting the wild boar and waterfowl. But these rumors are not particularly relevant, and it is certain that among people of his own class in the neighborhood he passed for a stern and even austere man, observant of his religious obligations, and keeping strictly to himself. There was no talk of any familiarity with the women on his estate, though at that time the nobility were very free with their peasants. Some people said he had never looked at a woman since his wife's death; but such things are hard to prove, and the evidence on this point was not worth much.

Well, in his sixty-second year, Yves de Cornault went to the *pardon* at Locronan, and saw there a young lady of Douarnenez, who had ridden over pillion behind her father to do her duty to the saint. Her name was Anne de Barrigan, and she came of good old Breton stock, but much less great and powerful than that of Yves de Cornault; and her father had squandered his fortune at cards, and lived almost like a peasant in his little granite manor on the moors. . . . . I have said I would add nothing of my own to this bald statement of a strange case; but I must interrupt myself here to describe the young lady who rode up to the lych-gate of Locronan at the very moment when the Baron de Cornault was also dismounting there. I take my description from a faded drawing in red crayon, sober and truthful enough to be by a late pupil of the Clouets, which hangs in Lanrivain's study, and is said to be a portrait of Anne de Barrigan. It is unsigned and has no mark of identity but the initials A. B., and the date 16—, the year after her marriage. It represents a young woman with a small oval face, almost pointed, yet wide enough for a full mouth with a tender depression at the corners. The nose is small, and the eyebrows are set rather high, far apart, and as lightly penciled as the eyebrows in a Chinese painting. The forehead is high and serious, and the hair, which one feels to be fine and thick and fair, is drawn off it and lies close like a cap. The eyes are neither large nor small, hazel probably, with a look at once shy and steady. A pair of beautiful long hands are crossed below the lady's breast. . . .

The chaplain of Kerfol, and other witnesses, averred that when the Baron came back from Locronan he jumped from his horse, ordered another to be instantly saddled, called to a young page to come with him, and rode away that same evening to the south. His steward followed the next morning with coffers laden on a pair of pack mules. The following week Yves de Cornault rode back to Kerfol, sent for his vassals and tenants, and told them he was to be married at All Saints to Anne de Barrigan of Douarnenez. And on All Saints' Day the marriage took place.

As to the next few years, the evidence on both sides seems to show that they passed happily for the couple. No one was found to say that Yves de Cornault had been unkind to his wife, and it was plain to all that he was content with his bargain. Indeed, it was admitted by the chaplain

84

and other witnesses for the prosecution that the young lady had a softening influence on her husband, and that he became less exacting with his
tenants, less harsh to peasants and dependents, and less subject to the fits
of gloomy silence which had darkened his widowhood. As to his wife, the
only grievance her champions could call up in her behalf was that Kerfol
was a lonely place, and that when her husband was away on business at
Rennes or Morlaix—whither she was never taken—she was not allowed
so much as to walk in the park unaccompanied. But no one asserted that
she was unhappy, though one servant woman said she had surprised her
crying, and had heard her say that she was a woman accursed to have no
child, and nothing in life to call her own. But that was a natural enough
feeling in a wife attached to her husband; and certainly it must have been
a great grief to Yves de Cornault that she bore no son. Yet he never made
her feel her childlessness as a reproach—she admits this in her evidence—
but seemed to try to make her forget it by showering gifts and favors on
her. Rich though he was, he had never been openhanded; but nothing was
too fine for his wife, in the way of silks or gems or linen, or whatever else
she fancied. Every wandering merchant was welcome at Kerfol, and when
the master was called away he never came back without bringing his wife
a handsome present—something curious and particular—from Morlaix or
Rennes or Quimper. One of the waiting women gave, in cross-examina-
tion, an interesting list of one year's gifts, which I copy. From Morlaix, a
carved ivory junk, with Chinamen at the oars, that a strange sailor had
brought back as a votive offering for Notre Dame de la Clarté, above
Ploumanac'h; from Quimper, an embroidered gown, worked by the nuns
of the Assumption; from Rennes, a silver rose that opened and showed an
amber Virgin with a crown of garnets; from Morlaix, again, a length of
Damascus velvet shot with gold, bought of a Jew from Syria; and for
Michaelmas that same year, from Rennes, a necklet or bracelet of round
stones—emeralds and pearls and rubies—strung like beads on a fine gold
chain. This was the present that pleased the lady best, the woman said.
Later on, as it happened, it was produced at the trial, and appears to have
struck the Judges and the public as a curious and valuable jewel.

The very same winter, the Baron absented himself again, this time
as far as Bordeaux, and on his return he brought his wife something even

odder and prettier than the bracelet. It was a winter evening when he rode up to Kerfol and, walking into the hall, found her sitting by the hearth, her chin on her hand, looking into the fire. He carried a velvet box in his hand and, setting it down, lifted the lid and let out a little golden brown dog.

Anne de Cornault exclaimed with pleasure as the little creature bounded toward her. "Oh, it looks like a bird or a butterfly!" she cried as she picked it up; and the dog put its paws on her shoulders and looked at her with eyes "like a Christian's." After that she would never have it out of her sight, and petted and talked to it as if it had been a child—as indeed it was the nearest thing to a child she was to know. Yves de Cornault was much pleased with his purchase. The dog had been brought to him by a sailor from an East India merchantman, and the sailor had bought it of a pilgrim in a bazaar at Jaffa, who had stolen it from a nobleman's wife in China: a perfectly permissible thing to do, since the pilgrim was a Christian and the nobleman a heathen doomed to hell-fire. Yves de Cornault had paid a long price for the dog, for they were beginning to be in demand at the French court, and the sailor knew he had got hold of a good thing; but Anne's pleasure was so great that, to see her laugh and play with the little animal, her husband would doubtless have given twice the sum.

So far, all the evidence is at one, and the narrative plain sailing; but now the steering becomes difficult. I will try to keep as nearly as possible to Anne's own statements, though toward the end, poor thing. . . .

Well, to go back. The very year after the little brown dog was brought to Kerfol, Yves de Cornault, one winter night, was found dead at the head of a narrow flight of stairs leading down from his wife's rooms to a door opening on the court. It was his wife who found him and gave the alarm, so distracted, poor wretch, with fear and horror—for his blood was all over her—that at first the roused household could not make out what she was saying, and thought she had suddenly gone mad. But there, sure enough, at the top of the stairs lay her husband, stone dead, and head foremost, the blood from his wounds dripping down to the steps below him. He had been dreadfully scratched and gashed about the face and throat, as if with curious pointed weapons; and one of his legs had a deep tear in it which had cut an artery, and probably caused his death. But how did he come there, and who had murdered him?

His wife declared that she had been asleep in her bed, and hearing his cry had rushed out to find him lying on the stairs; but this was immediately questioned. In the first place, it was proved that from her room she could not have heard the struggle on the stairs, owing to the thickness of the walls and the length of the intervening passage; then it was evident that she had not been in bed and asleep, since she was dressed when she roused the house, and her bed had not been slept in. Moreover, the door at the bottom of the stairs was ajar, and it was noticed by the chaplain (an observant man) that the dress she wore was stained with blood about the knees, and that there were traces of small bloodstained hands low down on the staircase walls, so that it was conjectured that she had really been at the postern door when her husband fell and, feeling her way up to him in the darkness on her hands and knees, had been stained by his blood dripping down on her. Of course it was argued on the other side that the blood marks on her dress might have been caused by her kneeling down by her husband when she rushed out of her room; but there was the open door below, and the fact that the finger marks in the staircase all pointed upward.

The accused held to her statement for the first two days, in spite of its improbability; but on the third day word was brought to her that Hervé de Lanrivain, a young nobleman of the neighborhood, had been arrested for complicity in the crime. Two or three witnesses thereupon came forward to say that it was known throughout the country that Lanrivain had formerly been on good terms with the lady of Cornault; but that he had been absent from Brittany for over a year, and people had ceased to associate their names. The witnesses who made this statement were not of a very reputable sort. One was an old herb-gatherer suspected of witchcraft, another a drunken clerk from a neighboring parish, the third a half-witted shepherd who could be made to say anything; and it was clear that the prosecution was not satisfied with its case, and would have liked to find more definite proof of Lanrivain's complicity than the statement of the herb-gatherer, who swore to having seen him climbing the wall of the park on the night of the murder. One way of patching out incomplete proofs in those days was to put some sort of pressure, moral or physical, on the accused person. It is not clear what pressure was put on Anne de Cornault; but on the third day, when she was brought in court, she "appeared weak and wandering," and after being encouraged to collect herself and speak the truth, on her honor and the wounds of her Blessed Redeemer, she confessed that she had in fact gone down the stairs to speak with Hervé de Lanrivain (who denied everything), and had been surprised there by the sound of her husband's fall. That was better; and the prosecution rubbed its hands with satisfaction. The satisfaction increased when various dependents living at Kerfol were induced to say—with apparent sincerity—that during the year or two preceding his death their master had once more grown uncertain and irascible, and subject to the fits of brooding silence which his household had learned to dread before his second marriage. This seemed to show that things had not been going well at Kerfol; though no one could be found to say that there had been any signs of open disagreement between husband and wife.

Anne de Cornault, when questioned as to her reason for going down at night to open the door to Hervé de Lanrivain, made an answer which must have sent a smile around the court. She said it was because she was lonely and wanted to talk with the young man. Was this the only reason? she was asked; and replied: "Yes, by the Cross over your Lordships' heads." "But why at midnight?" the court asked. "Because I could see him in no other way." I can see the exchange of glances across the ermine collars under the Crucifix.

Anne de Cornault, further questioned, said that her married life had been extremely lonely: "desolate" was the word she used. It was true that her husband seldom spoke harshly to her; but there were days when he did not speak at all. It was true that he had never struck or threatened her; but he kept her like a prisoner at Kerfol, and when he rode away to Morlaix or Quimper or Rennes he set so close a watch on her that she could not pick a flower in the garden without having a waiting woman at her heels. "I am no Queen, to need such honors," she once said to him; and he had answered that a man who has a treasure does not leave the key in the lock when he goes out. "Then take me with you," she urged; but to this he said that towns were pernicious places, and young wives better off at their own firesides.

"But what did you want to say to Hervé de Lanrivain?" the court asked; and she answered: "To ask him to take me away."

"Ah—you confess that you went down to him with adulterous thoughts?"

"No."

"Then why did you want him to take you away?"

"Because I was afraid for my life."

"Of whom were you afraid?"

"Of my husband."

"Why were you afraid of your husband?"

"Because he had strangled my little dog."

Another smile must have passed around the courtroom: in days when any nobleman had a right to hang his peasants—and most of them exercised it—pinching a pet animal's windpipe was nothing to make a fuss about.

At this point one of the Judges, who appears to have had a certain sympathy for the accused, suggested that she should be allowed to explain herself in her own way; and she thereupon made the following statement.

The first years of her marriage had been lonely; but her husband had not been unkind to her. If she had had a child she would not have been unhappy; but the days were long, and it rained too much.

It was true that her husband, whenever he went away and left her, brought her a handsome present on his return; but this did not make up for the loneliness. At least nothing had, till he brought her the little brown dog from the East: after that she was much less unhappy. Her husband seemed pleased that she was so fond of the dog; he gave her leave to put her jeweled bracelet around its neck, and to keep it always with her.

One day she had fallen asleep in her room, with the dog at her feet, as his habit was. Her feet were bare and resting on his back. Suddenly she was waked by her husband: he stood beside her, smiling not unkindly.

"You look like my great-grandmother, Juliane de Cornault, lying in the chapel with her feet on a little dog," he said.

The analogy sent a chill through her, but she laughed and answered: "Well, when I am dead you must put me beside her, carved in marble, with my dog at my feet."

"Oho—we'll wait and see," he said, laughing also, but with his black brows close together. "The dog is the emblem of fidelity."

"And do you doubt my right to lie with mine at my feet?"

"When I'm in doubt I find out," he answered. "I am an old man," he added, "and people say I make you lead a lonely life. But I swear you shall have your monument if you earn it."

"And I swear to be faithful," she returned, "if only for the sake of having my little dog at my feet."

Not long afterward he went on business to the Quimper Assizes; and while he was away his aunt, the widow of a great nobleman of the duchy, came to spend a night at Kerfol on her way to the *pardon* of Ste. Barbe. She was a woman of piety and consequence, and much respected by Yves de Cornault, and when she proposed to Anne to go with her to Ste. Barbe no one could object, and even the chaplain declared himself in favor of the pilgrimage. So Anne set out for Ste. Barbe, and there for the first time she talked with Hervé de Lanrivain. He had come once or twice to Kerfol with his father, but she had never before exchanged a dozen words with him. They did not talk for more than five minutes now: it was under the chestnuts, as the procession was coming out of the chapel. He said: "I pity you," and she was surprised, for she had not supposed that anyone thought her an object of pity. He added: "Call for me when you need me," and she smiled a little, but was glad afterward, and thought often of the meeting.

She confessed to having seen him three times afterward: not more. How or where she would not say—one had the impression that she feared to implicate someone. Their meetings had been rare and brief; and at the last he had told her that he was starting the next day for a foreign country, on a mission which was not without peril and might keep him for many months absent. He asked her for a remembrance, and she had none to give him but the collar about the little dog's neck. She was sorry afterward that she had given it, but he was so unhappy at going that she had not had the courage to refuse.

Her husband was away at the time. When he returned a few days later he picked up the animal to pet it, and noticed that its collar was missing. His wife told him that the dog had lost it in the undergrowth of the park, and that she and her maids had hunted a whole day for it. It was true, she explained to the court, that she had made the maids search for the necklet—they all believed the dog had lost it in the park. . . .

Her husband made no comment, and that evening at supper he was in his usual mood, between good and bad: you could never tell which. He talked a good deal, describing what he had seen and done at Rennes; but now and then he stopped and looked hard at her, and when she went to bed she found her little dog strangled on her pillow. The little thing was dead, but still warm; she stooped to lift it, and her distress turned to horror when she discovered that it had been strangled by twisting twice round its throat the necklet she had given to Lanrivain.

The next morning at dawn she buried the dog in the garden, and hid the necklet in her breast. She said nothing to her husband, then or later, and he said nothing to her; but that day he had a peasant hanged for stealing a faggot in the park, and the next day he nearly beat to death a young horse he was breaking.

Winter set in, and the short days passed, and the long nights, one by one; and she heard nothing of Hervé de Lanrivain. It might be that her husband had killed him; or merely that he had been robbed of the necklet. Day after day by the hearth among the spinning maids, night after night alone on her bed, she wondered and trembled. Sometimes at table her husband looked across at her and smiled; and then she felt sure that Lanrivain was dead. She dared not try to get news of him, for she was sure her husband would find out if she did: she had an idea that he could find out anything. Even when a witch woman who was a noted seer, and could show you the whole world in her crystal, came to the castle for a night's shelter, and the maids flocked to her, Anne held back.

The winter was long and black and rainy. One day, in Yves de Cornault's absence, some gypsies came to Kerfol with a troop of performing dogs. Anne bought the smallest and cleverest, a white dog with a feathery coat and one blue and one brown eye. It seemed to have been ill-treated by the gypsies, and clung to her plaintively when she took it from them. That evening her husband came back, and when she went to bed she found the dog strangled on her pillow.

After that she said to herself that she would never have another dog; but one bitter cold evening a poor lean greyhound was found whining at the castle gate, and she took him in and forbade the maids to speak of him to her husband. She hid him in a room that no one went to, smuggled food to him from her own plate, made him a warm bed to lie on and petted him like a child.

Yves de Cornault came home, and the next day she found the greyhound strangled on her pillow. She wept in secret, but said nothing, and resolved that even if she met a dog dying of hunger she would never bring him into the castle; but one day she found a young sheep dog, a brindled puppy with good blue eyes, lying with a broken leg in the snow of the park. Yves de Cornault was at Rennes, and she brought the dog in, warmed and fed it, tied up its leg and hid it in the castle till her husband's return. The day before, she gave it to a peasant woman who lived a long way off, and paid her handsomely to care for it and say nothing; but that night she heard a whining and scratching at her door, and when she opened it the lame puppy, drenched and shivering, jumped up on her with little sobbing barks. She hid him in her bed, and the next morning was about to have him taken back to the peasant woman when she heard her husband ride into the court. She shut the dog in a chest, and went down to receive him. An hour or two later, when she returned to her room, the puppy lay strangled on her pillow. . . .

After that she dared not make a pet of any other dog; and her loneliness became almost unendurable. Sometimes, when she crossed the court of the castle, and thought no one was looking, she stopped to pat the old pointer at the gate. But one day as she was caressing him her husband came out of the chapel; and the next day the old dog was gone. . . .

This curious narrative was not told in one sitting of the court, or received without impatience and incredulous comment. It was plain that the Judges were surprised by its puerility, and that it did not help the accused in eyes of the public. It was an odd tale, certainly; but what did it prove? That Yves de Cornault disliked dogs, and that his wife, to gratify her own fancy, persistently ignored this dislike. As for pleading this trivial disagreement as an excuse for her relations—whatever their nature—with her supposed accomplice, the argument was so absurd that her own lawyer manifestly regretted having let her make use of it, and tried several times to cut short her story. But she went on to the end, with a kind of hypnotized insistence, as though the scenes she evoked were so real to her that she had forgotten where she was and imagined herself to be reliving them.

At length the Judge who had previously shown a certain kindness to her said (leaning forward a little, one may suppose, from his row of dozing colleagues): "Then you would have us believe that you murdered your husband because he would not let you keep a pet dog?"

"I did not murder my husband."

"Who did, then? Hervé de Lanrivain?"

"No."

"Who then? Can you tell us?"

"Yes, I can tell you. The dogs—" At that point she was carried out of the court in a swoon.

It was evident that her lawyer tried to get her to abandon this line of defense. Possibly her explanation, whatever it was, had seemed convincing when she poured it out to him in the heat of their first private colloquy; but now that it was exposed to the cold daylight of judicial scrutiny, and the banter of the town, he was thoroughly ashamed of it, and would have sacrificed her without a scruple to save his professional reputation. But the obstinate Judge—who perhaps, after all, was more inquisitive than kindly—evidently wanted to hear the story out, and she was ordered, the next day, to continue her deposition.

She said that after the disappearance of the old watchdog nothing particular happened for a month or two. Her husband was much as usual: she did not remember any special incident. But one evening a peddler woman came to the castle and was selling trinkets to the maids. She had no heart for trinkets, but she stood looking on while the women made their choice. And then, she did not know how, but the peddler coaxed her into buying for herself a pear-shaped pomander with a strong scent in it—she had once seen something of the kind on a gypsy woman. She had no desire for the pomander, and did not know why she had bought it. The peddler said that whoever wore it had the power to read the future; but she did not really believe that, or care much either. However, she bought the thing and took it up to her room, where she sat turning it about in her hand. Then the strange scent attracted her and she began to wonder what kind of spice was in the box. She opened it and found a grey bean rolled in a strip of paper; and on the paper she saw a sign she knew, and a message from Hervé de Lanrivain, saying that he was at home again and would be at the door in the court that night after the moon had set. . . .

She burned the paper and sat down to think. It was nightfall, and her husband was at home. . . . She had no way of warning Lanrivain, and there was nothing to do but to wait. . . .

At this point I fancy the drowsy courtroom beginning to wake up. Even to the oldest hand on the bench there must have been a certain relish in picturing the feelings of a woman on receiving such a message at nightfall from a man living twenty miles away, to whom she had no means of sending a warning. . . .

She was not a clever woman, I imagine; and as the first result of her cogitation she appears to have made the mistake of being, that evening, too kind to her husband. She could not ply him with wine, according to the traditional expedient, for though he drank heavily at times he had a strong head; and when he drank beyond its strength it was because he chose to, and not because a woman coaxed him. Not his wife, at any rate—she was an old story by now. As I read the case, I fancy there was no feeling for her left in him but the hatred occasioned by his supposed dishonor.

At any rate, she tried to call up her old graces; but early in the evening he complained of pains and fever, and left the hall to go up to the closet where he sometimes slept. His servant carried him a cup of hot wine, and brought back word that he was sleeping and not to be disturbed; and an hour later, when Anne lifted the tapestry and listened at his door, she heard his loud regular breathing. She thought it might be a feint, and stayed a long time barefooted in the passage, her ear to the crack; but the breathing went on too steadily and naturally to be other than that of a man in a sound sleep. She crept back to her room reassured, and stood in the window watching the moon set through the trees of the park. The sky was misty and starless, and after the moon went down the night was black as pitch. She knew the time had come, and stole along the passage, past her husband's door—where she stopped again to listen to his breathing—to the top of the stairs. There she paused a moment, and assured herself that no one was following her; then she began to go down the stairs in the darkness. They were so steep and winding that she had to go very slowly, for fear of stumbling. Her one thought was to get the door unbolted, tell Lanrivain to make his escape, and hasten back to her room. She had tried the bolt earlier in the evening, and managed to put a little grease on it; but nevertheless, when she drew it, it gave a squeak . . . not loud, but it made her heart stop; and the next minute, overhead, she heard a noise. . . .

"What noise?" the prosecution interposed.

"My husband's voice calling out my name and cursing me."

"What did you hear after that?"

"A terrible scream and a fall."

"Where was Hervé de Lanrivain at this time?"

"He was standing outside in the court. I just made him out in the darkness. I told him for God's sake to go, and then I pushed the door shut."

"What did you do next?"

"I stood at the foot of the stairs and listened."

"What did you hear?"

"I heard dogs snarling and panting." (Visible discouragement of the bench, boredom of the public, and exasperation of the lawyer for the defense. Dogs again—! But the inquisitive Judge insisted.)

"What dogs?"

She bent her head and spoke so low that she had to be told to repeat her answer: "I don't know."

"How do you mean—you don't know?"

"I don't know what dogs. . . ."

The Judge again intervened: "Try to tell us exactly what happened. How long did you remain at the foot of the stairs?"

"Only a few minutes."

"And what was going on meanwhile overhead?"

"The dogs kept on snarling and panting. Once or twice he cried out. I think he moaned once. Then he was quiet."

"Then what happened?"

"Then I heard a sound like the noise of a pack when the wolf is thrown to them—gulping and lapping."

(There was a groan of disgust and repulsion through the court, and another attempted intervention by the distracted lawyer. But the inquisitive Judge was still inquisitive.)

"And all the while you did not go up?"

"Yes—I went up then—to drive them off."

"The dogs?"

"Yes."

"Well—?"

"When I got there it was quite dark. I found my husband's flint and steel and struck a spark. I saw him lying there. He was dead."

"And the dogs?"

"The dogs were gone."

"Gone—where to?"

"I don't know. There was no way out—and there were no dogs at Kerfol."

She straightened herself to her full height, threw her arms above her head, and fell down on the stone floor with a long scream. There was a moment of confusion in the courtroom. Someone on the bench was heard to say: "This is clearly a case for the ecclesiastical authorities"—and the prisoner's lawyer doubtless jumped at the suggestion.

After this, the trial loses itself in a maze of cross-questioning and squabbling. Every witness who was called corroborated Anne de Cornault's statement that there were no dogs at Kerfol: had been none for several months. The master of the house had taken a dislike to dogs, there was no denying it. But, on the other hand, at the inquest, there had been long and bitter discussions as to the nature of the dead man's wounds. One of the surgeons called in had spoken of marks that looked like bites. The suggestion of witchcraft was revived, and the opposing lawyers hurled tomes of necromancy at each other.

At last Anne de Cornault was brought back into court—at the insistance of the same Judge—and asked if she knew where the dogs she spoke of could have come from. On the body of her Redeemer she swore that she did not. Then the Judge put his final question: "If the dogs you think you heard had been known to you, do you think you would have recognized them by their barking?"

"Yes."

"Did you recognize them?"

"Yes."

"What dogs do you take them to have been?"

"My dead dogs," she said in a whisper. . . . She was taken out of court, not to reappear there again. There was some kind of ecclesiastical investigation, and the end of the business was that the Judges disagreed with each other, and with the ecclesiastical committee, and that Anne de Cornault was finally handed over to the keeping of her husband's family, who shut her up in the keep of Kerfol, where she is said to have died many years later, a harmless madwoman.

So ends her story. As for that of Hervé de Lanrivain, I had only to apply to his collateral descendant for its subsequent details. The evidence against the young man being insufficient, and his family influence in the duchy considerable, he was set free, and left soon afterward for Paris. He was probably in no mood for a worldly life, and he appears to have come almost immediately under the influence of the famous M. Arnauld d'Andilly and the gentlemen of Port Royal. A year or two later he was received into their Order, and without achieving any particular distinction he followed its good and evil fortunes till his death some twenty years later. Lanrivain showed me a portrait of him by a pupil of Philippe de Champaigne: sad eyes, an impulsive mouth and a narrow brow. Poor

Hervé de Lanrivain: it was a grey ending. Yet as I looked at his stiff and sallow effigy, in the dark dress of the Jansenists, I almost found myself envying his fate. After all, in the course of his life two great things had happened to him: he had loved romantically, and he must have talked with Pascal. . . .

Arthur Conan Doyle

SILVER BLAZE

"I am afraid, Watson, that I shall have to go," said Holmes as we sat down together to our breakfast one morning.

"Go! Where to?"

"To Dartmoor; to King's Pyland."

I was not surprised. Indeed, my only wonder was that he had not already been mixed up in this extraordinary case, which was the one topic of conversation through the length and breadth of England. For a whole day my companion had rambled about the room with his chin upon his chest and his brows knitted, charging and recharging his pipe with the strongest black tobacco, and absolutely deaf to any of my questions or remarks. Fresh editions of every paper had been sent up by our news agent, only to be glanced over and tossed down into a corner. Yet, silent as he was, I knew perfectly well what it was over which he was brooding. There was but one problem before the public which could challenge his powers of analysis, and that was the singular disappearance of the favourite for the Wessex Cup, and the tragic murder of its trainer. When, therefore, he suddenly announced his intention of setting out for the scene of the drama, it was only what I had both expected and hoped for.

"I should be most happy to go down with you if I should not be in the way," said I.

"My dear Watson, you would confer a great favour upon me by coming. And I think that your time will not be misspent, for there are points about the case which promise to make it an absolutely unique one. We have, I think, just time to catch our train at Paddington, and I will go further into the matter upon our journey. You would oblige me by bringing with you your very excellent field-glass."

And so it happened that an hour or so later I found myself in the corner of a first-class carriage flying along enroute for Exeter, while Sherlock Holmes, with his sharp, eager face framed in his ear-flapped travelling-cap, dipped rapidly into the bundle of fresh papers which he had procured at Paddington. We had left Reading far behind us before he thrust the last one of them under the seat and offered me his cigar-case.

"We are going well," said he, looking out of the window and glancing at his watch. "Our rate at present is fifty-three and a half miles an hour."

"I have not observed the quarter-mile posts," said I.

"Nor have I. But the telephone posts upon this line are sixty yards apart, and the calculation is a simple one. I presume that you have looked into this matter of the murder of John Straker and the disappearance of Silver Blaze?"

"I have seen what the *Telegraph* and the *Chronicle* have to say."

"It is one of those cases where the art of the reasoner should be used rather for the sifting of details than for the acquiring of fresh evidence. The tragedy has been so uncommon, so complete, and of such personal importance to so many people that we are suffering from a plethora of surmise, conjecture, and hypothesis. The difficulty is to detach the framework of fact—of absolute undeniable fact—from the embellishments of theorists and reporters. Then, having established ourselves upon this sound basis, it is our duty to see what inferences may be drawn and what are the special points upon which the whole mystery turns. On Tuesday evening I received telegrams from both Colonel Ross, the owner of the horse, and from Inspector Gregory, who is looking after the case, inviting my cooperation."

"Tuesday evening!" I exclaimed. "And this is Thursday morning. Why didn't you go down yesterday?"

"Because I made a blunder, my dear Watson—which is, I am afraid, a more common occurrence than anyone would think who only knew me through your memoirs. The fact is that I could not believe it possible that the most remarkable horse in England could long remain concealed, especially in so sparsely inhabited a place as the north of Dartmoor. From hour to hour yesterday I expected to hear that he had been found, and that his abductor was the murderer of John Straker. When, however, another morning had come and I found that beyond the arrest of young Fitzroy Simpson nothing had been done, I felt that it was time for me to take action. Yet in some ways I feel that yesterday has not been wasted."

"You have formed a theory, then?"

"At least I have got a grip of the essential facts of the case. I shall enumerate them to you, for nothing clears up a case so much as stating it to another person, and I can hardly expect your cooperation if I do not show you the position from which we start."

I lay back against the cushions, puffing at my cigar, while Holmes, leaning forward, with his long, thin forefinger checking off the points upon the palm of his left hand, gave me a sketch of the events which had led to our journey.

"Silver Blaze," said he, "is from the Somomy stock and holds as brilliant a record as his famous ancestor. He is now in his fifth year and has brought in turn each of the prizes of the turf to Colonel Ross, his fortunate owner. Up to the time of the catastrophe he was the first favourite for the Wessex Cup, the betting being three to one on him. He has always, however, been a prime favourite with the racing public and has never yet disappointed them, so that even at those odds enormous sums of money have been laid upon him. It is obvious, therefore, that there were many people who had the strongest interest in preventing Silver Blaze from being there at the fall of the flag next Tuesday.

"The fact was, of course, appreciated at King's Pyland, where the colonel's training stable is situated. Every precaution was taken to guard the favourite. The trainer, John Straker, is a retired jockey who rode in Colonel Ross's colours before he became too heavy for the weighing-chair. He has served the colonel for five years as jockey and for seven as trainer, and has always shown himself to be a zealous and honest servant. Under him were three lads, for the establishment was a small one, containing only four horses in all. One of these lads sat up each night in the stable, while the others slept in the loft. All three bore excellent characters. John Straker, who is a married man, lived in a small villa about two hundred yards from the stables. He has no children, keeps one maidservant, and is comfortably off. The country round is very lonely, but about half a mile to the north there is a small cluster of villas which have been built by a Tavistock contractor for the use of invalids and others who may wish to enjoy the pure Dartmoor air. Tavistock itself lies two miles to the west, while across the moor, also about two miles distant, is the larger training establishment of Mapleton, which belongs to Lord Backwater and is managed by Silas Brown. In every other direction the moor is a complete wilderness, inhabited only by a few roaming gypsies. Such was the general situation last Monday night when the catastrophe occurred.

"On that evening the horses had been exercised and watered as usual, and the stables were locked up at nine o'clock. Two of the lads walked up to the trainer's house, where they had supper in the kitchen, while the third, Ned Hunter, remained on guard. At a few minutes after nine the maid, Edith Baxter, carried down to the stables his supper, which consisted of a dish of curried mutton. She took no liquid, as there was a water-tap in the stables, and it was the rule that the lad on duty should drink nothing else. The maid carried a lantern with her, as it was very dark and the path ran across the open moor.

"Edith Baxter was within thirty yards of the stables when a man appeared out of the darkness and called to her to stop. As she stepped into the circle of yellow light thrown by the lantern she saw that he was a person of gentlemanly bearing, dressed in a gray suit of tweeds, with a cloth cap. He wore gaiters and carried a heavy stick with a knob to it. She was most impressed, however, by the extreme pallor of his face and by the nervousness of his manner. His age, she thought, would be rather over thirty than under it.

" 'Can you tell me where I am?' he asked. 'I had almost made up my mind to sleep on the moor when I saw the light of your lantern.'

" 'You are close to the King's Pyland training stables,' said she.

" 'Oh, indeed! What a stroke of luck!' he cried. 'I understand that a stable-boy sleeps there alone every night. Perhaps that is his supper which you are carrying to him. Now I am sure that you would not be too proud to earn the price of a new dress, would you?' He took a piece of white paper folded up out of his waistcoat pocket. 'See that the boy has this to-night, and you shall have the prettiest frock that money can buy.'

"She was frightened by the earnestness of his manner and ran past him to the window through which she was accustomed to hand the meals. It was already opened, and Hunter was seated at the small table inside. She had begun to tell him of what had happened when the stranger came up again.

" 'Good evening,' said he, looking through the window. 'I wanted to have a word with you.' The girl has sworn that as he spoke she noticed the corner of the little paper packet protruding from his closed hand.

" 'What business have you here?' asked the lad.

" 'It's business that may put something into your pocket,' said the other. 'You've two horses in for the Wessex Cup—Silver Blaze and Bayard. Let me have the straight tip and you won't be a loser. Is it a fact that at the weights Bayard could give the other a hundred yards in five furlongs, and that the stable have put their money on him?'

" 'So, you're one of those damned touts!' cried the lad. 'I'll show you how we serve them in King's Pyland.' He sprang up and rushed across the stable to unloose the dog. The girl fled away to the house, but as she ran she looked back and saw that the stranger was leaning through the window. A minute later, however, when Hunter rushed out with the hound he was gone, and though he ran all around the buildings he failed to find any trace of him."

"One moment," I asked. "Did the stable-boy, when he ran out with the dog, leave the door unlocked behind him?"

"Excellent, Watson, excellent!" murmured my companion. "The importance of the point struck me so forcibly that I sent a special wire to Dartmoor yesterday to clear the matter up. The boy locked the door before he left it. The window, I may add, was not large enough for a man to get through.

"Hunter waited until his fellow-grooms had returned, when he sent a message to the trainer and told him what had occurred. Straker was excited at hearing the account, although he does not seem to have quite realized its true significance. It left him, however, vaguely uneasy, and Mrs. Straker, waking at one in the morning, found that he was dressing. In reply to her inquiries, he said that he could not sleep on account of his anxiety about the horses, and that he intended to walk down to the stables to see that all was well. She begged him to remain at home, as she could hear the rain pattering against the window, but in spite of her entreaties he pulled on his large mackintosh and left the house.

"Mrs. Straker awoke at seven in the morning to find that her husband had not yet returned. She dressed herself hastily, called the maid, and set off for the stables. The door was open; inside, huddled together upon a chair, Hunter was sunk in a state of absolute stupor, the favourite's stall was empty, and there were no signs of his trainer.

"The two lads who slept in the chaff-cutting loft above the harness-room were quickly aroused. They had heard nothing during the night, for they are both sound sleepers. Hunter was obviously under the influence of some powerful drug, and as no sense could be got out of him, he was left to sleep it off while the two lads and the two women ran out in search of the absentees. They still had hopes that the trainer had for some reason taken out the horse for early exercise, but on ascending the knoll near the house, from which all the neighbouring moors were visible, they not only could see no signs of the missing favourite, but they perceived something which warned them that they were in the presence of a tragedy.

"About a quarter of a mile from the stables John Straker's overcoat was flapping from a furze-bush. Immediately beyond there was a bowl-shaped depression in the moor, and at the bottom of this was found the dead body of the unfortunate trainer. His head had been shattered by a savage blow from some heavy weapon, and he was wounded on the thigh, where there was a long, clean cut, inflicted evidently by some very sharp instrument. It was clear, however, that Straker had defended himself vigorously against his assailants, for in his right hand he held a small knife, which was clotted with blood up to the handle, while in his left he clasped a red-and-black silk cravat, which was recognized by the maid as having been worn on the preceding evening by the stranger who had visited the stables. Hunter, on recovering from his stupor, was also quite positive as to the ownership of the cravat. He was equally certain that the same stranger had, while standing at the window, drugged his curried mutton, and so deprived the stables of their watchman. As to the missing horse, there were abundant proofs in the mud which lay at the bottom of the fatal hollow that he had been there at the time of the struggle. But from that morning he has disappeared, and although a large reward has been offered, and all the gypsies of Dartmoor are on the alert, no news has come of him. Finally, an analysis has shown that the remains of his supper left by the stable-lad contained an appreciable quantity of powdered opium, while the people at the house partook of the same dish on the same night without any ill effect.

"Those are the main facts of the case, stripped of all surmise, and stated as baldly as possible. I shall now recapitulate what the police have done in the matter.

"Inspector Gregory, to whom the case has been committed, is an extremely competent officer. Were he but gifted with imagination he might rise to great heights in his profession. On his arrival he promptly found and arrested the man upon whom suspicion naturally rested. There was little difficulty in finding him, for he inhabited one of those villas which I have mentioned. His name, it appears, was Fitzroy Simpson. He was a man of excellent birth and education, who had squandered a fortune upon the turf, and who lived now by doing a little quiet and genteel book-making in the sporting clubs of London. An examination of his betting-book shows that bets to the amount of five thousand pounds had been registered by him against the favourite. On being arrested he volunteered the statement that he had come down to Dartmoor in the hope of getting some information about the King's Pyland horses, and also about Desborough, the second favourite, which was in charge of Silas Brown at the Mapleton stables. He did not attempt to deny that he had acted as described upon the evening before, but declared that he had no sinister designs and had simply wished to obtain first-hand information. When confronted with his cravat he turned very pale and was utterly unable to account for its presence in the hand of the murdered man. His wet clothing showed that he had been out in the storm of the night before, and his stick, which was a penang-lawyer weighted with lead, was just such a weapon as might, by repeated blows, have inflicted the terrible injuries to which the trainer had succumbed. On the other hand, there was no wound upon his person, while the state of Straker's knife would show that one at least of his assailants must bear his mark upon him. There you have it all in a nutshell, Watson, and if you can give me any light I shall be infinitely obliged to you."

I had listened with the greatest interest to the statement which Holmes, with characteristic clearness, had laid before me. Though most of the facts were familiar to me, I had not sufficiently appreciated their relative importance, nor their connection to each other.

"Is it not possible," I suggested, "that the incised wound upon Straker may have been caused by his own knife in the convulsive struggles which follow any brain injury?"

"It is more than possible: it is probable," said Holmes. "In that case one of the main points in favour of the accused disappears."

"And yet," said I, "even now I fail to understand what the theory of the police can be."

"I am afraid that whatever theory we state has very grave objections to it," returned my companion. "The police imagine, I take it, that this Fitzroy Simpson, having drugged the lad, and having in some way obtained a duplicate key, opened the stable door and took out the horse, with the intention, apparently, of kidnapping him altogether. His bridle is missing, so that Simpson must have put this on. Then, having left the door open behind him, he was leading the horse away over the moor when he was either met or overtaken by the trainer. A row naturally ensued. Simpson beat out the trainer's brains with his heavy stick without receiving any injury from the small knife which Straker used in self-defence, and then the thief either led the horse on to some secret hiding-place, or else it may have bolted during the struggle, and be now wandering out on the moors. That is the case as it appears to the police, and improbable as it is, all other explanations are more improbable still. However, I shall very quickly test the matter when I am once upon the spot, and until then I cannot really see how we can get much further than our present position."

It was evening before we reached the little town of Tavistock, which lies, like the boss of a shield, in the middle of the huge circle of Dartmoor. Two gentlemen were awaiting us in the station—the one a tall, fair man with lion-like hair and beard and curiously penetrating light blue eyes; the other a small, alert person, very neat and dapper, in a frock-coat and gaiters, with trim little side-whiskers and an eyeglass. The latter was Colonel Ross, the well-known sportsman; the other, Inspector Gregory; a man who was rapidly making his name in the English detective service.

"I am delighted that you have come down, Mr. Holmes," said the colonel. "The inspector here has done all that could possibly be suggested, but I wish to leave no stone unturned in trying to avenge poor Straker and in recovering my horse."

"Have there been any fresh developments?" asked Holmes.

"I am sorry to say that we have made very little progress," said the inspector. "We have an open carriage outside, and as you would no doubt like to see the place before the light fails, we might talk it over as we drive."

A minute later we were all seated in a comfortable landau and were rattling through the quaint old Devonshire city. Inspector Gregory was full of his case and poured out a stream of remarks, while Holmes threw in an occasional question or interjection. Colonel Ross leaned back with his arms folded and his hat tilted over his eyes, while I listened with interest to the dialogue of the two detectives. Gregory was formulating his theory, which was almost exactly what Holmes had foretold in the train.

"The net is drawn pretty close round Fitzroy Simpson," he remarked, "and I believe myself that he is our man. At the same time I recognize that the evidence is purely circumstantial, and that some new development may upset it."

"How about Straker's knife?"

"We have quite come to the conclusion that he wounded himself in his fall."

"My friend Dr. Watson made that suggestion to me as we came down. If so, it would tell against this man Simpson."

"Undoubtedly. He has neither a knife nor any sign of a wound. The evidence against him is certainly very strong. He had a great interest in the disappearance of the favourite. He lies under suspicion of having poisoned the stable-boy; he was undoubtedly out in the storm; he was armed with a heavy stick, and his cravat was found in the dead man's hand. I really think we have enough to go before a jury."

Holmes shook his head. "A clever counsel would tear it all to rags," said he. "Why should he take the horse out of the stable? If he wished to injure it, why could he not do it there? Has a duplicate key been found in his possession? What chemist sold him the powdered opium? Above all, where could he, a stranger to the district, hide a horse, and such a horse as this? What is his own explanation as to the paper which he wished the maid to give to the stable-boy?"

"He says that it was a ten-pound note. One was found in his purse. But your other difficulties are not so formidable as they seem. He is not a stranger to the district. He has twice lodged at Tavistock in the summer. The opium was probably brought from London. The key, having served its purpose, would be hurled away. The horse may be at the bottom of one of the pits or old mines upon the moor."

"What does he say about the cravat?"

"He acknowledges that it is his and declares that he had lost it. But a new element has been introduced into the case which may account for his leading the horse from the stable."

Holmes pricked up his ears.

"We have found traces which show that a party of gypsies encamped on Monday night within a mile of the spot where the murder took place. On Tuesday they were gone. Now, presuming that there was some understanding between Simpson and these gypsies, might he not have been leading the horse to them when he was overtaken, and may they not have him now?"

"It is certainly possible."

"The moor is being scoured for these gypsies. I have also examined every stable and outhouse in Tavistock, and for a radius of ten miles."

"There is another training-stable quite close, I understand?"

"Yes, and that is a factor which we must certainly not neglect. As Desborough, their horse, was second in the betting, they had an interest in the disappearance of the favourite. Silas Brown, the trainer, is known to have had large bets upon the event, and he was no friend to poor Straker. We have, however, examined the stables, and there is nothing to connect him with the affair."

"And nothing to connect this man Simpson with the interests of the Mapleton stables?"

"Nothing at all."

Holmes leaned back in the carriage, and the conversation ceased. A few minutes later our driver pulled up at a neat little red-brick villa with overhanging eaves which stood by the road. Some distance off, across a paddock, lay a long gray-tiled outbuilding. In every other direction the low curves of the moor, bronze-coloured from the fading ferns, stretched away to the sky-line, broken only by the steeples of Tavistock, and by a cluster of houses away to the westward which marked the Mapleton stables. We all sprang out with the exception of Holmes, who continued to lean back with his eyes fixed upon the sky in front of him, entirely absorbed in his own thoughts. It was only when I touched his arm that he roused himself with a violent start and stepped out of the carriage.

"Excuse me," said he, turning to Colonel Ross, who had looked at him in some surprise. "I was day-dreaming." There was a gleam in his eye and a suppressed excitement in his manner which convinced me, used as I was to his ways, that his hand was upon a clue, though I could not imagine where he had found it.

"Perhaps you would prefer at once to go on to the scene of the crime, Mr. Holmes?" said Gregory.

"I think that I should prefer to stay here a little and go into one or two questions of detail. Straker was brought back here, I presume?"

"Yes, he lies upstairs. The inquest is to-morrow."

"He has been in your service some years, Colonel Ross?"

"I have always found him an excellent servant."

"I presume that you made an inventory of what he had in his pockets at the time of his death, Inspector?"

"I have the things themselves in the sitting-room if you would care to see them."

"I should be very glad." We all filed into the front room and sat round the central table while the inspector unlocked a square tin box and laid a small heap of things before us. There was a box of vestas, two inches of tallow candle, an A D P brier-root pipe, a pouch of sealskin with half an ounce of long-cut Cavendish, a silver watch with a gold chain, five sovereigns in gold, an aluminum pencil-case, a few papers, and an ivory-handled knife with a very delicate, inflexible blade marked Weiss & Co., London.

"This is a very singular knife," said Holmes, lifting it up and examining it minutely. "I presume, as I see blood-stains upon it, that it is the one which was found in the dead man's grasp. Watson, this knife is surely in your line?"

"It is what we call a cataract knife," said I.

"I thought so. A very delicate blade devised for very delicate work. A strange thing for a man to carry with him upon a rough expedition, especially as it would not shut in his pocket."

"The tip was guarded by a disc of cork which we found beside his body," said the inspector. "His wife tells us that the knife had lain upon the dressing-table, and that he had picked it up as he left the room. It was a poor weapon, but perhaps the best that he could lay his hands on at the moment."

"Very possibly. How about these papers?"

"Three of them are receipted hay-dealers' accounts. One of them is a letter of instructions from Colonel Ross. This other is a milliner's account for thirty-seven pounds fifteen made out by Madame Lesurier, of Bond Street, to William Derbyshire. Mrs. Straker tells us that Derbyshire was a friend of her husband's, and that occasionally his letters were addressed here."

"Madame Derbyshire had somewhat expensive tastes," remarked Holmes, glancing down the account. "Twenty-two guineas is rather heavy for a single costume. However, there appears to be nothing more to learn, and we may now go down to the scene of the crime."

As we emerged from the sitting-room a woman, who had been waiting in the passage, took a step forward and laid her hand upon the inspector's sleeve. Her face was haggard and thin and eager, stamped with the print of a recent horror.

"Have you got them? Have you found them?" she panted.

"No, Mrs. Straker. But Mr. Holmes here has come from London to help us, and we shall do all that is possible."

"Surely I met you in Plymouth at a garden-party some little time ago, Mrs. Straker?" said Holmes.

"No, sir; you are mistaken."

"Dear me! Why, I could have sworn to it. You wore a costume of dove-coloured silk with ostrich-feather trimming."

"I never had such a dress, sir," answered the lady.

"Ah, that quite settles it," said Holmes. And with an apology he followed the inspector outside. A short walk across the moor took us to the hollow in which the body had been found. At the brink of it was the furze-bush upon which the coat had been hung.

"There was no wind that night, I understand," said Holmes.

"None, but very heavy rain."

"In that case the overcoat was not blown against the furze-bushes, but placed there."

"Yes, it was laid across the bush."

"You fill me with interest. I perceive that the ground has been trampled up a good deal. No doubt many feet have been here since Monday night."

"A piece of matting has been laid here at the side, and we have all stood upon that."

"Excellent."

"In this bag I have one of the boots which Straker wore, one of Fitzroy Simpson's shoes, and a cast horseshoe of Silver Blaze."

"My dear Inspector, you surpass yourself!" Holmes took the bag, and, descending into the hollow, he pushed the matting into a more central position. Then stretching himself upon his face and leaning his chin upon his hands, he made a careful study of the trampled mud in front of him. "Hullo!" said he suddenly. "What's this?" It was a wax vesta, half burned, which was so coated with mud that it looked at first like a little chip of wood.

"I cannot think how I came to overlook it," said the inspector with an expression of annoyance.

"It was invisible, buried in the mud. I only saw it because I was looking for it."

"What! you expected to find it?"

"I thought it not unlikely."

He took the boots from the bag and compared the impressions of each of them with marks upon the ground. Then he clambered up to the rim of the hollow and crawled about among the ferns and bushes.

"I am afraid that there are no more tracks," said the inspector. "I have examined the ground very carefully for a hundred yards in each direction."

"Indeed!" said Holmes, rising. "I should not have the impertinence to do it again after what you say. But I should like to take a little walk over the moor before it grows dark that I may know my ground to-morrow, and I think that I shall put this horseshoe into my pocket for luck."

Colonel Ross, who had shown some signs of impatience at my companion's quiet and systematic method of work, glanced at his watch. "I wish you would come back with me, Inspector," said he. "There are several points on which I should like your advice, and especially as to whether we do not owe it to the public to remove our horse's name from the entries for the cup."

"Certainly not," cried Holmes with decision. "I should let the name stand."

The colonel bowed. "I am very glad to have had your opinion, sir," said he. "You will find us at poor Straker's house when you have finished your walk, and we can drive together into Tavistock."

He turned back with the inspector, while Holmes and I walked slowly across the moor. The sun was beginning to sink behind the stable of Mapleton, and the long, sloping plain in front of us was tinged with gold, deepening into rich, ruddy browns where the faded ferns and brambles caught the evening light. But the glories of the landscape were all wasted upon my companion, who was sunk in the deepest thought.

"It's this way, Watson," said he at last. "We may leave the question of who killed John Straker for the instant and confine ourselves to finding out what has become of the horse. Now, supposing that he broke away during or after the tragedy, where could he have gone to? The horse is a very gregarious creature. If left to himself his instincts would have been either to return to King's Pyland or go over to Mapleton. Why should he run wild upon the moor? He would surely have been seen by now. And why should gypsies kidnap him? These people always clear out when they hear of trouble, for they do not wish to be pestered by the police. They could not hope to sell such a horse. They would run a great risk and gain nothing by taking him. Surely that is clear."

"Where is he, then?"

"I have already said that he must have gone to King's Pyland or to Mapleton. He is not at King's Pyland. Therefore he is at Mapleton. Let us take that as a working hypothesis and see what it leads us to. This part of the moor, as the inspector remarked, is very hard and dry. But it falls away towards Mapleton, and you can see from here that there is a long hollow over yonder, which must have been very wet on Monday night. If our supposition is correct, then the horse must have crossed that, and there is the point where we should look for his tracks."

We had been walking briskly during this conversation, and a few more minutes brought us to the hollow in question. At Holmes's request I walked down the bank to the right, and he to the left, but I had not taken fifty paces before I heard him give a shout and saw him waving his hand to me. The track of a horse was plainly outlined in the soft earth in front of him, and the shoe which he took from his pocket exactly fitted the impression.

"See the value of imagination," said Holmes. "It is the one quality which Gregory lacks. We imagined what might have happened, acted upon the supposition, and find ourselves justified. Let us proceed."

We crossed the marshy bottom and passed over a quarter of a mile of dry, hard turf. Again the ground sloped, and again we came on the tracks. Then we lost them for half a mile, but only to pick them up once more quite close to Mapleton. It was Holmes who saw them first, and he stood pointing with a look of triumph upon his face. A man's track was visible beside the horse's.

"The horse was alone before," I cried.

"Quite so. It was alone before. Hullo, what is this?"

The double track turned sharp off and took the direction of King's Pyland. Holmes whistled, and we both followed along after it. His eyes were on the trail, but I happened to look a little to one side and saw to my surprise the same tracks coming back again in the opposite direction.

"One for you, Watson," said Holmes when I pointed it out. "You have saved us a long walk, which would have brought us back on our own traces. Let us follow the return track."

We had not to go far. It ended at the paving of asphalt which led up to the gates of the Mapleton stables. As we approached, a groom ran out from them.

"We don't want any loiterers about here," said he.

"I only wished to ask a question," said Holmes, with his finger and thumb in his waistcoat pocket. "Should I be too early to see your master, Mr. Silas Brown, if I were to call at five o'clock to-morrow morning?"

"Bless you, sir, if anyone is about he will be, for he is always the first stirring. But here he is, sir, to answer your questions for himself. No, sir, no, it is as much as my place is worth to let him see me touch your money. Afterwards, if you like."

As Sherlock Holmes replaced the half-crown which he had drawn from his pocket, a fierce-looking elderly man strode out from the gate with a hunting-crop swinging in his hand.

"What's this, Dawson!" he cried. "No gossiping! Go about your business! And you, what the devil do you want here?"

"Ten minutes' talk with you, my good sir," said Holmes in the sweetest of voices.

"I've no time to talk to every gadabout. We want no strangers here. Be off, or you may find a dog at your heels."

Holmes leaned forward and whispered something in the trainer's ear. He started violently and flushed to the temples.

"It's a lie!" he shouted. "An infernal lie!"

"Very good. Shall we argue about it here in public or talk it over in your parlour?"

"Oh, come in if you wish to."

Holmes smiled. "I shall not keep you more than a few minutes, Watson," said he. "Now, Mr. Brown, I am quite at your disposal."

It was twenty minutes, and the reds had all faded into grays before Holmes and the trainer reappeared. Never have I seen such a change as had been brought about in Silas Brown in that short time. His face was ashy pale, beads of perspiration shone upon his brow, and his hands shook until the hunting-crop wagged like a branch in the wind. His bullying, overbearing manner was all gone too, and he cringed along at my companion's side like a dog with its master.

"Your instructions will be done. It shall all be done," said he.

"There must be no mistake," said Holmes, looking round at him. The other winced as he read the menace in his eyes.

"Oh, no, there shall be no mistake. It shall be there. Should I change it first or not?"

Holmes thought a little and then burst out laughing. "No, don't," said he, "I shall write to you about it. No tricks, now, or—"

"Oh, you can trust me, you can trust me!"

"Yes, I think I can. Well, you shall hear from me to-morrow." He turned upon his heel, disregarding the trembling hand which the other held out to him, and we set off for King's Pyland.

"A more perfect compound of the bully, coward, and sneak than Master Silas Brown I have seldom met with," remarked Holmes as we trudged along together.

"He has the horse, then?"

"He tried to bluster out of it, but I described to him so exactly what his actions had been upon that morning that he is convinced that I was watching him. Of course you observed the peculiarly square toes in the impressions, and that his own boots exactly corresponded to them. Again, of course no subordinate would have dared to do such a thing. I described to him how, when according to his custom he was the first down, he perceived a strange horse wandering over the moor. How he went out to it, and his astonishment at recognizing, from the white forehead which has given the favourite its name, that chance had put in his power the only horse which could beat the one upon which he had put his money. Then I described how his first impulse had been to lead him back to King's Pyland, and how the devil had shown him how he could hide the horse until the race was over, and how he had led it back and concealed it at Mapleton. When I told him every detail he gave it up and thought only of saving his own skin."

"But his stables had been searched?"

"Oh, an old horse-faker like him has many a dodge."

"But are you not afraid to leave the horse in his power now, since he has every interest in injuring it?"

"My dear fellow, he will guard it as the apple of his eye. He knows that his only hope of mercy is to produce it safe."

"Colonel Ross did not impress me as a man who would be likely to show much mercy in any case."

"The matter does not rest with Colonel Ross. I follow my own methods and tell as much or as little as I choose. That is the advantage of being unofficial. I don't know whether you observed it, Watson, but the colonel's manner has been just a trifle cavalier to me. I am inclined now to have a little amusement at his expense. Say nothing to him about the horse."

"Certainly not without your permission."

"And of course this is all quite a minor point compared to the question of who killed John Straker."

"And you will devote yourself to that?"

"On the contrary, we both go back to London by the night train."

I was thunderstruck by my friend's words. We had only been a few hours in Devonshire, and that he should give up an investigation which he had begun so brilliantly was quite incomprehensible to me. Not a word more could I draw from him until we were back at the trainer's house. The colonel and the inspector were awaiting us in the parlour.

"My friend and I return to town by the night-express," said Holmes. "We have had a charming little breath of your beautiful Dartmoor air."

The inspector opened his eyes, and the colonel's lip curled in a sneer.

"So you despair of arresting the murderer of poor Straker," said he.

Holmes shrugged his shoulders. "There are certainly grave difficulties in the way," said he. "I have every hope, however, that your horse will start upon Tuesday, and I beg that you will have your jockey in readiness. Might I ask for a photograph of Mr. John Straker?"

The inspector took one from an envelope and handed it to him.

"My dear Gregory, you anticipate all my wants. If I might ask you to wait here for an instant, I have a question which I should like to put to the maid."

"I must say that I am rather disappointed in our London consultant," said Colonel Ross bluntly as my friend left the room. "I do not see that we are any further than when he came."

"At least you have his assurance that your horse will run," said I.

"Yes, I have his assurance," said the colonel with a shrug of his shoulders. "I should prefer to have the horse."

I was about to make some reply in defence of my friend when he entered the room again.

"Now, gentlemen," said he, "I am quite ready for Tavistock."

As we stepped into the carriage one of the stable-lads held the door open for us. A sudden idea seemed to occur to Holmes, for he leaned forward and touched the lad upon the sleeve.

"You have a few sheep in the paddock," he said. "Who attends to them?"

"I do, sir."

"Have you noticed anything amiss with them of late?"

"Well, sir, not of much account, but three of them have gone lame, sir."

I could see that Holmes was extremely pleased, for he chuckled and rubbed his hands together.

"A long shot, Watson, a very long shot," said he, pinching my arm. "Gregory, let me recommend to your attention this singular epidemic among the sheep. Drive on, coachman!"

Colonel Ross still wore an expression which showed the poor opinion which he had formed of my companion's ability, but I saw by the inspector's face that his attention had been keenly aroused.

"You consider that to be important?" he asked.

"Exceedingly so."

"Is there any point to which you would wish to draw my attention?"

"To the curious incident of the dog in the night-time."

"The dog did nothing in the night-time."

"That was the curious incident," remarked Sherlock Holmes.

Four days later Holmes and I were again in the train, bound for Winchester to see the race for the Wessex Cup. Colonel Ross met us by appointment outside the station, and we drove in his drag to the course beyond the town. His face was grave, and his manner was cold in the extreme.

"I have seen nothing of my horse," said he.

"I suppose that you would know him when you saw him?" asked Holmes.

The colonel was very angry. "I have been on the turf for twenty years and never was asked such a question as that before," said he. "A child would know Silver Blaze with his white forehead and his mottled off-foreleg."

"How is the betting?"

"Well, that is the curious part of it. You could have got fifteen to one yesterday, but the price has become shorter and shorter, until you can hardly get three to one now."

"Hum!" said Holmes. "Somebody knows something, that is clear."

As the drag drew up in the enclosure near the grandstand I glanced at the card to see the entries.

> Wessex Plate [it ran] 50 sovs. each h ft with 1000 sovs. added, for four and five year olds. Second, £300. Third, £200. New course (one mile and five furlongs).
> 1. Mr. Heath Newton's The Negro. Red cap, Cinnamon jacket.
> 2. Colonel Wardlaw's Pugilist. Pink cap, Blue and black jacket.
> 3. Lord Backwater's Desborough. Yellow cap and sleeves.
> 4. Colonel Ross's Silver Blaze. Black cap. Red jacket.
> 5. Duke of Balmoral's Iris. Yellow and black stripes.
> 6. Lord Singleford's Rasper. Purple cap. Black sleeves.

"We scratched our other one and put all hopes on your word," said the colonel. "Why, what is that? Silver Blaze favourite?"

"Five to four against Silver Blaze!" roared the ring. "Five to four against Silver Blaze! Five to fifteen against Desborough! Five to four on the field!"

"There are the numbers up," I cried. "They are all six there."

"All six there? Then my horse is running," cried the colonel in great agitation. "But I don't see him. My colours have not passed."

"Only five have passed. This must be he."

As I spoke a powerful bay horse swept out from the weighing enclosure and cantered past us, bearing on its back the well-known black and red of the colonel.

"That's not my horse," cried the owner. "That beast has not a white hair upon its body. What is this that you have done, Mr. Holmes?"

"Well, well, let us see how he gets on," said my friend imperturbably. For a few minutes he gazed through my field-glass. "Capital! An excellent start!" he cried suddenly. "There they are, coming round the curve!"

From our drag we had a superb view as they came up the straight. The six horses were so close together that a carpet could have covered them, but halfway up the yellow of the Mapleton stable showed to the front. Before they reached us, however, Desborough's bolt was shot, and the colonel's horse, coming away with a rush, passed the post a good six lengths before its rival, the Duke of Balmoral's Iris making a bad third.

"It's my race, anyhow," gasped the colonel, passing his hand over his eyes. "I confess that I can make neither head nor tail of it. Don't you think that you have kept up your mystery long enough, Mr. Holmes?"

"Certainly, Colonel, you shall know everything. Let us all go round and have a look at the horse together. Here he is," he continued as we made our way into the weighing enclosure, where only owners and their friends find admittance. "You have only to wash his face and his legs in spirits of wine, and you will find that he is the same old Silver Blaze as ever."

"You take my breath away!"

"I found him in the hands of a faker and took the liberty of running him just as he was sent over."

"My dear sir, you have done wonders. The horse looks very fit and well. It never went better in its life. I owe you a thousand apologies for having doubted your ability. You have done me a great service by recovering my horse. You would do me a greater still if you could lay your hands on the murderer of John Straker."

"I have done so," said Holmes quietly.

The colonel and I stared at him in amazement. "You have got him! Where is he, then?"

"He is here."

"Here! Where?"

"In my company at the present moment."

The colonel flushed angrily. "I quite recognize that I am under obligations to you, Mr. Holmes," said he, "but I must regard what you have just said as either a very bad joke or an insult."

Sherlock Holmes laughed. "I assure you that I have not associated you with the crime, Colonel," said he. "The real murderer is standing immediately behind you." He stepped past and laid his hand upon the glossy neck of the thoroughbred.

"The horse!" cried both the colonel and myself.

"Yes, the horse. And it may lessen his guilt if I say that it was done in self-defence, and that John Straker was a man who was entirely unworthy of your confidence. But there goes the bell, and as I stand to win a little on this next race, I shall defer a lengthy explanation until a more fitting time."

We had the corner of a Pullman car to ourselves that evening as we whirled back to London, and I fancy that the journey was a short one to Colonel Ross as well as to myself as we listened to our companion's narrative of the events which had occurred at the Dartmoor training-stables upon that Monday night, and the means by which he had unravelled them.

"I confess," said he, "that any theories which I had formed from the newspaper reports were entirely erroneous. And yet there were indications there, had they not been overlaid by other details which concealed their true import. I went to Devonshire with the conviction that Fitzroy Simpson was the true culprit, although, of course, I saw that the evidence against him was by no means complete. It was while I was in the carriage, just as we reached the trainer's house, that the immense significance of the curried mutton occurred to me. You may remember that I was distrait and remained sitting after you had all alighted. I was marvelling in my own mind how I could possibly have overlooked so obvious a clue."

"I confess," said the colonel, "that even now I cannot see how it helps us."

"It was the first link in my chain of reasoning. Powdered opium is by no means tasteless. The flavour is not disagreeable, but it is perceptible. Were it mixed with any ordinary dish the eater would undoubtedly detect it and would probably eat no more. A curry was exactly the medium which would disguise this taste. By no possible supposition could this stranger, Fitzroy Simpson, have caused curry to be served in the trainer's family that night, and it is surely too monstrous a coincidence to suppose that he happened to come along with powdered opium upon the very night when a dish happened to be served which would disguise the flavour. That is unthinkable. Therefore Simpson becomes eliminated from the case, and our attention centres upon Straker and his wife, the only two people who could have chosen curried mutton for supper that night. The opium was added after the dish was set aside for the stable-boy, for the others had the same for supper with no ill effects. Which of them, then, had access to that dish without the maid seeing them?

"Before deciding that question I had grasped the significance of the silence of the dog, for one true inference invariably suggests others. The Simpson incident had shown me that a dog was kept in the stables, and yet, though someone had been in and had fetched out a horse, he had not barked enough to arouse the two lads in the loft. Obviously the midnight visitor was someone whom the dog knew well.

"I was already convinced, or almost convinced, that John Straker went down to the stables in the dead of the night and took out Silver Blaze. For what purpose? For a dishonest one, obviously, or why should he drug his own stable-boy? And yet I was at a loss to know why. There have been cases before now where trainers have made sure of great sums of money by laying against their own horses through agents and then preventing them from winning by fraud. Sometimes it is a pulling jockey. Sometimes it is some surer and subtler means. What was it here? I hoped that the contents of his pockets might help me to form a conclusion.

"And they did so. You cannot have forgotten the singular knife which was found in the dead man's hand, a knife which certainly no sane man would choose for a weapon. It was, as Dr. Watson told us, a form of knife which is used for the most delicate operations known in surgery. And it was to be used for a delicate operation that night. You must know, with your wide experience of turf matters, Colonel Ross, that it is possible to make a slight nick upon the tendons of a horse's ham, and to do it subcutaneously, so as to leave absolutely no trace. A horse so treated would develop a slight lameness, which would be put down to a strain in exercise or a touch of rheumatism, but never to foul play."

"Villain! Scoundrel!" cried the colonel.

"We have here the explanation of why John Straker wished to take the horse out on to the moor. So spirited a creature would have certainly roused the soundest of sleepers when it felt the prick of the knife. It was absolutely necessary to do it in the open air."

"I have been blind!" cried the colonel. "Of course that was why he needed the candle and struck the match."

"Undoubtedly. But in examining his belongings I was fortunate enough to discover not only the method of the crime but even its motives. As a man of the world, Colonel, you know that men do not carry other people's bills about in their pockets. We have most of us quite enough to do to settle our own. I at once concluded that Straker was leading a double life and keeping a second establishment. The nature of the bill showed that there was a lady in the case, and one who had expensive tastes. Liberal as you are with your servants, one can hardly expect that they can buy twenty-guinea walking dresses for their ladies. I questioned Mrs. Straker as to the dress without her knowing it, and, having satisfied myself that it had never reached her, I made a note of the milliner's address and felt that by calling there with Straker's photograph I could easily dispose of the mythical Derbyshire.

"From that time on all was plain. Straker had led out the horse to a hollow where his light would be invisible. Simpson in his flight had dropped his cravat, and Straker had picked it up—with some idea, perhaps, that he might use it in securing the horse's leg. Once in the hollow, he had got behind the horse and had struck a light; but the creature, frightened at the sudden glare, and with the strange instinct of animals feeling that some mischief was intended, had lashed out, and the steel shoe had struck Straker full on the forehead. He had already, in spite of the rain, taken off his overcoat in order to do his delicate task, and so, as he fell, his knife gashed his thigh. Do I make it clear?"

"Wonderful!" cried the colonel. "Wonderful! You might have been there!"

"My final shot was, I confess, a very long one. It struck me that so astute a man as Straker would not undertake this delicate tendon-nicking without a little practice. What could be practise on? My eyes fell upon the sheep, and I asked a question which, rather to my surprise, showed that my surmise was correct.

"When I returned to London I called upon the milliner, who had recognized Straker as an excellent customer of the name of Derbyshire, who had a very dashing wife, with a strong partiality for expensive dresses. I have no doubt that this woman had plunged him over head and ears in debt, and so led him into this miserable plot."

"You have explained all but one thing," cried the colonel. "Where was the horse?"

"Ah, it bolted, and was cared for by one of your neighbours. We must have an amnesty in that direction, I think. This is Clapham Junction, if I am not mistaken, and we shall be in Victoria in less than ten minutes. If you care to smoke a cigar in our rooms, Colonel, I shall be happy to give you any other details which might interest you."

Sarah Orne Jewett

THE COON DOG

In the early dusk of a warm September evening the bats were flitting to and fro, as if it were still summer, under the great elm that overshadowed Isaac Brown's house, on the Dipford road. Isaac Brown himself, and his old friend and neighbor, John York, were leaning against the fence.

"Frost keeps off late, don't it?" said John York. "I laughed when I first heard about the circus comin'; I thought 't was so unusual late in the season. Turned out well, however. Everybody I noticed was returnin' with a palm-leaf fan. Guess they found 'em useful under the tent; it was a master hot day. I saw old lady Price with her hands full o' those free advertisin' fans, as if she was layin' in a stock against next summer. Well, I expect she'll live to enjoy 'em."

"I was right here where I'm standin' now, and I see her as she was goin' by this mornin'," said Isaac Brown, laughing and settling himself comfortably against the fence as if they had chanced upon a welcome subject of conversation. "I hailed her, same's I generally do. 'Where are you bound today, ma'am?' says I.

" 'I'm goin' over as fur as Dipford Center,' says she. 'I'm goin' to see my poor dear 'Liza Jane. I want to 'suage her grief; her husband, Mr. 'Bijah Topliff, has passed away.'

" 'So much the better,' says I.

" 'No; I never l'arnt about it till yesterday,' says she; an' she looked up at me real kind of pleasant, and begun to laugh.

" 'I hear he's left property,' says she, tryin' to pull her face down solemn. I give her the fifty cents she wanted to borrow to make up her carfare and other expenses, an' she stepped off like a girl down tow'ds the depot.

"This afternoon, as you know, I'd promised the boys that I'd take 'em over to see the menagerie, and nothin' wouldn't do none of us any good but we must see the circus too; an' when we'd just got posted on one o' the best high seats, Mother she nudged me, and I looked right down front two, three rows, an' if there wa'n't Mis' Price, spectacles an' all, with her head right up in the air, havin' the best time you ever see. I laughed right out. She hadn't taken no time to see 'Lizy Jane; she wa'n't 'suagin' no grief for nobody till she'd seen the circus. 'There,' says I, 'I do like to have anybody keep their young feelin's.' "

"Mis' Price come over to see our folks before breakfast," said John York. "Wife said she was inquirin' about the circus, but she wanted to know first if they couldn't oblige her with a few trinkets o'mournin', seein' as how she'd got to pay a mournin' visit. Wife thought 'twas a bosom-pin, or somethin' like that, but turned out she wanted the skirt of a dress; 'most anything would do, she said."

"I thought she looked extra well startin' off," said Isaac, with an indulgent smile. "The Lord provides very handsome for such, I do declare! She ain't had no visible means o' support these ten or fifteen years back, but she don't freeze up in winter no more than we do."

"Nor dry up in summer," interrupted his friend; "I never did see such an able hand to talk."

"She's good company, and she's obliging an' useful when the women folks have their extra work progressin'," continued Isaac Brown kindly. " 'Tain't much for a well-off neighborhood like this to support that old chirpin' cricket. My mother used to say she kind of helped the work along by 'livenin' of it. Here she comes now; must have taken the last train, after she had supper with 'Lizy Jane. You stay still; we're goin' to hear all about it."

The small, thin figure of Mrs. Price had to be hailed twice before she could be stopped.

"I wish you a good evenin', neighbors," she said. "I have been to the house of mournin'."

"Find 'Liza Jane in, after the circus?" asked Isaac Brown, with equal seriousness. "Excellent show, wasn't it, for so late in the season?"

"Oh, beautiful; it was beautiful, I declare," answered the pleased spectator readily. "Why, I didn't see you, nor Mis' Brown. Yes; I felt it best to refresh my mind an' wear a cheerful countenance. When I see 'Liza Jane I was able to divert her mind consid'able. She was glad I went. I told her I'd made an effort, knowin' 'twas so she had to lose the a'ternoon. 'Bijah left property, if he did die away from home on a foreign shore."

"You don't mean that 'Bijah Topliff's left anything!" exclaimed John York with interest, while Isaac Brown put both hands deep into his pockets, and leaned back in a still more satisfactory position against the gatepost.

"He enjoyed poor health," answered Mrs. Price, after a moment of deliberation, as if she must take time to think. " 'Bijah never was one that scattereth, nor yet increaseth. 'Liza Jane's got some memories o' the past that's a good deal better than others; but he died somewhere out in Connecticut, or so she heard, and he's left a very val'able coon dog—one he set a great deal by. 'Liza Jane said, last time he was to home, he priced that dog at fifty dollars. 'There now, 'Liza Jane,' says I, right to her, when she told me, 'if I could git fifty dollars for that dog, I certain' would.

Perhaps some o' the circus folks would like to buy him; they've taken in a stream o' money this day. But 'Liza Jane ain't never inclined to listen to advice. 'Tis a dreadful poor-spirited-lookin' creatur'. I don't want no right o' dower in him, myself."

"A good coon dog's worth somethin', certain," said John York, handsomely.

"If he *is* a good coon dog," added Isaac Brown. "I wouldn't have parted with old Rover, here, for a good deal of money when he was right in his best days; but a dog like him's like one of the family. Stop an' have some supper, won't ye, Mis' Price?"—as the thin old creature was flitting off again. At that same moment this kind invitation was repeated from the door of the house; and Mrs. Price turned in, unprotesting and always sociably inclined, at the open gate.

It was a month later, and a whole autumn's length colder, when the two men were coming home from a long tramp through the woods. They had been making a solemn inspection of a wood lot that they owned together, and had now visited their landmarks and outer boundaries, and settled the great question of cutting or not cutting some large pines. When it was well decided that a few years' growth would be no disadvantage to the timber, they had eaten an excellent cold luncheon and rested from their labors.

"I don't feel a day older'n I ever did when I get out in the woods this way," announced John York, who was a prim, dusty-looking little man, a prudent person, who had been selectman of the town at least a dozen times.

"No more do I," agreed his companion, who was large and jovial and openhanded, more like a lucky sea captain than a farmer. After pounding a slender walnut tree with a heavy stone, he had succeeded in getting down a pocketful of late-hanging nuts, and was now snapping them back, one by one, to a venturesome chipmunk among some little frostbitten beeches. Isaac Brown had a wonderfully pleasant way of getting on with all sorts of animals, even men. After a while they rose and went their way, these two companions, stopping here and there to look at a possible woodchuck's hole, or to strike a few hopeful blows at a hollow tree with the light axe which Isaac had carried to blaze new marks on some of the line trees on the farther edge of their possessions. Sometimes they stopped to admire the size of an old hemlock, or to talk about thinning out the young pines. At last they were not very far from the entrance to the great tract of woodland. The yellow sunshine came slanting in much brighter against the tall tree trunks, spotting them with golden light high among the still branches.

Presently they came to a great ledge, frost-split and cracked into mysterious crevices.

"Here's where we used to get all the coons," said John York. "I haven't seen a coon this great while, spite o' your courage knocking on the trees up back here. You know that night we got the four fat ones? We started 'em somewheres near here, so the dog could get after 'em when they came out at night to go foragin'."

"Hold on, John"; and Mr. Isaac Brown got up from the log where he had just sat down to rest, and went to the ledge, and looked carefully all about. When he came back he was much excited, and beckoned his friend away, speaking in a stage whisper.

"I guess you'll see a coon before you're much older," he exclaimed. "I've thought it looked lately as if there'd been one about my place, and there's plenty o' signs here, right in their old haunts. Couple o' hen's heads an' a lot o' feathers—"

"Might be a fox," interrupted John York.

"Might be a coon," answered Mr. Isaac Brown. "I'm goin' to have him, too. I've been lookin' at every old hollow tree I passed, but I never thought o' this place. We'll come right off tomorrow night, I guess, John, an' see if we can't get him. 'Tis an extra handy place for 'em to den; in old times the folks always called it a good place; they've been so scarce o' these late years that I've thought little about 'em. Nothin' I ever liked so well as a coon hunt. Gorry! he must be a big old fellow, by his tracks! See here, in this smooth dirt; just like a baby's footmark."

"Trouble is, we lack a good dog," said John York anxiously, after he had made an eager inspection. "I don't know where in the world to get one, either. There ain't no such a dog about as your Rover, but you've let him get spoilt; these days I don't see him leave the yard. You ought to keep the womenfolks from overfeedin' of him so. He ought to have lasted a good spell longer. He's no use for huntin' now, that's certain."

Isaac accepted the rebuke meekly. John York was a calm man, but he now grew very fierce under such a provocation. Nobody likes to be hindered in a coonhunt.

"Oh, Rover's too old, anyway," explained the affectionate master regretfully. "I've been wishing all this afternoon I'd brought him; but I didn't think anything about him as we came away, I've got so used to seeing him layin' about the yard. 'Twould have been a real treat for old Rover, if he could have kept up. Used to be at my heels the whole time. He couldn't follow us, anyway, up here."

"I shouldn't wonder if he could," insisted John, with a humorous glance at his old friend, who was much too heavy and huge of girth for quick transit over rough ground. John York himself had grown lighter as he had grown older.

"I'll tell you one thing we could do," he hastened to suggest. "There's that dog of 'Bijah Topliff's. Don't you know the old lady told us, that day she went over to Dipford, how high he was valued? Most o' 'Bijah's important business was done in the fall, goin' out by night, gunning with fellows from the mills. He was just the kind of a worthless do-nothing that's sure to have an extra knowin' smart dog. I expect 'Liza Jane's got him now. Let one o' my boys go over!"

"Why, 'Liza Jane's come, bag and baggage, to spend the winter with her mother," exclaimed Isaac Brown, springing to his feet like a boy. "I've had it in mind to tell you, two or three times this afternoon, and then something else has flown it out of my head. I let my John Henry take the long-tailed wagon an' go down to the depot this mornin' to fetch her an' her goods up. The old lady come in early, while we were to breakfast, and to hear her lofty talk you'd have thought 't would taken a couple o' four-horse teams to move her. I told John Henry he might take that wagon and fetch up what light stuff he could, and see how much else there was, an' then I could make further arrangements. She said 'Liza Jane'd see me well satisfied, an' rode off, pleased to death. I see 'em returnin' about eight, after the train was in. They'd got 'Liza Jane with 'em, smaller'n ever; and there was a trunk tied up with a rope, and a small roll of beddin' and braided mats, and a quilted rockin' chair. The old lady was holdin' on tight to a birdcage with nothin' in it. Yes; an' I see the dog, too, in behind. He appeared kind of timid. He's a yaller dog, but he ain't stump-tailed. They hauled up out front o' the house, and Mother and I went right out; Mis' Price always expects to have notice taken. She was in great spirits. Said 'Liza Jane concluded to sell off most of her stuff rather'n have the care of it. She'd told the folks that Mis' Topliff had a beautiful sofa and a lot of nice chairs, and two framed pictures that would fix up the house complete, and invited us all to come over and see 'em. There, she seemed just as pleased returnin' with the birdcage. Disappointments don't appear to trouble her no more than a butterfly. I kind of like the old creatur'; I don't mean to see her want."

"They'll let us have the dog," said John York. "I don't know but I'll give a quarter for him, and we'll let 'em have a good piece o' the coon."

"You really comin' 'way up here by night, coonhuntin'?" asked Isaac Brown, looking reproachfully at his more agile companion.

"I be," answered John York.

"I was dre'tful afraid you was only talking, and might back out," returned the cheerful heavyweight, with a chuckle. "Now we've got things all fixed, I feel more like it than ever. I tell you, there's just boy enough left inside of me. I'll clean up my old gun tomorrow mornin' and you look right after your'n. I dare say the boys have took good care of 'em for us, but they don't know what we do about huntin', and we'll bring 'em all along and show 'em a little fun."

"All right," said John York, as soberly as if they were going to look after a piece of business for the town; and they gathered up the axe and other light possessions, and started toward home.

The two friends, whether by accident or design, came out of the woods some distance from their own houses, but very near to the low-storied little gray dwelling of Mrs. Price. They crossed the pasture, and climbed over the toppling fence at the foot of her small sandy piece of land, and knocked at the door. There was a light already in the kitchen. Mrs. Price and Eliza Jane Topliff appeared at once, eagerly hospitable.

"Anybody sick?" asked Mrs. Price, with instant sympathy. "Nothin' happened, I hope?"

"Oh, no," said both the men.

"We came to talk about hiring your dog tomorrow night," explained Isaac Brown, feeling for the moment amused at his eager errand. "We got on track of a coon just now, up in the woods, and we thought we'd give our boys a little treat. You shall have fifty cents, an' welcome, and a good piece o' the coon."

"Yes, Squire Brown; we can let you have the dog as well as not," interrupted Mrs. Price, delighted to grant a favor. "Poor departed 'Bijah, he set everything by him as a coon dog. He always said a dog's capital was all in his reputation."

"You'll have to be dreadful careful an' not lose him," urged Mrs. Topliff. "Yes, sir; he's a proper coon dog as ever walked the earth, but he's terrible weak-minded about followin' 'most anybody. 'Bijah used to travel off twelve or fourteen miles after him to git him back, when he wa'n't able. Somebody'd speak to him decent, or fling a whiplash as they drove by, an' off he'd canter on three legs right after the wagon. But 'Bijah said he wouldn't trade him for no coon dog he ever was acquainted with. Trouble is, coons is awful sca'ce."

"I guess he ain't out of practice," said John York, amiably; "I guess he'll know when he strikes the coon. Come, Isaac, we must be gittin' along tow'ds home. I feel like eatin' a good supper. You tie him up tomorrow afternoon, so we shall be sure to have him," he turned to say to Mrs. Price, who stood smiling at the door.

"Land sakes, dear, he won't git away; you'll find him right there betwixt the woodbox and the stove, where he is now. Hold the light, 'Liza Jane; they can't see their way out to the road. I'll fetch him over to ye in good season," she called out, by way of farewell; " 't will save ye third of a mile extra walk. No, 'Liza Jane, you'll let me do it, if you please. I've got a mother's heart. The gentlemen will excuse us for showin' feelin'. You're all the child I've got, an' your prosperity is the same as mine."

*   *   *

The great night of the coon hunt was frosty and still, with only a dim light from the new moon. John York and his boys, and Isaac Brown, whose excitement was very great, set forth across the fields toward the dark woods. The men seemed younger and gayer than the boys. There was a burst of laughter when John Henry Brown and his little brother appeared with the coon dog of the late Mr. Abijah Topliff, which had promptly run away home again after Mrs. Price had coaxed him over in the afternoon. The captors had tied a string round his neck, at which they pulled vigorously from time to time to urge him forward. Perhaps he found the night too cold; at any rate, he stopped short in the frozen furrows every few minutes, lifting one foot and whining a little. Half a dozen times he came near to tripping up Mr. Isaac Brown and making him fall at full length.

"Poor Tiger! Poor Tiger!" said the good-natured sportsman, when somebody said that the dog didn't act as if he were much used to being out at night. "He'll be all right when he once gets track of the coon." But when they were fairly in the woods, Tiger's distress was perfectly genuine. The long rays of light from the old-fashioned lanterns of pierced tin went wheeling round and round, making a tall ghost of every tree, and strange shadows went darting in and out behind the pines. The woods were like an interminable pillared room where the darkness made a high ceiling. The clean frosty smell of the open fields was changed for a warmer air, damp with the heavy odor of moss and fallen leaves. There was something wild and delicious in the forest at that hour of night. The men and boys tramped on silently in single file, as if they followed the flickering light instead of carrying it. The dog fell back by instinct, as did his companions, into the easy familiarity of forest life. He ran beside them, and watched eagerly as they chose a safe place to leave a coat or two and a basket. He seemed to be an affectionate dog, now that he had made acquaintance with his masters.

"Seems to me he don't exactly know what he's about," said one of the York boys scornfully; "we must have struck that coon's track somewhere, comin' in."

"We'll get through talkin', an' heap up a little somethin' for a fire, if you'll turn to and help," said his father. "I've always noticed that nobody can give so much good advice about a piece o' work as a new hand. When you've treed as many coons as your Uncle Brown an' me, you won't feel so certain. Isaac, you be the one to take the dog up round the ledge, there. He'll scent the coon quick enough then. We'll 'tend to this part o' the business."

"You may come too, John Henry," said the indulgent father, and they set off together silently with the coon dog. He followed well enough now; his tail and ears were drooping even more than usual, but he whimpered along as bravely as he could, much excited, at John Henry's heels, like one of those great soldiers who are all unnerved until the battle is well begun.

A minute later the father and son came hurrying back, breathless, and stumbling over roots and bushes. The fire was already lighted, and sending a great glow higher and higher among the trees.

"He's off! He's struck a track! He was off like a major!" wheezed Mr. Isaac Brown.

"Which way'd he go?" asked everybody.

"Right out toward the fields. Like's not the old fellow was just starting after more of our fowls. I'm glad we come early, he can't have got far yet. We can't do nothin' but wait now, boys. I'll set right down here."

"Soon as the coon trees, you'll hear the dog sing, now I tell you!" said John York, with great enthusiasm. "That night your father an' me got those four busters we've told you about, they come right back here to the ledge. I don't know but they will now. 'Twas a dreadful cold night, I know. We didn't get home till past three o'clock in the mornin', either. You remember, don't you, Isaac?"

"I do," said Isaac. "How old Rover worked that night! Couldn't see out of his eyes nor hardly wag his clever old tail, for two days; thorns in both his fore paws, and the last coon took a piece right out of his off shoulder."

"Why didn't you let Rover come tonight, father?" asked the younger boy. "I think he knew somethin' was up. He was jumpin' 'round at a great rate when I come out of the yard."

"I didn't know but he might make trouble for the other dog," answered Isaac, after a moment's silence. He felt almost disloyal to the faithful creature, and had been missing him all the way. " 'Sh! there's a bark!'' And they all stopped to listen.

The fire was leaping higher; they all sat near it, listening and talking by turns. There is apt to be a good deal of waiting in a coon hunt.

"If Rover was young as he used to be, I'd resk him to tree any coon that ever run," said the regretful master. "This smart creature o' Topliff's can't beat him, I know. The poor old fellow's eyesight seems to be going. Two—three times he's run out at me right in broad day, an' barked when I come up the yard toward the house, and I did pity him dreadfully; he was so 'shamed when he found out what he'd done. Rover's a dog that's got an awful lot o' pride. He went right off out behind the long barn the last time, and wouldn't come in for nobody when they called him to supper till I went out myself and made it up with him. No; he can't see very well now, Rover can't."

"He's heavy, too; he's got too unwieldy to tackle a smart coon, I expect, even if he could do the tall runnin'," said John York, with sympathy. "They have to get a master grip with their teeth, through a coon's thick pelt this time o' year. No; the young folks gets all the good chances after a while;" and he looked round indulgently at the chubby faces of his boys, who fed the fire, and rejoiced in being promoted to the society of their elders on equal terms. "Ain't it time we heard from the dog?" And they all listened, while the fire snapped and the sap whistled in some green sticks.

"I hear him," said John Henry suddenly; and faint and far away there came the sound of a desperate bark. There is a bark that means attack and there is a bark that means only foolish excitement.

"They ain't far off!" said Isaac. "My gracious, he's right after him! I don't know's I expected that poor-looking dog to be so smart. You can't tell by their looks. Quick as he scented the game up here in the rocks, off he put. Perhaps it ain't any matter if they ain't stump-tailed, long 's they're yaller dogs. He didn't look heavy enough to me. I tell you, he means business. Hear that bark!"

"They all bark alike after a coon," John York was as excited as anybody. "Git the guns laid out to hand, boys; I told you we'd ought to follow," he commanded. "If it's the old fellow that belongs here, he may put in any minute." But there was again a long silence and state of suspense; the chase had turned another way. There were faint distant yaps. The fire burned low and fell together with a shower of sparks. The smaller boys began to grow chilly and sleepy, when there was a thud and rustle and snapping of twigs close at hand, then the gasp of a breathless dog. Two dim shapes rushed by; a shower of bark fell, and a dog began to sing at the foot of the great twisted pine not fifty feet away.

"Hooray for Tiger!" yelled the boys; but the dog's voice filled all the woods. It might have echoed to the mountain tops. There was the old coon; they could all see him halfway up the tree, flat to the great limb. They heaped the fire with dry branches till it flared high. Now they lost him in a shadow as he twisted about the tree. John York fired, and Isaac Brown fired, while John Henry started to climb a neighboring oak; but at last it was Isaac who brought the coon to ground with a lucky shot, and the dog stopped his deafening bark and frantic leaping in the underbrush, and after an astonishing moment of silence, crept out, a proud victor, to his prouder master's feet.

"Goodness alive, who's this? Good for you, old handsome! Why, I'll be hanged if it ain't old Rover, boys; *it's old Rover!*" But Isaac could not speak another word. They all crowded round the wistful, clumsy old dog, whose eyes shone bright, though his breath was all gone. Each man patted him, and praised him, and said they ought to have mistrusted all the time that it could be nobody but he. It was some minutes before Isaac Brown could trust himself to do anything but pat the sleek old head that was always ready to his hand.

"He must have overheard us talkin'; I guess he'd have come if he'd dropped dead halfway," proclaimed John Henry, like a prince of the reigning house; and Rover wagged his tail as if in honest assent, as he lay at his master's side. They sat together, while the fire was brightened again to make a good light for the coon-hunt supper; and Rover had a good half of everything that found its way into his master's hand. It was toward midnight when the triumphal procession set forth toward home, with the two lanterns, across the fields.

* * *

The next morning was bright and warm after the hard frost of the night before. Old Rover was asleep on the doorstep in the sun, and his master stood in the yard, and saw neighbor Price come along the road in her best array, with a gay holiday air.

"Well, now," she said eagerly, "you wa'n't out very late last night, was you? I got up myself to let Tiger in. He come home, all beat out, about a quarter past nine. I expect you hadn't no kind of trouble gittin' the coon. The boys was tellin' me he weighed 'most thirty pounds."

"Oh, no kind o' trouble," said Isaac, keeping the great secret gallantly. "You got the things I sent over this morning?"

"Bless your heart, yes! I'd a sight rather have all that good pork an' potatoes than any o' your wild meat," said Mrs. Price, smiling with prosperity. "You see, now, 'Liza Jane she's given in. She didn't re'lly know but 't was all talk of 'Bijah 'bout that dog's bein' wuth fifty dollars. She says she can't cope with a huntin' dog same 's he could, an' she 's given me the money you an' John York sent over this mornin'; an' I didn't know but what you'd lend me another half a dollar, so I could both go to Dipford Center an' return, an' see if I couldn't make a sale o' Tiger right over there where they all know about him. It's right in the coon season; now's my time, ain't it?"

"Well, gettin' a little late," said Isaac, shaking with laughter as he took the desired sum of money out of his pocket. "He seems to be a clever dog round the house."

"I don't know 's I want to harbor him all winter," answered the excursionist frankly, striking into a good traveling gait as she started off toward the railroad station.

John Updike

DEATHS OF
DISTANT FRIENDS

Though I was between marriages for several years, in a disarray that preoccupied me completely, other people continued to live and to die. Len, an old golf partner, overnight in the hospital for what they said was a routine examination, dropped dead in the lavatory, having just placed a telephone call to his hardware store saying he would be back behind the counter in the morning. He owned the store and could leave a clerk in charge on sunny afternoons. His swing was too quick, and he kept his weight back on his right foot, and the ball often squirted off to the left without getting into the air at all; but he sank some gorgeous putts in his day, and he always dressed with a nattiness that seemed to betoken high hopes for his game. In buttercup-yellow slacks, sky-blue turtleneck, and tangerine cashmere cardigan he would wave from the practice green as, having driven out from Boston through clouds of grief and sleeplessness and moral confusion, I would drag my cart across the asphalt parking lot, my cleats scraping, like a monster's claws, at every step.

Though Len had known and liked Julia, the wife I had left, he never spoke of my personal condition or of the fact that I drove an hour out from Boston to meet him instead of, as formerly, ten minutes down the road. Golf in that interim was a haven; as soon as I stepped off the first tee in pursuit of my drive, I felt enclosed in a luminous wide sanctuary, safe from women, stricken children, solemn lawyers, disapproving old acquaintances—the entire offended social order. Golf had its own order, and its own love, as the three or four of us staggered and shouted our way toward each hole, laughing at misfortune and applauding the rare strokes of relative brilliance. Sometimes the summer sky would darken and a storm arise, and we would cluster in an abandoned equipment shed or beneath a tree that seemed less tall and vulnerable to lightning than its brothers. Our natural nervousness and our impatience at having the excitements of golf interrupted would in this space of shelter focus into an almost amorous heat—the breaths and sweats of middle-aged men packed together in the pattering rain like cattle in a boxcar. Len's face bore a number of spots of actinic keratosis; he was going to have them surgically removed before they turned into skin cancer. Who would have thought that the lightning bolt of a coronary would fall across his plans and clean remove him from my tangled life? Never again (no two snowflakes or fingerprints, no two heartbeats traced on the oscilloscope, and no two golf swings are exactly alike) would I see his so hopefully addressed drive ("Hello dere, ball," he would joke, going into his waggle and squat) squirt off low to the left in that unique way of his, and hear him exclaim in angry frustration (he was a born-again Baptist, and had developed a personal language of avoided curses), "Ya dirty ricka-fric!"

I drove out to Len's funeral and tried to tell his son, "Your father was a great guy," but the words fell flat in that cold, bare Baptist church. Len's gaudy colors, his Christian effervescence, his hopeful and futile swing, our crowing back and forth, our fellowship within the artificial universe composed of variously resistant lengths and types of grass were all tints of life too delicate to capture, and had flown.

A time later, I read in the paper that Miss Amy Merrymount, ninety-one, had at last passed away, as a dry leaf passes into leaf mold. She had always seemed ancient; she was one of those New Englanders, one of the last, who spoke of Henry James as if he had just left the room. She possessed letters, folded and unfolded almost into pieces, from James to her parents, in which she was mentioned, not only as a little girl but as a young lady "coming into her 'own,' into a liveliness fully rounded." She lived in a few rooms, crowded with antiques, of a great inherited country house of which she was constrained to rent out the larger portion. Why she had never married was a mystery that sat upon her lightly in old age; the slender smooth beauty that sepia photographs remembered, the breeding and intelligence and (in a spiritual sense) ardor she still possessed must have intimidated as many suitors as these virtues attracted and must have given her, in her own eyes, in an age when the word *inviolate* still had force and renunciation a certain prestige, a value whose winged moment of squandering never quite arose. Also, she had a sardonic dryness to her voice and something restless and dismissive in her manner. She was a keen self-educator; she kept up with new developments in art and science, took up organic foods and political outrage when they became fashionable, and liked to have young people about her. When Julia and I moved to town with our babies and fresh faces, we became part of her tea circle, and in an atmosphere of tepid but mutual enchantment maintained acquaintance for twenty years.

Perhaps not so tepid: now I think Miss Merrymount loved us, or at least loved Julia, who always took on a courteous brightness, a soft daughterly shine, in those underheated and window-lit rooms crowded with spindly, feathery heirlooms once spread through the four floors of a Back Bay town house. In memory the glow of my former wife's firm chin and exposed throat and shoulders merges with the ghostly smoothness of those old framed studio photos of the Merrymount sisters—there were three, of whom two died sadly young, as if bequeathing their allotment of years to the third, the survivor sitting with us in her gold-brocaded wing chair. Her face had become unforeseeably brown with age, and totally wrinkled, like an Indian's, with something in her dark eyes of glittering Indian cruelty. "I found her rather disappointing," she might dryly say of an absent mutual acquaintance, or, of one who had been quite dropped from her circle, "She wasn't absolutely first-rate."

The search for the first-rate had been a pastime of her generation. I cannot think, now, of whom she utterly approved, except Father Daniel Berrigan and Sir Kenneth Clark. She saw them both on television. Her eyes with their opaque glitter were failing, and for her cherished afternoons of reading (while the light died outside her windows and a little fire of birch logs danced in the brass-skirted fireplace) were substituted scheduled hours tuned in to educational radio and television. In those last years, Julia would go and read to her—Austen, *Middlemarch,* Joan Didion, some Proust and Mauriac in French, when Miss Merrymount decided that Julia's accent passed muster. Julia would practice a little on me, and, watching her lips push forward and go small and tense around the French sounds like the lips of an African mask of ivory, I almost fell in love with her again. Affection between women is a touching, painful, exciting thing for a man, and in my vision of it—tea yielding to sherry in those cluttered rooms where twilight thickened until the white pages being slowly turned and the patient melody of Julia's voice were the sole signs of life—love was what was happening between this gradually dying old lady and my wife, who had gradually become middle-aged, our children grown into absent adults, her voice nowhere else hearkened to as it was here. No doubt there were confidences, too, between the pages. Julia always returned from Miss Merrymount's, to make my late dinner, looking younger and even blithe, somehow emboldened.

In that awkward postmarital phase when old friends still feel obliged to extend invitations one doesn't yet have the presence of mind to decline, I found myself at a large gathering at which Miss Merrymount was present. She was now quite blind and invariably accompanied by a young person, a round-faced girl hired as companion and guide. The fragile old lady, displayed like peacock feathers under a glass bell, had been established in a wing chair in a corner of the room beyond the punch bowl. At my approach, she sensed a body coming near and held out her withered hand, but when she heard my voice her hand dropped. "You have done a dreadful thing," she said, all on one long intake of breath. Her face turned away, showing her hawk-nosed profile, as though I had offended her sight. The face of her young companion, round as a radar dish, registered slight shock; but I smiled, in truth not displeased. There is a relief at judgment, even adverse. It is good to think that somewhere a seismograph records our quakes and slippages. I imagine Miss Merrymount's death, not too many months after this, as a final, serenely flat line on the hospital monitor attached to her. Something sardonic in that flat line, too—of unviolated rectitude, of magnificent patience with a world that for over ninety years failed to prove itself other than disappointing. By this time, Julia and I were at last divorced.

Everything of the abandoned home is lost, of course—the paintings on the walls, the way shadows and light contend in this or that corner, the gracious burst of evening warmth from the radiators. The pets. Canute was a male golden retriever we had acquired as a puppy when the children were still a tumbling, preteen pack. Endlessly amiable, as his breed tends to be, he suffered all, including castration, as if life were a steady hail of blessings. Curiously, not long before he died, my youngest child, who sings in a female punk group that has just started up, brought Canute to the house where now I live with Lisa as my wife. He sniffed around politely and expressed with only a worried angle of his ears the wonder of his old master reconstituted in this strange-smelling home; then he collapsed with a heavy sigh onto the kitchen floor. He looked fat and seemed lethargic. My daughter, whose hair is cut short and dyed mauve in patches, said that the dog roamed at night and got into the neighbors' garbage, and even into one neighbor's horse feed. This sounded like mismanagement to me. Julia's new boyfriend is a middle-aged former Dartmouth quarterback, a golf and tennis and backpack freak, and she is hardly ever home, so busy is she keeping up with him and trying to learn new games. The house and lawn are neglected; the children drift in and out with their friends and once in a while clean out the rotten food in the refrigerator. Lisa, sensing my suppressed emotions, said something tactful and bent down to scratch Canute behind one ear.

Since the ear was infected and sensitive, he feebly snapped at her, then thumped the kitchen floor with his tail, in apology.

Like me when snubbed by Miss Merrymount, my wife seemed more pleased than not, encountering a touch of resistance, her position in the world as it were confirmed. She discussed dog antibiotics with my daughter, and at a glance one could not have been sure who was the older, though it was clear who had the odder hair. It is true, as the cliché runs, that Lisa is young enough to be my daughter. But now that I am fifty, every female under thirty-five is young enough to be my daughter. Most of the people in the world are young enough to be my daughter.

A few days after his visit, Canute disappeared, and a few days later he was found far out on the marshes near my old house, his body bloated. The dog officer's diagnosis was a heart attack. Can that happen, I wondered, to four-footed creatures? The thunderbolt had hit my former pet by moonlight, his heart full of marshy joy and his stomach fat with garbage, and he had lain for days with ruffling fur while the tides went in and out. The image makes me happy, like the sight of a sail popping full of wind and tugging its boat swiftly out from shore. In truth—how terrible to acknowledge—all three of these deaths make me happy, in a way. Witnesses to my disgrace are being removed. The world is growing lighter. Eventually there will be none to remember me as I was in those embarrassing, disarrayed years when I scuttled without a shell, between houses and wives, a snake between skins, a monster of selfishness, my grotesque needs naked and pink, my social presence beggarly and vulnerable. The deaths of others carry us off bit by bit, until there will be nothing left; and this, too, will be, in a way, a mercy.

James Michener

LUCIFER AND HEY-YOU

The golden age of the eastern shore of the Chesapeake Bay came in that four-decade span from 1880 to 1920 when the rest of the nation allowed the marshy counties to sleep undisturbed. True, in these years the world experienced panic and wars, revolutions and contested elections, but these had almost no impact on the somnolent estuaries and secluded coves. Roads now connected the important towns situated at the heads of rivers, but they were narrow and dusty, and it took wagons days to cover what a speedy boat could negotiate in an hour. When roads paved with white oyster shells did arrive, at the end of this happy age, they were usually one-car width only and formed not a reasonable means of transportation but a lively invitation to suicide.

There was, of course, occasional excitement, but it rarely came from the outside world. A black male servant was accused of assaulting a white woman, and a lynching party (composed mainly of Turlocks and Cavenys) broke into the jail with the intention of stringing the accused from an oak tree, but Judge Hathaway Steed proposed to have no such blot on his jurisdiction; armed only with a family pistol, he confronted the mob and ordered it to disperse.

The Eastern Shore baseball league, composed of six natural rivals, including Easton, Crisfield, Chestertown and Patamoke, flourished and became notorious for having produced Home Run Baker, who would hit in one year the unheard-of total of twelve round-trippers. A luxurious ferryboat left Baltimore every Saturday and Sunday at seven-thirty in the morning to transport day-trippers to a slip at Claiborne, where the throngs would leave the ship and crowd into the cars of the Baltimore, Chesapeake and Atlantic Railroad for a two-hour race across the peninsula to Ocean City on the Atlantic. At four-forty-five in the afternoon the railroad cars would refill, the train would chug its way back to Claiborne, passengers would reboard the ferry and arrive back at Baltimore at ten-thirty at night—all for one dollar and fifty cents.

One of the adventures that caused the most excitement occurred in 1887, when a ship commanded by Captain Thomas Lightfoot, a trouble-maker if there ever was one, docked at Patamoke with its cargo of ice sawed from the freshwater ponds of Labrador. When the sawdust had been washed away, and the blue-green cakes were stored in icehouses along the riverfront, Captain Lightfoot produced an object that was to cause as much long-lasting trouble as the golden apple that Paris was required to award to the most beautiful goddess.

"I've somethin' extra for you," Lightfoot announced as he directed one of his black stevedores to fetch the item from below. "Before it appears I wish to inform you that it is for sale, ten dollars cash."

A moment later the stevedore appeared on deck leading by a leash one of the most handsome dogs ever seen in Maryland. He was jet-black, sturdy in his front quarters, sleek and powerful in his hind, with a face so intelligent that it seemed he might speak at any moment. His movements were quick, his dark eyes following every development nearby, yet his disposition appeared so equable that he seemed always about to smile.

"He's called a Labrador," Lightfoot said. "Finest huntin' dog ever developed."

"He's what?" Jake Turlock snapped.

"Best huntin' dog known."

"Can't touch a Chesapeake retriever," Turlock said, referring to the husky red dog bred especially for bay purposes.

"This dog," said Lightfoot, "will take your Chesapeake and teach him his ABC's."

"That dog ain't worth a damn," Turlock said. "Too stocky up front." But there was something about this new animal that captivated Tim Caveny, whose red Chesapeake had just died without ever fulfilling the promise he had shown as a pup—"Fine in the water and persistent in trackin' downed birds, but not too bright. Downright stupid, if you ask me." This new black dog displayed a visible intelligence that gave every sign of further development, and Caveny announced, "I'd like to see him."

Captain Lightfoot, suspecting that in Caveny he had found his pigeon, turned the Labrador loose, and with an almost psychic understanding that his future lay with this Irishman, the dog ran to Caveny, leaned against his leg and nuzzled his hand.

It was an omen. Tim's heart was lost, and he said, "I'll take him."

"Mr. Caveny, you just bought the best Labrador ever bred." With grandiloquent gestures the captain turned the animal over to his new owner. The dog, sensing that he had found a permanent master, stayed close to Tim, licking his hand and looking up with dark eyes overflowing with affection.

Tim paid the ten dollars, then reached down and patted his new hunting companion. "Come on, Lucifer," he said.

"That's a hell of a name for a dog," Turlock growled.

"He's black, ain't he?"

"If he's black, call him Blackie."

"He's Old Testament black," Tim said. And to Captain Lightfoot's surprise, he recited: " 'How art thou fallen from heaven, O Lucifer, son of the morning!' " Turning his back to the others, he stooped over the dog, ruffled his head and said in a low voice, "You'll be up in the morning, Lucifer, early, early."

Lightfoot then startled the crowd by producing three other dogs of this new breed, one male and two females, and these, too, he sold to the hunters of Patamoke, assuring each purchaser: "They can smell ducks, and they've never been known to lose a cripple."

"To me they look like horse manure," Jake Turlock said.

"They what?" Caveny demanded.

"I said," Turlock repeated, "that your black dog looks like a horse turd."

Slowly Tim handed the leash he had been holding to a bystander. Then with a mighty swipe, he knocked Turlock to the wet and salty boards of the wharf. The waterman stumbled in trying to regain his footing, and while he was off balance Caveny saw a chance to deliver an uppercut that almost knocked him into the water. Never one to allow a fallen foe an even chance, Caveny leaped across the planking and kicked the waterman in his left armpit, lifting him well into the air. This was a mistake, because when Turlock landed, his hand fell upon some lumber stacked for loading onto Captain Lightfoot's ship, and after he had quickly tested three or four clubs he found one to his liking, and with it delivered such a blow to the Irishman's head that the new owner of the Labrador staggered back and fell into the Choptank.

In this way the feud between Tim Caveny, owner of a black Labrador, and Jake Turlock, owner of a red Chesapeake, began.

The first test of the two dogs came in the autumn of 1888 at the dove shoot on the farm of old Lyman Steed, who had spent his long life running one of the Refuge plantations and had now retired to a stretch of land near Patamoke.

Nineteen first-class hunters of the area convened at regular intervals during the dove season to shoot this most interesting of the small game birds—gentlemen like Lyman Steed, middle-class shopkeepers and rough watermen like Jake Turlock and Tim Caveny. A dove shoot was one of the most republican forms of sport so far devised. Here a man's worth was determined by two criteria: the way he fired his gun and how he managed his dog.

Each hunter was allowed to bring one dog to the shoot, and the animal had to be well trained, because the birds came charging in at low altitude, swerved and dodged in unbelievable confusion and, on the lucky occasions when they were hit, fell maliciously in unpredictable spots. If there was a swamp nearby, as on the Steed farm, the doves would fall there. If there were brambles, the dying doves seemed to seek them out, and the only practical way for a hunter to retrieve his dove, if he hit one, was to have a dog trained to leap forward when he saw a dove fall from the sky and find it no matter where it dropped. The dog must also lift the fallen bird gently in its teeth, carry it without bruising it against thorns, and drop it at the feet of his master. A dove hunt was more a test of dog than of master.

Jake Turlock had a well-trained beast, a large, surly red-haired Chesapeake, specially bred to work the icy waters of the bay in fall and winter. These dogs were unusual in that they grew a double matting of hair and produced an extra supply of oil to lubricate it. They could swim all day, loved to dive into the water for a fallen goose and were particularly skilled in breaking their way through thin ice. Like most of his breed, Jake's Chesapeake had a vile temper and would allow himself to be worked only by his master. Every other gunner in the field was his enemy and their dogs were beneath his contempt, but he was kept obedient by Jake's stern cry: "Hey-You, heel!"

His name was Hey-You. Jake had started calling him that when he first arrived at the Turlock shack, a fractious, bounding pup giving no evidence that he could ever be trained. In fact, Jake had thought so little of him that he delayed giving him a proper name. "Hey-You! Get the dove!" The pup would look quizzical, wait, consider whether he wanted to obey or not, then leap off when Jake kicked him.

So during his useless youth he was plain "Hey-You, into the water for the goose!" But at the age of three, after many kicks and buffetings, he suddenly developed into a marvelous hunting dog, a raider like his master, a rough-and-tumble uncivilized beast who seemed made for the Chesapeake. "Hey-You! Go way down and fetch the dove!" So when this red-haired dog swaggered onto the dove field that October day, he was recognized as one of the best ever trained in the Patamoke area.

Lucifer, Tim Caveny's Labrador, was an unknown quantity, for he had never before participated in a dove shoot; furthermore he had been trained in a manner quite different from the way Hey-You had been treated. "My children were raised with love," the Irishman said, "and my dog was trained the same way." From the moment Lucifer came down off Captain Lightfoot's ice ship, he had known nothing but love.

His glossy coat was kept nourished by a daily supply of fat from the Caveny table, and his nails were trimmed. In return he gave the Caveny family his complete affection. "I believe that dog would lay down his life for me," Mrs. Caveny told her neighbors, for when she fed him he always looked up at her with his great black eyes and rubbed against her hand. A peddler came to the door one day unexpectedly and in a frightening manner; Lucifer's hackles rose, and he leaned forward tensely, waiting for a sign. Startled at seeing the man, Mrs. Caveny emitted a short gasp, whereupon Lucifer shot like a thunderbolt for the man's throat.

"Down, Lucifer!" she cried and he stopped almost in midair.

But whether he could discipline himself to retrieve doves was another matter. Jake Turlock predicted widely, "The stupid Irishman has spoiled his dog, if'n he was any good to begin with." Other hunters who had trained their beasts more in the Turlock tradition agreed, adding, "He ain't gonna get much out of that what-you-call-it Labrador."

But Caveny persisted, talking to Lucifer in sweet Irish phrases, trying to convince the animal that glory awaited him on the dove field. "Luke, you and me will get more doves than this town ever seen. Luke, when I say 'Fetch the dove!' you're to go direct to the spot you think it fell. Then run out in wider and wider circles." Whether the dog would do this was uncertain, but Tim had tried with all his guile to get the animal in a frame of mind conducive to success. Now, as he led him to Lyman Steed's farm, he prayed that his lessons had been in the right direction, but when he turned the last corner and saw the other eighteen men with their Chesapeakes awaiting him, eager to see what he had accomplished with this strange dog, his heart fluttered and he felt dizzy.

Pulling gently on the rope attached to the dog's collar, he brought him back, kneeled beside him and whispered in his lilting brogue, "Lucifer, you and me is on trial. They're all watchin' us." He stroked the dog's glistening neck and said, "At my heel constantly, little fellow. You don't move till I fire. And when I do, Luke, for the love of a merciful God, find that dove. Soft mouth, Luke, soft mouth and drop him at my toes, like you do with the rag dolls."

As if he knew what his master was saying, Luke turned and looked at Tim impatiently, as if to say, I know my job—I'm a Labrador.

The field contained about twenty acres and had recently been harvested, so that it provided a large, flat, completely open area, but it was surrounded by a marsh on one side, a large blackberry bramble on another, and a grove of loblollies covering a thicket of underbrush on a third. The doves would sweep in over the loblollies, drop low, hear gunfire and veer back over the brambles. The placement of gunners was an art reserved for Judge Hathaway Steed, who hunted in an expensive Harris tweed jacket imported from London.

The judge had been a hunter all his life, raised Chesapeakes and sold them to his friends. He had acquired much better intuition concerning doves than he had of the law, and now he proposed to place his eighteen subordinates strategically, about sixty yards apart and in a pattern that pretty well covered the perimeter of the field. Toward the end of his assignments he came to Tim Caveny. "You there, with the what-you-call-it dog."

"Labrador," Caveny said, tipping his hat respectfully, as his father had done in the old country when the squire spoke.

"Since we can't be sure a dog like that can hunt . . ."

"He can hunt."

The judge ignored this. "Take that corner," he said, and Tim wanted to complain that doves rarely came to that corner, but since he was on trial he kept his mouth shut, but he was most unhappy when he saw Jake Turlock receive one of the best positions.

Then everyone stopped talking, for down the road edging the field came a carriage driven by a black man. On the seat beside him sat a very old gentleman with a shotgun across his knees. This was Lyman Steed, owner of the field. He was eighty-seven years old and so frail that a stranger would have wondered how he could lift a gun, let alone shoot it. Behind him, eyes and ears alert, rode a large red Chesapeake.

The carriage came to a halt close to where Hathaway Steed was allocating the spots, and the black driver descended, unfolded a canvas chair and lifted the old man down into it. "Where do we sit today?" Steed asked in a high, quavering voice.

"Take him over by the big tree," Hathaway said, and the black man carried the chair and its contents to the spot indicated. There he scraped the ground with his foot, making a level platform, and on it he placed the owner of the farm and one of the best shots in this meet. "We's ready," the black man cried, and the judge gave his last instructions: "If you see a dove that the men near you don't, call 'Mark!' Keep your dogs under control. And if the dove flies low, absolutely no shooting in the direction of the man left or right."

The men took their positions. It was half after one in the afternoon. The sun was high and warm; insects droned. The dogs were restless, but each stayed close to his master, and some men wondered whether there would be any doves, because on some days they failed to show.

But not today. From the woods came six doves, flying low in their wonderfully staggered pattern, now in this direction, now swooping in that. Jake Turlock, taken by surprise, fired and hit nothing. "Mark!" he shouted at the top of his voice. Tim Caveny fired and hit nothing. "Mark!" he bellowed. In swift, darting patterns the doves dived and swirled and twisted, and three other hunters fired at them, to no avail, but as the birds tried to leave the field old Lyman Steed had his gun waiting. With a splendid shot he hit his target, and his big Chesapeake leaped out before the bird hit the ground and retrieved it before the dove could even flutter. Bearing it proudly in his mouth, but not touching its flesh with his teeth, he trotted back, head high, to his master and laid the bird at the old man's feet.

"That's how it's done," Tim Caveny whispered to his Labrador.

There was a long wait and the hunters began to wonder if they would see any more doves, but Hathaway Steed, walking the rounds to police the action, assured each man as he passed, "We're going to see flocks."

He was right. At about two-thirty they started coming in. "Mark!" one hunter shouted as they passed him before he could fire. Jake Turlock was waiting and knocked one down, whereupon Hey-You leaped out into the open field, pounced on the fallen bird and brought it proudly back. Jake looked at Tim, but the Irishman kept his eyes on the sky. He did whisper to Lucifer, "Any dog can retrieve in an open field. Wait till one falls in the brambles."

On the next flight Tim got no chance to shoot, but Turlock did, and this time he hit a bird that had come over the field, heard the shooting and doubled back. This dove fell into the brambles. "Fetch the dove!" Jake told his Chesapeake, but the bushes were too thick. That bird was lost.

But now another dove flew into Tim's range, and when he fired, this one also fell into brambles. "Fetch the dove!" Tim said calmly, his heart aching for a good retrieve.

Lucifer plunged directly for the fallen bird but could not penetrate the thick and thorny briars. Unlike Turlock's Chesapeake, he did not quit, for he heard his master calling softly, "Circle, Luke! Circle!" and he ran in wide circles until he found a path back to the brambles. But again he was stopped, and again his master cried, "Circle, Luke!" And this time he found an entrance that allowed him to roam freely, but with so much ranging that he had lost an accurate guide to the fallen bird. Still he heard his master's voice imploring, "Circle, Luke!" and he knew that this meant he still had a chance.

So in the depth of the bramble patch, but below the reach of the thorns, he ran and scrambled and clawed and finally came upon Caveny's bird. He gave a quiet yup, and when Tim heard this his heart expanded. Lucifer had passed his first big test, but on the way out of the patch the dog smelled another fallen bird, Turlock's, and he brought this one too.

When he laid the two doves at Tim's feet, the Irishman wanted to kneel and kiss his rough black head, but he knew that all the hunters in his area were watching, so in a manly way he patted the dog, then prepared for his moment of triumph.

It was a custom in dove shooting that if a hunter downed a bird that his dog could not retrieve but another man's dog did, the second hunter was obligated to deliver the dove to the man who had downed it. It was a nice tradition, for it allowed the second man to make a show of carrying the dove to its rightful owner while all the other hunters observed his act of sportsmanship. Implied in the gesture was the comment "My dog can retrieve and yours can't."

Proudly Tim Caveny walked the hundred-odd yards to where Jake Turlock was standing. Lucifer started to follow, but Tim cried sharply, "Stay!" and the dog obeyed. The other hunters took note of this, then watched as Tim gravely delivered the bird, but at this moment another hunter shouted "Mark!" and a whole covey flew over.

Automatically Jake and Tim fired, and two birds fell. Jake's Hey-You was on the spot, of course, and proudly ran out to recover the dove his master had knocked down. Lucifer was standing far from where his master had shot and was so obedient to the earlier command "Stay" that he did not move. But when Tim yelled, "Fetch the dove," he rushed directly to the fallen bird and carried it not to where Tim was standing but back to his assigned location.

The hunter next to Tim on the down side of the field called, "You got yourself a dog, Tim."

When Caveny returned to his location and saw the dove neatly laid beside his pouch, he desperately wanted to smother the dark beast with his affection, but he said merely, "Good dog, Luke."

"Mark!" came the call and up went the guns.

The day was a triumph. Luke hunted in marshland as well as he had in the brambles. He proved he had a soft mouth. He circled well in woods, and on the open field he was superb. And with it all he displayed the sweet disposition of the Labradors and the Cavenys.

It was the tradition on these dove shoots for one member at the end of the day to provide refreshments. At a quarter to five, religiously, the hunting ceased. The dogs were put back on leashes, and if the owners had come by wagon, were stowed in back while their masters ate cold duck and drank Baltimore beer. Turlock and Caveny, having come on foot, tied their dogs to trees, and as they did so the former muttered, "Doves ain't nothin', Caveny. It's what a dog does in ice that counts."

"Lucifer will handle ice," Tim said confidently.

"On the bay proper, my Chesapeake is gonna eat 'im up. Out there they got waves."

"Your Labrador looks like a breed to be proud of," old Lyman Steed said as the black servant carried him into position to share the duck.

"Has possibilities," Judge Hathaway Steed said. "But we won't know till we see him after geese."

Each man complimented Tim on what he had accomplished with his strange dog, but each also predicted, "Probably won't be much on the bay. Hair's not thick enough."

Tim did not argue, but when he got Lucifer home he hugged him and gave him chicken livers, and whispered, "Lucifer, geese is just doves, grown bigger. You'll love the water, cold or not." During the whole dove season, during which this fine black dog excelled, Tim repeated his assurances: "You're gonna do the same with geese."

The test came in November. As the four men and their dogs holed up in a blind at the Turlock marshes, Jake reminded them, "Geese ain't so plentiful now. Can't afford any mistakes, man or dog." He was right. Once the Choptank and its sister rivers had been home for a million geese; now the population had diminished to less than four hundred thousand, and bagging them became more difficult. Jake, a master of the goose call, tried from dawn till ten in the morning to lure the big birds down, but failed. The hunters had a meager lunch, and toward dusk, when it seemed that the day was a failure, nine geese wheeled in, lowered the pitch of their wings, spread their feet and came right at the blind. Guns blazed, and before the smoke had cleared, Jake's Chesapeake had leaped out of the blind with powerful swimming motions and retrieved the goose that his master had appeared to kill. Lucifer went into the water, too, but many seconds after Hey-You, and he was both splashy and noisy in making his retrieve of Tim's goose.

"Sure doesn't like cold water," Jake said contemptuously.

"Neither did yours, when he started," Tim said.

"A Chesapeake is born lovin' water, colder the better."

It became obvious to the hunters, after eight mornings in the blind, that while Tim Caveny's new dog was exceptional with doves on warm days, he left much to be desired as a real hunter in the only form of the sport that mattered—goose on water. He displayed a discernible reluctance to plunge into cold waves, and they began to wonder whether he would go into ice at all.

Talk at the store centered on his deficiencies: "This here Labrador is too soft. Can't hold a candle to a Chesapeake for hard work when it matters. You ask me, I think Caveny bought hisself a loser." Some hunters told him this to his face.

Tim listened and said nothing. In his lifetime he had had four major dogs, all of them Chesapeakes, and he understood the breed almost as well as Jake Turlock did, but he had never owned a dog with the charm of Lucifer, the warmth, the love, and that meant something—"I come home, the room's bigger when that dog's in it."

"Point is," the men argued, "a huntin' dog oughtn't to be in a room in the first place. His job is outside."

"You don't know Lucifer. Besides, he's sired the best lot of pups in the region. This breed is bound to catch on."

The Patamoke hunters were a suspicious clan. The most important thing in their lives, more important than wife or church or political party, was the totality of the hunting season: "You got to have the right gun, the right mates, the right spot, the right eye for the target and, above all, the right dog. And frankly, I doubt the Labrador." The pups did not sell.

Tim had faith. He talked with Lucifer constantly, encouraging him to leap more quickly into the cold water. He showed what ice was like, and how the dog must break it with his forepaws to make a path for himself to the downed goose. Using every training trick the Choptank had ever heard of, he tried to bring this handsome dog along step by step.

He failed. In January, when real ice formed along the edges of the river, the men went hunting along the banks of the bay itself, and when

Jake Turlock knocked down a beautiful goose, it fell on ice about two hundred yards from the blind—"Hey-You, get the bird!"

And the big Chesapeake showed what a marvelous breed he was by leaping into the free water, swimming swiftly to the edge of the ice, then breaking a way for himself right to the goose. Clutching the big bird proudly in his jaws, he plunged back into the icy water, pushed aside the frozen chunks and returned to the blind, entering it with a mighty water-spraying leap.

"That's what I call a dog," Jake said proudly, and the men agreed.

Lucifer did not perform so well. He retrieved his goose, all right, but hesitantly and almost with protest. He didn't want to leap into the water in the first place; he was not adept at breaking ice; and when he returned to the blind, he ran along the ice for as long as possible before going back to the freezing water.

"He did get the goose," Jake admitted condescendingly, and for the rest of that long day on the Chesapeake the two dogs performed in this way, with Hey-You doing as well as a water dog could and Lucifer just getting by.

Tim never spoke a harsh word. Lucifer was his dog, a splendid, loving, responsive animal, and if he didn't like cold water, that was a matter between him and his master. And toward dusk the dog found an opportunity to repay Tim's confidence. Jake had shot a big goose, which had fallen into a brambled sort of marsh from which Hey-You could not extract it. The dog tried, swam valiantly in various directions, but achieved nothing.

In the meantime Lucifer remained in the blind, trembling with eagerness, and Tim realized that his Labrador knew where the goose was. After Hey-You had returned with nothing, Tim said softly, "Luke, there's a bird out there. Show them how to get it."

Like a flash, the black dog leaped into the water, splashed his way through the semi-ice into the rushy area—and found nothing. "Luke!" Tim bellowed. "Circle. Circle." So the dog ran and splashed and swam in noisy circles and still found nothing, but he would not quit, for his master kept pleading, "Luke, circle!"

And then he found the goose, grabbed it in his gentle mouth and swam proudly back to the blind. As he was about to place the goose at Tim's feet the Irishman said quietly, "No!" and the dog was so attentive to his master that he froze, wanting to know what he had done wrong.

"Over there," Tim said, and Luke took the goose to Jake and placed it at his feet.

The feud between the two watermen continued. The men at the store fired it with unkind comments about Lucifer's deficiencies, but once or twice Caveny caught a hint that their animosity was weakening, for at some unexpected moment a man would see in Tim's dog a quality that made him catch his breath. Outwardly every hunter would growl, "I want my dog to be rough and able to stand the weather and ready to leap at anyone attackin' me," but inwardly he would also want the dog to love him. And the way in which Lucifer stayed close to Tim, anxious to detect every nuance in the Irishman's mood, tantalized the men at the store. All they would grant openly was "Maybe Tim's got somethin' in that black dog." But Jake Turlock would not admit even that. "What he's got is a good lapdog, and that's about it. As for me, I'm interested solely in huntin'."

Aside from this disagreement over dogs, and a fistfight now and then, the two watermen maintained a respectful friendship. They hunted together, fished together and worked the oyster beds in season. But it was the big gun that cemented their partnership, giving it substance and allowing it to blossom.

In these decades when the Eastern Shore thrived, the city of Baltimore also flourished. Some discriminating critics considered it the best city in America, combining the new wealth of the North with the old gentility of the South. The city offered additional rewards: a host of German settlers who gave it intellectual distinction; numerous Italians who gave it warmth. But for most observers, its true excellence derived from the manner in which its hotels and restaurants maintained a tradition of savory cooking: Southern dishes, Northern meats, Italian spices and German beer.

In 1888 the noblest hotel of them all had opened, the Rennert, eight stories high with an additional three stories to provide a dome at one end, a lofty belvedere at the other. It was a grand hostelry that boasted, "Our cooks are Negro. Our waiters wear white gloves." From the day of its opening, it became noted for the sumptuousness of its cuisine: "Eighteen kinds of game. Fourteen ways to serve oysters. And the best wild duck in America." To dine at the Rennert was to share the finest the Chesapeake could provide.

Jake Turlock and Tim Caveny had never seen the new hotel, but it was to play a major role in their lives. Its black chefs demanded the freshest oysters, and these were delivered daily during the season by Choptank watermen who packed their catch in burlap bags, speeding them across the bay by special boat. When the boat was loaded with oysters, its principal cargo, the captain could usually find space on deck for a few last-minute barrels crammed with ducks: mallards, redheads, canvasbacks, and, the juiciest of all, the black. It was in the providing of these ducks for the Rennert that Jake and Tim began to acquire a little extra money, which they saved for the larger project they had in mind.

One night at the store, after arguing about the comparative merits of their dogs, Jake said, "I know me a man's got a long gun he might want to dispose of."

Caveny was excited. "If you can get the gun, I can get me a couple of skiffs."

Turlock replied: "Suppose we get the gun and the skiffs, I know me a captain who'll ferry our ducks to the Rennert. Top dollar."

Caveny completed the fantasying by adding, "We put aside enough money, we can get Paxmore to build us our own boat. Then we're in business."

So the pair sailed upriver to the landing of a farm owned by an old man named Greef Twombly, and there they propositioned him: "You ain't gonna have much use for your long gun, Greef. We aim to buy it."

"What you gonna use for money?" the toothless old fellow asked.

"We're gonna give you ten dollars cash, which Tim Caveny has in his pocket right now, and another forty when we start collectin' ducks."

"Barrel of that gun was made from special forged iron. My grandfather brought it from London, sixty-two years ago."

"It's been used."

"More valuable now than when he got it home."

"We'll give you sixty."

"Sixty-five and I'll think about it."

"Sixty-five it is and we get possession now."

Twombly rocked back and forth, considering aspects of the deal, then led them to one of the proudest guns ever to sweep the ice at midnight. It was a monstrous affair, eleven feet six inches long, about a hundred and ten pounds in weight, with a massive stock that could not possibly fit into a man's shoulder, which was a good thing because if anyone tried to hold this cannon when it fired, the recoil would tear his arm away.

"You ever fire one of these?" the old man asked.

"No, but I've heard," Turlock said.

"Hearin' ain't enough, son. You charge it with three quarters of a pound of black powder in here, no less, or she won't carry. Then you pour in a pound and a half of Number Six Shot, plus one fistful. You tamp her down with greasy wadding, like this, and you're ready. Trigger's kept real tight so you can't explode her by accident, because if you did, it would rip the side off'n a house."

The two watermen admired the huge barrel, the sturdy fittings and the massive oak stock; as they inspected their purchase, the old man said, "You know how to fit her into a skiff?"

"I've seen," Turlock said.

But Twombly wanted to be sure these new men understood the full complexity of this powerful gun, so he asked them to carry it to the landing, where he had a fourteen-foot skiff with an extremely pointed bow and almost no dead rise, chocks occupying what normally would have been the main seat and a curious burlap contraption built into the stern area.

Deftly the old hunter let himself down into the skiff, kneeling in the stern. He then produced a double-ended paddle like the ones Eskimos used, and also two extremely short single-handed paddles. Adjusting his weight and testing the double paddle, he told Jake, "You can hand her down."

When the two watermen struggled with the preposterous weight of the gun, the old man said, "It ain't for boys." He accepted the gun into the skiff, dropped its barrel between the chocks, flipped a wooden lock, which secured it, then fitted the heavy butt into a socket made of burlap bagging filled with pine needles.

"What you do," Twombly said, "is use your big paddle to ease you into position, but when you come close to the ducks you stow it and take out your two hand paddles, like this." And with the two paddles that looked like whisk brooms, he silently moved the skiff about.

"When you get her into position, you lie on your belly, keep the hand paddles close by and sight along the barrel of the gun. You don't point the gun; you point the skiff. And when you get seventy, eighty ducks in range, you put a lot of pressure on this trigger and—"

The gun exploded with a power that seemed to tear a hole in the sky. The kickback came close to ripping out the stern of the skiff, but the pine needles absorbed it, while a veritable cloud of black smoke curled upward.

"First time I ever shot that gun in daylight," the old man said. "It's a killer."

"You'll sell?"

"You're Lafe Turlock's grandson, ain't you?"

"I am."

"I had a high regard for Lafe. Gun's yourn."

"You'll get your fifty-five," Jake promised.

"I better," the old man said ominously.

Caveny produced the two skiffs he had promised, and their mode of operation became standardized: as dusk approached, Jake would inspect his skiff to be sure he had enough pine needles in the burlap to absorb the recoil; he also cleaned the huge gun, prepared his powder and checked his supply of shot. Tim in the meantime was preparing his own skiff and feeding the two dogs.

Hey-You ate like a pig, gulping down whatever Caveny produced, but Lucifer was more finicky—there were certain things, like chicken guts, he would not eat. But the two animals had learned to exist together, each with his own bowl, growling with menace if the other approached. They had never engaged in a real fight; Hey-You would probably have killed Lucifer had one been joined, but they did nip at each other and a kind of respectful discipline was maintained.

Whenever they saw Jake oiling the gun, they became tense, would not sleep and spied on every action of their masters. As soon as it became clear that there was to be duck hunting, they bounded with joy and kept close to the skiff in which Caveny would take them onto the water.

Duck hunting with a big gun was an exacting science best performed in the coldest part of winter with no moon, for then the watermen enjoyed various advantages: they could cover the major part of their journey by sliding their skiffs across the ice; when they reached areas of open water they would find the ducks clustered in great rafts; and the lack of moonlight enabled them to move close without being seen. The tactic required the utmost silence; even the crunch of a shoe on frost would spook the ducks. The dogs especially had to remain silent, perched in Caveny's skiff, peering into the night.

When the two skiffs reached open water, about one o'clock in the morning with the temperature at 12 degrees, Tim kept a close watch on the necks of the two dogs; almost always the first indication that ducks were in the vicinity came when the hackles rose on Hey-You. He was so attuned to the bay that one night Tim conceded graciously, "Jake, your dog can see ducks at a hundred yards in pitch-black," and Turlock replied, "That's why he's a huntin' dog, not a lapdog—like some I know."

When the ducks were located, vast collections huddling in the cold, Turlock took command. Easing his skiff into the icy water, he adjusted his double-ended paddle, stayed on his knees to keep the center of gravity low, and edged toward the restive fowl. Sometimes it took him an hour to cover a quarter of a mile; he kept the barrel of his gun smeared with lampblack to prevent its reflecting such light as there might be, and in cold darkness he inched forward.

Now he discarded his two-handled paddle and lay flat on his belly, his cheek alongside the stock of the great gun, his hands working the short paddles. It was a time of tension, for the slightest swerve or noise would alert the ducks and they would be off.

Slowly, slowly he began to point the nose of the skiff at the heart of the congregation, and when he had satisfied himself that the muzzle of the gun was pointed in the right direction, he brought his short paddles in and took a series of deep breaths. Then, with his right cheek close to the stock but not touching it, and his right hand at the trigger, he extended his forefinger, grasped the heavy trigger—and waited. Slowly the skiff drifted and steadied, and when everything was in line, he pulled the trigger.

He was never prepared for the magnitude of the explosion that ripped through the night. It was monstrous, like the fire of a cannon, but in the brief flash it produced he would always see ducks being blown out of the water as if a hundred expert gunners had fired at them.

Now Caveny became the focus. Paddling furiously, he sped his skiff through the dark water, the two dogs quivering with desire to leap into the waves to retrieve the ducks. But he wanted to bring them much closer to where the birds lay, and to do so he enforced stern discipline. "No! No!"—that was all he said, but the two dogs obeyed, standing on their hind feet, their forepaws resting on the dead rise like twin figureheads, one red, one black.

"Fetch!" he shouted, and the dogs leaped into the water and began their task of hauling the ducks to the two skiffs. Hey-You always going to Turlock's and Lucifer to Caveny's.

Since Tim's job was to maintain his shotgun and knock down cripples, he was often too busy to bother with his dog, so the Labrador had perfected a tactic whereby he paddled extra hard with his hind legs, reared out of the water and tossed his ducks into the Caveny skiff.

In this way the two watermen, with one explosion of their big gun, sometimes got themselves as many as sixty canvasbacks, ten or twelve blacks and a score of others. On rare occasions they would be able to fire twice in one night, and then their profit was amazing.

As soon as the two skiffs reached Patamoke, the watermen packed their catch in ventilated barrels, which waited lined up on the wharf.

There they purchased from other night gunners enough additional ducks to make full barrels, which they handed over to the captain of the boat running oysters to the Rennert, and at the end of each month they received from the hotel a check for their services.

One wintry February night the two watermen crept out to a spacious lagoon in the ice; there must have been three thousand ducks rafted there beneath a frozen late-rising moon. Caveny became aware of how cold it was when Lucifer left his spot on the gunwale and huddled in the bottom of the skiff. Hey-You turned twice to look at his cowardly companion, then moved to the middle of the bow as if obliged to do the work of two.

Jake, seeing this tremendous target before him—more ducks in one spot than they had ever found before—decided that he would use not a pound and a half of shot, but almost twice as much. "I'll rip a tunnel through the universe of ducks." But to propel such a heavy load he required an extraheavy charge, so into the monstrous gun he poured more than a pound of black powder. He also rammed home a double wadding. "This is gonna be a shot to remember. Rennert's will owe us enough money to pay for our boat."

Cautiously he moved his lethal skiff into position, waited, took a deep breath and pulled the trigger.

Whoooom! The gun produced a flash that could have been seen for miles and a bang that reverberated across the bay. The tremendous load of shot slaughtered more than a hundred and ten ducks and seven geese. It also burst out the back of Jake's skiff, knocked him unconscious and threw him a good twenty yards aft into the dark and icy waters.

The next minutes were a nightmare. Caveny, having seen his partner fly through the air during the brief flash of the explosion, started immediately to paddle in the direction of where the body might have fallen, but the two dogs, trained during their entire lives to retrieve fallen birds, found themselves involved with the greatest fall of ducks they had ever encountered, and they refused to bother with a missing man.

"Goddammit!" Caveny yelled. "Leave them ducks alone and find Jake!"

But the dogs knew better. Back and forth they swam on their joyous mission, gathering ducks at a rate they had never imagined in their twitching dreams.

"Jake! Where in hell are you?"

In the icy darkness he could find no way of locating the drowning man; all he knew was the general direction of Jake's fall, and now, in some desperation—with almost no chance of finding his mate—he began sweeping the area.

Lucifer swam noisily to the skiff, almost reprimanding Tim for having moved it away from the fallen ducks, and threw two ducks into the boat. Then he swam casually a few yards and, grabbing the unconscious Turlock by the arm, hauled him to the skiff before returning to the remaining ducks.

When Tim finally succeeded in dragging Jake aboard, he could think of nothing better to do than to slap the unconscious man's face with his icy glove, and after a few minutes Jake revived. Bleary-eyed, he tried to determine where he was, and when at last he perceived that he was in Caveny's skiff and not in his own, he bellowed, "What have you done with the gun?"

"I been savin' you!" Tim yelled back, distraught by the whole affair and by the mangled ducks that kept piling into his skiff.

"To hell with me. Save the gun!"

So now the two watermen began paddling furiously and with no plan, trying to locate the other skiff, and after much fruitless effort Jake had the brains to shout, "Hey-You! Where are you?"

And from a direction they could not have anticipated, a dog barked, and when they paddled toward the sound they found a sorely damaged skiff almost sinking from the weight of its big gun and the many ducks Hey-You had fetched.

On the doleful yet triumphant return to Patamoke, Tim Caveny could not help pointing out that it had been his Labrador who had saved Turlock's life, but Jake growled through the ice festooning his chin, "Granted, but it was Hey-You that saved the gun, and that's what's important."

Connie Willis

THE LAST OF THE WINNEBAGOS

O n the way out to Tempe I saw a
dead jackal in the road. I was in the far left lane of Van Buren, ten lanes
away from it, and its long legs were facing away from me, the squarish
muzzle flat against the pavement so it looked narrower than it really was,
and for a minute I thought it was a dog.

I had not seen an animal in the road like that for fifteen years. They
can't get onto the divideds, of course, and most of the multiways are
fenced. And people are more careful of their animals.

The jackal was probably somebody's pet. This part of Phoenix was
mostly residential, and after all this time, people still think they can turn
the nasty, carrion-loving creatures into pets. Which was no reason to have

hit it and, worse, left it there. It's a felony to strike an animal and another one to not report it, but whoever had hit it was long gone.

I pulled the Hitori over onto the center shoulder and sat there awhile, staring at the empty multiway. I wondered who had hit it and whether they had stopped to see if it was dead.

Katie had stopped. She had hit the brakes so hard she sent the jeep into a skid that brought it up against the ditch, and jumped out of the jeep. I was still running toward him, floundering in the snow. We made it to him almost at the same time. I knelt beside him, the camera dangling from my neck, its broken case hanging half open.

"I hit him," Katie had said. "I hit him with the jeep."

I looked in the rearview mirror. I couldn't even see over the pile of camera equipment in the back seat with the eisenstadt balanced on top. I got out. I had come nearly a mile, and looking back, I couldn't see the jackal, though I knew now that's what it was.

"McCombe! David! Are you there yet?" Ramirez's voice said from inside the car.

I leaned in. "No," I shouted in the general direction of the phone's mike. "I'm still on the multiway."

"Mother of God, what's taking you so long? The governor's conference is at twelve, and I want you to go out to Scottsdale and do a layout on the closing of Taliesin West. The appointment's for ten. Listen, McCombe, I got the poop on the Amblers for you. They bill themselves as 'One Hundred Percent Authentic,' but they're not. Their RV isn't really a Winnebago, it's an Open Road. It *is* the last RV on the road, though, according to Highway Patrol. A man named Eldridge was touring with one, also *not* a Winnebago, a Shasta, until March, but he lost his license in Oklahoma for using a tanker lane, so this is it. Recreation vehicles are banned in all but four states. Texas has legislation in committee, and Utah has a full-divided bill coming up next month. Arizona will be next, so takes lots of pictures, Davey boy. This may be your last chance. And get some of the zoo."

"What about the Amblers?" I said.

"Their name *is* Ambler, believe it or not. I ran a lifeline on them. He was a welder. She was a bank teller. No kids. They've been doing this since eighty-nine when he retired. Nineteen years. David, are you using the eisenstadt?''

We had been through this the last three times I'd been on a shoot. "I'm not *there* yet," I said.

"Well, I want you to use it at the governor's conference. Set it on his desk if you can."

I intended to set it on a desk, all right. One of the desks at the back, and let it get some nice shots of the rear ends of reporters as they reached wildly for a little clear air-space to shoot their pictures in, some of them holding their vidcams in their upstretched arms and aiming them in what they hope is the right direction because they can't see the governor at all, let it get a nice shot of one of the reporter's arms as he knocked it face-down on the desk.

"This one's a new model. It's got a trigger. It's set for faces, full-lengths, and vehicles."

So great. I come home with a hundred-frame cartridge full of passersby and tricycles. How the hell did it know when to click the shutter or which one the governor was in a press conference of eight hundred people, full-length *or* face? It was supposed to have all kinds of fancy lightmetrics and computer-composition features, but all it could really do was mindlessly snap whatever passed in front of its idiot lens, just like the highway speed cameras.

It had probably been designed by the same government types who'd put the highway cameras along the road instead of overhead so that all it takes is a little speed to reduce the new side-license plates to a blur, and people go faster than ever. A great camera, the eisenstadt. I could hardly wait to use it.

"Sun-co's very interested in the eisenstadt," Ramirez said. She didn't say goodbye. She never does. She just stops talking and then starts up again later. I looked back in the direction of the jackal.

The multiway was completely deserted. New cars and singles don't use the undivided multiways much, even during rush hours. Too many of the little cars have been squashed by tankers. Usually there are at least a few obsoletes and renegade semis taking advantage of the Patrol's being on the dividers, but there wasn't anybody at all.

I got back in the car and backed up even with the jackal. I turned off the ignition but didn't get out. I could see the trickle of blood from its mouth from here. A tanker went roaring past out of nowhere, trying to beat the cameras, straddling the three middle lanes and crushing the jackal's rear half to a bloody mush. It was a good thing I hadn't been trying to cross the road. He never would have even seen me.

I started the car and drove to the nearest off-ramp to find a phone. There was one at an old 7-Eleven on McDowell.

"I'm calling to report a dead animal on the road," I told the woman who answered the Society's phone.

"Name and number?"

"It's a jackal," I said. "It's between Thirtieth and Thirty-Second on Van Buren. It's in the far right lane."

"Did you render emergency assistance?"

"There was no assistance to be rendered. It was dead."

"Did you move the animal to the side of the road?"

"No."

"Why not?" she said, her tone suddenly sharper, more alert.

Because I thought it was a dog. "I didn't have a shovel," I said, and hung up.

I got out to Tempe by eight-thirty, in spite of the fact that every tanker in the state suddenly decided to take Van Buren. I got pushed out onto the shoulder and drove on that most of the way.

The Winnebago was set up in the fairgrounds between Phoenix and Tempe, next to the old zoo. The flyer had said they would be open from nine to nine, and I had wanted to get most of my pictures before they opened, but it was already a quarter to nine, and even if there were no cars in the dusty parking lot, I was probably too late.

It's a tough job being a photographer. The minute most people see a camera, their real faces close like a shutter in too much light, and all that's left is their camera face, their public face. It's a smiling face, except in the case of Saudi terrorists or senators, but, smiling or not, it shows no real emotion. Actors, politicians, people who have their pictures taken all the time are the worst. The longer the person's been in the public eye, the easier it is for me to get great vidcam footage and the harder it is to get anything approaching a real photograph, and the Amblers had been at this for nearly twenty years. By a quarter to nine they would already have their camera faces on.

I parked down at the foot of the hill next to the clump of ocotillas and yucca where the zoo sign had been, pulled my Nikon longshot out of the mess in the back seat, and took some shots of the sign they'd set up by the multiway: "See a Genuine Winnebago. One Hundred Percent Authentic."

The Genuine Winnebago was parked longways against the stone banks of cacti and palms at the front of the zoo. Ramirez had said it wasn't a real Winnebago, but it had the identifying W with its extending stripes running the length of the RV, and it seemed to me to be the right shape, though I hadn't seen one in at least ten years.

I was probably the wrong person for this story. I had never had any great love for RV's, and my first thought when Ramirez called with the assignment was that there are some things that should be extinct, like mosquitoes and lane dividers, and RV's are right at the top of the list. They had been everywhere in the mountains when I'd lived in Colorado, crawling along in the left-hand lane, taking up two lanes even in the days when a lane was fifteen feet wide, with a train of cursing cars behind them.

I'd been behind one on Independence Pass that had stopped cold while a ten-year-old got out to take pictures of the scenery with an Instamatic, and one of them had tried to take the curve in front of my house and ended up in my ditch, looking like a beached whale. But that was always a bad curve.

An old man in an ironed short-sleeved shirt came out the side door and around to the front end and began washing the Winnebago with a sponge and a bucket. I wondered where he had gotten the water. According to Ramirez's advance work, which she'd sent me over the modem about the Winnebago, it had maybe a fifty-gallon water tank, tops, which is barely enough for drinking water, a shower, and maybe washing a dish or two, and there certainly weren't any hookups here at the zoo, but he was swilling water onto the front bumper and even over the tires as if he had more than enough.

I took a few shots of the RV standing in the huge expanse of parking lot and then hit the longshot to full for a picture of the old man working on the bumper. He had large reddish-brown freckles on his arms and the top of his bald head, and he scrubbed away at the bumper with a vengeance. After a minute he stopped and stepped back, and then called to his wife. He looked worried, or maybe just crabby. I was too far away to tell if he had snapped out her name impatiently or simply called her to come and look, and I couldn't see his face. She opened the metal side door, with its narrow louvered window, and stepped down onto the metal step.

The old man asked her something, and she, still standing on the step, looked out toward the multiway and shook her head, and then came around to the front, wiping her hands on a dishtowel, and they both stood there looking at his handiwork.

They were One Hundred Percent Authentic, even if the Winnebago wasn't, down to her flowered blouse and polyester slacks, probably also one hundred percent, and the cross-stitched rooster on the dishtowel. She had on brown leather slip-ons like I remembered my grandmother wearing, and I was willing to bet she had set her thinning white hair on bobby pins. Their bio said they were in their eighties, but I would have put them in their nineties, although I wondered if they were too perfect and therefore fake, like the Winnebago. But she went on wiping her hands on the dishtowel the way my grandmother had when she was upset, even though I couldn't see if her face was showing any emotion, and that action at least was authentic.

She apparently told him the bumper looked fine because he dropped the dripping sponge into the bucket and went around behind the Winnebago. She went back inside, shutting the metal door behind her even though it had to be already at least a hundred and ten out, and they hadn't even bothered to park under what scanty shade the palms provided.

I put the longshot back in the car. The old man came around the front with a big plywood sign. He propped it against the vehicle's side. "The Last of the Winnebagos," the sign read in somebody's idea of what Indian writing should look like. "See a vanishing breed. Admission— Adults—$8.00, Children under twelve—$5.00 Open 9 A.M. to Sunset." He strung up a row of red and yellow flags, and then picked up the bucket and started toward the door, but halfway there he stopped and took a few steps down the parking lot to where I thought he probably had a good view of the road, and then went back, walking like an old man, and took another swipe at the bumper with the sponge.

"Are you done with the RV yet, McCombe?" Ramirez said on the car phone.

I slung the camera into the back. "I just got here. Every tanker in Arizona was on Van Buren this morning. Why the hell don't you have me do a piece on abuses of the multiway system by water-haulers?"

"Because I want you to get to Tempe alive. The governor's press conference has been moved to one, so you're okay. Have you used the eisenstadt yet?"

"I told you, I just got here. I haven't even turned the damned thing on."

"You don't turn it on. It self-activates when you set it bottom down on a level surface."

Great. It had probably already shot its 100-frame cartridge on the way here.

"Well, if you don't use it on the Winnebago, make sure you use it at the governor's conference," she said. "By the way, have you thought any more about moving to investigative?"

That was why Sun-co was really so interested in the eisenstadt. It had been easier to send a photographer who could write stories than it had to send a photographer and a reporter, especially in the little one-seater Hitoris they were ordering now, which was how I got to be a photojournalist. And since that had worked out so well, why send either? Send an eisenstadt and a DAT deck and you won't need an Hitori and way-mile credits to get them there. You can send them through the mail. They can sit unnoticed on the old governor's desk, and after a while somebody in a one-seater who wouldn't have to be either a photographer or a reporter can sneak in to retrieve them and a dozen others.

"No," I said, glancing back up the hill. The old man gave one last swipe to the front bumper and then walked over to one of the zoo's old stone-edged planters and dumped the bucket in on a tangle of prickly pear, which would probably think it was a spring shower and bloom before I made it up the hill. "Look, if I'm going to get any pictures before the turistas arrive, I'd better go."

"I wish you'd think about it. And use the eisenstadt this time. You'll like it once you try it. Even *you'll* forget it's a camera."

"I'll bet," I said. I looked back down the multiway. Nobody at all was coming now. Maybe that was what all the Amblers' anxiety was about—I should have asked Ramirez what their average daily attendance was and what sort of people used up credits to come this far out and see an old beat-up RV. The curve into Tempe alone was three point two miles. Maybe nobody came at all. If that was the case, I might have a chance of getting some decent pictures. I got in the Hitori and drove up the steep drive.

"Howdy," the old man said, all smiles, holding out his reddish-brown freckled hand to shake mine. "Name's Jake Ambler. And this here's Winnie," he said, patting the metal side of the RV, "Last of the Winnebagos. Is there just the one of you?"

"David McCombe," I said, holding out my press pass. "I'm a photographer. Sun-co. Phoenix *Sun,* Tempe-Mesa *Tribune,* Glendale *Star,* and affiliated stations. I was wondering if I could take some pictures of your vehicle?" I touched my pocket and turned the taper on.

"You bet. We've always cooperated with the media, Mrs. Ambler and me. I was just cleaning old Winnie up," he said. "She got pretty dusty on the way down from Globe." He didn't make any attempt to tell his wife I was there, even though she could hardly avoid hearing us, and she didn't open the metal door again. "We been on the road now with Winnie for almost twenty years. Bought her in 1989 in Forest City, Iowa, where they were made. The wife didn't want to buy her, didn't know if she'd like traveling, but now she's the one wouldn't part with it."

He was well into his spiel now, an open, friendly, I-have-nothing-to-hide expression on his face that hid everything. There was no point in taking any stills, so I got out the vidcam and shot the TV footage while he led me around the RV.

"This up here," he said, standing with one foot on the flimsy metal ladder and patting the metal bar around the top, "is the luggage rack, and this is the holding tank. It'll hold thirty gallons and has an automatic electric pump that hooks up to any waste hookup. Empties in five minutes, and you don't even get your hands dirty." He held up his fat pink hands palms forward as if to show me. "Water tank," he said, slapping a silver metal tank next to it. "Holds forty gallons, which is plenty for just the two of us. Interior space is a hundred fifty cubic feet with six feet four of headroom. That's plenty even for a tall guy like yourself."

He gave me the whole tour. His manner was easy, just short of slap-on-the-back hearty, but he looked relieved when an ancient VW bug came chugging catty-cornered up through the parking lot. He must have thought they wouldn't have any customers either.

A family piled out, Japanese tourists, a woman with short black hair, a man in shorts, two kids. One of the kids had a ferret on a leash.

"I'll just look around while you tend to the paying customers," I told him.

I locked the vidcam in the car, took the longshot, and went up toward the zoo. I took a wide-angle of the zoo sign for Ramirez. I could see it now—she'd run a caption like, "The old zoo stands empty today. No sound of lion's roar, of elephant's trumpeting, or children's laughter, can be heard here. The old Phoenix Zoo, last of its kind, while just outside its gates stands yet another last of its kind. Story on page 10." Maybe it would be a good idea to let the eisenstadts and the computers take over.

I went inside. I hadn't been out here in years. In the late eighties there had been a big flap over zoo policy. I had taken the pictures, but I hadn't covered the story since there were still such things as reporters back then. I had photographed the cages in question and the new zoo director who had caused all the flap by stopping the zoo's renovation project cold and giving the money to a wildlife protection group.

"I refuse to spend money on cages when in a few years we'll have nothing to put in them. The timber wolf, the California condor, the grizzly bear, are in imminent danger of becoming extinct, and it's our responsibility to save them, not make a comfortable prison for the last survivors."

The Society had called him an alarmist, which just goes to show you how much things can change. Well, he was an alarmist, wasn't he?

The grizzly bear isn't extinct in the wild—it's Colorado's biggest tourist draw, and there are so many whooping cranes Texas is talking about limited hunting.

In all the uproar, the zoo had ceased to exist, and the animals all went to an even more comfortable prison in Sun City—sixteen acres of savannah land for the zebras and lions, and snow manufactured daily for the polar bears.

They hadn't really been cages, in spite of what the zoo director said. The old capybara enclosure, which was the first thing inside the gate, was a nice little meadow with a low stone wall around it. A family of prairie dogs had taken up residence in the middle of it.

I went back to the gate and looked down at the Winnebago. The family circled the Winnebago, the man bending down to look underneath the body. One of the kids was hanging off the ladder at the back of the RV. The ferret was nosing around the front wheel Jake Ambler had so carefully scrubbed down, looking like it was about ready to lift its leg, if ferrets do that. The kid yanked on its leash and then picked it up in his arms. The mother said something to him. Her nose was sunburned.

Katie's nose had been sunburned. She had had that white cream on it, that skiers used to use. She was wearing a parka and jeans and bulky pink-and-white moonboots that she couldn't run in, but she still made it to Aberfan before I did. I pushed past her and knelt over him.

"I hit him," she said bewilderedly. "I hit a dog."

"Get back in the jeep, damn it!" I shouted at her. I stripped off my sweater and tried to wrap him in it. "We've got to get him to the vet."

"Is he dead?" Katie said, her face as pale as the cream on her nose.

"No!" I had shouted. "No, he isn't dead."

The mother turned and looked up toward the zoo, her hand shading her face. She caught sight of the camera, dropped her hand, and smiled, a toothy, impossible smile. People in the public eye are the worst, but even people having a snapshot taken close down somehow, and it isn't just the phony smile. It's as if that old superstition is true, and cameras do really steal the soul.

I pretended to take her picture and then lowered the camera. The zoo director had put up a row of tombstone-shaped signs in front of the gate, one for each endangered species. They were covered with plastic, which hadn't helped much. I wiped the streaky dust off the one in front of me. "Canis latrans," it said, with two green stars after it. "Coyote. North American wild dog. Due to large-scale poisoning by ranchers, who saw it as a threat to cattle and sheep, the coyote is nearly extinct in the wild." Underneath there was a photograph of a ragged coyote sitting on its haunches and an explanation of the stars. Blue—endangered species. Yellow—endangered habitat. Red—extinct in the wild.

After Misha died, I had come out here to photograph the dingo and the coyotes and the wolves, but they were already in the process of moving the zoo, so I couldn't get any pictures, and it probably wouldn't have done any good. The coyote in the picture had faded to a greenish-yellow and its yellow eyes were almost white, but it stared out of the picture looking as hearty and unconcerned as Jake Ambler, wearing its camera face.

The mother had gone back to the bug and was herding the kids inside. Mr. Ambler walked the father back to the car, shaking his shining bald head, and the man talked some more, leaning on the open door, and then got in and drove off. I walked back down.

If he was bothered by the fact that they had only stayed ten minutes and that, as far as I had been able to see, no money had changed hands, it didn't show in his face. He led me around to the side of the RV and pointed to a chipped and faded collection of decals along the painted bar of the W. "These here are the states we've been in." He pointed to the one nearest the front. "Every state in the Union, plus Canada and Mexico. Last state we were in was Nevada."

Up this close it was easy to see where he had painted out the name of the original RV and covered it with the bar of red. The paint had the dull look of unauthenticity. He had covered up the "Open Road" with a burnt-wood plaque that read, "The Amblin' Amblers."

He pointed at a bumper sticker next to the door that said, "I got lucky in Vegas at Caesar's Palace," and had a picture of a naked showgirl. "We couldn't find a decal for Nevada. I don't think they make them anymore. And you know something else you can't find? Steering wheel covers. You know the kind. That keep the wheel from burning your hands when it gets hot?"

"Do you do all the driving?" I asked.

He hesitated before answering, and I wondered if one of them didn't have a license. I'd have to look it up in the lifeline. "Mrs. Ambler spells me sometimes, but I do most of it. Mrs. Ambler reads the map. Damn maps nowadays are so hard to read. Half the time you can't tell what kind of road it is. They don't make them like they used to."

We talked for a while more about all the things you couldn't find a decent one of anymore and the sad state things had gotten in generally, and then I announced I wanted to talk to Mrs. Ambler, got the vidcam and the eisenstadt out of the car, and went inside the Winnebago.

She still had the dishtowel in her hand, even though there couldn't possibly be space for that many dishes in the tiny RV. The inside was even smaller than I had thought it would be, low enough that I had to duck and so narrow I had to hold the Nikon close to my body to keep from hitting the lens on the passenger seat. It felt like an oven inside, and it was only nine o'clock in the morning.

I set the eisenstadt down on the kitchen counter, making sure its concealed lens was facing out. If it would work anywhere, it would be here. There was basically nowhere for Mrs. Ambler to go that she could get out of range. There was nowhere I could go either, and sorry, Ramirez, there are just some things a live photographer can do better than a preprogrammed one, like stay out of the picture.

"This is the galley," Mrs. Ambler said, folding her dishtowel and hanging it from a plastic ring on the cupboard below the sink with the cross-stitch design showing. It wasn't a rooster after all. It was a poodle wearing a sunbonnet and carrying a basket. "Shop on Wednesday," the motto underneath said.

"As you can see, we have a double sink with a hand-pump faucet. The refrigerator is LP-electric and holds four cubic feet. Back here is the dinette area. The table folds up into the rear wall, and we have our bed. And this is our bathroom."

She was as bad as her husband. "How long have you had the Winnebago?" I said to stop the spiel. Sometimes, if you can get people talking about something besides what they intended to talk about, you can disarm them into something like a natural expression.

"Nineteen years," she said, lifting up the lid of the chemical toilet. "We bought it in 1989. I didn't want to buy it—I didn't like the idea of selling our house and going gallivanting off like a couple of hippies, but Jake went ahead and bought it, and now I wouldn't trade it for anything. The shower operates on a forty-gallon pressurized water system." She stood back so I could get a picture of the shower stall, so narrow you wouldn't have to worry about dropping the soap. I dutifully took some vidcam footage.

"You live here full-time then?" I said, trying not to let my voice convey how impossible that prospect sounded. Ramirez had said they were from Minnesota. I had assumed they had a house there and only went on the road for part of the year.

"Jake says the great outdoors is our home," she said. I gave up trying to get a picture of her and snapped a few high-quality detail stills for the papers: the "Pilot" sign taped on the dashboard in front of the driver's seat, the crocheted granny-square afghan on the uncomfortable-looking couch, a row of salt and pepper shakers in the back windows—Indian children, black scottie dogs, ears of corn.

"Sometimes we live on the open prairies and sometimes on the seashore," she said. She went over to the sink and hand-pumped a scant two cups of water into a little pan and set it on the two-burner stove. She took down two turquoise melmac cups and flowered saucers and a jar of freeze-dried coffee and spooned a little into the cups. "Last year we were in the Colorado Rockies. We can have a house on a lake or in the desert, and when we get tired of it, we just move on. Oh, my, the things we've seen."

I didn't believe her. Colorado had been one of the first states to ban recreational vehicles, even before the gas crunch and the multiways. It had banned them on the passes first and then shut them out of the national forests, and by the time I left they weren't even allowed on the interstates.

Ramirez had said RV's were banned outright in forty-seven states. New Mexico was one, Utah had heavy restricks, and daytime travel was forbidden in all the western states. Whatever they'd seen, and it sure wasn't Colorado, they had seen it in the dark or on some unpatrolled multiway, going like sixty to outrun the cameras. Not exactly the foot-loose and fancy-free life they tried to paint.

The water boiled. Mrs. Ambler poured it into the cups, spilling a little on the turquoise saucers. She blotted it up with the dishtowel. "We came down here because of the snow. They get winter so early in Colorado."

"I know," I said. It had snowed two feet, and it was only the middle of September. Nobody even had their snow tires on. The aspens hadn't turned yet, and some of the branches broke under the weight of the snow. Katie's nose was still sunburned from the summer.

"Where did you come from just now?" I asked her.

"Globe," she said, and opened the door to yell to her husband. "Jake! Coffee!" She carried the cups to the table-that-converts-into-a-bed. "It has leaves that you can put in it so it seats six," she said.

I sat down at the table so she was on the side where the eisenstadt could catch her. The sun was coming in through the cranked-open back windows, already hot. Mrs. Ambler got onto her knees on the plaid cushions and let down a woven cloth shade, carefully, so it wouldn't knock the salt and pepper shakers off.

There were some snapshots stuck up between the ceramic ears of corn. I picked one up. It was a square Polaroid from the days when you had to peel off the print and glue it to a stiff card: The two of them, looking exactly the way they did now, with that friendly, impenetrable camera smile, were standing in front of a blur of orange rock—the Grand Canyon? Zion? Monument Valley? Polaroid had always chosen color over definition. Mrs. Ambler was holding a little yellow blur in her arms that could have been a cat but wasn't. It was a dog.

"That's Jake and me at Devil's Tower," she said, taking the picture away from me. "And Taco. You can't tell from this picture, but she was the cutest little thing. A chihuahua." She handed it back to me and rummaged behind the salt and pepper shakers. "Sweetest little dog you ever saw. This will give you a better idea."

The picture she handed me was considerably better, a matte print done with a decent camera. Mrs. Ambler was holding the chihuahua in this one, too, standing in front of the Winnebago.

"She used to sit on the arm of Jake's chair while he drove and when we came to a red light she'd look at it, and when it turned green she'd bark to tell him to go. She was the smartest little thing."

I looked at the dog's flaring, pointed ears, its bulging eyes and rat's snout. The dogs never come through. I took dozens of picture, there at the end, and they might as well have been calendar shots. Nothing of the real dog at all. I decided it was the lack of muscles in their faces—they could not smile, in spite of what their owners claimed. It is the muscles in the face that make people leap across the years in pictures. The expressions on dogs' faces were what breeding had fastened on them—the gloomy bloodhound, the alert collie, the rakish mutt—and anything else was wishful thinking on the part of the doting master, who would also swear that a colorblind chihuahua with a brain pan the size of a Mexican jumping bean could tell when the light changed.

My theory of the facial muscles doesn't really hold water, of course. Cats can't smile either, and they come through. Smugness, slyness, disdain—all of those expressions come through beautifully, and they don't have any muscles in their faces either, so maybe it's love that you can't capture in a picture because love was the only expression dogs were capable of.

I was still looking at the picture. "She is a cute little thing," I said and handed it back to her. "She wasn't very big, was she?"

"I could carry Taco in my jacket pocket. We didn't name her Taco. We got her from a man in California that named her that," she said, as if she could see herself that the dog didn't come through in the picture. As if, had she named the dog herself, it would have been different. Then the name would have been a more real name, and Taco would have, by default, become more real as well. As if a name could convey what the picture didn't—all the things the little dog did and was and meant to her.

Names don't do it either, of course. I had named Aberfan myself. The vet's assistant, when he heard it, typed it in as Abraham.

"Age?" he had said calmly, even though he had no business typing all this into a computer, he should have been in the operating room with the vet.

"You've got that in there, damn it," I shouted.

He looked calmly puzzled. "I don't know any Abraham . . ."

"Aberfan, damn it. Aberfan!"

"Here it is," the assistant said imperturbably.

Katie, standing across the desk, looked up from the screen. "He had the newparvo and lived through it?" she said bleakly.

"He had the newparvo and lived through it," I said, "until you came along."

"I had an Australian shepherd," I told Mrs. Ambler.

Jake came into the Winnebago, carrying the plastic bucket. "Well, it's about time," Mrs. Ambler said, "Your coffee's getting cold."

"I was just going to finish washing off Winnie," he said. He wedged the bucket into the tiny sink and began pumping vigorously with the heel of his hand. "She got mighty dusty coming down through all that sand."

"I was telling Mr. McCombe here about Taco," she said, getting up and taking him the cup and saucer. "Here, drink your coffee before it gets cold."

"I'll be in in a minute," he said. He stopped pumping and tugged the bucket out of the sink.

"Mr. McCombe had a dog," she said, still holding the cup out to him. "He had an Australian shepherd. I was telling him about Taco."

"He's not interested in that," Jake said. They exchanged one of those warning looks that married couples are so good at. "Tell him about the Winnebago. That's what he's here for."

Jake went back outside. I screwed the longshot's lens cap on and put the vidcam back in its case. She took the little pan off the miniature stove and poured the coffee back into it. "I think I've got all the pictures I need," I said to her back.

She didn't turn around. "He never liked Taco. He wouldn't even let her sleep on the bed with us. Said it made his legs cramp. A little dog like that that didn't weigh anything."

I took the longshot's lens cap back off.

"You know what we were doing the day she died? We were out shopping. I didn't want to leave her alone, but Jake said she'd be fine. It was ninety degrees that day, and he just kept on going from store to store, and when we got back she was dead." She set the pan on the stove and turned on the burner. "The vet said it was the newparvo, but it wasn't. She died from the heat, poor little thing."

I set the Nikon down gently on the formica table and estimated the settings.

"When did Taco die?" I asked her, to make her turn around.

"Ninety," she said. She turned back to me, and I let my hand come down on the button in an almost soundless click, but her public face was still in place: apologetic now, smiling, a little sheepish. "My, that was a long time ago."

I stood up and collected my cameras. "I think I've got all the pictures I need," I said again. "If I don't, I'll come back out."

"Don't forget your briefcase," she said, handing me the eisenstadt. "Did your dog die of the newparvo, too?"

"He died fifteen years ago," I said. "In ninety-three."

She nodded understandingly. "The third wave," she said.

I went outside. Jake was standing behind the Winnebago, under the back window, holding the bucket. He shifted it to his left hand and held out his right hand to me. "You get all the pictures you needed?" he asked.

"Yeah," I said. "I think your wife showed me about everything." I shook his hand.

"You come on back out if you need any more pictures," he said, and sounded, if possible, even more jovial, open-handed, friendly than he had before. "Mrs. Ambler and me, we always cooperate with the media."

"Your wife was telling me about your chihuahua," I said, more to see the effect on him than anything else.

"Yeah, the wife still misses that little dog after all these years," he said, and he looked the way she had, mildly apologetic, still smiling. "It died of the newparvo. I told her she ought to get it vaccinated, but she kept putting it off." He shook his head. "Of course, it wasn't really her fault. You know whose fault the newparvo really was, don't you?"

Yeah, I knew. It was the communists' fault, and it didn't matter that all their dogs had died, too, because he would say their chemical warfare had gotten out of hand or that everybody knows commies hate dogs. Or maybe it was the fault of the Japanese, though I doubted that. He was, after all, in a tourist business. Or the Democrats or the atheists or all of them put together, and even that was One Hundred Percent Authentic—portrait of the kind of man who drives a Winnebago—but I didn't want to hear it. I walked over to the Hitori and slung the eisenstadt in the back.

"You know who really killed your dog, don't you?" he called after me.

"Yes," I said, and got in the car.

I went home, fighting my way through a fleet of red-painted water tankers who weren't even bothering to try to outrun the cameras and thinking about Taco. My grandmother had had a chihuahua. Perdita. Meanest dog that ever lived. Used to lurk behind the door waiting to take Labrador-sized chunks out of my leg. And my grandmother's. It developed some lingering chihuahuan ailment that made it incontinent and even more ill-tempered, if that was possible.

Toward the end, it wouldn't even let my grandmother near it, but she refused to have it put to sleep and was unfailingly kind to it, even though I never saw any indication that the dog felt anything but unrelieved spite toward her. If the newparvo hadn't come along, it probably would still have been around making her life miserable.

I wondered what Taco, the wonder dog, able to distinguish red and green at a single intersection, had really been like, and if it had died of heat prostration. And what it had been like for the Amblers, living all that time in a hundred and fifty cubic feet together and blaming each other for their own guilt.

I called Ramirez as soon as I got home, breaking in without announcing myself, the way she always did. "I need a lifeline," I said.

"I'm glad you called," she said. "You got a call from the Society. And how's this as a slant for your story? 'The Winnebago and the Winnebagos.' They're an Indian tribe. In Minnesota, I think—why the hell aren't you at the governor's conference?"

"I came home," I said. "What did the Society want?"

"They didn't say. They asked for your schedule. I told them you were with the governor in Tempe. Is this about a story?"

"Yeah."

"Well, you run a proposal past me before you write it. The last thing the paper needs is to get in trouble with the Society."

"The lifeline's for Katherine Powell." I spelled it.

She spelled it back to me. "Is she connected with the Society story?"

"No."

"Then what is she connected with? I've got to put something on the request-for-info."

"Put down background."

"For the Winnebago story?"

"Yes," I said. "For the Winnebago story. How long will it take?"

"That depends. When do you plan to tell me why you ditched the governor's conference? *And* Taliesin West. Jesus Maria, I'll have to call the *Republic* and see if they'll trade footage. I'm sure they'll be thrilled to have shots of an extinct RV. That is, assuming you got any shots. You did make it out to the zoo, didn't you?"

"Yes. I got vidcam footage, stills, the works. I even used the eisenstadt."

"Mind sending your pictures in while I look up your old flame, or is that too much to ask? I don't know how long this will take. It took me two days to get clearance on the Amblers. Do you want the whole thing—pictures, documentation?"

"No. Just a resume. And a phone number."

She cut out, still not saying goodbye. If phones still had receivers, Ramirez would be a great one for hanging up on people. I highwired the vidcam footage and the eisenstadts in to the paper and then fed the eisenstadt cartridge into the developer. I was more than a little curious about what kind of pictures it would take, in spite of the fact that it was trying to do me out of a job. At least it used high-res film and not some damn two hundred thousand–pixel TV substitute. I didn't believe it could compose, and I doubted if the eisenstadt would be able to do foreground-background either, but it might, under certain circumstances, get a picture I couldn't.

The doorbell rang. I answered the door. A lanky young man in a Hawaiian shirt and baggies was standing on the front step, and there was another man in a Society uniform out in the driveway.

"Mr. McCombe?" he said, extending a hand. "Jim Hunter. Humane Society."

I don't know what I'd expected—that they wouldn't bother to trace the call? That they'd let somebody get away with leaving a dead animal on the road?

"I just wanted to stop by and thank you on behalf of the Society for phoning in that report on the jackal. Can I come in?"

He smiled, an open, friendly, smug smile, as if he expected me to be stupid enough to say, "I don't know what you're talking about," and slam the screen door on his hand.

"Just doing my duty," I said, smiling back at him.

"Well, we really appreciate responsible citizens like you. It makes our job a whole lot easier." He pulled a folded readout from his shirt pocket. "I just need to double-check a couple of things. You're a reporter for Sun-co, is that right?"

"Photo-journalist," I said.

"And the Hitori you were driving belongs to the paper?"

I nodded.

"It has a phone. Why didn't you use it to make the call?"

The uniform was bending over the Hitori.

"I didn't realize it had a phone. The paper just bought the Hitoris. This is only the second time I've had one out."

Since they knew the paper had had phones put in, they also knew what I'd just told them. I wondered where they'd gotten the info. Public phones were supposed to be tap-free, and if they'd read the license number off one of the cameras, they wouldn't know who'd had the car unless they'd talked to Ramirez, and if they'd talked to her, she wouldn't have been talking blithely about the last thing she needed being trouble with the Society.

"You didn't know the car had a phone," he said, "so you drove to—" He consulted the readout, somehow giving the impression he was taking notes. I'd have bet there was a taper in the pocket of that shirt. "—The 7-Eleven at McDowell and Fortieth Street, and made the call from there. Why didn't you give the Society rep your name and address?"

"I was in a hurry," I said. "I had two assignments to cover before noon, the second out in Scottsdale."

"Which is why you didn't render assistance to the animal either. Because you were in a hurry."

You bastard, I thought. "No," I said. "I didn't render assistance because there wasn't any assistance to be rendered. The—it was dead."

"And how did you know that, Mr. McCombe?"

"There was blood coming out of its mouth," I said.

I had thought that that was a good sign, that he wasn't bleeding anywhere else. The blood had come out of Aberfan's mouth when he tried to lift his head, just a little trickle, sinking into the hard-packed snow. It had stopped before we even got him into the car. "It's all right, boy," I told him. "We'll be there in a minute."

Katie started the jeep, killed it, started it again, backed it up to where she could turn around.

Aberfan lay limply across my lap, his tail against the gear shift. "Just lie still, boy," I said. I patted his neck. It was wet, and I raised my hand and looked the palm, afraid it was blood. It was only water from the melted snow. I dried his neck and the top of his head with the sleeve of my sweater.

"How far is it?" Katie said. She was clutching the steering wheel with both hands and sitting stiffly forward in the seat. The windshield wipers flipped back and forth, trying to keep up with the snow.

"About five miles," I said, and she stepped on the gas pedal and then let up on it again as we began to skid. "On the right side of the highway."

Aberfan raised his head off my lap and looked at me. His gums were gray, and he was panting, but I couldn't see any more blood. He tried to lick my hand. "You'll make it, Aberfan," I said. "You made it before, remember?"

"But you didn't get out of the car and go check, to make sure it was dead?" Hunter said.

"No."

"And you don't have any idea who hit the jackal?" he said, and made it sound like the accusation it was.

"No."

He glanced back at the uniform, who had moved around the car to the other side. "Whew," Hunter said, shaking his Hawaiian collar, "it's like an oven out here. Mind if I come in?" which meant the uniform needed more privacy. Well, then, by all means, give him more privacy. The sooner he sprayed print-fix on the bumper and tires and peeled off the incriminating traces of jackal blood that weren't there and stuck them in the evidence bags he was carrying in the pockets of that uniform, the sooner they'd leave. I opened the screen door wider.

"Oh, this is great," Hunter said, still trying to generate a breeze with his collar. "These old adobe houses stay so cool." He glanced around the room at the developer and the enlarger, the couch, the dry-mounted photographs on the wall. "You don't have any idea who might have hit the jackal?"

"I figure it was a tanker," I said. "What else would be on Van Buren that time of morning?"

I was almost sure it had been a car or a small truck. A tanker would have left the jackal a spot on the pavement. But a tanker would get a license suspension and two weeks of having to run water into Santa Fe instead of Phoenix, and probably not that. Rumor at the paper had it the Society was in the water board's pocket. If it was a car, on the other hand, the Society would take away the car and stick its driver with a prison sentence.

"They're all trying to beat the cameras," I said. "The tanker probably didn't even know it'd hit it."

"What?" he said.

"I said, it had to be a tanker. There isn't anything else on Van Buren during rush hour."

I expected him to say, "Except for you," but he didn't. He wasn't even listening. "Is this your dog?" he said.

He was looking at the photograph of Perdita. "No," I said. "That was my grandmother's dog."

"What is it?"

A nasty little beast. And when it died of the newparvo, my grandmother had cried like a baby. "A chihuahua."

He looked around at the other walls. "Did you take all these pictures of dogs?" His whole manner had changed, taking on a politeness that made me realize just how insolent he had intended to be before. The one on the road wasn't the only jackal around.

"Some of them," I said. He was looking at the photograph next to it. "I didn't take that one."

"I know what this one is," he said, pointing at it. "It's a boxer, right?"

"An English bulldog," I said.

"Oh, right. Weren't those the ones that were exterminated? For being vicious?"

"No," I said.

He moved on to the picture over the developer, like a tourist in a museum. "I bet you didn't take this one either," he said, pointing at the high shoes, the old-fashioned hat on the stout old woman holding the dogs in her arms.

"That's a photograph of Beatrix Potter, the English children's author," I said. "She wrote *Peter Rabbit*."

He wasn't interested. "What kind of dogs are those?"

"Pekingese."

"It's a great picture of them."

It is, in fact, a terrible picture of them. One of them has wrenched his face away from the camera, and the other sits grimly in her owner's hand, waiting for its chance. Obviously neither of them liked having its picture taken, though you can't tell that from their expressions. They reveal nothing in their little flat-nosed faces, in their black little eyes.

Beatrix Potter, on the other hand, comes through beautifully, in spite of the attempt to smile for the camera and the fact that she must have had to hold onto the Pekes for dear life, or maybe because of that. The fierce, humorous love she felt for her fierce, humorous little dogs is all there in her face. She must never, in spite of *Peter Rabbit* and its attendant fame, have developed a public face. Everything she felt was right there, unprotected, unshuttered. Like Katie.

"Are any of these your dog?" Hunter asked. He was standing looking at the picture of Misha that hung above the couch.

"No," I said.

"How come you don't have any pictures of your dog?" he asked, and I wondered how he knew I had had a dog and what else he knew.

"He didn't like having his picture taken."

He folded up the readout, stuck it in his pocket, and turned around to look at the photo of Perdita again. "He looks like he was a real nice little dog," he said.

The uniform was waiting on the front step, obviously finished with whatever he had done to the car.

"We'll let you know if we find out who's responsible," Hunter said, and they left. On the way out to the street the uniform tried to tell him what he'd found, but Hunter cut him off. The suspect has a house full of photographs of dogs, therefore he didn't run over a poor facsimile of one on Van Buren this morning. Case closed.

I went back over to the developer and fed the eisenstadt film in. "Positives, one two three order, five seconds," I said, and watched as the pictures came up on the developer's screen. Ramirez had said the eisenstadt automatically turned on whenever it was set upright on a level surface. She was right. It had taken a half-dozen shots on the way out to Tempe. Two shots of the Hitori it must have taken when I set it down to load the car, open door of same with prickly pear in the foreground, a blurred shot of palm trees and buildings with a minuscule, sharp-focused glimpse of the traffic on the expressway. Vehicles and people. There was a great shot of the red tanker that had clipped the jackal and ten or so of the yucca I had parked next to at the foot of the hill.

It had gotten two nice shots of my forearm as I set it down on the kitchen counter of the Winnebago and some beautifully composed still lifes of Melmac with Spoons. Vehicles and people. The rest of the pictures were dead losses: my back, the open bathroom door, Jake's back, and Mrs. Ambler's public face.

Except the last one. She had been standing right in front of the eisenstadt, looking almost directly into the lens. "When I think of that poor thing, all alone," she had said, and by the time she turned around she had her public face back on, but for a minute there, looking at what she thought was a briefcase and remembering, there she was, the person I had tried all morning to get a picture of.

I took it into the living room and sat down and looked at it awhile.

"So you knew this Katherine Powell in Colorado," Ramirez said, breaking in without preamble, and the highwire slid silently forward and began to print out the lifeline. "I always suspected you of having some deep dark secret in your past. Is she the reason you moved to Phoenix?"

I was watching the highwire advance the paper. Katherine Powell, 4628 Dutchman Drive, Apache Junction. Forty miles away.

"Holy Mother, you were really cradle-robbing. According to my calculations, she was seventeen when you lived there."

Sixteen.

"Are you the owner of the dog?" the vet had asked her, his face slackening into pity when he saw how young she was.

"No," she said. "I'm the one who hit him."

"My God," he said. "How old are you?"

"Sixteen," she said, and her face was wide open. "I just got my license."

"Aren't you even going to tell me what she has to do with this Winnebago thing?" Ramirez said.

"I moved down here to get away from the snow," I said, and cut out without saying goodbye.

The lifeline was still rolling silently forward. Hacker at Hewlett-Packard. Fired in ninety-nine, probably during the unionization. Divorced. Two kids. She had moved to Arizona five years after I did. Management programmer for Toshiba. Arizona driver's license.

I went back to the developer and looked at the picture of Mrs. Ambler. I had said dogs never came through. That wasn't true. Taco wasn't in the blurry snapshots Mrs. Ambler had been so anxious to show me, in the stories she had been so anxious to tell. But she was in this picture, reflected in the pain and love and loss on Mrs. Ambler's face. I could see her plain as day, perched on the arm of the driver's seat, barking impatiently when the light turned green.

I put a new cartridge in the eisenstadt and went out to see Katie.

I had to take Van Buren—it was almost four o'clock, and the rush hour would have started on the dividers—but the jackal was gone anyway. The Society is efficient. Like Hitler and his Nazis.

"Why don't you have any pictures of your dog?" Hunter had asked. The question could have been based on the assumption that anyone who would fill his living room with photographs of dogs must have had one of his own, but it wasn't. He had known about Aberfan, which meant he'd had access to my lifeline, which meant all kinds of things. My lifeline was privacy-coded, so I had to be notified before anybody could get access, except, it appeared, the Society. A reporter I knew at the paper, Dolores Chiwere, had tried to do a story a while back claiming that the Society had an illegal link to the lifeline banks, but she hadn't been able to come up with enough evidence to convince her editor. I wondered if this counted.

The lifeline would have told them about Aberfan but not about how he died. Killing a dog wasn't a crime in those days, and I hadn't pressed charges against Katie for reckless driving or even called the police.

"I think you should," the vet's assistant had said. "There are less than a hundred dogs left. People can't just go around killing them."

"My God, man, it was snowing and slick," the vet had said angrily, "and she's just a kid."

"She's old enough to have a license," I said, looking at Katie. She was fumbling in her purse for her driver's license. "She's old enough to have been on the roads."

Katie found her license and gave it to me. It was so new it was still shiny. Katherine Powell. She had turned sixteen two weeks ago.

"This won't bring him back," the vet had said, and taken the license out of my hand and given it back to her. "You go on home now."

"I need her name for the records," the vet's assistant had said.

She had stepped forward. "Katie Powell," she had said.

"We'll do the paperwork later," the vet had said firmly.

They never did do the paperwork, though. The next week the third wave hit, and I suppose there hadn't seemed any point.

I slowed down at the zoo entrance and looked up into the parking lot as I went past. The Amblers were doing a booming business. There were at least five cars and twice as many kids clustered around the Winnebago.

"Where the hell are you?" Ramirez said. "And where the hell are your pictures? I talked the *Republic* into a trade, but they insisted on scoop rights. I need your stills now!"

"I'll send them in as soon as I get home," I said. "I'm on a story."

"The hell you are! You're on your way out to see your old girlfriend. Well, not on the paper's credits, you're not."

"Did you get the stuff on the Winnebago Indians?" I asked her.

"Yes. They were in Wisconsin, but they're not anymore. In the mid-seventies there were sixteen hundred of them on the reservation and about forty-five hundred altogether, but by 1990, the number was down to five hundred, and now they don't think there are any left, and nobody knows what happened to them."

I'll tell you what happened to them, I thought. Almost all of them were killed in the first wave, and people blamed the government and the Japanese and the ozone layer, and after the second wave hit, the Society passed all kinds of laws to protect the survivors, but it was too late, they were already below the minimum survival population limit, and then the third wave polished off the rest of them, and the last of the Winnebagos sat in a cage somewhere, and if I had been there I would probably have taken his picture.

"I called the Bureau of Indian Affairs," Ramirez said, "and they're supposed to call me back, and you don't give a damn about the Winnebagos. You just wanted to get me off the subject. What's this story you're on?"

I looked around the dashboard for an exclusion button.

"What the hell is going on, David? First you ditch two big stories, now you can't even get your pictures in. Jesus, if something's wrong, you can tell me. I want to help. It has something to do with Colorado, doesn't it?"

I found the button and cut her off.

Van Buren got crowded as the afternoon rush spilled over off the divideds. Out past the curve, where Van Buren turns into Apache Boulevard, they were putting in new lanes. The cement forms were already up on the eastbound side, and they were building the wooden forms up in two of the six lanes on my side.

The Amblers must have just beaten the workmen, though at the rate the men were working right now, leaning on their shovels in the hot afternoon sun and smoking stew, it had probably taken them six weeks to do this stretch.

Mesa was still open multiway, but as soon as I was through downtown, the construction started again, and this stretch was nearly done—forms up on both sides and most of the cement poured. The Amblers couldn't have come in from Globe on this road. The lanes were barely wide enough for the Hitori, and the tanker lanes were gated. Superstition is full-divided, and the old highway down from Roosevelt is, too, which meant they hadn't come in from Globe at all. I wondered how they had come in—probably in some tanker lane on a multiway.

"Oh, my, the things we've seen," Mrs. Ambler had said. I wondered how much they'd been able to see skittering across the dark desert like a couple of kangaroo mice, trying to beat the cameras.

The roadworkers didn't have the new exit signs up yet, and I missed the exit for Apache Junction and had to go halfway to Superior, trapped in my narrow, cement-sided lane, till I hit a change-lanes and could get turned around.

Katie's address was in Superstition Estates, a development pushed up as close to the base of Superstition Mountain as it could get. I thought about what I would say to Katie when I got there. I had said maybe ten sentences altogether to her, most of them shouted directions, in the two hours we had been together. In the jeep on the way to the vet's I had talked to Aberfan, and after we got there, sitting in the waiting room, we hadn't talked at all.

It occurred to me that I might not recognize her. I didn't really remember what she looked like—only the sunburned nose and that terrible openness, and now, fifteen years later, it seemed unlikely that she would have either of them. The Arizona sun would have taken care of the first, and she had gotten married and divorced, been fired, had who knows what else happen to her in fifteen years to close her face. In which case, there had been no point in my driving all the way out here. But Mrs. Ambler had had an almost impenetrable public face, and you could still catch her off-guard. If you got her talking about the dogs. If she didn't know she was being photographed.

Katie's house was an old-style passive solar, with flat black panels on the roof. It looked presentable, but not compulsively neat. There wasn't any grass—tankers won't waste their credits coming this far out, and Apache Junction isn't big enough to match the bribes and incentives of Phoenix or Tempe—but the front yard was laid out with alternating patches of black lava chips and prickly pear. The side yard had a parched-looking palo verde tree, and there was a cat tied to it. A little girl was playing under the tree with toy cars.

I took the eisenstadt out of the back and went up to the front door and rang the bell. At the last moment, when it was too late to change my mind, walk away, because she was already opening the screen door, it occurred to me that she might not recognize me, that I might have to tell her who I was.

Her nose wasn't sunburned, and she had put on the weight a six-teen-year-old puts on to get to be thirty, but otherwise she looked the same as she had that day in front of my house. And her face hadn't completely closed. I could tell, looking at her, that she recognized me and that she had known I was coming. She must have put a notify on her lifeline to have them warn her if I asked her whereabouts. I thought about what that meant.

She opened the screen door a little, the way I had to the Humane Society. "What do you want?" she said.

I had never seen her angry, not even when I turned on her at the vet's. "I wanted to see you," I said.

I had thought I might tell her I had run across her name while I was working on a story and wondered if it was the same person or that I was doing a piece on the last of the passive solars. "I saw a dead jackal on the road this morning," I said.

"And you thought I killed it?" she said. She tried to shut the screen door.

I put out my hand without thinking to stop her. "No," I said. I took my hand off the door. "No, of course I don't think that. Can I come in? I just want to talk to you."

The little girl had come over, clutching her toy cars to her pink T-shirt, and was standing off to the side, watching curiously.

"Come on inside, Jana," Katie said, and opened the screen door a fraction wider. The little girl scooted through. "Go on in the kitchen," she said. "I'll fix you some Kool-Aid." She looked up at me. "I used to have nightmares about your coming. I'd dream that I'd go to the door and there you'd be."

"It's really hot out here," I said and knew I sounded like Hunter. "Can I come in?"

She opened the screen door all the way. "I've got to make my daughter something to drink," she said, and led the way into the kitchen, the little girl dancing in front of her.

"What kind of Kool-Aid do you want?" Katie asked her, and she shouted, "Red!"

The kitchen counter faced the stove, refrigerator, and water cooler across a narrow aisle that opened out into an alcove with a table and chairs. I put the eisenstadt down on the table and then sat down myself so she wouldn't suggest moving into another room.

Katie reached a plastic pitcher down from one of the shelves and stuck it under the water tank to fill it. Jana dumped her cars on the counter, clambered up beside them, and began opening the cupboard doors.

"How old's your little girl?" I asked.

Katie got a wooden spoon out of the drawer next to the stove and brought it and the pitcher over to the table. "She's four," she said. "Did you find the Kool-Aid?" she asked the little girl.

"Yes," the little girl said, but it wasn't Kool-Aid. It was a pinkish cube she peeled a plastic wrapping off of. It fizzed and turned a thinnish red when she dropped it in the pitcher. Kool-Aid must have become extinct, too, along with Winnebagos and passive solar. Or else changed beyond recognition. Like the Humane Society.

Katie poured the red stuff into a glass with a cartoon whale on it. "Is she your only one?" I asked.

"No, I have a little boy," she said, but warily, as if she wasn't sure she wanted to tell me, even though if I'd requested the lifeline I already had access to all this information. Jana asked if she could have a cookie and then took it and her Kool-Aid back down the hall and outside. I could hear the screen door slam.

Katie put the pitcher in the refrigerator and leaned against the kitchen counter, her arms folded across her chest. "What do you want?"

She was just out of range of the eisenstadt, her face in the shadow of the narrow aisle.

"There was a dead jackal on the road this morning," I said. I kept my voice low so she would lean forward into the light to try and hear me. "It'd been hit by a car, and it was lying funny, at an angle. It looked like a dog. I wanted to talk to somebody who remembered Aberfan, somebody who knew him."

"I didn't know him," she said. "I only killed him, remember? That's why you did this, isn't it, because I killed Aberfan?"

She didn't look at the eisenstadt, hadn't even glanced at it when I set it on the table, but I wondered suddenly if she knew what I was up to. She was still carefully out of range. And what if I said to her, "That's right. That's why I did this, because you killed him, and I didn't have any pictures of him. You owe me. If I can't have a picture of Aberfan, you at least owe me a picture of you remembering him."

Only she didn't remember him, didn't know anything about him except what she had seen on the way to the vet's, Aberfan lying on my lap and looking up at me, already dying. I had had no business coming here, dredging all this up again. No business.

"At first I thought you were going to have me arrested," Katie said, "and then after all the dogs died, I thought you were going to kill me."

The screen door banged. "Forgot my cars," the little girl said and scooped them into the tail of her T-shirt. Katie tousled her hair as she went past, and then folded her arms again.

" 'It wasn't my fault,' I was going to tell you when you came to kill me," she said. " 'It was snowy. He ran right in front of me. I didn't even see him.' I looked up everything I could find about newparvo. Preparing for the defense. How it mutated from parvovirus and from cat distemper before that and then kept on mutating, so they couldn't come up with a vaccine. How even before the third wave they were below the minimum survival population. How it was the fault of the people who owned the last survivors because they wouldn't risk their dogs to breed them. How the scientists didn't come up with a vaccine until only the jackals were left. 'You're wrong,' I was going to tell you. 'It was the puppy mill owners' fault that all the dogs died. If they hadn't kept their dogs in such unsanitary conditions, it never would have gotten out of control in the first place.' I had my defense all ready. But you'd moved away."

Jana banged in again, carrying the empty whale glass. She had a red smear across the whole lower half of her face. "I need some more," she said, making "some more" into one word. She held the glass in both hands while Katie opened the refrigerator and poured her another glassful.

"Wait a minute, honey," she said. "You've got Kool-Aid all over you," and bent to wipe Jana's face with a paper towel.

Katie hadn't said a word in her defense while we waited at the vet's, not, "It was snowy," or, "He ran right out in front of me," or, "I didn't even see him." She had sat silently beside me, twisting her mittens in her lap, until the vet came out and told me Aberfan was dead, and then she had said, "I didn't know there were any left in Colorado. I thought they were all dead."

And I had turned to her, to a sixteen-year-old not even old enough to know how to shut her face, and said, "Now they all are. Thanks to you."

"That kind of talk isn't necessary," the vet had said warningly.

I had wrenched away from the hand he tried to put on my shoulder. "How does it feel to have killed one of the last dogs in the world?" I had shouted at her. "How does it feel to be responsible for the extinction of an entire species?"

The screen door banged again. Katie was looking at me, still holding the reddened paper towel.

"You moved away," she said, "and I thought maybe that meant you'd forgiven me, but it didn't, did it?" She came over to the table and wiped at the red circle the glass had left. "Why did you do it? To punish me? Or did you think that's what I'd been doing the last fifteen years, roaring around the roads murdering animals?"

"What?" I said.

"The Society's already been here."

"The Society?" I said, not understanding.

"Yes," she said, still looking at the red-stained towel. "They said you had reported a dead animal on Van Buren. They wanted to know where I was this morning between eight and nine A.M."

I nearly ran down a roadworker on the way back into Phoenix. He leaped for the still-wet cement barrier, dropping the shovel he'd been leaning on all day, and I ran right over it.

The Society had already been there. They had left my house and gone straight to hers. Only that wasn't possible, because I hadn't even called Katie then. I hadn't even seen the picture of Mrs. Ambler yet. Which meant they had gone to see Ramirez after they left me, and the last thing Ramirez and the paper needed was trouble with the Society.

"I thought it was suspicious when he didn't go to the governor's conference," she had told them, "and just now he called and asked for a lifeline on this person here. Katherine Powell, 4628 Dutchman Drive. He knew her in Colorado."

"Ramirez!" I shouted at the car phone. "I want to talk to you!" There wasn't any answer.

I swore at her for a good ten miles before I remembered I had the exclusion button on. I punched it off. "Ramirez, where the hell are you?"

"I could ask you the same question," she said. She sounded even angrier than Katie, but not as angry as I was. "You cut me off, you won't tell me what's going on."

"So you decided you had it figured out for yourself, and you told your little theory to the Society."

"What?" she said, and I recognized that tone, too. I had heard it in my own voice when Katie told me the Society had been there. Ramirez hadn't told anybody anything, she didn't even know what I was talking about, but I was going too fast to stop.

"You told the Society I'd asked for Katie's lifeline, didn't you?" I shouted.

"No," she said. "I didn't. Don't you think it's time you told me what's going on?"

"Did the Society come see you this afternoon?"

"No. I told you. They called this morning and wanted to talk to you. I told them you were at the governor's conference."

"And they didn't call back later?"

"No. Are you in trouble?"

I hit the exclusion button. "Yes," I said. "Yes, I'm in trouble."

Ramirez hadn't told them. Maybe somebody else at the paper had, but I didn't think so. There had after all been Dolores Chiwere's story about them having illegal access to the lifelines. "How come you don't have any pictures of your dog?" Hunter had asked me, which meant they'd read my lifeline, too. So they knew we had both lived in Colorado, in the same town, when Aberfan died.

"What did you tell them?" I had demanded of Katie. She had been standing there in the kitchen still messing with the Kool-Aid-stained towel, and I had wanted to yank it out of her hands and make her look at me. "What did you tell the Society?"

She looked up at me. "I told them I was on Indian School Road, picking up the month's programming assignments from my company. Unfortunately, I could just as easily have driven in on Van Buren."

"About Aberfan!" I shouted. "What did you tell them about Aberfan?"

She looked steadily at me. "I didn't tell them anything. I assumed you'd already told them."

I had taken hold of her shoulders. "If they come back, don't tell them anything. Not even if they arrest you. I'll take care of this. I'll . . ."

But I hadn't told her what I'd do because I didn't know. I had run out of her house, colliding with Jana in the hall on her way in for another refill, and roared off for home, even though I didn't have any idea what I would do when I got there.

Call the Society and tell them to leave Katie alone, that she had nothing to do with this? That would be even more suspicious than everything else I'd done so far, and you couldn't get much more suspicious than that.

I had seen a dead jackal on the road (or so I said), and instead of reporting it immediately on the phone right there in my car, I'd driven to a convenience store two miles away. I'd called the Society, but I'd refused to give them my name and number. And then I'd canceled two shoots without telling my boss and asked for the lifeline of one Katherine Powell, whom I had known fifteen years ago and who could have been on Van Buren at the time of the accident.

The connection was obvious, and how long would it take them to make the connection that fifteen years ago was when Aberfan had died?

Apache was beginning to fill up with rush hour overflow and a whole fleet of tankers. The overflow obviously spent all their time driving dividers—nobody bothered to signal that they were changing lanes. Nobody even gave an indication that they knew what a lane was. Going around the curve from Tempe and onto Van Buren they were all over the road. I moved over into the tanker lane.

My lifeline didn't have the vet's name on it. They were just getting started in those days, and there was a lot of nervousness about invasion of privacy. Nothing went on-line without the person's permission, especially not medical and bank records, and the lifelines were little more than puff bios: family, occupation, hobbies, pets. The only things on the lifeline besides Aberfan's name were the date of his death and my address at the time, but that was probably enough. There were only two vets in town.

The vet hadn't written Katie's name down on Aberfan's record. He had handed her driver's license back to her without even looking at it, but Katie had told her name to the vet's assistant. He might have written it down. There was no way I could find out. I couldn't ask for the vet's lifeline because the Society had access to the lifelines. They'd get to him before I could. I could maybe have the paper get the vet's records for me, but I'd have to tell Ramirez what was going on, and the phone was probably tapped, too. And if I showed up at the paper, Ramirez would confiscate the car. I couldn't go there.

Wherever the hell I was going, I was driving too fast to get there. When the tanker ahead of me slowed down to ninety, I practically climbed up his back bumper. I had gone past the place where the jackal had been hit without ever seeing it. Even without the traffic, there probably hadn't been anything to see. What the Society hadn't taken care of, the overflow probably had, and anyway, there hadn't been any evidence to begin with. If there had been, if the cameras had seen the car that hit it, they wouldn't have come after me. And Katie.

The Society couldn't charge her with Aberfan's death—killing an animal hadn't been a crime back then—but if they found out about Aberfan they would charge her with the jackal's death, and it wouldn't matter if a hundred witnesses, a hundred highway cameras had seen her on Indian School Road. It wouldn't matter if the print-fix on her car was clean. She had killed one of the last dogs, hadn't she? They would crucify her.

I should never have left Katie. "Don't tell them anything," I had told her, but she had never been afraid of admitting guilt. When the receptionist had asked her what had happened, she had said, "I hit him," just like that, no attempt to make excuses, to run off, to lay the blame on someone else.

I had run off to try to stop the Society from finding out that Katie had hit Aberfan, and meanwhile the Society was probably back at Katie's, asking her how she'd happened to know me in Colorado, asking her how Aberfan died.

I was wrong about the Society. They weren't at Katie's house. They were at mine, standing on the porch, waiting for me to let them in.

"You're a hard man to track down," Hunter said.

The uniform grinned. "Where you been?"

"Sorry," I said, fishing my keys out of my pocket. "I thought you were all done with me. I've already told you everything I know about the incident."

Hunter stepped back just far enough for me to get the screen door open and the key in the lock. "Officer Segura and I just need to ask you a couple more questions."

"Where'd you go this afternoon?" Segura asked.

"I went to see an old friend of mine."

"Who?"

"Come on, come on," Hunter said. "Let the guy get in his own front door before you start badgering him with a lot of questions."

I opened the door. "Did the cameras get a picture of the tanker that hit the jackal?" I asked.

"Tanker?" Segura said.

"I told you," I said, "I figure it had to be a tanker. The jackal was lying in the tanker lane." I led the way into the living room, depositing my keys on the computer and switching the phone to exclusion while I talked. The last thing I needed was Ramirez bursting in with, "What's going on? Are you in trouble?"

"It was probably a renegade that hit it, which would explain why he didn't stop." I gestured at them to sit down.

Hunter did. Segura started for the couch and then stopped, staring at the photos on the wall above it. "Jesus, will you look at all the dogs!" he said. "Did you take all these pictures?"

"I took some of them. That one in the middle is Misha."

"The last dog, right?"

"Yes," I said.

"No kidding. The very last one."

No kidding. She was being kept in isolation at the Society's research facility in St. Louis when I saw her. I had talked them into letting me shoot her, but it had to be from outside the quarantine area. The picture had an unfocused look that came from shooting it through a wire mesh—reinforced window in the door, but I wouldn't have done any better if they'd let me inside. Misha was past having any expression to photograph. She hadn't eaten in a week at that point. She lay with her head on her paws, staring at the door, the whole time I was there.

"You wouldn't consider selling this picture to the Society, would you?"

"No, I wouldn't."

He nodded understandingly. "I guess people were pretty upset when she died."

Pretty upset. They had turned on anyone who had anything to do with it—the puppy mill owners, the scientists who hadn't come up with a vaccine, Misha's vet—and a lot of others who hadn't. And they had handed over their civil rights to a bunch of jackals who were able to grab them because everybody felt so guilty. Pretty upset.

"What's this one?" Segura asked. He had already moved on to the picture next to it.

"It's General Patton's bull terrier Willie."

They fed and cleaned up after Misha with those robot arms they used to use in the nuclear plants. Her owner, a tired-looking woman, was allowed to watch her through the wire-mesh window but had to stay off to the side because Misha flung herself barking against the door whenever she saw her.

"You should make them let you in," I had told her. "It's cruel to keep her locked up like that. You should make them let you take her back home."

"And let her get the newparvo?" she said.

There was nobody left for Misha to get the newparvo from, but I didn't say that. I set the light readings on the camera, trying not to lean into Misha's line of vision.

"You know what killed them, don't you?" she said. "The ozone layer. All those holes. The radiation got in and caused it."

It was the communists, it was the Mexicans, it was the government. And the only people who acknowledged their guilt weren't guilty at all.

"This one here looks kind of like a jackal," Segura said. He was looking at a picture I had taken of a German shepherd after Aberfan died. "Dogs were a lot like jackals, weren't they?"

"No," I said, and sat down on the shelf in front of the developer's screen, across from Hunter. "I already told you everything I know about the jackal. I saw it lying in the road, and I called you."

"You said when you saw the jackal it was in the far right lane," Hunter said.

"That's right."

"And you were in the far left lane?"

"I was in the far left lane."

They were going to take me over my story, point by point, and when I couldn't remember what I'd said before, they were going to say, "Are you sure that's what you saw, Mr. McCombe? Are you sure you didn't see the jackal get hit? Katherine Powell hit it, didn't she?"

"You told us this morning you stopped, but the jackal was already dead. Is that right?" Hunter asked.

"No," I said.

Segura looked up. Hunter touched his hand casually to his pocket and then brought it back to his knee, turning on the taper.

"I didn't stop for about a mile. Then I backed up and looked at it, but it was dead. There was blood coming out of its mouth."

Hunter didn't say anything. He kept his hands on his knees and waited—an old journalist's trick, if you wait long enough, they'll say something they didn't intend to, just to fill the silence.

"The jackal's body was at a peculiar angle," I said, right on cue. "The way it was lying, it didn't look like a jackal. I thought it was a dog." I waited till the silence got uncomfortable again. "It brought back a lot of terrible memories," I said. "I wasn't even thinking. I just wanted to get away from it. After a few minutes I realized I should have called the Society, and I stopped at the 7-Eleven."

I waited again, till Segura began to shoot uncomfortable glances at Hunter, and then started in again. "I thought I'd be okay, that I could go ahead and work, but after I got to my first shoot, I knew I wasn't going to make it, so I came home." Candor. Openness. If the Amblers can do it, so can you. "I guess I was still in shock or something. I didn't even call my boss and have her get somebody to cover the governor's conference. All I could think about was—" I stopped and rubbed my hand across my face. "I needed to talk to somebody. I had the paper look up an old friend of mine, Katherine Powell."

I stopped, I hoped this time for good. I had admitted lying to them and confessed to two crimes: leaving the scene of the accident and using press access to get a lifeline for personal use, and maybe that would be enough to satisfy them. I didn't want to say anything about going out to see Katie. They would know she would have told me about their visit and decide this confession was an attempt to get her off, and maybe they'd been watching the house and knew it anyway, and this was all wasted effort.

The silence dragged on. Hunter's hands tapped his knees twice and then subsided. The story didn't explain why I'd picked Katie, who I hadn't seen in fifteen years, who I knew in Colorado, to go see, but maybe, maybe they wouldn't make the connection.

"This Katherine Powell," Hunter said, "you knew her in Colorado, is that right?"

"We lived in the same little town."

We waited.

"Isn't that when your dog died?" Segura said suddenly. Hunter shot him a glance of pure rage, and I thought, it isn't a taper he's got in that shirt pocket. It's the vet's records, and Katie's name is on them.

"Yes," I said. "He died in September of eighty-nine."

Segura opened his mouth.

"In the third wave?" Hunter asked before he could say anything.

"No," I said. "He was hit by a car."

They both looked genuinely shocked. The Amblers could have taken lessons from them. "Who hit it?" Segura asked, and Hunter leaned forward, his hand moving reflexively toward his pocket.

"I don't know," I said. "It was a hit and run. Whoever it was just left him lying there in the road. That's why when I saw the jackal, it . . . that was how I met Katherine Powell. She stopped and helped me. She helped me get him into her car, and we took him to the vet's, but it was too late."

Hunter's public face was pretty indestructible, but Segura's wasn't. He looked surprised and enlightened and disappointed all at once.

"That's why I wanted to see her," I said unnecessarily.

"Your dog was hit on what day?" Hunter asked.

"September thirtieth."

"What was the vet's name?"

He hadn't changed his way of asking the questions, but he no longer cared what the answers were. He had thought he'd found a connection, a cover-up, but here we were, a couple of dog lovers, a couple of good Samaritans, and his theory had collapsed. He was done with the interview, he was just finishing up, and all I had to do was be careful not to relax too soon.

I frowned. "I don't remember his name. Cooper, I think."

"What kind of car did you say hit your dog?"

"I don't know," I said, thinking, not a jeep. Make it something besides a jeep. "I didn't see him get hit. The vet said it was something big, a pickup maybe. Or a Winnebago."

And I knew who had hit the jackal. It had all been right there in front of me—the old man using up their forty-gallon water supply to wash the bumper, the lies about their coming in from Globe—only I had been too intent on keeping them from finding out about Katie, on getting the picture of Aberfan, to see it. It was like the damned parvo. When you had it licked in one place, it broke out somewhere else.

"Were there any identifying tire tracks?" Hunter said.

"What?" I said. "No. It was snowing that day." It had to show in my face, and he hadn't missed anything yet. I passed my hand over my eyes. "I'm sorry. These questions are bringing it all back."

"Sorry," Hunter said.

"Can't we get this stuff from the police report?" Segura asked.

"There wasn't a police report," I said. "It wasn't a crime to kill a dog when Aberfan died."

It was the right thing to say. The look of shock on their faces was the real thing this time, and they looked at each other in disbelief instead of at me. They asked a few more questions and then stood up to leave. I walked them to the door.

"Thank you for your cooperation, Mr. McCombe," Hunter said. "We appreciate what a difficult experience this has been for you."

I shut the screen door between us. The Amblers would have been going too fast, trying to beat the cameras because they weren't even supposed to be on Van Buren. It was almost rush hour, and they were in the tanker lane, and they hadn't even seen the jackal till they hit it, and then it was too late. They had to know the penalty for hitting an animal was jail and confiscation of the vehicle, and there wasn't anybody else on the road.

"Oh, one more question," Hunter said from halfway down the walk. "You said you went to your first assignment this morning. What was it?"

Candid. Open. "It was out at the old zoo. A sideshow kind of thing."

I watched them all the way out to their car and down the street. Then I latched the screen, pulled the inside door shut, and locked it, too. It had been right there in front of me—the ferret sniffing the wheel, the bumper, Jake anxiously watching the road. I had thought he was looking for customers, but he wasn't. He was expecting to see the Society drive up. "He's not interested in that," he had said when Mrs. Ambler said she had been telling me about Taco. He had listened to our whole conversation, standing under the back window with his guilty bucket, ready to come back in and cut her off if she said too much, and I hadn't tumbled to any of it. I had been so intent on Aberfan I hadn't even seen it when I looked right through the lens at it. And what kind of an excuse was that? Katie hadn't even tried to use it, and she was learning to drive.

I went and got the Nikon and pulled the film out of it. It was too late to do anything about the eisenstadt pictures or the vidcam footage, but I didn't think there was anything in them. Jake had already washed the bumper by the time I'd taken those pictures.

I fed the longshot film into the developer. "Positives, one two three order, fifteen seconds," I said, and waited for the image to come on the screen.

I wondered who had been driving. Jake, probably. "He never liked Taco," she had said, and there was no mistaking the bitterness in her voice. "I didn't want to buy the Winnebago."

They would both lose their licenses, no matter who was driving, and the Society would confiscate the Winnebago. They would probably not send two octogenarian specimens of Americana like the Amblers to prison. They wouldn't have to. The trial would take six months, and Texas already had legislation in committee.

The first picture came up. A light-setting shot of an ocotillo.

Even if they got off, even if they didn't end up taking away the Winnebago for unauthorized use of a tanker lane or failure to purchase a sales tax permit, the Amblers had six months left at the outside. Utah was all ready to pass a full-divided bill, and Arizona would be next. In spite of the road crews' stew-slowed pace, Phoenix would be all-divided by the time the investigation was over, and they'd be completely boxed in. Permanent residents of the zoo. Like the coyote.

A shot of the zoo sign, half-hidden in the cactus. A close-up of the Amblers' balloon-trailing sign. The Winnebago in the parking lot.

"Hold," I said. "Crop." I indicated the areas with my finger. "Enlarge to full screen."

The longshot takes great pictures, sharp contrast, excellent detail. The developer only had a five hundred thousand–pixel screen, but the dark smear on the bumper was easy to see, and the developed picture would be much clearer. You'd be able to see every splatter, every grayish-yellow hair. The Society's computers would probably be able to type the blood from it.

"Continue," I said, and the next picture came on the screen. Artsy shot of the Winnebago and the zoo entrance. Jake washing the bumper. Red-handed.

Maybe Hunter had bought my story, but he didn't have any other suspects, and how long would it be before he decided to ask Katie a few more questions? If he thought it was the Amblers, he'd leave her alone.

The Japanese family clustered around the waste-disposal tank. Closeup of the decals on the side. Interiors—Mrs. Ambler in the gallery, the upright-coffin shower stall, Mrs. Ambler making coffee.

No wonder she had looked that way in the eisenstadt shot, her face full of memory and grief and loss. Maybe in the instant before they hit it, it had looked like a dog to her, too.

All I had to do was tell Hunter about the Amblers, and Katie was off the hook. It should be easy. I had done it before.

"Stop," I said to a shot of the salt-and-pepper collection. The black and white scottie dogs had painted, red-plaid bows and red tongues. "Expose," I said. "One through twenty-four."

The screen went to question marks and started beeping. I should have known better. The developer could handle a lot of orders, but asking it to expose perfectly good film went against its whole memory, and I didn't have time to give it the step-by-steps that would convince it I meant what I said.

"Eject," I said. The scotties blinked out. The developer spat out the film, rerolled into its protective case.

The doorbell rang. I switched on the overhead and pulled the film out to full length and held it directly under the light. I had told Hunter an RV hit Aberfan, and he had said on the way out, almost an after-thought, "That first shoot you went to, what was it?" And after he left, what had he done, gone out to check on the sideshow kind of thing, gotten Mrs. Ambler to spill her guts? There hadn't been time to do that and get back. He must have called Ramirez. I was glad I had locked the door.

I turned off the overhead. I rerolled the film, fed it back into the developer, and gave it a direction it could handle. "Permanganate bath, full strength, one through twenty-four. Remove one hundred percent emulsion. No notify."

The screen went dark. It would take the developer at least fifteen minutes to run the film through the bleach bath, and the Society's com-puters could probably enhance a picture out of two crystals of silver and thin air, but at least the detail wouldn't be there. I unlocked the door.

It was Katie.

She held up the eisenstadt. "You forgot your briefcase," she said.

I stared blankly at it. I hadn't even realized I didn't have it. I must have left it on the kitchen table when I went tearing out, running down little girls and stewed roadworkers in my rush to keep Katie from getting involved. And here she was, and Hunter would be back any minute, saying, "That shoot you went on this morning, did you take any pictures?"

"It isn't a briefcase," I said.

"I wanted to tell you," she said, and stopped. "I shouldn't have accused you of telling the Society I'd killed the jackal. I don't know why you came to see me today, but I know you're not capable of—"

"You have no idea what I'm capable of," I said. I opened the door enough to reach for the eisenstadt. "Thanks for bringing it back. I'll get the paper to reimburse your way-mile credits."

Go home. Go home. If you're here when the Society comes back, they'll ask you how you met me, and I just destroyed the evidence that could shift the blame to the Amblers. I took hold of the eisenstadt's handle and started to shut the door.

She put her hand on the door. The screen door and the fading light made her look unfocused, like Misha. "Are you in trouble?"

"No," I said. "Look, I'm very busy."

"Why did you come to see me?" she asked. "Did you kill the jackal?"

"No," I said, but I opened the door and let her in.

I went over to the developer and asked for a visual status. It was only on the sixth frame. "I'm destroying evidence," I said to Katie. "I took a picture this morning of the vehicle that hit it, only I didn't know it was the guilty party until a half an hour ago." I motioned for her to sit down on the couch. "They're in their eighties. They were driving on a road they weren't supposed to be on, in an obsolete recreation vehicle, worrying about the cameras and the tankers. There's no way they could have seen it in time to stop. The Society won't see it that way, though. They're determined to blame somebody, anybody, even though it won't bring them back."

She set her canvas carryit and the eisenstadt down on the table next to the couch. "The Society was here when I got home," I said. "They'd figured out we were both in Colorado when Aberfan died. I told them it was a hit and run, and you'd stopped to help me. They had the vet's records, and your name was on them."

I couldn't read her face. "If they come back, you tell them that you gave me a ride to the vet's." I went back to the developer. The longshot film was done. "Eject," I said, and the developer spit it into my hand. I fed it into the recycler.

"McCombe! Where the hell are you?" Ramirez's voice exploded into the room, and I jumped and started for the door, but she wasn't there. The phone was flashing. "McCombe! This is important!"

Ramirez was on the phone and using some override I didn't even know existed. I went over and pushed it back to access. The lights went out. "I'm here," I said.

"You won't believe what just happened!" She sounded outraged. "A couple of terrorist types from the Society just stormed in here and confiscated the stuff you sent me!"

All I'd sent her was the vidcam footage and the shots from the eisenstadt, and there shouldn't have been anything on those. Jake had already washed the bumper. "What stuff?" I said.

"The prints from the eisenstadt!" she said, still shouting. "Which I didn't have a chance to look at when they came in because I was too busy trying to work a trade on your governor's conference, not to mention trying to track you down! I had hardcopies made and sent the originals straight down to composing with your vidcam footage. I finally got to them half an hour ago, and while I'm sorting through them, this Society creep just grabs them away from me. No warrants, no 'would you mind?,' nothing. Right out of my hand. Like a bunch of—"

"Jackals," I said. "You're sure it wasn't the vidcam footage?" There wasn't anything in the eisenstadt shots except Mrs. Ambler and Taco, and even Hunter couldn't have put that together, could he?

"Of course I'm sure," Ramirez said, her voice bouncing off the walls. "It was one of the prints from the eisenstadt. I never even saw the vidcam stuff. I sent it straight to composing. I told you."

I went over to the developer and fed the cartridge in. The first dozen shots were nothing, stuff the eisenstadt had taken from the back seat of the car. "Start with frame ten," I said. "Positives. One two three order. Five seconds."

"What did you say?" Ramirez demanded.

"I said, did they say what they were looking for?"

"Are you kidding? I wasn't even there as far as they were concerned. They split up the pile and started through them on *my* desk."

The yucca at the foot of the hill. More yucca. My forearm as I set the eisenstadt down on the counter. My back.

"Whatever it was they were looking for, they found it," Ramirez said.

I glanced at Katie. She met my gaze steadily, unafraid. She had never been afraid, not even when I told her she had killed all the dogs, not even when I showed up on her doorstep after fifteen years.

"The one in the uniform showed it to the other one," Ramirez was saying, "and said, 'You were wrong about the woman doing it. Look at this.' "

"Did you get a look at the picture?"

Still life of cups and spoons. Mrs. Ambler's arm. Mrs. Ambler's back.

"I tried. It was a truck of some kind."

"A truck? Are you sure? Not a Winnebago?"

"A truck. What the hell is going on over there?"

I didn't answer. Jake's back. Open shower door. Still life with Sanka. Mrs. Ambler remembering Taco.

"What woman are they talking about?" Ramirez said. "The one you wanted the lifeline on?"

"No," I said. The picture of Mrs. Ambler was the last one on the cartridge. The developer went back to the beginning. Bottom half of the Hitori. Open car door. Prickly pear. "Did they say anything else?"

"The one in the uniform pointed to something on the hardcopy and said, 'See. There's his number on the side. Can you make it out?' "

Blurred palm trees and the expressway. The tanker hitting the jackal.

"Stop," I said. The image froze.

"What?" Ramirez said.

It was a great action shot, the back wheels passing right over the mess that had been the jackal's hind legs. The jackal was already dead, of course, but you couldn't see that or the already drying blood coming out of its mouth because of the angle. You couldn't see the truck's license number either because of the speed the tanker was going, but the number was there, waiting for the Society's computers. It looked like the tanker had just hit it.

"What did they do with the picture?" I asked.

"They took it into the chief's office. I tried to call up the originals from composing, but the chief had already sent for them *and* your vidcam footage. Then I tried to get you, but I couldn't get past your damned exclusion."

"Are they still in there with the chief?"

"They just left. They're on their way over to your house. The chief told me to tell you he wants 'full cooperation,' which means hand over the negatives and any other film you just took this morning. He told *me* to keep my hands off. No story. Case closed."

"How long ago did they leave?"

"Five minutes. You've got plenty of time to make me a print. Don't highwire it. I'll come pick it up."

"What happened to, 'The last thing I need is trouble with the Society'?"

"It'll take them at least twenty minutes to get to your place. Hide it somewhere the Society won't find it."

"I can't," I said, and listened to her furious silence. "My developer's broken. It just ate my longshot film," I said, and hit the exclusion button again.

"You want to see who hit the jackal?" I said to Katie, and motioned her over to the developer. "One of Phoenix's finest."

She came and stood in front of the screen, looking at the picture. If the Society's computers were really good, they could probably prove the jackal was already dead, but the Society wouldn't keep the film long enough for that. Hunter and Segura had probably already destroyed the highwire copies. Maybe I should offer to run the cartridge sheet through the permanganate bath for them when they got here, just to save time.

I looked at Katie. "It looks guilty as hell, doesn't it?" I said. "Only it isn't." She didn't say anything, didn't move. "It would have killed the jackal if it had hit it. It was going at least ninety. But the jackal was already dead."

She looked across at me.

"The Society would have sent the Amblers to jail. It would have confiscated the house they've lived in for fifteen years for an accident that was nobody's fault. They didn't even see it coming. It just ran right out in front of them."

Katie put her hand up to the screen and touched the jackal's image.

"They've suffered enough," I said, looking at her. It was getting dark. I hadn't turned on any lights, and the red image of the tanker made her nose look sunburned.

"All these years she's blamed him for her dog's death, and he didn't do it," I said. "A Winnebago's a hundred square feet on the inside. That's about as big as this developer, and they've lived inside it for fifteen years, while the lanes got narrower and the highways shut down, hardly enough room to breathe, let alone live, and her blaming him for something he didn't do."

In the ruddy light from the screen she looked sixteen.

"They won't do anything to the driver, not with the tankers hauling thousands of gallons of water into Phoenix every day. Even the Society won't run the risk of a boycott. They'll destroy the negatives and call the case closed. And the Society won't go after the Amblers," I said. "Or you."

I turned back to the developer. "Go," I said, and the image changed. Yucca. Yucca. My forearm. My back. Cups and spoons.

"Besides," I said. "I'm an old hand at shifting the blame." Mrs. Ambler's arm. Mrs. Ambler's back. Open shower door. "Did I ever tell you about Aberfan?"

Katie was still watching the screen, her face pale now from the light blue one hundred percent formica shower stall.

"The Society already thinks the tanker did it. The only one I've got to convince is my editor." I reached across to the phone and took the exclusion off. "Ramirez," I said, "wanta go after the Society?"

Jake's back. Cups, spoons, and Sanka.

"I did," Ramirez said in a voice that could have frozen the Salt River, "but your developer was broken, and you couldn't get me a picture."

Mrs. Ambler and Taco.

I hit the exclusion button again and left my hand on it. "Stop," I said. "Print." The screen went dark, and the print slid out into the tray. "Reduce frame. Permanganate bath by one percent. Follow on screen." I took my hand off. "What's Dolores Chiwere doing these days, Ramirez?"

"She's working investigative. Why?"

I didn't answer. The picture of Mrs. Ambler faded a little, a little more.

"The Society *does* have a link to the lifelines!" Ramirez said, not quite as fast as Hunter, but almost. "That's why you requested your old girlfriend's line, isn't it? You're running a sting."

I had been wondering how to get Ramirez off Katie's trail, and she had done it herself, jumping to conclusions just like the Society. With a little effort, I could convince Katie, too: Do you know why I really came to see you today? To catch the Society. I had to pick somebody the Society couldn't possibly know about from my lifeline, somebody I didn't have any known connection with.

Katie watched the screen, looking like she already half-believed it. The picture of Mrs. Ambler faded some more. Any known connection.

"Stop," I said.

"What about the truck?" Ramirez demanded. "What does it have to do with this sting of yours?"

"Nothing," I said. "And neither does the water board, which is an even bigger bully than the Society. So do what the chief says. Full cooperation. Case closed. We'll get them on lifeline tapping."

She digested that, or maybe she'd already hung up and was calling Dolores Chiwere. I looked at the image of Mrs. Ambler on the screen. It had faded enough to look slightly overexposed but not enough to look tampered with. And Taco was gone.

I looked at Katie. "The Society will be here in another fifteen minutes," I said, "which gives me just enough time to tell you about Aberfan." I gestured at the couch. "Sit down."

She came and sat down. "He was a great dog," I said. "He loved the snow. He'd dig through it and toss it up with his muzzle and snap at the snowflakes, trying to catch them."

Ramirez had obviously hung up, but she would call back if she couldn't track down Chiwere. I put the exclusion back on and went over to the developer. The image of Mrs. Ambler was still on the screen. The bath hadn't affected the detail that much. You could still see the wrinkles, the thin white hair, but the guilt, or blame, the look of loss and love, was gone. She looked serene, almost happy.

"There are hardly any good pictures of dogs," I said. "They lack the necessary muscles to take good pictures, and Aberfan would lunge at you as soon as he saw the camera."

I turned the developer off. Without the light from the screen, it was almost dark in the room. I turned on the overhead.

"There were less than a hundred dogs left in the United States, and he'd already had the newparvo once and nearly died. The only pictures I had of him had been taken when he was asleep. I wanted a picture of Aberfan playing in the snow."

I leaned against the narrow shelf in front of the developer's screen. Katie looked the way she had at the vet's, sitting there with her hands clenched, waiting for me to tell her something terrible.

"I wanted a picture of him playing in the snow, but he always lunged at the camera," I said, "so I let him out in the front yard, and then I sneaked out the side door and went across the road to some pine trees where he wouldn't be able to see me. But he did."

"And he ran across the road," Katie said. "And I hit him."

She was looking down at her hands. I waited for her to look up, dreading what I would see in her face. Or not see.

"It took me a long time to find out where you'd gone," she said to her hands. "I was afraid you'd refuse me access to your lifeline. I finally saw one of your pictures in a newspaper, and I moved to Phoenix, but after I got here I was afraid to call you for fear you'd hang up on me."

She twisted her hands the way she had twisted her mittens at the vet's. "My husband said I was obsessed with it, that I should have gotten over it by now, everybody else had, that they were only dogs anyway."

She looked up, and I braced my hands against the developer. "He said forgiveness wasn't something somebody else could give you, but I didn't want you to forgive me exactly. I just wanted to tell you I was sorry."

There hadn't been any reproach, any accusation in her face when I told her she was responsible for the extinction of a species that day at the vet's, and there wasn't now. Maybe she didn't have the facial muscles for it, I thought bitterly.

"Do you know why I came to see you today?" I said angrily. "My camera broke when I tried to catch Aberfan. I didn't get any pictures." I grabbed the picture of Mrs. Ambler out of the developer's tray and flung it at her. "Her dog died of newparvo. They left it in the Winnebago, and when they came back, it was dead."

"Poor thing," she said, but she wasn't looking at the picture. She was looking at me.

"She didn't know she was having her picture taken. I thought if I got you talking about Aberfan, I could get a picture like that of you."

And surely now I would see it, the look I had really wanted when I set the eisenstadt down on Katie's kitchen table, the look I still wanted, even though the eisenstadt was facing the wrong way, the look of betrayal the dogs had never given us. Not even Misha. Not even Aberfan. How does it feel to be responsible for the extinction of an entire species?

I pointed at the eisenstadt. "It's not a briefcase. It's a camera. I was going to take your picture without your even knowing it."

She had never known Aberfan. She had never known Mrs. Ambler either, but in that instant before she started to cry she looked like both of them. She put her hand up to her mouth. "Oh," she said, and the love, the loss was there in her voice, too. "If you'd had it then, it wouldn't have happened."

I looked at the eisenstadt. If I had had it, I could have set it on the porch and Aberfan would never have even noticed it. He would have burrowed through the snow and tossed it up with his nose, and I could have thrown snow up in big glittering sprays that he would have leaped at, and it never would have happened. Katie Powell would have driven past, and I would have stopped to wave at her, and she, sixteen years old and just learning to drive, would maybe even have risked taking a mittened hand off the steering wheel to wave back, and Aberfan would have wagged his tail into a blizzard and then barked at the snow he'd churned up.

He wouldn't have caught the third wave. He would have lived to be an old dog, fourteen or fifteen, too old to play in the snow anymore, and even if he had been the last dog in the world I would not have let them lock him up in a cage, I would not have let them take him away. If I had had the eisenstadt.

No wonder I hated it.

It had been at least fifteen minutes since Ramirez called. The Society would be here any minute. "You shouldn't be here when the Society comes," I said, and Katie nodded and smudged the tears off her cheeks and stood up, reaching for her carryit.

"Do you ever take pictures?" she said, shouldering the carryit. "I mean, besides for the papers?"

"I don't know if I'll be taking pictures for them much longer. Photojournalists are becoming an extinct breed."

"Maybe you could come take some pictures of Jana and Kevin. Kids grow up so fast, they're gone before you know it."

"I'd like that," I said. I opened the screen door for her and looked both ways down the street at the darkness. "All clear," I said, and she went out. I shut the screen door between us.

She turned and looked at me one last time with her dear, open face that even I hadn't been able to close. "I miss them," she said.

I put my hand up to the screen. "I miss them, too."

I watched her to make sure she turned the corner and then went back in the living room and took down the picture of Misha. I propped it against the developer so Segura would be able to see it from the door. In a month or so, when the Amblers were safely in Texas and the Society had forgotten about Katie, I'd call Segura and tell him I might be willing to sell it to the Society, and then in a day or so I'd tell him I'd changed my mind. When he came out to try to talk me into it, I'd tell him about Perdita and Beatrix Potter, and he would tell me about the Society.

Chiwere and Ramirez would have to take the credit for the story—I didn't want Hunter putting anything else together—and it would take more than one story to break them, but it was a start.

Katie had left the print of Mrs. Ambler on the couch. I picked it up and looked at it a minute and then fed it into the developer. "Recycle," I said.

I picked up the eisenstadt from the table by the couch and took the film cartridge out. I started to pull the film out to expose it, and then shoved it into the developer instead and turned it on. "Positives, one two three order, five seconds."

I had apparently set the camera on its activator again—there were ten shots or so of the back seat of the Hitori. Vehicles and people. The pictures of Katie were all in shadow. There was a Still Life of Kool-Aid Pitcher with Whale Glass and another one of Jana's toy cars, and some near-black frames that meant Katie had laid the eisenstadt face-down when she brought it to me.

"Two seconds," I said, and waited for the developer to flash the last shots so I could make sure there wasn't anything else on the cartridge and then expose it before the Society got here. All but the last frame was of the darkness that was all the eisenstadt could see lying on its face. The last one was of me.

The trick in getting good pictures is to make people forget they're being photographed. Distract them. Get them talking about something they care about.

"Stop," I said, and the image froze.

Aberfan was a great dog. He loved to play in the snow, and after I had murdered him, he lifted his head off my lap and tried to lick my hand.

The Society would be here any minute to take the longshot film and destroy it, and this one would have to go, too, along with the rest of the cartridge. I couldn't risk Hunter's being reminded of Katie. Or Segura taking a notion to do a print-fix and peel on Jana's toy cars.

It was too bad. The eisenstadt takes great pictures. "Even you'll forget it's a camera," Ramirez had said in her spiel, and that was certainly true. I was looking straight into the lens.

And it was all there, Misha and Taco and Perdita and the look he gave me on the way to the vet's while I stroked his poor head and told him it would be all right, that look of love and pity I had been trying to capture all these years. The picture of Aberfan.

The Society would be here any minute. "Eject," I said, and cracked the cartridge open, and exposed it to the light.

Patrick F. McManus

STRANGE MEETS
MATILDA JEAN

I had always wanted to have a dog I could be proud of, but instead I had Strange. All my friends were proud of their dogs. They bragged constantly about how Sport or Biff or Rags or Pal had run off a burglar, saved a little girl from drowning, brought in their father's newspaper, warned the family just in time that the house was on fire, rounded up cows, pointed pheasants, retrieved ducks, and performed such amazing and entertaining tricks that I had a hard time believing the dog didn't have a movie contract.

Strange, on the other hand, would have welcomed burglars with open paws, and stood watch while they looted the house. He never saved anybody from anything. He enjoyed chasing cows, but merely for the sport. He considered pointing impolite. If he retrieved a duck, it was for his own use. Any tricks he knew he kept to himself.

He was a connoisseur of the disgusting. He turned up his nose at my grandmother's cooking, then dined happily on cow chips, year-old roadkill, and the awful offal of neighborhood butcherings. Occasionally, he scrawled his territorial signature on the leg of a complete stranger, as though it were a mobile fireplug. (*"Bad dog! Sorry about your pant leg, mister. Now, as I was saying, would it be all right if I fish the crick behind your place? I'll close the gates."*) Strange was also an enthusiastic crotch-sniffer, causing visitors to gyrate like belly dancers in their efforts to escape his probing nose, all the while trying to carry on a normal conversation, as if nothing embarrassing were happening down below.

Concern for the sensibilities of the reader prevents me from mentioning some of my dog's more disgusting hobbies, except to say they involved highly noxious fumes, chickens, human legs, embarrassing itch, and various slurpy aspects of what passes for dog hygiene. Strange apparently held the view that his hobbies were vastly entertaining to the public at large. Whenever we had dinner guests he would run through his repertoire of the disgusting in front of the dining-room window.

"How did you like that one?" he would ask, smiling in at us, as though expecting a standing ovation.

"No dessert for me, thanks," our guests would respond. Strange was a major social liability.

"There's nothing worse," my grandmother once commented, "than an egg-sucking dog."

"Strange don't suck eggs," I said proudly, desperate to find something favorable about my dog.

"I stand corrected," Gram said. "There is something worse." She and Strange didn't relate well.

We never thought of Strange as *our* dog. He was his own dog. What I disliked most about him was his arrogance. If I threw a stick and told him "Fetch," he would give me this insolent stare, which said, "Fetch it yourself, dumbo. You threw it." Then he would flip a cigarette butt at me, blow out a stream of smoke, and slouch back into his doghouse. (Well no, of course, he didn't really smoke cigarettes, but that was the essence of his attitude, as though he had watched too many movies about hard-boiled detectives.) Strange clearly thought of himself as a big tough canine, even though he was probably the smallest dog in our neighborhood. He was rather sickly looking, too, with chronically bloodshot eyes and a loose, leering mouth. Eating year-old roadkill probably does that to you. I can't imagine what a vet would have recommended for a dog like Strange. Probably a parole officer.

Strange swaggered about our place as though he owned it. You could almost see him thinking, "I won this house in a crap game, and there ain't nobody telling me what to do on my own property." After one of his particularly obnoxious offenses, often involving deadly toxic fumes, my grandmother would grab him by two handfuls of hide and send him flying outside, whereupon Strange would turn and snarl at her, "Try that again, old woman, and you'll hear from my lawyer." Then he would take out his vengeance on a chicken or squirrel or anything he could find that was smaller than himself. He reigned supreme in the confines of our yard.

Then one day my sister, Troll, brought home a huge yellow tomcat. The cat was half as big as she was. It was the cat version of an offensive all-pro tackle, and looked as if it ate scrap iron for breakfast. Its purr rattled dishes in the cupboard. Sex education not yet having been introduced in our schools, my sister named the burly yellow beast *Matilda Jean!* I was so disgusted with the name I almost gagged, but she said it was her cat, she'd name it anything she pleased.

"How do you know it's a tomcat, anyway?" she sniffed at me.

Troll had me there. We went to the same school. It just *looked* like a tom.

Although Matilda Jean was thoroughly gentle and affectionate with members of the family, he obviously was a fighter. One ear had been gnawed half off, patches of fur were missing, and numerous scars recorded the history of a violent, brawling past. Matilda Jean lounged around the house all the first day at his new home, but that evening he got up, stretched, rippled his shoulder and neck muscles like yellow waves on a pond, strode to the door, and asked to be let out.

Later that night, as we were preparing for bed, a terrible cat fight broke out on the roof of our house. It raged back and forth over the roof, up one side and down the other. We rushed out to save poor Matilda Jean and chase off the intruder. We needn't have bothered. Suddenly, a tangled, writhing, screeching knot of cats toppled off the roof and thumped to the ground. Matilda Jean landed on his back at the bottom and for a moment was stunned. The intruder, a big black-and-white model owned by our neighbors, saw its chance. It pulled itself together, a fairly complicated task, matching up the various parts, and streaked off into the night. Matilda Jean got up, rippled his muscles, and climbed back to the roof, apparently taking upon himself the responsibility of protecting us from any shifty-eyed scoundrels who might happen by.

Strange had been away from home for two days. We thought nothing of it, since he regularly went off carousing with his cronies. When he didn't show up the day after the cat fight, however, I began to worry. He wasn't much of a dog, but he was all the dog I had. "Maybe something happened to him," I said to Gram.

"There you go again," she said, "getting my hopes up."

I went out to see if Strange had slipped in unnoticed and was sacked out in his doghouse sleeping off a hangover. The doghouse was empty. Then I saw him, sauntering down the road, occasionally glancing over his shoulder to check whether he was being tailed, possibly by the vice squad. He stopped at the gate and scanned the yard in search of a chicken or squirrel available for assault and battery. The yard was empty.

Matilda Jean peered intently down from the roof, on the lookout for shifty-eyed scoundrels. Strange, of course, fit the description. The cat dropped to the ground a few feet from the startled dog.

It is difficult to know what goes through a dog's mind, but I suspect the few cognitive processes available to Strange were assessing the situation something like this: *A cat! What's a fool cat doing on my property? Dogs chase cats. I'm a dog. Therefore, I will chase this cat and teach it a good lesson. The cat will start running any second. Get ready!*

Matilda Jean didn't start running. His back arched, his hair bristled, his tail lashed back and forth like a ragged yellow whip.

Strange eyed the cat calmly. *So, it's a fight the pussycat wants. Well, he's come to the right place!* He clamped a cigar in his teeth, struck a match on the seat of his pants, lit the cigar, and flicked the match away. Eyes squinted, he smiled grimly around the cigar as he loosened the guns in his holsters. *Draw, cat!*

"Woof!" he said.

"*KILLLLLLLLLLLLL!*" Matilda Jean screamed.

Finally, my dog did something I could brag about. The next day at school I casually mentioned that my dog was really something. "You won't believe what he did last night."

My friends stared at me in astonishment. "You don't mean Strange, do you?" one of them said. "You got another dog?"

"Nope!" I said. "It was Strange. What happened, Troll brought home this big old tomcat, and Strange and it got in a heck of a fight. And you won't believe this, but right in the middle of the fight, the cat and Strange went right up that tamarack tree in our yard. Strange raced up it just like a squirrel. Man, it was something to see! That ol' cat was so surprised it almost fell out of the tree!"

"Wow!" somebody said. "No kidding, you mean Strange actually chased a cat up a tree and climbed up after it?"

People always get so distracted by petty details. What did it matter, who chased whom? The important thing was, *my dog climbed a tree!*

Ring Lardner

DOGS

Every little wile you hear people talking about a man that they don't nobody seem to have much use for him on acct. of him not paying his debts or beating his wife or something and everybody takes a rap at him about this and that until finely one of the party speaks up and says they must be some good in him because he likes animals.

"A man can't be all bad when he is so kind to dogs." That is what they generally always say and that is the reason you see so many men stop on the st. when they see a dog and pet it because they figure that may be somebody will be looking at them do it, and the next time they are getting panned, why who ever seen it will speak up and say:

"He can't be all bad because he likes dogs."

Well friends when you come right down to cases they's about as much sence to this as a good many other delusions that we got here in this country, like for inst. the one about nobody wanting to win the first pot and the one about the whole lot of authors not being able to do their best work unlest they are ½ pickled.

But if liking animals ain't a virtue in itself I don't see how it proves that a man has got any virtues, and personly if I had a daughter and she wanted to get marred and I asked her what kind of a bird the guy was and she said she don't know nothing about him except that one day she seen him kiss a leopard, why I would hold up my blessing till a few of the missing precincts was heard from.

But as long as our best people has got it in their skull that a friendly feeling toward dumb brutes takes the curse off of a bad egg, why I or nobody else is going to be a sucker enough to come out and admit that all the horses, rams, and oxen in the world could drop dead tomorrow morning without us batting an eye.

Pretty near everybody wants to be well thought of and if liking dogs or sheep is a helping along these lines, why even if I don't like them, I wouldn't never loose a opportunity to be seen in their company and act as if I was haveing the time of my life.

But while I was raised in a kennel, you might say, and some of my most intimate childhood friends was of the canine gender, still in all I believe dogs is better in some climates than others, the same as oysters, and I don't think it should ought to be held against a man if he don't feel the same towards N.Y. dogs as he felt towards Michigan dogs, and I am free to confess that the 4 dogs who I have grew to know personly here on Long Island has failed to arouse tender yearnings anyways near similar to those inspired by the flea bearers of my youth.

And in case they should be any tendency on the part of my readers to denounce me for failing to respond whole heartily to the wiles of the Long Island breed let me present a brief sketch of some so as true lovers of the canine tribe can judge for themselfs if the fault is all mind.

No. I

This was the dainty boy that belonged to Gene Buck and it was a bull dog no bigger than a 2 car garage and it wouldn't harm a hair of nobody's head only other animals and people. Children were as safe with this pet as walking in the Pittsburgh freight yards and he wouldn't think of no more wronging a cat than scratching himself.

In fairness to Mr. Buck I'll state that a pal of his give him the dog as a present without no comment. Well they wasn't no trouble till Gene had the dog pretty near $^1/_2$ hr. when they let him out. He was gone 10 minutes during which Gene received a couple of phone calls announcing more in anger than in sorrow the sudden deaths of 2 adjacent cats of noble berth so when the dog come back Gene spanked him and give him a terrible scolding and after that he didn't kill no more cats except when he got outdoors.

But the next day De Wolf Hopper come over to call and brought his kid which the dog thought would look better with one leg and it took 5 people to get him not to operate, so after that Gene called up the supt. of a dogs reform school and the man said he would take him and cure him of the cat habit by trying one of his victims around his neck and leaving it there for a wk. but he didn't know how to cure the taste for young Hoppers unlest De Wolf could spare the kid the wk. after they was finished with the cat.

This proposition fell through but anyway Gene sent the dog to the reformatory and is still paying board for same.

No. 2

The people that lived 3 houses from the undersigned decided to move to England where it seems like you can't take dogs no more so they asked us did we want the dog as it was very nice around children and we took it and sure enough it was OK in regards to children but it shared this new owners feeling towards motorcycles and every time one went past the house the dog would run out and spill the contents, and on Sundays when the traffic was heavy they would sometimes be as many as 4 or 5 motorcycle jehus standing on their heads in the middle of the road.

One of them finely took offence and told on the dog and the justice of the peace called me up and said I would have to kill it within 24 hrs. and the only way I could think of to do same was drown it in the bath tub and if you done that, why the bath tub wouldn't be no good no more because it was a good sized dog and no matter how often you pulled the stopper it would still be there.

No. 3

The next-door neighbors has a pro-German police dog that win a blue ribbon once but now it acts as body guard for the lady of the house and one day we was over there and the host says to slap his Mrs. on the arm and see what happened so I slapped her on the arm and I can still show you what happened.

When you dance with mine hostess this sweet little pet dances right along with you and watches your step and if you tred on my lady's toe he fines you a mouth full and if you and her is partners in a bridge game he lays under the table and you either bid right and play right or you get nipped.

No. 4

This is our present incumbrance which we didn't ask for him and nobody give him to us but here he is and he has got the insomnia and he has picked a spot outside my window to enjoy it but not only that but he has learnt that if you jump at a screen often enough it will finely give way and the result is that they ain't a door or window on the first floor that you couldn't drive a rhinoceros through it and all the bugs that didn't already live in the house is moveing in and bringing their family.

That is a true record of the dogs who I have met since takeing up my abode in Nassau county so when people ask me do I like dogs I say I'm crazy about them and I think they are all right in their place but it ain't Long Island.

Bill Pronzini and
Jeffrey Wallmann

COYOTE AND
QUARTER MOON

With the Laurel County Deputy Sheriff beside her, Jill Quarter-Moon waited for the locksmith to finish unlatching the garage door. Inside, the dog—a good-sized Doberman; she had identified it through the window—continued its frantic barking.

The house to which the garage belonged was only a few years old, a big ranch-style set at the end of a cul-de-sac and somewhat removed from its neighbors in the expensive Oregon Estates development. Since it was a fair Friday morning in June, several of the neighbors were out and mingling in a wide crescent around the property; some of them Jill recognized from her previous visit here. Two little boys were chasing each other around her Animal Regulation Agency truck, stirring up a pair of other barking dogs nearby. It only added to the din being raised by the Doberman.

At length the locksmith finished and stepped back. "It's all yours," he said.

"You'd better let me go in with you," the deputy said to Jill.

There was a taint of chauvinism in his offer, but she didn't let it upset her. She was a mature twenty-six, and a full-blooded Umatilla Indian, and she was comfortable with both her womanhood and her role in society. She was also strikingly attractive, in the light-skinned way of Pacific Northwest Indians, with hip-length brown hair and a long willowy body. Some men, the deputy being one of them, seemed to feel protective, if not downright chivalric, toward her. Nothing made her like a man less than being considered a pretty-and-helpless female.

She shook her head at him and said, "No thanks. I've got my tranquilizer dart gun."

"Suit yourself, then." The deputy gave her a disapproving frown and stepped back out of her way. "It's your throat."

Jill drew a heavy padded glove over her left hand, gripped the dart gun with her right. Then she caught hold of the door latch and depressed it. The Doberman stopped barking; all she could hear from inside were low growls. The dog sensed that someone was coming in, and when she opened the door it would do one of two things: back off and watch her, or attack. She had no way of telling beforehand which it would be.

The Doberman had been locked up inside the garage for at least thirty-six hours. That was how long ago it had first started howling and barking and upsetting the neighbors enough so that one of them had complained to the Agency. The owner of the house, Jill had learned in her capacity as field agent, was named Edward Benham; none of the neighbors knew him—he'd kept to himself during the six months he had lived here—and none of them knew anything at all about his dog. Benham hadn't answered his door, nor had she been able to reach him by telephone or track down any local relatives. Finally she had requested, through the Agency offices, a court order to enter the premises. A judge had granted it, and along with the deputy and the locksmith, here she was to release the animal.

She hesitated a moment longer with her hand on the door latch. If the Doberman backed off, she stood a good chance of gentling it enough to lead it out to the truck; she had a way with animals, dogs in particular—something else she could attribute to her Indian heritage. But if it attacked she would have no choice except to shoot it with the tranquilizer gun. An attack-trained, or even an untrained but high-strung, Doberman could tear your throat out in a matter of seconds.

Taking a breath, she opened the door and stepped just inside the entrance. She was careful to act natural, confident; too much caution could be as provoking to a nervous animal as movements too bold or too sudden. Black and short-haired, the Doberman was over near one of the walls—yellowish eyes staring at her, fangs bared and gleaming in the light from the open doorway and the single dusty window. But it stood its ground, forelegs spread, rear end flattened into a crouch.

"Easy," Jill said soothingly. "I'm not going to hurt you."

She started forward, extending her hand, murmuring the words of a lullaby in Shahaptian dialect. The dog cocked its head, ears perked, still growling, still tensed—but it continued to stay where it was and its stub of a tail began to quiver. That was a good sign, Jill knew. No dog wagged its tail before it attacked.

As her eyes became more accustomed to the half light, she could see that there were three small plastic bowls near the Doberman; each of them had been gnawed and deeply scratched. The condition of the bowls told her that the dog had not been fed or watered during the past thirty-six hours. She could also see that in one corner was a wicker sleeping basket about a foot and a half in diameter, and that on a nearby shelf lay a curry comb. These things told her something else, but just what it meant she had no way of knowing yet.

"Easy, boy . . . calm," she said in English. She was within a few paces of the dog now and it still showed no inclination to jump at her. Carefully she removed the thick glove, stretched her hand out so that the Doberman could better take her scent. "That's it, just stay easy, stay easy . . ."

237

The dog stopped growling. The tail stub began to quiver faster, the massive head came forward and she felt the dryness of its nose as it investigated her hand. The yellow eyes looked up at her with what she sensed was a wary acceptance.

Slowly she put away the tranquilizer gun and knelt beside the animal, murmuring the lullaby again, stroking her hand around its neck and ears. When she felt it was ready to trust her she straightened and patted the dog, took a step toward the entrance. The Doberman followed. And kept on following as she retraced her path toward the door.

They were halfway there when the deputy appeared in the doorway. "You all right in there, lady?" he called.

The Doberman bristled, snarled again low in its throat. Jill stopped and stood still. "Get away, will you?" she said to the deputy, using her normal voice, masking her annoyance so the dog wouldn't sense it. "Get out of sight. And find a hose or a faucet, get some water puddled close by. This animal is dehydrated."

The deputy retreated. Jill reached down to stroke the Doberman another time, then led it slowly out into the sunlight. When they emerged she saw that the deputy had turned on a faucet built into the garage wall; he was backed off to one side now, one hand on the weapon holstered at his side, like an actor in a B movie. The dog paid no attention to him or to anyone else. It went straight for the water and began to lap at it greedily. Jill went with it, again bent down to soothe it with her hands and voice.

While she was doing that she also checked the license and rabies tags attached to its collar, making a mental note of the numbers stamped into the thin aluminum. Now that the tenseness of the situation had eased, anger was building within her again at the way the dog had been abused. Edward Benham, whoever he was, would pay for that, she thought. She'd make certain of it.

The moment the Doberman finished drinking, Jill stood and faced the bystanders. "All of you move away from the truck," she told them. "And keep those other dogs quiet."

"You want me to get the back open for you?" the deputy asked.

"No. He goes up front with me."

"Up front? Are you crazy, lady?"

"This dog has been cooped up for a long time," Jill said. "If I put him back, in the cage, he's liable to have a fit. And he might never trust me again. Up front I can open the window, talk to him, keep him calmed down.

The deputy pursed his lips reprovingly. But as he had earlier, he said, "It's your throat," and backed off with the others.

When the other dogs were still Jill caught hold of the Doberman's collar and led it down the driveway to the truck. She opened the passenger door, patted the seat. The Doberman didn't want to go in at first, but she talked to it, coaxing, and finally it obeyed. She shut the door and went around and slid in under the wheel.

"Good boy," she told the dog, smiling. "We showed them, eh?"

Jill put the truck in gear, turned it around, and waved at the scowling deputy as she passed him by.

At the Agency—a massive old brick building not far from the university—she turned the Doberman over to Sam Wyatt, the resident veterinarian, for examination and treatment. Then she went to her desk in the office area reserved for field agents and sat down with the Benham case file.

The initial report form had been filled out by the dispatcher who had logged the complaint from one of Benham's neighbors. That report listed the breed of Benham's dog as an Alaskan husky, female—not a Doberman, male. Jill had been mildly surprised when she went out to the house and discovered that the trapped dog was a Doberman. But then, the Agency was a bureaucratic organization, and like all bureaucratic organizations it made mistakes in paperwork more often than it ought to. It was likely that the dispatcher, in checking the registry files for the Benham name, had either pulled the wrong card or miscopied the information from the right one.

But Jill kept thinking about the sleeping basket and the curry comb inside the garage. The basket had been too small for the Doberman but about the right size for a female husky. And curry combs were made for long-haired, not short-haired dogs.

The situation puzzled as well as angered her. And made her more than a little curious. One of the primary character traits of the Umatilla was inquisitiveness, and Jill had inherited it along with her self-reliance and her way with animals. She had her grandmother to thank for honing her curiosity, though, for teaching her never to accept any half-truth or partial answer. She could also thank her grandmother who had been born in the days when the tribe lived not on the reservation in northeastern Oregon but along the Umatilla River—the name itself meant "many rocks" or "water rippling over sand"—for nurturing her love for animals and leading her into her present job with the Agency. As far back as Jill could remember, the old woman had told and retold the ancient legends about "the people"—the giant creatures, Salmon and Eagle and Fox and the greatest of all, Coyote, the battler of monsters, who ruled the earth before the human beings were created, before all animals shrank to their present size.

But she was not just curious about Benham for her own satisfaction: she had to have the proper data for her report. If the Agency pressed charges for animal abuse, which was what she wanted to see happen, and a heavy fine was to be levied against Benham, all pertinent information had to be correct.

She went to the registry files and pulled the card on Edward Benham. The dispatcher, it turned out, *hadn't* made a mistake after all: the breed of dog listed as being owned by Benham was an Alaskan husky, female. Also, the license and rabies tag numbers on the card were different from those she had copied down from the Doberman's collar.

One good thing about bureaucratic organizations, she thought, was that they had their filing systems cross-referenced. So she went to the files arranged according to tag numbers and looked up the listed owner of the Doberman.

The card said: *Fox Hollow Kennels, 1423 Canyon Road, Laurel County, Oregon.*

Jill had heard of Fox Hollow Kennels; it was a fairly large place some distance outside the city, operated by a man named Largo or Fargo, which specialized in raising a variety of purebred dogs. She had been there once on a field investigation that had only peripherally concerned the kennel. She was going to make her second visit, she decided, within the next hour.

The only problem with that decision was that her supervisor, Lloyd Mortisse, vetoed it when she went in to tell him where she was going. Mortisse was a lean, mournful-looking man in his late forties, with wild gray hair that reminded Jill of the beads her grandmother had strung into ornamental baskets. He was also a confirmed bureaucrat, which meant that he loved paperwork, hated anything that upset the routine, and was suspicious of the agents' motives every time they went out into the field.

"Call up Fox Hollow," he told her. "You don't need to go out there; the matter doesn't warrant it."

"I think it does."

"You have other work to do, Ms. Quarter-Moon."

"Not as important as this, Mr. Mortisse."

She and Mortisse were constantly at odds. There was a mutual animosity, albeit low-key, based on his part by a certain condescension— either because she was a woman or an Indian, or maybe both—and on her part by a lack of respect. It made for less than ideal working conditions.

He said, "And I say it's not important enough for you to neglect your other duties."

"Ask that poor Doberman how important it is."

"I repeat, you're not to pursue the matter beyond a routine telephone call," Mortisse told her sententiously. "Now is that understood?"

"Yes. It's understood."

Jill pivoted, stalked out of the office, and kept right on stalking through the rear entrance and out to her truck. Twenty minutes later she was turning onto the long gravel drive, bordered by pine and Douglas fir, that led to the Fox Hollow Kennels.

She was still so annoyed at Mortisse, and preoccupied with Edward Benham, that she almost didn't see the large truck that came barreling toward her along the drive until it was too late. As it was, she managed to swerve off onto the soft shoulder just in time, and to answer the truck's horn blast with one of her own. It was an old Ford stakebed, she saw as it passed her and braked for the turn onto Canyon Road, with the words *Fox Hollow Kennels* on the driver's door. Three slat-and-wire crates were tied together on the bed, each of which contained what appeared to be a mongrel dog. The dogs had begun barking at the sound of the horns and she could see two of them pawing at the wire mesh.

Again she felt both her curiosity and her anger aroused. Transporting dogs in bunches via truck wasn't exactly inhuman treatment, but it was still a damned poor way to handle animals. And what was an American Kennel Club-registered outfit which specialized in purebreds doing with mongrels?

Jill drove up the access drive and emerged into a wide gravel parking area. The long whitewashed building that housed Fox Hollow's office was on her right, with a horseshoe arrangement of some thirty kennels and an exercise yard behind it. Pine woods surrounded the complex, giving it a rustic atmosphere.

When she parked and got out, the sound of more barking came to her from the vicinity of the exercise yard. She glanced inside the office, saw that it was empty, and went through a swing-gate that led to the back. There, beside a low fence, a man stood tossing dog biscuits into the concrete run on the other side, where half a dozen dogs—all of these purebred setters—crowded and barked together. He was in his late thirties, average-sized, with bald head and nondescript features, wearing Levi's and a University of Oregon sweatshirt. Jill recognized him as the owner, Largo or Fargo.

"Mr. Largo?" she said.

He turned, saying, "The name is Fargo." Then he set the food sack down and wiped his hands on his Levi's. His eyes were speculative as he studied both her and her tan Agency uniform. "Something I can do for you, miss?"

Jill identified herself. "I'm here about a dog," she said, "a male Doberman, about three years old. It was abandoned inside a house in Oregon Estates at least two days ago; we went in and released it this morning. The house belongs to a man named Benham, Edward Benham, but the Doberman is registered to Fox Hollow."

Fargo's brows pulled down. "Benham, did you say?"

"That's right. Edward Benham. Do you know him?"

"Well, I don't recognize the name."

"Is it possible you sold him the Doberman?"

"I suppose it is," Fargo said. "Some people don't bother to change the registration. Makes a lot of trouble for all of us when they don't."

"Yes, it does. Would you mind checking your records?"

"Not at all."

He led her around and inside the kennel office. It was a cluttered room that smelled peculiarly of dog, dust, and cheap men's cologne. An open door on the far side led to an attached workroom; Jill could see a bench littered with tools, stacks of lumber, and several slat-and-wire crates of the type she had noticed on the truck, some finished and some under construction.

Along one wall was a filing cabinet and Fargo crossed to it, began to rummage inside. After a time he came out with a folder, opened it, consulted the papers it held, and put it away again. He turned to face Jill.

"Yep," he said, "Edward Benham. He bought the Doberman about three weeks ago. I didn't handle the sale myself, one of my assistants took care of it. That's why I didn't recognize the name."

"Is your assistant here now?"

"No, I gave him a three-day weekend to go fishing."

"Is the Doberman the only animal Benham has bought from you?"

"As far as the records show, it is."

"Benham is the registered owner of a female Alaskan husky," Jill said. "Do you know anyone who specializes in that breed?"

"Not offhand. Check with the American Kennel Club; they might be able to help you."

"I'll do that." Jill paused. "I passed your truck on the way in, Mr. Fargo. Do you do a lot of shipping of dogs?"

"Some, yes. Why?"

"Just curious. Where are those three today bound?"

"Portland." Fargo made a deliberate point of looking at his watch. "If you'll excuse me, I've got work to do . . ."

"Just one more thing. I'd like to see your American Kennel Club registration on the Doberman you sold Benham."

"Can't help you there, I'm afraid," Fargo said. "There wasn't any AKC registration on that Doberman."

"No? Why not? He's certainly a purebred."

"Maybe so, but the animal wasn't bred here. We bought it from a private party who didn't even know the AKC existed."

"What was this private party's name?"

"Adams. Charles Adams. From out of state—California. That's why Fox Hollow was the first to register the dog with you people."

Jill decided not to press the matter, at least not with Fargo personally. She had other ways of finding out information about him, about Fox Hollow, and about Edward Benham. She thanked Fargo for his time, left the office, and headed her truck back to the Agency.

When she got there she went first to see Sam Wyatt, to check on the Doberman's health. There was nothing wrong with the animal, Wyatt told her, except for minor malnutrition and dehydration. It had been fed, exercised, and put into one of the larger cages.

She looked in on it. The dog seemed glad to see her; the stub of a tail began to wag when she approached the cage. She played her fingers through the mesh grille, let the Doberman nuzzle them.

While she was doing that the kennel attendant, a young redhead named Lena Stark, came out of the dispensary. "Hi, Jill," she said. "The patient looks pretty good, doesn't he?"

"He'll look a lot better when we find him a decent owner."

"That's for sure."

"Funny thing—he's registered to the Fox Hollow Kennels, but they say he was sold to one Edward Benham. It was Benham's garage he was locked up in."

"Why is that funny?"

"Well, purebred Dobermans don't come cheap. Why would anybody who'd pay for one suddenly go off and desert him?"

"I guess that is kind of odd," Lena admitted. "Unless Benham was called out of town on an urgent matter or something. That would explain it."

"Maybe," Jill said.

"Some people should never own pets, you know? Benham should have left the dog at Fox Hollow; at least they care about the welfare of animals."

"Why do you say that?"

"Because every now and then one of their guys comes in and takes most of our strays."

"Oh? For what reason?"

"They train them and then find homes for them in other parts of the state. A pretty nice gesture, don't you think?"

"Yes," Jill said thoughtfully. "A pretty nice gesture."

She went inside and straight to the filing room, where she pulled the Fox Hollow folder. At her desk she spread out the kennel's animal licensing applications and studied them. It stood to reason that there would be a large number and there were; but as she sifted through them Jill was struck by a peculiarity. Not counting the strays Fox Hollow had "adopted" from the Agency, which by law had to be vaccinated and licensed before being released, there were less than a dozen dogs brought in and registered over the past twelve months. For a kennel which claimed to specialize in purebreds, this was suspiciously odd. Yet no one else had noticed it in the normal bureaucratic shuffle, just as no one had paid much attention to Fox Hollow's gathering of Agency strays.

And why *was* Fox Hollow in the market for so many stray dogs? Having met Fargo, she doubted that he was the humanitarian type motivated by a desire to save mongrels from euthanasia, a dog's fate if kept unclaimed at the Agency for more than four days. No, it sounded as if he were in some sort of strange wholesale pet business—as if the rest of the state, not to mention the rest of the country, didn't have their own animal overpopulation problems.

But where did Edward Benham, and the Doberman, fit in? Jill reviewed the Benham file again, but it had nothing new to tell her. She wished she knew where he'd gone, or of some way to get in touch with him. The obvious way, of course, was through his place of employment; unfortunately, however, pet license applications did not list employment of owners, only home address and telephone number. Nor had any of his neighbors known where he worked.

Briefly she considered trying to bluff information out of one of the credit-reporting companies in the city. Benham had bought rather then rented or leased his house, which meant that he probably carried a mortgage, which meant credit, which meant an application listing his employment. The problem was that legitimate members of such credit companies used special secret numbers to identify themselves when requesting information, so any ruse she might attempt would no doubt fail, and might even backfire and land her in trouble with Mortisse.

Then she thought of Pete Olafson, the office manager for Mid-Valley Adjustment Bureau, a local bad-debt collection service. Mid-Valley could certainly belong to a credit-reporting company. And she knew Pete pretty well, had dated him a few times in recent months. There wasn't any torrid romance brewing between her and the sandy-haired bachelor, but she knew he liked her a good deal—maybe enough to bend the rules a little and check Benham's credit as a favor.

She looked up Mid-Valley's number, dialed it, and was talking to Pete fifteen seconds later. "You must be a mindreader, Jill," he said after she identified herself. "I was going to call you later. The University Theater is putting on 'Our Town' tomorrow night and I've wangled a couple of free passes. Would you like to go?"

"Sure. If you'll do me a favor in return."

Pete sighed dramatically. "Nothing is free these days, it seems. Okay, what is it?"

"I want to know where a man named Edward Benham is employed. Could you track down his credit applications and find out from them?"

"I can if he's got credit somewhere."

"Well, he owns his own home, out in Oregon Estates. The name is Benham, B-e-n-h-a-m, Edward. How fast can you find out for me?"

"It shouldn't take long. Sit tight; I'll get back to you."

* * *

Jill replaced the handset and sat with her chin propped in one palm brooding. If the lead to Edward Benham through Pete didn't pan out, then what? Talk to his neighbors again? Through them she could find out the name of the real estate agent who had sold Benham his home . . . but it was unlikely that they would divulge personal information about him, since she had no official capacity. Talk to Fargo again? That probably wouldn't do her any good either. . . .

The door to Lloyd Mortisse's private office opened; Jill saw him thrust his wild-maned head out and look in her direction. It was not a look of pleasure. "Ms. Quarter-Moon," he said. "Come into my office, please."

Jill complied. Mortisse shut the door behind her, sat down at his desk, and glared at her. "I thought," he said stiffly, "that I told you not to go out to Fox Hollow Kennels."

Surprised, Jill asked, "How did you know about that?"

"Mr. Fargo called me. He wanted to know why you were out there asking all sorts of questions. He wasn't particularly pleased by your visit; neither am I. Why did you disobey me?"

"I felt the trip was necessary."

"Oh, you felt it was necessary. I see. That makes it all right, I suppose."

"Look, Mr. Mortisse—"

"I do not like disobedience," Mortisse said. "I won't stand for it again, is that clear? Nor will I stand for you harassing private facilities like Fox Hollow. This Agency's sole concern in the Benham matter is to house the Doberman for ninety-six hours or until it is claimed. And I'll be the one, not you, to decide if any misdemeanor animal-abuse charges are to be filed against Mr. Benham."

Jill thought that it was too bad these weren't the old days, when one of the Umatilla customs in tribal disputes was to hold a potlatch—a fierce social competition at which rival chiefs gave away or destroyed large numbers of blankets, coppers, and slaves in an effort to outdo and therefore vanquish each other. She would have liked nothing better than to challenge Mortisse in this sort of duel, using bureaucratic attitudes and red tape as the throwaway material. She also decided there was no point in trying to explain her suspicions to him; he would only have said in his supercilious way that none of it was Agency business. If she was going to get to the bottom of what was going on at Fox Hollow, she would have to do it on her own.

"Do you understand?" Mortisse was saying. "You're to drop this matter and attend to your assigned duties. And you're not to disobey a direct order again, under any circumstances."

"I understand," Jill said thinly. "Is that all?"

"That's all."

She stood and left the office, resisting an impulse to slam the door. The wall clock said that it was 4:10—less than an hour until quitting time for the weekend. All right, she thought as she crossed to her desk. I'll drop the matter while I'm on Agency time. But what I do and where I go on my own time is *my* business, Mortisse or no Mortisse.

It was another ten minutes, during which time she typed up a pair of two-day-old reports, before Pete Olafson called her back. "Got what you asked for, Jill," he said. "Edward Benham has a pretty fair credit rating, considering he's modestly employed."

"What does he do?"

"He's a deliveryman, it says here. For a kennel."

Jill sat up straight. "Kennel?"

"That's right," Pete said. "Place called Fox Hollow outside the city. Is that what you're after?"

"It's a lot more than I expected," Jill told him. Quickly she arranged tomorrow night's date with him, then replaced the receiver and sat mulling over this latest bit of news.

If she had needed anything more to convince her that something was amiss at Fox Hollow, this was it. Fargo had claimed he didn't know Edward Benham; now it turned out that Benham worked for Fargo. Why had he lied? What was he trying to cover up? And where was Benham? And where did the Doberman fit in?

She spent another half hour at her desk, keeping one eye on the clock and pretending to work while she sorted through questions, facts, and options in her mind. At ten minutes of five, when she couldn't take any more of the inactivity, she went out into the kennel area to see Lena Stark.

"Release the Doberman to me, will you, Lena?" she asked. "I'll bring him back later tonight and check him in with the night attendant."

"Why do you want him?"

"I like his looks and I want to get better acquainted. If it turns out neither Fox Hollow nor Benham decides to claim him, I may just adopt him myself."

"I don't know, Jill . . ."

"He's all right, isn't he? Sam Wyatt said he was."

"Sure, he's fine. But the rules—"

"Oh, hang the rules. Nobody has to know except you and me and the night attendant. I'll take full responsibility."

"Well . . . okay, I guess you know what you're doing."

Lena opened the cage and the Doberman came out, stubby tail quivering, and nuzzled Jill's hand. She led it out through the rear door, into the parking lot to where her compact was parked. Obediently, as if delighted to be free and in her company, the dog jumped onto the front seat and sat down with an expectant look.

Jill stroked its ears as she drove out of the lot. "I don't want to keep calling you 'boy'," she said. "I think I'll give you a name, even if it's only temporary. How about Tyee?" In the old Chinook jargon, the mixed trade language of Indians and whites in frontier days, *tyee* was the word for chief. "You like that? Tyee?"

The dog cocked its head and made a rumbly sound in its throat.

"Good," Jill said. "Tyee it is."

She drove across the city and into Oregon Estates. Edward Benham's house, she saw when she braked at the end of the cul-de-sac, looked as deserted as it had this morning. This was confirmed when she went up and rang the doorbell several times without getting a response.

She took Tyee with her and let him sniff around both front and back. The Doberman showed none of the easy familiarity of a dog on its own turf; rather, she sensed a wary tenseness in the way he moved and keened the air. And when she led him near the garage he bristled, Jill thought. But then why had he been locked in Benham's garage?

She would have liked to go inside for a better look around, but the locksmith had relocked the doors, as dictated by law, before leaving the premises that morning. The house was securely locked too, as were each of the windows. And drawn drapes and blinds made it impossible to see into any of the rooms from outside.

Jill took Tyee back to her compact. She sat for a time, considering. Then she started the engine and pointed the car in an easterly direction.

It was just seven o'clock when she came up the access drive to Fox Hollow Kennels and coasted to a stop on the gravel parking area near the main building. There were no other vehicles around, a *Closed* sign was propped in one dusty pane of the front door, and the complex had a deserted aura; even the dogs in the near kennels were quiet.

She got out, motioning for Tyee to stay where he was on the front seat. The setting sun hung above the tops of the pines straight ahead, bathing everything in a dark-orange radiance. Jill judged that there was about an hour of daylight left, which meant that an hour was all she would have to look around. Prowling in daylight was risky enough, though if she were seen she might be able to bluff her way out of trouble by claiming she had brought Tyee back to his registered owner. If she were caught here after dark, no kind of bluff would be worth much.

The office door was locked, but when she shook it, it rattled loosely in its frame. Jill bent for a closer look at the latch. It was a spring-type lock, rather than a deadbolt. She straightened again, gnawing at her lower lip. Detectives in movies and on TV were forever opening spring locks with credit cards or pieces of celluloid; there was no reason why she couldn't do the same thing. No reason, that was, except that it was illegal and would cost her her job, if not a prison term, were she to be caught. She could imagine Lloyd Mortisse smiling like a Cheshire Cat at news of her arrest.

But she was already here, and the need to sate her curiosity was overpowering. The debate with her better judgment lasted all of ten seconds. Then she thought: Well, fools rush in—and she went back to the car to get a credit card from her purse.

Less than a minute of maneuvering with the card rewarded her with a sharp click as the lock snapped free. The door opened under her hand. Enough of the waning orange sunlight penetrated through the windows, she saw when she stepped inside, so that she didn't need any other kind of light. She went straight to the filing cabinets, began to shuffle through the folders inside.

The kennel records were in something of a shambles; Jill realized quickly that it would take hours, maybe even days, to sort through all the receipts, partial entries, and scraps of paper. But one file was complete enough to hold her attention and to prove interesting. It consisted of truck expenses—repair bills, oil company credit card receipts, and the like—and what intrigued her was that, taken together, they showed that the Fox Hollow delivery truck consistently traveled to certain towns in Oregon, northern California, and southern Washington. Forest Grove, Corvallis, Portland, McMinnville, Ashland, La Grande, Arcata, Kirkland. . . . These, and a few others, comprised a regular route.

Which might explain why Edward Benham was nowhere to be found at the moment; some of the towns were at least an overnight's drive away, and it was Benham's signature that was on most of the receipts. But the evident truck route also raised more questions. Why such long hauls for a small kennel? Why to some points out of state? And why to these particular towns, when there were numerous others of similar size along the way?

"Curiouser and curiouser," Jill murmured to herself.

She shut the file drawers and turned to the desk. Two of the drawers were locked; she decided it would be best not to try forcing them. None of the other drawers, nor any of the clutter spread across the top, told her anything incriminating or enlightening.

The door to the adjacent workroom was closed, but when she tried the knob it opened right up. That room was dimmer but there was still enough daylight filtering in to let her see the tools, workbench, stacks of lumber, finished and unfinished crates. She picked through the farrago of items on the bench; caught up slats and corner posts of an unassembled cage, started to put them down again. Then, frowning, she studied one of the wooden posts more carefully.

The post was hollow. So were the others; the inner lengths of all four had been bored out by a large drill bit. When fitted into the frame of a fully constructed cage the posts would appear solid, their holes concealed by the top and bottom sections. Only when the cage was apart, like now, would the secret compartments be exposed, to be filled or emptied.

Of what?

Jill renewed her search. In a back corner were three rolls of cage wire—and caught on a snag of mesh on one roll was a small cellophane bag. The bag was out of easy sight and difficult to reach, but she managed to retrieve it. It looked new, unopened, and it was maybe 3×5 inches in size. The kind of bag—

And then she knew. All at once, with a kind of wrenching insight, she understood what the bag was for, why the corner posts were hollowed out, what Fox Hollow was involved in. And it was ugly enough and frightening enough to make her feel a chill of apprehension, make her want to get away from there in a hurry. It was more than she had bargained for—considerably more.

She ran out of the workroom, still clutching the cellophane bag in her left hand. At the office door she peered through the glass before letting herself out, to make sure the parking area remained deserted. Then she set the button-lock on the knob, stepped outside, pulled the door shut, and started across to her compact.

Tyee was gone.

She stopped, staring in at the empty front seat. She had left the driver's window all the way down and he must have jumped out. Turning, she peered through gathering shadows toward the kennels. But the dogs were still quiet back there, and they wouldn't be if the Doberman had gone prowling in that direction. Where, then? Back down the drive? The pine woods somewhere?

Jill hesitated. The sense of urgency and apprehension demanded that she climb into the car, Tyee or no Tyee, and drive away pronto. But she couldn't just leave him here while she went to tell her suspicions to the country sheriff. The law would not come out here tonight no matter what she told them; they'd wait until tomorrow, when the kennel was open for business and when they could obtain a search warrant. And once she left here herself she had no intention of coming back again after dark.

She moved away from the car, toward the dark line of evergreens beyond. It was quiet here, with dust settling, and sounds carried some distance; the scratching noises reached her ears when she was still twenty paces from the woods. She'd heard enough dogs digging into soft earth to recognize the sound and she quickened her pace. Off to one side was a beaten-down area, not quite a path, and she went into the trees at that point. The digging sounds grew louder. Then she saw Tyee, over behind a decayed moss-festooned log, making earth and dry needles fly out behind him with his forepaws.

"What are you doing?" she called to him. "Come here, Tyee."

The Doberman kept on digging, paying no attention to her. She hurried over to him, around the bulky shape of the log. And then she stopped abruptly, made a startled gasping sound.

A man's arm and clenched hand lay partially uncovered in the soft ground.

Tyee was still digging, still scattering dirt and pine needles. Jill stood frozen, watching part of a broad back encased in a khaki shirt appear.

Now she knew what had happened to Edward Benham.

She made herself move, step forward and catch hold of the Doberman's collar. He resisted at first when she tried to tug him away from the shallow grave and what was in it; but she got a firmer grip and pulled harder, and finally he quit struggling. She dragged him around the log, back out of the trees.

Most of the daylight was gone now; the sky was grayish, streaked with red, like bloody fingermarks on faded cloth. A light wind had come up and she felt herself shiver as she took the Doberman toward her compact. She was anything but a shrinking violet, but what she had found at Fox Hollow tonight was enough to frighten Old Chief Joseph or any of the other venerable Shahaptian warriors. The sooner she was sitting in the safety of the Laurel County Sheriff's office, the better she—

And the sudden figure of a man came out from behind her car.

She was ten feet from the driver's door, her right hand on Tyee's collar, and the man just rose up into view like Nashlah, the legendary monster of the Columbia River. Jill made an involuntary cry, stiffened into a standstill. The Doberman seemed to go as tense as she did; a low rumble sounded in his throat as the man came toward them.

Fargo. With a gun in his hand.

"You just keep on holding that dog," he said. He stopped fifteen feet away, holding the gun out at arm's length. "You're both dead if you let go his collar."

She was incapable of speech for five or six seconds. Then she made herself say, "There's no need for that gun, Mr. Fargo. I'm only here to return the Doberman. . . ."

"Sure you are. Let's not play games. You're here because you're a damned snoop. And I'm here because you tripped a silent alarm connected to my house when you broke into the office."

It was not in Jill's nature to panic in a crisis; she got a grip on her fear and held it down, smothered it. "The office door was unlocked," she said. "Maybe you think you locked it when you left but you didn't. I just glanced inside."

"I don't buy that either," Fargo said. "I saw you come out of the office; I left my car down the road and walked up here through the trees. I saw you go into the woods over there, too."

"I went to find the dog, that's all."

"But that's not what you found, right? He's got dirt all over his forepaws—he's been doing some digging. You found Benham. And now you know too much about everything."

"I don't know what you're talking about."

"I say you do. So does that cellophane bag you're carrying."

Jill looked down at her left hand; she had forgotten all about the bag. And she had never even considered the possibility of a silent alarm system. She had a lot to learn about being a detective—if she survived to profit by her mistakes.

"All right," she said. "It's drugs, isn't it? That's the filthy business you're in."

"You got it."

"Selling drugs to college kids all over the Pacific Northwest," she said. That was the significance of the towns on the Fox Hollow shipping route: they were all college or university towns. Humboldt State in Arcata, Lewis & Clark in Portland, Linfield College in McMinnville, Eastern Oregon College in La Grande. And the state university right here in this city. That was also why Fox Hollow had taken so many stray dogs from the Agency; they needed a constant supply to cover their shipment of drugs—cocaine and heroin, probably, the kind usually packaged and shipped in small cellophane bags—to the various suppliers along their network. "Where does it come from? Canada?"

"Mexico," Fargo said. "They bring it up by ship, we cut and package and distribute it."

"To kennels in those other cities, I suppose."

"That's right. They make a nice cover."

"What happens to the dogs you ship?"

"What do you think happens to them? Dogs don't matter when you're running a multi-million-dollar operation. Neither do snoops like you. Nobody fouls up this kind of operation and gets away with it."

Tyee growled again, shifted his weight; Jill tightened her grip on his collar. "Did Benham foul it up? Is that why he's dead?"

"He tried to. His percentage wasn't enough for him and he got greedy; he decided to hijack a shipment for himself—substitute milk sugar and then make off with the real stuff. When he left here on Wednesday for Corvallis he detoured over to his house and made the switch. Only one of the crates had the drugs in it, like always; he had to let the dog out of that one to get at the shipment and it turned on him, tried to bite him."

"This dog, the Doberman."

"Yeah. He managed to lock it up inside his garage, but that left him with an empty crate and he couldn't deliver an empty, not without making the Corvallis contact suspicious. So he loaded his own dog, the Husky, inside the crate and delivered it instead. But our man checked the dope anyway, discovered the switch, and called me. I was waiting for Benham when he got back here."

"And you killed him."

Fargo shrugged. "I had no choice."

"Like you've got no choice with me?"

He shrugged again. "I forgot all about the Doberman, that was my mistake. If I hadn't, I wouldn't have you on my hands. But it just didn't occur to me the dog would raise a ruckus and a nosy Agency worker would decide to investigate."

"Why did you lie to me before about knowing Benham?"

"I didn't want you doing any more snooping. I figured if I gave you that story about selling him the Doberman, you'd come up against a dead-end and drop the whole thing. Same reason I called your supervisor: I thought he'd make you drop it. Besides, you had no official capacity. It was your word against mine."

"Lying to me was your second mistake," Jill said. "If you kill me, it'll be your third."

"How do you figure that?"

"I told somebody I came out here tonight. He'll go to the county sheriff if I disappear, and they'll come straight to you."

"That's a bluff," Fargo said. "And I don't bluff. You didn't tell anybody about coming here; nobody knows but you and me. And pretty soon it'll just be me." He made a gesture with the gun. "Look at it this way. You're only one person, but I got a lot of people depending on me: others in the operation, all those kids we supply."

All those kids, Jill thought, and there was a good hot rage inside her now. College kids, some of them still in their teens. White kids, black kids—Indian kids. She had seen too many Indian youths with drug habits; she had talked to the parents of a sixteen-year-old boy who had died from an overdose of heroin on the Umatilla reservation, of a seventeen-year-old girl, an honor student, killed in a drug raid at Trout Lake near the Warm Springs development. Any minority, especially its restless and sometimes disenchanted youth, was susceptible to drug exploitation;

and Indians were a minority long oppressed in their own country. That was why she hated drugs, and hated these new oppressors, the drug dealers like Fargo, even more.

Fargo said, "Okay, we've done enough talking—no use in prolonging things. Turn around, walk into the woods."

"So you can bury me next to Benham?"

"Never mind that. Just move."

"No," she said, and she let her body go limp, sank onto her knees. She dropped the cellophane bag as she did so and then put that hand flat on the gravel beside her, keeping her other hand on Tyee's collar. The Doberman, sensing the increase of tension between her and Fargo, had his fangs bared now, growling steadily.

"What the hell?" Fargo said. "Get up."

Jill lowered her chin to her chest and began to chant in a soft voice—a Shahaptian prayer.

"I said get up!"

She kept on chanting.

Fargo took two steps toward her, a third, a fourth. That put less than five feet of ground between them. "I'll shoot you right where you are, I mean it—"

She swept up a handful of gravel, hurled it at his face, let go of Tyee's collar, and flung herself to one side.

The gun sent off and she heard the bullet strike the ground near her head, felt the sting of a pebble kicked up against her cheek. Then Fargo screamed, and when Jill rolled over she saw that Tyee had done what she'd prayed he would—attacked Fargo the instant he was released. He had driven the man backward and knocked him down and was shaking his captured wrist as if it were a stick; the gun had popped loose and sailed off to one side. Fargo cried out again, tried to club the Doberman with his free hand. Blood from where Tyee's teeth had bitten into his wrist flowed down along his right arm.

Jill scrambled to her feet, ran to where the gun lay and scooped it up. But before she could level it at Fargo, he jacknifed his body backwards, trying to escape from the Doberman, and cracked his head against the front bumper of her compact; she heard the thunking sound it made in the stillness, saw him go limp. Tyee still straddled the inert form, growling, shaking the bloody wrist.

She went over there, caught the dog's collar again, talked to him until he let go of Fargo and backed off with her. But he stood close, alert, alternately looking at the unconscious man and up at her. She knelt and hugged him, and there were tears in her eyes. She disliked women who cried, particularly self-sufficient Indian women, but sometimes . . . sometimes it was a necessary release.

"You know who you are?" she said to him. "You're not Tyee, you're Coyote. You do battle with monsters and evil beings and you save Indians from harm."

The Doberman licked her hand.

"The Great One isn't supposed to return until the year 2000, when the world changes again and all darkness is gone; but you're here already and I won't let you go away. You're mine and I'm yours from now on—Coyote and Quarter-Moon."

Then she stood, shaking but smiling, and went to re-pick the lock on the office door so she could call the Laurel County sheriff.

Jack London

THE LAW OF CLUB AND FANG

Buck's first day on the Dyea beach was like a nightmare. Every hour was filled with shock and surprise. He had been suddenly jerked from the heart of civilization and flung into the heart of things primordial. No lazy, sun-kissed life was this, with nothing to do but loaf and be bored. Here was neither peace, nor rest, nor a moment's safety. All was confusion and action, and every moment life and limb were in peril. There was imperative need to be constantly alert; for these dogs and men were not town dogs and men. They were savages, all of them, who knew no law but the law of club and fang.

He had never seen dogs fight as these wolfish creatures fought, and his first experience taught him an unforgettable lesson. It is true, it was a vicarious experience, else he would not have lived to profit by it. Curly was the victim. They were camped near the log store, where she, in her friendly way, made advances to a husky dog the size of a full-grown wolf, though not half so large as she. There was no warning, only a leap in like a flash, a metallic clip of teeth, a leap out equally swift, and Curly's face was ripped open from eye to jaw.

It was the wolf manner of fighting, to strike and leap away; but there was more to it than this. Thirty or forty huskies ran to the spot and surrounded the combatants in an intent and silent circle. Buck did not comprehend that silent intentness, nor the eager way with which they were licking their chops. Curly rushed her antagonist, who struck again and leaped aside. He met her next rush with his chest, in a peculiar fashion that tumbled her off her feet. She never regained them. This was what the onlooking huskies had waited for. They closed in upon her, snarling and yelping, and she was buried, screaming with agony, beneath the bristling mass of bodies.

So sudden was it, and so unexpected, that Buck was taken aback. He saw Spitz run out his scarlet tongue in a way he had of laughing; and he saw François, swinging an axe, spring into the mess of dogs. Three men with clubs were helping him to scatter them. It did not take long. Two minutes from the time Curly went down, the last of her assailants were clubbed off. But she lay there limp and lifeless in the bloody, trampled snow, almost literally torn to pieces, the swart half-breed standing over her and cursing horribly. The scene often came back to Buck to trouble him in his sleep. So that was the way. No fairplay. Once down, that was the end of you. Well, he would see to it that he never went down. Spitz ran out his tongue and laughed again, and from that moment Buck hated him with a bitter and deathless hatred.

Before he had recovered from the shock caused by the tragic passing of Curly, he received another shock. François fastened upon him an arrangement of straps and buckles. It was a harness, such as he had seen the grooms put on the horses at home. And as he had seen horses work, so he was set to work, hauling François on a sled to the forest that fringed the valley, and returning with a load of firewood. Though his dignity was sorely hurt by thus being made a draught animal, he was too wise to rebel. He buckled down with a will and did his best, though it was all new and strange. François was stern, demanding instant obedience, and by virtue of his whip receiving instant obedience; while Dave, who was an experienced wheeler, nipped Buck's hind quarters whenever he was in error. Spitz was the leader, likewise experienced, and while he could not always get at Buck, he growled sharp reproof now and again, or cunningly threw his weight in the traces to jerk Buck into the way he should go. Buck learned easily, and under the combined tuition of his two mates and François made remarkable progress. Ere they returned to camp he knew enough to stop at "ho," to go ahead at "mush," to swing wide on the bends, and to keep clear of the wheeler when the loaded sled shot downhill at their heels.

"T'ree vair' good dogs," François told Perrault. "Dat Buck, heem pool lak hell. I tich heem queek as anyt'ing."

By afternoon, Perrault, who was in a hurry to be on the trail with his despatches, returned with two more dogs. "Billee" and "Joe" he called them, two brothers, and true huskies both. Sons of the one mother though they were, they were as different as day and night. Billee's one fault was his excessive good nature, while Joe was the very opposite, sour and introspective, with a perpetual snarl and a malignant eye. Buck received them in comradely fashion, Dave ignored them, while Spitz proceeded to thrash first one and then the other. Billee wagged his tail appeasingly, turned to run when he saw that appeasement was of no avail, and cried (still appeasingly) when Spitz's sharp teeth scored his flank. But no matter how Spitz circled, Joe whirled around on his heels to face him, mane bristling, ears laid back, lips writhing and snarling, jaws clipping together as fast as he could snap, and eyes diabolically gleaming—the incarnation of belligerent fear. So terrible was his appearance that Spitz was forced to forego disciplining him; but to cover his own discomfiture he turned upon the inoffensive and wailing Billee and drove him to the confines of the camp.

By evening Perrault secured another dog, an old husky, long and lean and gaunt, with a battle-scarred face and a single eye which flashed a warning of prowess that commanded respect. He was called Sol-leks, which means the Angry One. Like Dave, he asked nothing, gave nothing, expected nothing; and when he marched slowly and deliberately into their midst, even Spitz left him alone. He had one peculiarity which Buck was unlucky enough to discover. He did not like to be approached on his blind side. Of this offence Buck was unwittingly guilty, and the first knowledge he had of his indiscretion was when Sol-leks whirled upon him and slashed his shoulder to the bone for three inches up and down. Forever after Buck avoided his blind side, and to the last of their comradeship had no more trouble. His only apparent ambition, like Dave's, was to be left alone; though, as Buck was afterward to learn, each of them possessed one other and even more vital ambition.

That night Buck faced the great problem of sleeping. The tent, illumined by a candle, glowed warmly in the midst of the white plain; and when he, as a matter of course, entered it, both Perrault and François bombarded him with curses and cooking utensils, till he recovered from his consternation and fled ignominiously into the outer cold. A chill wind was blowing that nipped him sharply and bit with especial venom into his wounded shoulder. He lay down on the snow and attempted to sleep, but the frost soon drove him shivering to his feet. Miserable and disconsolate, he wandered about among the many tents, only to find that one place was as cold as another. Here and there savage dogs rushed upon him, but he bristled his neck-hair and snarled (for he was learning fast), and they let him go his way unmolested.

Finally an idea came to him. He would return and see how his own team mates were making out. To his astonishment, they had disappeared. Again he wandered about through the great camp, looking for them, and again he returned. Were they in the tent? No, that could not be, else he would not have been driven out. Then where could they possibly be? With drooping tail and shivering body, very forlorn indeed, he aimlessly circled the tent. Suddenly the snow gave way beneath his fore legs and he sank down. Something wriggled under his feet. He sprang back, bristling and snarling, fearful of the unseen and unknown. But a friendly little yelp reassured him, and he went back to investigate. A whiff of warm air ascended to his nostrils, and there, curled up under the snow in a snug ball, lay Billee. He whined placatingly, squirmed and wriggled to show his good will and intentions, and even ventured, as a bribe for peace, to lick Buck's face with his warm wet tongue.

Another lesson. So that was the way they did it, eh? Buck confidently selected a spot, and with much fuss and waste effort proceeded to dig a hole for himself. In a trice the heat from his body filled the confined space and he was asleep. The day had been long and arduous, and he slept soundly and comfortably, though he growled and barked and wrestled with bad dreams.

Nor did he open his eyes till roused by the noises of the waking camp. At first he did not know where he was. It had snowed during the night and he was completely buried. The snow walls pressed him on every side, and a great surge of fear swept through him—the fear of the wild thing for the trap. It was a token that he was harking back through his own life to the lives of his forbears; for he was a civilized dog, an unduly civilized dog, and of his own experience knew no trap and so could not of himself fear it. The muscles of his whole body contracted spasmodically and instinctively, the hair on his neck and shoulders stood on end, and with a ferocious snarl he bounded straight up into the blinding day, the snow flying about him in a flashing cloud. Ere he landed on his feet, he saw the white camp spread out before him and knew where he was and remembered all that had passed from the time he went for a stroll with Manuel to the hole he had dug for himself the night before.

A shout from François hailed his appearance. "Wot I say?" the dog driver cried to Perrault. "Dat Buck for sure learn queek as anyt'ing."

Perrault nodded gravely. As courier for the Canadian Government, bearing important despatches, he was anxious to secure the best dogs, and he was particularly gladdened by the possession of Buck.

Three more huskies were added to the team inside an hour, making a total of nine, and before another quarter of an hour had passed they were in harness and swinging up the trail toward the Dyea Cañon. Buck was glad to be gone, and though the work was hard he found he did not particularly despise it. He was surprised at the eagerness which animated the whole team and which was communicated to him; but still more surprising was the change wrought in Dave and Sol-leks. They were new dogs, utterly transformed by the harness. All passiveness and unconcern had dropped from them. They were alert and active, anxious that the work should go well, and fiercely irritable with whatever, by delay or confusion, retarded that work. The toil of the traces seemed the supreme expression of their being, and all that they lived for and the only thing in which they took delight.

Dave was wheeler or sled dog, pulling in front of him was Buck, then came Sol-leks; the rest of the team was strung out ahead, single file, to the leader, which position was filled by Spitz.

Buck had been purposely placed between Dave and Sol-leks so that he might receive instruction. Apt scholar that he was, they were equally apt teachers, never allowing him to linger long in error, and enforcing their teaching with their sharp teeth. Dave was fair and very wise. He never nipped Buck without cause, and he never failed to nip him when he stood in need of it. As François's whip backed him up, Buck found it to be cheaper to mend his ways than to retaliate. Once, during a brief halt, when he got tangled in the traces and delayed the start, both Dave and Sol-leks flew at him and administered a sound trouncing. The resulting tangle was even worse, but Buck took good care to keep the traces clear thereafter; and ere the day was done, so well had he mastered his work, his mates about ceased nagging him. François's whip snapped less frequently, and Perrault even honored Buck by lifting up his feet and carefully examining them.

It was a hard day's run, up the Cañon, through Sheep Camp, past the Scales and the timber line, across glaciers and snowdrifts hundreds of feet deep, and over the great Chilcoot Divide, which stands between the salt water and the fresh and guards forbiddingly the sad and lonely North. They made good time down the chain of lakes which fills the craters of extinct volcanoes, and late that night pulled into the huge camp at the head of Lake Bennett, where thousands of gold-seekers were building boats against the breakup of the ice in the spring. Buck made his hole in the snow and slept the sleep of the exhausted just, but all too early was routed out in the cold darkness and harnessed with his mates to the sled.

That day they made forty miles, the trail being packed; but the next day, and for many days to follow, they broke their own trail, worked harder, and made poorer time. As a rule, Perrault travelled ahead of the team, packing the snow with webbed shoes to make it easier for them. François, guiding the sled at the gee-pole, sometimes exchanged places with him, but not often. Perrault was in a hurry, and he prided himself on his knowledge of ice, which knowledge was indispensable, for the fall ice was very thin, and where there was swift water, there was no ice at all.

Day after day, for days unending, Buck toiled in the traces. Always, they broke camp in the dark, and the first gray of dawn found them hitting the trail with fresh miles reeled off behind them. And always they pitched camp after dark, eating their bit of fish, and crawling to sleep into the snow. Buck was ravenous. The pound and a half of sun-dried salmon, which was his ration for each day, seemed to go nowhere. He never had enough, and suffered from perpetual hunger pangs. Yet the other dogs, because they weighed less and were born to the life, received a pound only of the fish and managed to keep in good condition.

He swiftly lost the fastidiousness which had characterized his old life. A dainty eater, he found that his mates, finishing first, robbed him of his unfinished ration. There was no defending it. While he was fighting off two or three, it was disappearing down the throats of the others. To remedy this, he ate as fast as they; and, so greatly did hunger compel him, he was not above taking what did not belong to him. He watched and learned. When he saw Pike, one of the new dogs, a clever malingerer and thief, slyly steal a slice of bacon when Perrault's back was turned, he duplicated the performance the following day, getting away with the whole chunk. A great uproar was raised, but he was unsuspected, while Dub, an awkward blunderer who was always getting caught, was punished for Buck's misdeed.

This first theft marked Buck as fit to survive in the hostile Northland environment. It marked his adaptability, his capacity to adjust himself to changing conditions, the lack of which would have meant swift and terrible death. It marked, further, the decay or going to pieces of his moral nature, a vain thing and a handicap in the ruthless struggle for existence. It was all well enough in the Southland, under the law of love and fellowship, to respect private property and personal feelings; but in the Northland, under the law of club and fang, whoso took such things into account was a fool, and in so far as he observed them he would fail to prosper.

Not that Buck reasoned it out. He was fit, that was all, and unconsciously he accommodated himself to the new mode of life. All his days, no matter what the odds, he had never run from a fight. But the club of the man in the red sweater had beaten into him a more fundamental and primitive code. Civilized, he could have died for a moral consideration, say the defence of Judge Miller's riding-whip; but the completeness of his decivilization was now evidenced by his ability to flee from the defence of a moral consideration and so save his hide. He did not steal for joy of it, but because of the clamor of his stomach. He did not rob openly, but stole secretly and cunningly, out of respect for club and fang. In short, the things he did were done because it was easier to do them than not to do them.

His development (or retrogression) was rapid. His muscles became hard as iron and he grew callous to all ordinary pain. He achieved an internal as well as external economy. He could eat anything, no matter how loathsome or indigestible; and, once eaten, the juices of his stomach extracted the last least particle of nutriment; and his blood carried it to the farthest reaches of his body, building it into the toughest and stoutest of tissues. Sight and scent became remarkably keen, while his hearing developed such acuteness that in his sleep he heard the faintest sound and knew whether it heralded peace or peril. He learned to bite the ice out with his teeth when it collected between his toes; and when he was thirsty and there was a thick scum of ice over the water hole, he would break it by rearing and striking it with stiff fore legs. His most conspicuous trait was an ability to scent the wind and forecast it a night in advance. No matter how breathless the air when he dug his nest by tree or bank, the wind that later blew inevitably found him to leeward, sheltered and snug.

And not only did he learn by experience, but instincts long dead became alive again. The domesticated generations fell from him. In vague ways he remembered back to the youth of the breed, to the time the wild dogs ranged in packs through the primeval forest and killed their meat as they ran it down. It was no task for him to learn to fight with cut and slash and the quick wolf snap. In this manner had fought forgotten ancestors. They quickened the old life within him, and the old tricks which they had stamped into the heredity of the breed were his tricks. They came to him without effort or discovery, as though they had been his always. And when, on the still cold nights, he pointed his nose at a star and howled long and wolflike, it was his ancestors, dead and dust, pointing nose at star and howling down through the centuries and through him. And his cadences were their cadences, the cadences which voiced their woe and what to them was the meaning of the stillness, and the cold, and dark.

Thus, as token of what a puppet thing life is, the ancient song surged through him and he came into his own again; and he came because men had found a yellow metal in the North, and because Manuel was a gardener's helper whose wages did not lap over the needs of his wife and divers small copies of himself.

James Thurber

JOSEPHINE
HAS HER DAY

The Dickinsons' pup was a failure. A bull terrier, a female, and a failure. With all of life before her, she had suddenly gone into a decline.

"She is pining away," said Dick, "like a mid-Victorian lady whose cavalier rode off and never came back."

"No," said Ellen, "there's nothing romantic about her. She looks like a servant girl who has been caught stealing a bar pin."

The failure, which was spiritual as well as physical, was unaccountable. Three weeks before, the pup had been bright and waggly and rotund. Ellen, discovering it in a bird store yapping at the virulent green tail of an indignant lady parrot, had called it not only a little plum-plum, but also a little umpsy-dumpsy.

Thus one thing had led to another, including momentary forgetfulness of their original intention to buy a Scotch terrier, mitigation of the crime being a female and a bull terrier, and eventual purchase of the puppy. And now here she had been shipped to their summer cottage in the Adirondacks, covered with gloom and sulphur, the shadow of her former self. They sat above her, the first hour of her arrival, in grim judgment.

"Maybe she's just growing," said Dick hopefully.

"An idiot could see she's shrinking," said Ellen. "Of course, you would have a bull terrier."

"I don't think it is a bull terrier, now," said Dick.

"Well, it *was* a bull terrier. And a female, too! What ever possessed us!"

"You called her a little plum-plum," murmured Dick.

"And you bought her," retorted Ellen. "Well, she'll have to be fed, I suppose. There wasn't a thing to eat in that shipping box." She swooped up the little dog. Now that it was so thin and its excess skin so wrinkly, a curious black edging around its eyes and jaw completed an effect of the most profound melancholy.

The puppy gave only two depressed laps at the milk-soaked bread placed before her, and then wobbled over to the stove in the sitting room, revolved uncertainly three times, and closed her eyes with a pessimistic sigh.

"Well, sir, she's a nice doggy," said Dick generously, starting over to her, "yes, sir, she's a nice doggy." But his wife intervened.

"Mustn't do that," she warned. "It says in the puppy book not to disturb them at their normal sleeping hours." Mrs. Dickinson had bought a lovely puppy book, illustrated with pictures of bright and waggly puppies.

When they went to bed the puppy was sleeping soundly on a bed they fixed for it in a corner of the kitchen, apparently glad to rest after the long, jolting ride. This gladness, however, did not carry her through the night. When the stars were still bright the Dickinsons were aroused from sleep by a clamorous yelping, a wonderfully able and lusty yelping for such a despondent puppy.

"Good Lord!" groaned Dickinson. "Now what?"

"They are bound to yelp the first few nights," said his wife, sleepily.

"Doesn't it say anything in the book about their not disturbing us at our normal sleeping hours?" demanded Dickinson. "Can't I go out and shut her up, do you suppose?"

"No. It would encourage her to expect a response every time she howled, and if you humor them that way they would soon get the upper hand."

"Well, if she keeps this up she'll get it anyway," grumbled Dick as he stuffed the ends of his pillow into his ears. "The National Association of Puppies probably hired the man to write that book."

The next morning at his typewriter Dickinson felt his mind being drawn, slowly but relentlessly, away from the necessary concentration on his work. Something was striking into his brain like the measured thud of a distant drum. "Come . . . come . . . come."

It was his wife's voice emerging from the "secluded room." Gradually a note of exasperation crept in. It was followed by the sound of a slight scratching body being dragged across the floor. There were more "comes," a silence, and more scratching. Then very insistent "comes," but no scratching.

"Is she dead, dear?" called out Dick hopefully.

His wife came into the room, carrying the pessimistic-looking puppy, still saffron with the sulphur that, Dick hazarded, had been showered upon her in the interest of "bug prevention."

"She seems listless," said Mrs. Dickinson. "Do you suppose she was the runt of a litter? The book says to avoid the runts."

"Napoleon was a runt," observed Dick sagely.

"But not of a litter," responded his wife.

"By golly," exclaimed Dick suddenly. "I've got a name for her, anyway! We'll call her Josephine!"

"Josephine?"

"Yes. After the wife of Napoleon, the famous runt. She started well, but got sort of 'down and out.'"

Mrs. Dickinson dropped wearily into a chair and put the puppy on the floor. "Well, I've tried to make this thing come to me all morning, and she just sits and studies the floor with that darned frown."

"Maybe she just doesn't want to come," said Dick.

"That's no reason why she shouldn't. The book says it is almost certain—wait a minute, I'll read it to you." She opened the puppy book which she carried in one hand. "Here: 'It is almost certain that you will be unexpectedly delighted during the very first lesson by their sudden scampering comprehension and that you will perceive they accept your word as law.' "

They watched the little dog study the carpet with incurious attention.

"Lawless little beast," mused Dick. "Look out if she begins to trace the design of the carpet with her paw. It's a sure sign of the end."

"No such luck," said Ellen with some bitterness.

Dick leaned down nearer the puppy. "Josephine!" he cried loudly but firmly. The puppy looked up at him as a little old lady on a train, constantly afraid of being carried past her station, might look at her carefree traveling companions. "She knows her name, anyway, and if she didn't have this awful thing on her mind she might scamper with comprehension, or whatever it is they do."

"Oh, I don't think she has any mind," cried Mrs. Dickinson, irritably. "But there—the book says that calmness, toleration, and self-control are essential in training a puppy."

"That book certainly says a lot for such a little book," commented Dick.

"And for such a little puppy," said his wife scornfully, as she picked up Josephine and carried her outdoors.

As the days went on, Josephine seemed to have taken the stigma of runt literally, as a thing to be religiously lived up to. She remained undeveloped physically and, Mrs. Dickinson declared, mentally, too. She declined, with stolid indifference, in her lesson hour, to adhere to any of the rules of the puppy book. The gay enterprise of "fetch" seemed to create in her no emotion save perhaps a vague wonder as to why the bit of rolled-up paper was tossed about so often.

At length came a cold, drizzly Monday when the Dickinsons gave up. They had had the empress more than three weeks, and her favorite occupation was to sit near the stove, frowning dejectedly and quivering. Once she turned over a cold wood ash with her paw. But that was all.

"Let's give her away to some family around here," said Dick, finally. "They all have lots of kids who would be crazy to have her."

"Yes, and they all have lots of dogs," said Ellen, "big, virile, happy dogs. Besides, no one wants anything but a hound dog, a hunter, in this country."

"I still think we might find some family that would take her. Someone's dog may have died."

"Everybody has two or three dogs. They wouldn't all die."

"They might," said Dick, hopefully. "They might have been playing with the shotgun, not knowing it was loaded."

"Nobody would look at a runt, a female whatnot. They would laugh just to see us walking along with her."

"We won't walk—we'll hire the Blanchards' flivver and tour around hunting a home for her," said Dick, enlarging on his plan.

So the next morning, which dawned with a promising sun, they started off with Josephine, the condemned puppy that wouldn't grow and wouldn't learn, shivering and frowning at the wind in dismay. Every house they passed for several miles had a hound dog, or two or three, big-pawed, long-eared creatures, nosing about the grounds. At last, however, when they tried their luck on a dirt byroad, they saw a small brown house hanging on a hillside, from whose environs came no mournful baying.

Dick stopped the car a little way down the road, bundled the puppy in his arms and got out. There he paused. The bright sun had been overcome by one of those rapidly driving caravans of dark clouds that ride the ranges of the north in the springtime. It began to rain. Dick put up his coat collar.

"Why shall I say we don't want her?" he asked his wife.

"Oh, just act bighearted," she laughed cheerily. "They might think you are Santa Claus."

But Dick's confidence in his own scheme melted rapidly in the rain as he carried the distressed and quivering puppy toward the front gate of the silent, weathered house. As he reached the slate-colored mail box, which winds and rain had beaten to a dejected slant, the puppy began to behave in a singular fashion. Her insides, as Dick described it later, began to go up and down. He turned and carried Josephine quickly back to Mrs. Dickinson.

"She's dying," he said, handing her to his wife.

"Hiccups, silly," said Ellen. "She'll get over them. It's nothing."

"No decent family would want a dog with hiccups," said Dick, firmly.

So they decided to wait until the paroxysms were over. This meant an unusually long wait. Josephine proved to be an accomplished hiccuper. If an interval was so protracted as to give hope of cessation, the next hiccup was so violent as to threaten indefinite continuance. At length Dick knocked the ashes from his pipe determinedly, got out of the car and lifted Josephine down after him. He set her in the road. Then suddenly he leaped at her and barked.

The puppy plunged down into the ditch by the roadside, her ears flatly inside out in abject terror. Dick hurried after her and retrieved a very wet and very muddy Josephine.

"Have you lost your mind?" exclaimed his wife. But Dickinson held up Josephine and examined her carefully. There were no more hiccups.

"By golly," he said, "these home remedies are the goods."

He started for the house again, briskly, the dog under his arm. After a long time the door on which he gingerly knocked opened just wide enough to frame the hard, spare face of a woman.

"Well, what do you want?" she growled ominously. Josephine growled ominously, too.

"I—us—" began Dick. "That is . . . er . . . a . . . can you tell me how far it is to Dale?"

Dale was the town on the outskirts of which the Dickinsons lived, the town from which they had just come. The woman jerked her thumb.

"Two mile," she grunted.

Josephine growled. The woman slammed the door. Dick walked back to his wife.

"She said her husband won't have a dog about the place," he told her. "Seems his father was bitten by one and the boys all inherited this dread."

The kind-faced lady who came to the door of the next place lifted her hands in polite refusal. Land! she already had two dogs! And Rex had a sore on his leg. Did the gentleman know what to do for sores on the leg? Dick said proudly that Josephine never had sores on the leg. "Maybe Eli Madden, the storekeeper in Dale, would take it," added the lady after a moment. "His dog was gored by a bull a week back—well, no—two weeks come Monday. You might try there. Sometimes we think Rex was bit by a woodchuck." Dick said Josephine had never been bitten by a woodchuck, and thanked the lady.

They whirled back over the road to Madden's place, which was not far from their cottage. It happened that school was letting out and the streets were filled with children. They seemed suddenly with economy of movement to surround the Dickinsons as they got out of the car and put Josephine on the ground to stretch. She studied the insurmountable problem of dust with furrowed brow.

"Lookut the lion," yelled one boy. "Woo! woo!"

"What kind of a dog is it, mister?" asked another.

"Aw, that ain't no dog," jeered a third.

"This," said Dick, "is a very wonderful dog. We are walking around the world with it. It eats keys."

"Dick!" said his wife.

"Eats keys?" exclaimed the children in a grand chorus.

"Trunk keys, door keys, padlock keys—any kind of keys," said Dick. "It shakes them well before eating."

Mrs. Dickinson indignantly picked up Josephine and led the way into Madden's store. "Heavens!" she said to her husband as the door shut out the parting jeers of the skeptical children, "Don't ever do that again. It's bad enough to have such a dog without summoning spectators."

She walked to the counter as Eli Madden came into the store from a back room. "We understand," she said sweetly, "that you lost your dog recently and would like to have another one."

"Gored by a bull," said Madden.

"We have a splendid puppy here, an American hound terrier," pursued Mrs. Dickinson brightly. Dick coughed loudly and hurriedly.

"That is—a bull terrier, an American bull terrier," he said. "It's yours for the taking."

"I tell you," said Madden, picking up the dog and examining it as if it were a motor car part, "it's too young a dog for me to bother with. But Floyd Timmons might take her. Never seen a stray yit he wouldn't. If you say so I'll take her up when I go this evening. I drive right past Floyd's place."

"If you don't mind," said Mrs. Dickinson eagerly.

Just then Josephine sneezed.

"She ain't sick, is she?" asked Madden suspiciously.

"She never did that before," exclaimed Mrs. Dickinson.

"May be distemper," said Madden, spitting. Josephine sniffled and looked miserable.

"Well, has she got a cold?" cooed Mrs. Dickinson, picking her up. "Has she got a little cold?"

They arranged with Madden to bring the dog back when it was quite over its cold. But for a week Josephine sneezed and sniffled at frequent intervals and her nose remained very warm. Mrs. Dickinson fixed a warmer bed for her, heated the shawl on which she slept, and placed a blanket under that; she fed her meat broth every day and studied the puppy book carefully for further suggestions. On the eighth day Josephine was over her sniffling and seemed much brighter than she had ever been. She even romped a bit and tugged at an apron string that Mrs. Dickinson playfully shook in front of her. "That's a real bulldog trait," said Dick admiringly.

They took her out into the front yard and the puppy scampered about a little on the grass, and even barked, a plaintive bark, at a vagrant scrap of paper. While they were watching her with amusement a man drove up to the end of the walk in a buggy.

"Have you got a dog here you don't want?" he sang out cheerfully. "My name's Timmons." The Dickinsons rose from where they were sitting on the porch.

"Oh, yes," said Dickinson cordially, "yes—sure."

The man got out of his buggy and came toward the house. And immediately Josephine retreated a step toward her master and mistress and growled, a tiny, funny growl.

"Quite a watchdog," said the man. "Here, pup." He stooped down and picked her up. She yielded with a wild look at Mrs. Dickinson. "You still want to part with her?"

"We really want a Scotch terrier," Dick told him. "That's the reason we are giving her up."

"I see," said the man. He shifted the dog to an easier position.

"Be sure she has a warm place to sleep," said Mrs. Dickinson, following Timmons to his buggy. "We aren't letting her sleep outdoors yet. She doesn't stand cold very well. She has had a cold and just got over it. Maybe you would want to take along the bed she has been using?"

"Oh, we got plenty of warm stuff we can bed her down in. We'll keep her in the kitchen of nights until it warms up a bit."

"She shouldn't be fed much cooked meat," went on Mrs. Dickinson. "If you could see that she got some broth now and then and some lean meat, well cut up. Milk isn't so good for her, so we don't give her much of it."

Timmons tucked the dog into the robe by his side. Josephine peered with questioning eyes first at her new owner and then at her recent mistress.

"Now, I'd be willing to pay you a little something for her. You see, a bull terrier will come in handy with the cows when my other dogs git too old, or die off."

"Not at all," said Dick.

"Oh, no," said Mrs. Dickinson. "Her name is Josephine," she added.

"Oh, that's all right," said Timmons largely. He clucked to his horse and the buggy moved off. They had a glimpse of Josephine peering back from one end of the seat, and then a hand took her out of sight.

"Well, there's a big bother off your hands," said Dick cheerfully, and Mrs. Dickinson nodded assent.

Scarcely an hour of the next few days went by, however, without some remembrance of Josephine coming up between them. There was, for one thing, the puppy book, rather useless now; and the little bed in the corner to stumble over; and the stick with a piece of paper tied on one end that Mrs. Dickinson had made for a plaything; and puppy biscuits scattered about the house and grounds. After a week, however, Dickinson, absorbed in his work, had almost forgotten the dog. Then one noon at luncheon he was outlining to his wife a plot for a story. It was a tale of motored action, set in the mountain ways, with rumrunners and deputy sheriffs and a girl in a red roadster driving madly through it.

"Then," explained Dick, "as they near the old house, which they suppose abandoned, a dog suddenly barks—"

"I do hope he will feed her the right things," said Mrs. Dickinson.

Dick put the brakes to his careening motor cars.

"Who will feed what?"

"Josephine," said his wife.

"Still thinking of the empress, eh?"

"You know a man is so likely to be careless. I wish I could have spoken to his wife about her."

"She'll be all right," said Dick brightly, pushing the dish of strawberry jam nearer to Ellen. "And when we get that Scotty in New York this fall you'll forget all about her and be glad we got her a good home."

"She was mighty bright and fine that last day," mused his wife. "And she growled at him. But still, I suppose she would never grow."

"Never," agreed Dick. "She would have been cut dead by all the best dogs in New York."

"You know," said Ellen, after a time, as she began to stack up the dishes, "maybe it was because I nursed her through that sick spell. . . ." She sighed. Dick knew that sigh.

"How about running up to this chap's farm and finding out how she's getting along?" he asked. "We wouldn't have to let her see us."

"All right," said Ellen quickly. "We could just stop and ask how she is doing and I could tell his wife about the broth and lean meat."

So one afternoon they hired the Blanchards' machine again, stopped at Eli Madden's store to ask the way to Timmons' farm, and drove up the road until they sighted his name on a gray mailbox in front of a large, rambling farmhouse.

Timmons was kneeling in a small room of the barns, sorting over some implements, when Dickinson found him.

"Hello, Timmons," he said, with a worried crease in his forehead, "I just dropped in to ask about the dog."

"Darned if Norb Gibbs didn't take her," said Timmons, rising. "He stopped up here one day and he had a little likker on him. Norb's a mean man. He's the orneriest cuss in these parts. Well, sir, your dog was runnin' 'round in front of the house and Norb took a fancy to her. I said I didn't want to sell, seein' as she'd bin give to us, and he kidded me, like, and said well, no, you wouldn't want to sell a gift dog—he'd just take her. And he did. Laughed when I tried to stop him."

"Can't you have the sheriff or someone get the dog?" asked Dick.

"Sheriff's 'way off to the county seat and his deputy here is a little thick with Gibbs. Nobody ever crosses him much. He's a hard man."

With a gesture of annoyance Dickinson finally asked the farmer to say nothing of the dog's disappearance. It wouldn't do for the thing to be talked about in the village. Then he went back to rejoin his wife.

"Did you see her?" she smiled wistfully.

"No," said Dick, with a great effort at lightness. "But she's doing fine, Timmons said."

"I'm sure she is," said Mrs. Dickinson. "I've told Mrs. Timmons all about her idiosyncrasies. Well . . . I guess we must be getting back home. It looks a lot like rain."

And it did rain, a slow, depressing drizzle, as they returned, Dick hard put to it to affect an easy cheerfulness while his mind turned over and over the quandary into which Josephine—and he—had fallen. Perhaps it might be an easy matter to buy her back for Timmons. But how was he to arrange a meeting without his wife's knowing? Through his speculations ran alternately an undercurrent of exasperation at all this bother about an undesirable pup, a thin-lipped anger at the unknown brute's action, and a faint feeling of dread.

Schemes for recovering the puppy for Timmons kept formulating in his brain. He was still thinking of the problem when, next day, he walked to Madden's store to replenish his supply of tobacco. He decided to query the storekeeper about the haunts and habits of the unseen man who never left his thoughts.

"Norb Gibbs?" asked Madden. "Right there." He jerked his thumb.

Dickinson turned to observe a group of three men in one corner of the store, talking haltingly in low tones, two of them pulling at pipes, the third leaning idly against a counter.

"Oh, Norb!" called Madden.

Before Dickinson could arrange his thoughts or formulate a mode of procedure, one of the smokers turned slightly and looked at the storekeeper.

"Feller here wants to see you," continued Madden.

Dick felt his heart begin to beat rapidly and his hands at the fingertips became a little cold. The man who slouched over to him, scowling, was heavy and stockily set, with a great round face, scarred on one cheek. He was dressed in a corduroy suit, with leather boots laced to the knees. He was tremendously thick through the chest, and his wrists, where they showed under the sleeves, were scraggly black with hair. Dick stuffed his half-filled pipe into his pocket.

"You want me?" asked Gibbs, scratching his neck with big fingers of his right hand.

"Why—" began Dick. "I—yes. That is—you have a little dog I'd like to buy from you if I could."

"What dog?" demanded Gibbs.

"A puppy I believe you got from Mr. Timmons," said Dick with a wry attempt at a smile and a feeling that his voice was a little weak and that his tongue moved thickly.

"I got a pup from him," said Gibbs. "Yes." He planted his feet apart, put his pipe in one corner of his mouth, and pushed his hat a little from his forehead. "What about it?"

"Well," said Dickinson, "I gave him to Timmons and now he—that is—I—my wife and I believe we would like to have him—I mean *her*—back. How is she getting along?" He felt the question was a bit silly and out of place.

"Right well," drawled the big man. "I reckon she'll make me a good dog. Nope. Can't say I want to get shed of her."

"You wouldn't sell her?" asked Dick.

"Nope."

"How about fifty dollars?" Dick hazarded hopefully. The thought went through his mind that maybe Timmons would agree to help buy back the dog. He had offered to pay something for it.

"Don't need no money," said Gibbs curtly.

"I—I want the dog very much," said Dick.

"Well s'posin' you come get her," said Gibbs, his voice rising. "And when you come, come big."

He turned and looked at his companions, as if inviting them to enjoy the scene. They listened silently. Madden, weighing out some nails on a scale, looked up with lifted brows.

"I got a lot o' handy cordwood around the place I use on them as I don't want prowlin' about," continued Gibbs. With a loud laugh he walked back and rejoined his friends. Madden resumed weighing his nails. Dick felt his face grow hot.

"You won't give her up, then?" he asked thickly.

"I said you come and get her," glowered Gibbs, thumbing some tobacco into his short pipe and leaning against the counter. One of his friends moved over and made more room for him.

"Maybe I will," said Dick. He was quivering slightly and his legs felt strangely strained under him.

"And maybe you'll git a clout like I've had to give yer damn dog now and again," laughed the man, brutally, showing his teeth in a grin at his companions.

Things grew a little hazy in front of Dickinson—a little hazy and red. He realized, with something like a flash of fire in his brain, that this strange brute had beaten his dog . . . Josephine. . . .

In two bounds he was across the room, for he was lithe and quick, if no match for the other in strength. Before Gibbs could remove one ankle from the other, as he lounged against the counter—before he could take the pipe from his hand, Dickinson struck him full in the mouth with all the force of a long right swing.

They will talk about the fight that followed for many years to come. Gibbs, knocked to a sitting position between a bushel of potatoes and a heavy unopened barrel, was hampered by his weight and his heavy clothing, but when he got to his feet he rushed for Dickinson like an injured bull. The swoop of the oncoming giant was powerful. Dickinson turned and, in sheer fright, ran to the door. But there he suddenly whirled. With a quick, mad, desperate movement he hurled himself straight at the feet . of the charging form. Not for nothing had he dived like that at football dummies in his school days, battering his body at the swinging stuffed moleskins as a member of the scrub team—the fighting scrubs. He struck the man just above the ankles.

Gibbs went toppling clumsily over him and hit the floor with a terrific crash. He fell near a newly opened box of hammers, glistening with blue steel heads and white-labeled handles. Dick rolled over and picked himself up as the man grasped a hammer and turned on his knees. His throw was wild. The hammer crashed into an unlighted lamp high above a counter, and glass tinkled sharply as the lamp swung and creaked dismally. As Gibbs staggered to his feet, Dick jumped for a chair behind the large stove near one corner of the store. Apparently the man, another hammer in his hand, expected Dickinson to hide behind the stove, for he moved toward him with a triumphant leer on his lips.

But Dickinson did not hide. The fever of battle was on him. He darted out straight at his foe, swinging the chair up from the floor as he came. Gibbs, somewhat startled, brought his hammer stroke down squarely on the upturned legs of the chair, two of which caught him solidly under the arm. He swore and the hammer flew from his hand. His other hand went to an injured elbow as the chair dropped to the floor. He lurched for it, but Dick tackled him again and Gibbs went down on the upturned chair. Dick was behind him. With a well-directed shove of his foot he sent Gibbs into an even more ludicrous entanglement with the piece of furniture. After which he leaped upon him, hammering blows into the back of his head.

"Get up!" yelled Dick in a frenzy. "Get up, you dog stealer, you dog beater, you—!"

The man struggled to a sitting posture and rubbed blood with his sleeve from a gash under his eye. Only his unusually slow movements, his handicap of heaviness, prevented him from closing with Dick before the latter got over his frenzy of yelling, while he stood above the defenseless man, his arms flailing about him.

But now the fellow was on his knees, his heavy hands flat on the floor, and Dickinson's reason returned. He lurched for a counter and began to hurl things at the slowly moving terror. He threw boxes, cans, racks—everything he could get his hands on. Grapefruit and tomatoes began to fly. A can of peaches plumped roundly into Gibbs' chest. A seed rack bounded from his shoulders as the swishing packets clattered about the floor. The scoop of nails which the awe-struck Madden had abandoned for the floor behind the counter sang a rattling song past Gibbs' ear and spattered like shot over walls and floor. But Gibbs got to his feet and, warding off more missiles with the chair, moved forward—relentless, grim, terrible. "I'll kill ye!" he grunted in spasmodic breaths. "I'll break ye in two!"

"Come on!" howled Dick, a challenge that was half wild fear, for the counter was bare of anything else to throw. He backed rapidly for the door. His feet struck the overturned box of hammers and he sat down. Madly he reached out and picked up a hammer and threw it. It went wide. Gibbs, seeing his foe on the floor before him, towered high, flung the chair against the stove with a clanging crash and rushed. And Dick's second hammer, flung with all his remaining strength and a rasping sob in his throat, struck Norb Gibbs directly over the eye. With a look of surprise, he fell to the floor in a heap.

* * *

The next thing Dickinson knew, the store was filled with people. He was aware that a hundred questions were being asked by a hundred forms moving in and out around him. Then abruptly the crowd made way for a figure that moved hurriedly through the door.

"Sheriff Griggsby! It's the sheriff!"

The crazy thought went through Dickinson's mind that this must be a movie. Then he fainted.

When he came to, he found himself firmly held in the arm of the law. His eyes widened and a question formed in his mind. Had he killed Gibbs?

"You're going to take a ride with me," said the sheriff grimly. Dick shivered. "You and me," continued the sheriff, "are going up after that female bitch now. I like a man 'll fight all hell for his dog, even if it *ain't* his."

Late one October day, when the western windows of houses were burning with orange fire, the Dickinsons stopped on a bench in Central Park and sat down. A sturdy little terrier with a sleek brown coat and very bright eyes, whose ancestry, however, would admittedly have been difficult to trace, jumped up and sat down between them.

Presently a lady went by, leading in leash a handsome and well-groomed Scotch terrier, of evident aristocracy.

"There, but for the grace of Gibbs," mused Dickinson, "goes our Scotty."

His wife patted the little terrier by her side and looked after the retreating Scotty.

"Oh," she said, "it makes a good enough dog of its kind."

Mike Resnick

THE LAST DOG

The Dog—old, mangy, his vertebrae forming little ridges beneath the slack skin that covered his gaunt body—trotted through the deserted streets, nose to the ground. He was missing half an ear and most of his tail, and caked blood covered his neck like a scarf. He may have been gold once, or light brown, but now he looked like an old red brick, even down to the straw and mud that clung to those few portions of his body which still retained any hair at all.

Since he had no true perception of the passage of time, he had no idea when he had last eaten—except that it had been a long time ago. A broken radiator in an automobile graveyard had provided water for the past week, and kept him in the area long after the last of the rusty, translucent liquid was gone.

He was panting now, his breath coming in a never-ending series of short spurts and gasps. His sides ached, his eyes watered, and every now and then he would trip over the rubble of the decayed and ruined buildings that lined the tortuously fragmented street. The toes of his feet were covered by sores and calluses, and both his dew claws had long since been torn off.

He continued trotting, occasionally shivering from the cold breeze that whistled down the streets of the lifeless city. Once he saw a rat, but a premature whine of hunger had sent it scurrying off into the debris before he could catch it, and so he trotted, his stride a little shorter, his chest hurting a little more, searching for sustenance so that he would live another day to hunt again and eat again and live still another day.

Suddenly he froze, his mud-caked nostrils testing the wind, the pitiful stump of a tail held rigidly behind him. He remained motionless for almost a minute, except for a spasmodic quivering in one foreleg, then slunk into the shadows and advanced silently down the street.

He emerged at what had once been an intersection, stared at the thing across the street from him, and blinked. His eyesight, none too good even in the days of his youth and health, was insufficient to the task, and so he inched forward, belly to ground, flecks of saliva falling onto his chest.

The Man heard a faint shuffling sound and looked into the shadows, a segment of an old two-by-four in his hand. He, too, was gaunt and dirty, his hair unkempt, four teeth missing and another one half rotted away. His feet were wrapped in old rags, and the only thing that held his clothes together was the dirt.

"Who's there?" he said in a rasping voice.

The Dog, fangs bared, moved out from between buildings and began advancing, a low growl rumbling in his throat. The Man turned to face him, strengthening his grip on his makeshift warclub. They stopped when they were fifteen feet apart, tense and unmoving. Slowly the Man raised his club to striking position; slowly the Dog gathered his hind legs beneath him.

Then, without warning, a rat raced out of the debris and ran between them. Savage cries escaped the lips of both the Dog and the Man. The Dog pounced, but the Man's stick was even faster; it flew through the air and landed on the rat's back, pulping it to the ground and killing it instantly.

The Man walked forward to retrieve his weapon and his prey. As he reached down, the Dog emitted a low growl. The Man stared at him for a long moment; then, very slowly, very carefully, he picked up one end of the stick. He sawed with the other end against the smashed body of the rat until it split in half, and shoved one pulpy segment toward the Dog. The Dog remained motionless for a few seconds, then lowered his head, grabbed the blood-spattered piece of flesh and tissue, and raced off across the street with it. He stopped at the edge of the shadows, lay down, and began gnawing at his grisly meal. The Man watched him for a moment, then picked up his half of the rat, squatted down like some million-years-gone progenitor, and did the same.

When his meal was done the Man belched once, walked over to the still-standing wall of a building, sat with his back against it, laid his two-by-four across his thighs, and stared at the Dog. The Dog, licking forepaws that would never again be clean, stared back.

They slept thus, motionless, in the ghost city. When the Man awoke the next morning he arose, and the Dog did likewise. The Man balanced his stick across his shoulder and began walking, and after a moment the Dog followed him. The Man spent most of the day walking through the city, looking into the soft innards of stores and shops, occasionally cursing as dead store after dead store refused to yield up shoes, or coats, or food. At twilight he built a small fire in the rubble and looked around for the Dog, but could not find it.

The Man slept uneasily and awoke some two hours before sunrise. The Dog was sleeping about twenty feet away from him. The Man sat up abruptly, and the Dog, startled, raced off. Ten minutes later he was back, stopping about eighty feet distant, ready to race away again at an instant's warning, but back nonetheless.

The Man looked at the Dog, shrugged, and began walking in a northerly direction. By midday he had reached the outskirts of the city and, finding the ground soft and muddy, he dug a hole with his hands and his stick. He sat down next to it and waited as water slowly seeped into it. Finally he reached his hands down, cupping them together, and drew the precious fluid up to his lips. He did this twice more, then began walking again. Some instinct prompted him to turn back, and he saw the Dog eagerly lapping up what water remained.

He made another kill that night, a medium-sized bird that had flown into the second-floor room of a crumbling hotel and couldn't remember how to fly out before he pulped it. He ate most of it, put the rest into what remained of a pocket, and walked outside. He threw it on the ground and the Dog slunk out of the shadows, still tense but no longer growling. The Man sighed, returned to the hotel, and climbed up to the second floor. There were no rooms with windows intact, but he did find one with half a mattress remaining, and he collapsed upon it.

When he awoke, the Dog was lying in the doorway, sleeping soundly.

They walked, a little closer this time, through the remains of the forest that was north of the city. After they had proceeded about a dozen miles they found a small stream that was not quite dry and drank from it, the Man first and then the Dog. That night the man lit another fire and the Dog lay down on the opposite side of it. The next day the Dog killed a small, undernourished squirrel. He did not share it with the Man, but neither did he growl or bare his teeth as the Man approached. That night the Man killed an opossum, and they remained in the area for two days, until the last of the marsupial's flesh had been consumed.

They walked north for almost two weeks, making an occasional kill, finding an occasional source of water. Then one night it rained, and there was no fire, and the Man sat, arms hugging himself, beneath a large tree. Soon the Dog approached him, sat about four feet away, and then slowly, ever so slowly, inched forward as the rain struck his flanks. The Man reached out absently and stroked the Dog's neck. It was their first physical contact, and the Dog leaped back, snarling. The Man withdrew his hand and sat motionless, and soon the Dog moved forward again.

After a period of time that might have been ten minutes or perhaps two hours, the Man reached out once more, and this time, although the

Dog trembled and tensed, he did not pull away. The Man's long fingers slowly moved up the sore-covered neck, scratched behind the torn ears, gently stroked the scarred head. Finally the Man withdrew his hand and rolled over on his side. The Dog looked at him for a moment, then sighed and lay up against his emaciated body.

The Man awoke the next morning to the feeling of something warm and scaly pressed into his hand. It was not the cool, moist nose of the dogs of literature, because this was not a dog of literature. This was the Last Dog, and he was the Last Man, and if they looked less than heroic, at least there was no one around to see and bemoan how the mighty had fallen.

The Man patted the Dog's head, arose, stretched, and began walking. The Dog trotted at his side, and for the first time in many years the nub of his tail moved rapidly from side to side. They hunted and ate and drank and slept, then repeated the procedure again and again.

And then they came to the Other.

The Other looked like neither Man nor Dog, nor like anything else of earth, as indeed it was not. It had come from beyond Centauri, beyond Arcturus, past Antares, from deep at the core of the galaxy, where the stars pressed so close together that nightfall never came. It had come, and had seen, and had conquered.

"You!" hissed the Man, holding his stick at the ready.

"You are the last," said the Other. "For six years I have scoured and scourged the face of this planet, for six years I have eaten alone and slept alone and lived alone and hunted down the survivors of the war one by one, and you are the last. There is only you to be slain, and then I may go home."

And, so saying, it withdrew a weapon that looked strangely like a pistol, but wasn't.

The Man crouched and prepared to hurl his stick, but even as he did so a brick-red, scarred, bristling engine of destruction hurtled past him, leaping through space for the Other. The Other touched what passed for a belt, made a quick gesture in the air, and the Dog bounced back off of something that was invisible, unsensible, but tangible.

Then, very slowly, almost casually, the Other pointed its weapon at the Man. There was no explosion, no flash of light, no whirring of gears, but suddenly the Man grasped his throat and fell to the ground.

The Dog got up and limped painfully over to the Man. He nuzzled his face, whined once, and pawed at his body, trying to turn it over.

"It is no use," said the Other, although its lips no longer moved. "He was the last, and now he is dead."

The Dog whined again, and pushed the Man's lifeless head with his muzzle.

"Come, Animal," said the Other wordlessly. "Come with me and I shall feed you and tend to your wounds."

I will stay with the Man, said the Dog, also wordlessly.

"But he is dead," said the Other. "Soon you will grow hungry and weak."

I was hungry and weak before, said the Dog.

The Other took a step forward, but stopped as the Dog bared his
· teeth and growled.

"He was not worth your loyalty," said the Other.

He was my—The Dog's brain searched for a word, but the concept it sought was complex far beyond its meager abilities to formulate. *He was my friend.*

"He was my enemy," said the Other. "He was petty and barbarous and unscrupulous and all that is worst in a sentient being. He was Man."

Yes, said the Dog. *He was Man.* With another whimper, he lay down beside the body of the Man and rested his head on its chest.

"There are no more," said the Other. "And soon you will leave him."

The Dog looked up at the Other and snarled again, and then the Other was gone and the Dog was alone with the Man. He licked him and nuzzled him and stood guard over him for two days and two nights, and then, as the Other had said he would, he left to hunt for food and water.

And he came to a valley of fat, lazy rabbits and cool, clear ponds, and he ate and drank and grew strong, and his wounds began to scab over and heal, and his coat grew long and luxuriant.

And because he was only a Dog, it was not too long before he forgot that there had ever been such a thing as a Man, except on those chilly nights when he lay alone beneath a tree in the valley and dreamt of a bond that had been forged by a gentle touch upon the head or a soft word barely audible above the crackling of a small fire.

And, being a Dog, one day he forgot even that, and assumed that the emptiness within him came only from hunger. And when he grew old and feeble and sick, he did not seek out the Man's barren bones and lie down to die beside them, but rather he dug a hole in the damp earth near the pond and lay there, his eyes half closed, a numbness setting in at his extremities and working its way slowly toward his heart.

And just before the Dog exhaled his last breath, he felt a moment of panic. He tried to jump up, but found that he couldn't. He whimpered once, his eyes clouding over with fear and something else; and then it seemed to him that a bony, gentle hand was caressing his ears, and, with a single wag of his tail, the Last Dog closed his eyes for the last time and prepared to join a God of stubbled beard and torn clothes and feet wrapped in rags.

Farley Mowat

A MESS OF SKUNKS

Almost every dog eventually runs foul of a skunk. Most dogs learn something from the experience. The wiser ones may conclude that it is common sense to defer to skunks in future, and even those tykes that habitually pursue danger tend to be more circumspect after their first encounter.

Mutt was no fool. Neither was he feckless. And this makes it even more difficult to explain his inability to grasp the fact that mixing it with skunks was unrewarding. The only beast I know of that makes a practice of attacking skunks is the great horned owl, but it has almost no sense of smell, it does not normally live in houses, and furthermore it eats the skunks it kills. Mutt, on the other hand, could smell very well, he habitually lived in houses with other and more sensitive beings, and he did not eat raw meat.

I can find no rational explanation for his foolhardy attitude toward skunks. The fact remains that there was hardly a time after he had passed his second birthday when he was not accompanied by that familiar odor—sometimes of great intensity, sometimes no more than a faint, but unmistakable, miasma in the air.

It is noteworthy that his first encounter was delayed until he had entered his third year.

It happened in July. In order to escape from the savage heat of the prairie summer, we had hauled the caravan north into the forested part of Saskatchewan, to a small resort on Lotus Lake. Mother's association with the Church of England in Saskatoon had gained us the privilege of being permitted to park our caravan on an isolated beach that belonged to the church and that was normally reserved for members of the cloth and their immediate families.

It was a most pleasant site. The caravan was close to the water's edge, on a small and private cove. There was a dock, equipped with a diving board, for our personal use. Privacy was the watchword of the place and we took advantage of it to swim without benefit of bathing suits. We were circumspect about this, for we had no wish to shock our hosts—but we were equally determined not to wear clothing in the water, unless driven to it.

We were soon driven to it. There were many young people at the beach: young divines, and young daughters of elderly divines. They were all, apparently, addicted to moonlight canoe expeditions, and our secluded cove seemed to draw them irresistibly. A canoe at night can be a stealthy thing, and much of the pleasure of our nocturnal bathing was spoiled by the irritating necessity of keeping a careful watch.

My parents felt this irritation more than did Mutt or I. Mutt had nothing to hide in any case, and I had almost as little to worry about, for I was then only twelve years old. My parents began to forgo the pleasures of the unclothed evening swim, but Mutt and I were more resolute.

Mutt was a fine swimmer, and he greatly enjoyed diving. He actually preferred to go in off the board, and it was a remarkable thing to see him bouncing slowly up and down at the end of the plank, gaining momentum for his leap.

One evening he and I left the caravan, with Mutt well in the lead. By the time I reached the shore, Mutt was halfway out the plank, and it was then too late for me to do anything but watch.

The board was already occupied. A skunk was lying at the tip of it, dreamily staring down into the moonlit waters at the schools of plump little rock bass that flickered back and forth. Innocent as he then was, Mutt nevertheless showed incredible obtuseness—the first intimation of this curious weakness that was to become so painfully familiar to us in the future. He made no effort to investigate the skunk. He simply lowered his head, flung his ears back out of his eyes, and charged.

The skunk's defensive blast caught Mutt from a range of not more than three feet, and deflected him to one side so that he ran off into space with considerable momentum and hit the water a good distance from the dock. I think that he must have actually gone right over the canoe, for when he surfaced—screaming with pain and outrage and lashing the water blindly—it was the seaward side of the canoe that his paws encountered.

I had not been aware of the canoe until then, but neither I nor any other resident of that section of the beach was left long in ignorance of its proximity. Mutt's efforts to scramble aboard completed the discomfiture of a young couple who had already reaped the wind. The man, who was a clergyman-to-be, showed a nobility of soul commensurate with his vocation. But the young lady was the daughter of a vicar—and she ran true to type. Her language was not churchly and, although I had spent much time among the tough boys who lived on the wrong side of the tracks in Saskatoon, I was impressed by this girl's virtuosity.

Our annoyance with Mutt was tempered by a degree of gratitude, for during the remainder of our stay at Lotus Lake we were untroubled by young love under the moon. Our little bay had acquired a hard name locally.

We had had our period of grace; for after this first encounter, Mutt and skunks became almost inseparable. There was a brief surcease for us during the heart of winter, but with the first spring days and the emergence of the skunks from semihibernation, we took up our cross once more.

It seemed to make no difference where we might be, in the geographical sense. On one occasion we welcomed spring in an area where no skunk had been reported for thirty years. There were skunks that spring; so many of them that the locals marveled, and spoke in hushed voices of a visitation.

Mutt's popularity was endangered by this affinity for skunks and there were people who may have wished in their hearts that Mutt had never been. Foremost among them must have been the undertaker's assistant in Happy Home Cemetery on a June day in 1939.

Happy Home lies in the heart of metropolitan Toronto and is isolated from the nearest wilderness by miles of asphalt desert. Yet it is very green and, in the spring at least, lovely with bird song. It is well named, for with its trees and brooks it is an oasis in the gray desolation of the city. Almost anyone could be happy there. Certainly Mutt and I found it a happy place, for it was our retreat during the blighted year we lived in Toronto. We spent many hours in Happy Home, looking for birds or simply meandering among the willow trees. We harbored the dream that some day we should encounter another exile like ourselves—a pheasant, or perhaps a rabbit.

The June day of which I write was one of sweltering heat such as only the perspiring body of a great city can generate. Mutt and I had fled to Happy Home, where we wandered among the acres of gleaming headstones and imagined that each concealed the burrow of a gopher. We thought often of gophers and always with a sense of sad regret; and if we mentally populated Happy Home with the little rodents, we meant no disrespect.

After a time I heard the song of a yellow warbler in the trees beside an artificial pond, and I pursued it while Mutt, who was never much of a bird watcher, went snuffling off in the hope of finding a more interesting trail. Unexpectedly he found one and with a shrill yelp took up the chase. I turned in time to see his white rump wink out of sight among the trees.

"Rabbit—at last!" I thought and, not to be denied a glimpse of it, ran after Mutt.

When I emerged on the level burying ground beyond the pond, Mutt was already several hundred feet away. As usual his queer, lopsided gallop gave him the appearance of having a strong starboard drift, like a small sailing vessel with insufficient keel beating to weather against a stiff breeze. In point of fact Mutt was heading dead into the wind, and sailing fast and straight.

It was a light wind, but sufficient. It came gently over Mutt and on to me, and I halted in my tracks. I was a little bitter. I had so much wanted it to be a rabbit.

As I took in the scene ahead of me I saw a somber, penguinlike assembly in the distance. The sight of the funeral party shocked me into acute apprehension. I whistled frantically for Mutt, but he was deaf. Hot with the passions of his old madness, he loped resolutely on.

By this time he was rapidly approaching the funeral party from the rear, while the mourners remained all unaware. However, my whistle must have reached the ears of the undertaker's assistant, for this tall young man slowly turned about. He did not see me, for I had already resigned him to his fate and had retreated into the shelter of the willows. But he saw Mutt approaching like a dog possessed.

The skunk was a small one, probably born that spring, and it must have been distrait in those unfamiliar surroundings. Trotting nervously among the stones, it veered erratically as it attempted to decide whether Mutt or the large man in the top hat was the more formidable enemy. It was inconspicuous, and I doubt if either the undertaker's assistant or Mutt actually saw it. Mutt at least knew it was somewhere near. The assistant did not. He had begun to run toward Mutt, intending, evidently, to head him off. His mouth was working, and he looked indignant.

The three of them came together with perfect timing under the lee of a pink marble shaft.

It was a distressing incident, but not without some compensation, for it convinced my parents that the heart of a great city was not our chosen ground. It was directly responsible for my father's decision to move us to a village some forty miles away.

This village seemed like an odd little place to me, fresh from the untrammeled west. There was an atmosphere about it of dusty corsets, creaking whalebone, and the aggressive gentility which is assumed by so many eastern Canadian hamlets. I found myself ill at ease among the boys and girls of my own age, and I was baffled by their sober and resolute attitude of hostility. I did not understand the watchfulness of our neighbors and I could not find the means to penetrate the barrier of suspicion that surrounded us.

Our new house itself was probably much to blame for our cold reception. Its previous tenant was a sculptor, one who had little talent for his art, but who concealed this deficiency by being pugnaciously and preposterously "modernist." The house was cluttered with his experiments and we suspected that he had sold the place as the only possible means to escape from the children of his contorted ego. Most of the pieces were passionless repetitions of a nude female torso, but many others were quite inscrutable. I recall one piece in particular. It was a wood carving that resembled nothing quite so much as a bicycle wheel that had been savaged by a determined railroad locomotive. It was called *Holes in the Soul*. For some reason it irritated Mutt, and when we had banished it to the back yard, he would stand and stare at it by the hour with his teeth bared slightly in a grimace of distaste.

Nevertheless, it was not the character of the vanished sculptor that had damned the house. It was simply the fact that he was an artist, and therefore in almost any part of rural Ontario he and his domicile would have been suspect. There can be few places in the world that are so resolutely determined to defend themselves against any suspicion of culture as the villages of central Ontario. They have a steadfastness that St. Ignatius Loyola himself would have admired.

We blamed the house for the frigidity of our reception. Yet, despite its lurid past, it suited us. Its front door looked out sedately over the outskirts of a sedate community; but then the house rambled backward through sagging passages until the back door opened on an unconstrained stretch of countryside. These tangled fields were a haven, not only to Mutt and me, but to many other beasts—not least of which was a family of skunks.

We saw them almost daily, and with a special quality of resignation we awaited the inevitable; but, almost incredibly, it did not come. I do not know why this was so, except to hazard a guess that Mutt too must have felt the weight of our social isolation, and did not even have the heart for skunk conflict. There was no overt act of war, yet we remained uneasy and alert until the first heavy frosts assured us that the skunks had retreated to winter quarters.

The earth-floored basement of the house contained our winter supply of vegetables and preserves, together with a barrel of Prince Edward County apples. There was an outside cellarway, barred by a pair of massive doors, and these we closed and calked against the advent of the frost. My father and I spent a Sunday carefully sealing up the many holes in the foundation, and when we had finished hardly a mouse could have got in—or out.

We had with us at this time a maid named Hannah whom we had brought from the west. She was one of those solid, grain-fed women for which the prairies are justly famous, but she was not gifted with much brain. Nevertheless, she had a vivid, if erratic, imagination. No leap into the fantastic was beyond her, and when she noticed that the level in the apple barrel was falling with unusual rapidity, she exercised her imagination and laid a formal complaint against Mutt. It was a fascinating picture that she conjured up: Mutt, scrunched into the barrel, industriously munching apples through the long winter nights. We were almost sorry that it could not have been so.

With Mutt ruled out, Hannah was temporarily at a loss. But not for long. She was a persevering woman, and one day while we were having breakfast she startled us with a unique solution to the problem of the diminishing apple supply.

She was handing Father his plate of oatmeal, and with it she volunteered the information that:

"Them ghosts is et half all them apples up."

Father toyed delicately with the phrase for a little while, then dropped his eyes to his plate with a slight shudder. I was made of sterner stuff. "What ghosts?" I asked.

Hannah looked at me with placid condescension. "Them apple ghosts," she explained patiently. "He's et about most of them apples you got from Prince Henry's house and just kind of lays the cores around."

After this we were driven to make a full investigation, and Hannah was relieved, yet at the same time disappointed, when I was able to tell her that we had no ghosts—only a skunk.

He was a mild-mannered fellow who must have led an unexceptional life up until the time he got himself locked up for the winter in our cellar, for there was no odor clinging to his fur. He was under the preserve cabinet when the beam of my flashlight found him. He showed no resentment, but only blinked his eyes and ducked his head in an apologetic sort of way, neither frightened nor aggressive. He must have long since assumed that we meant him no harm.

For a few days we were foolish enough to consider ways and means of removing him. Mutt, apprised of the skunk's presence, had a plan of his own and he was so anxious to put it into effect that he almost scratched a hole through the cellar door. We did not trust his discretion.

We soon recovered our reason and concluded an armistice. We had far more apples than we needed, anyway, and since the skunk was obviously amicable, we decided to live and let live.

Things worked out very well. The skunk stayed in the vegetable room, ate such apples as he required, and bothered no one. We came to accept his presence tranquilly, and it was no uncommon thing for one of us to be rummaging in the potato bin, while a few feet away the skunk munched on an apple.

This harmonious state of affairs would probably have continued until spring, when the skunk could have gone voluntarily on his way, had it not been for a man whom none of us has ever met. I do not even recall his name, but I know that he lives in one of the southern states of the Union. He is of the expert genus who write books and articles about birds and animals with such assurance that the reader is convinced the author must be privy to the thoughts of the beasts. Shortly before Christmas this man published an article about skunks in one of the more famous sporting magazines.

I read the article, and was deeply impressed. The author had developed a foolproof principle for handling skunks, and he was generous enough to share his secret with the world. The essence of his method was a garden hose. He had discovered that a jet of water directed a few inches behind a skunk, and in such a way that the stream was deflected slightly upwards after contact with the ground, would safely move any skunk that ever lived. Reasoning skunk-fashion, the author explained why the method was so effective. "The skunk," he wrote, "under the impression that his discomfort stems from a natural source, will move briskly away without attempting retaliation."

Christmas holidays were due to begin in a week's time, and I was bored and disgruntled by the last days of school. Hannah and I were alone in the house, for my parents were in Oakville on a three-day state visit to my father's family. I put down the magazine and went downstairs.

In my own defense I can plead that I was least systematic. My first move was to pry open the outer cellar doors, and only then did I enter the basement and attach the garden hose to the laundry tap. When the hose was spluttering satisfactorily, I moved into the vegetable room and, having located the skunk, I brought the stream to bear upon the hard ground immediately to his rear.

There was a startled scurrying and the skunk shot out of the vegetable room, and sought sanctuary behind the old-fashioned hot-air furnace. I pursued him with the jet, chivying him slowly toward the cellarway and the open doors. He went, unhappily, but, even as my author had foretold, without attempt at retaliation. Victory was nearly mine, when I glanced up at the cellarway to assure myself that there was no obstacle in the skunk's way—and behold Mutt's face framed in that square of cold blue sky.

I realized that he was poised to leap, and my reason was momentarily paralyzed by a vision of the certain consequences which must follow. Acting instinctively, I raised the hose in order to bring it to bear on Mutt, but I forgot that the skunk was in the way, and the lifting stream caught him fair amidships and bowled him over. I hit Mutt too, but by then it was too late to matter much.

Tears of rage and agony were blinding me, but I no longer cared. While Mutt and the skunk skirmished around the perimeter of the basement I followed them, brandishing my hose indiscriminately. Sometimes a ricochet blast from the skunk would send me staggering back toward the cellar doors. Raging, I returned each time to the fray. Back and forth we went, into the vegetable room, behind the furnace, under the cellar stairs. The air grew murky and the single electric light bulb shone dimly through a rich and yellow haze.

Mutt was the first to call it quits, and to leave by the outside entrance. The skunk, exhausted and suffering from its own potency, followed close behind. I was left alone, the hose still spurting in my hand.

The silence was intense, until from somewhere far above me I heard Hannah's stentorian tones.

"Mother of God!" she cried. "Mother of God—I go!"

In the event, Hannah did not go, but only because we were so far from Saskatchewan, and she had no idea which way her lost home lay. There was no escape for any of us.

There was misery in that house for a long time. Despite the bitterness of the weather, the furnace had to be turned off, since it sucked up tangible fumes from the basement and circulated them freely. Even with all windows and doors wide to the winter winds, the basement remained a haunted place. The skunk oil, mixed with water, had permeated the dirt floor so deeply that I doubt if even yet it has entirely passed away.

As for our neighbors, far from rallying to us in this time of need, they drew yet further off. One of them was overheard to express the opinions of them all.

"What else can you expect," she said with smug complacency, "from people who would live in a place like that?" It was clear that skunks and culture were inextricably bound up together in her mind.

My parents did not punish me directly, but they insisted that I go back to school on the day after the event. I pleaded for mercy, but to no avail. I went off very slowly, and with bowed head.

It was a frigid day, and the school was overheated. Before the opening exercises ended, there was not an occupied desk within five feet of me. I sat on, a self-conscious island of misery, until at last the teacher—Miss

Leatherbottom was her name—called me forward and handed me a note. It was succinct. "Go home," it said.

The humiliation of that experience was a heavy load to bear, yet it was as nothing to the spiritual torment inflicted on me a few years later by Mutt and his passion for skunks.

My maternal grandparents owned a cottage and a lake in the remote highlands of Quebec, and here the family was accustomed to forgather in the summer months. It was a place of pleasant memory on the whole, for it was free of the horrors of most summer resorts. There were no thundering outboard motors piloted by fat and foolish men, hell bent at fifty miles an hour for nowhere. There were no rows of shoddy matchbox cottages clustered cheek by jowl along the shores—the sylvan counterpart of city slums. Instead there was a single unobtrusive log house, an even more unobtrusive boathouse and sleeping cabin combined, and then nothing but the ancient hills, black-shrouded in their forests, overlooking and solacing the waters of the lake.

For Mutt and me it was a blessed place after the horrors of Toronto, and the almost equal horrors of the Ontario village. It was also the scene of my first love.

The girl was the daughter of a wealthy doctor who owned a cottage on a nearby lake. She was not insensible to me, and she showed some taste for poetry, which, in those days, was my chief interest. I wrote verse of a somewhat melancholy vein, but she would listen patiently while I declaimed it. I recall one passage that seemed particularly to move her. It concerned the fate of an abandoned lover, and one verse went like this:

> Still his unseeing, dull and lidless stare
> Earnestly scans the long blue upper air;
> A corpse's gaze—save where a clinging fly
> Scuffs busily across the sunken eye.

I thought it was effective, and so did the young lady. Great things might have resulted from our association had it not been cruelly terminated within a week.

Each Saturday there was a dance in the nearby village of Kazabazua (you will find the name on any reputable map) and I had arranged to take my girl to one of these affairs. The explosion of a summer thunderstorm on the Friday night before the dance did not distress me as I lay abed, dreaming my dreams. Yet that storm had a shattering effect upon my life.

In its first wild rush it uprooted and toppled a magnificent old pine that had stood for two hundred years not far from the house. In its fall the old tree uncovered a family of skunks who had their burrow beneath its roots. The skunks immediately sought other shelter, and found it under the floor of the cabin where a space had been left open for ventilation purposes. Unfortunately, Mutt, whose fear of thunderstorms was still pathogenic, had long since occupied this sanctuary, and there was hardly room for all the new arrivals.

My parents and grandparents were sitting by the open fire when the old tree came down. Grandmother, who always tended to take acts of God as personal affronts, was outraged. She began to pace up and down the room, peering out at the wreckage as she passed the window, and she made a little speech.

"I refuse," she cried, "absolutely refuse to plant another tree. What point is there when they just blow down again?"

Grandfather wisely let this pass, but my parents were still trying to digest it when all four of them became aware of new sounds of natural discord. From below their feet came strange and muffled scuttling noises, some snorts, a muted growl or two, and a weird sort of chattering. Grandmother, who was seldom at a loss, was mystified. She pounded the floor with her foot and cried out:

"Now what's all that about?"

The floor boards were not tight. There was no subfloor and Grandmother got her answer. With a callous indifference that I still find hard to forgive, my four elders promptly evacuated the house to seek shelter in the sleeping cabin by the lake. They left me to my fate.

I woke soon afterwards. The turmoil underfoot was mounting in intensity and the stench was breathtaking. Clutching an eiderdown, and burying my nose in its folds, I scuttled to the door and began slithering down the steep path to the lakeside. The thunder muttered overhead and rain drove down with a vicious intensity. A flash of lightning illuminated my path and I beheld the white and frightened face of a skunk two or three paces ahead of me, and evidently in full flight from the Donnybrook under the house.

I could not stop. My bare feet scratched for traction on the steep and muddy path, but it was useless. Both the skunk and I were on a greased slide, and we fetched up at the bottom of the path almost inextricably entwined with one another in the eiderdown.

They would not have me in the sleeping cabin. Grandmother held the door shut. "He's your damned dog—go and sleep with *him*," she said, and there was an unaccustomed bitterness in her tone.

As a matter of fact I slept under an upturned rowboat for the rest of the night.

At the crack of dawn on Saturday morning I was in the lake laboring with a cake of carbolic soap. At intervals during that awful day I experimented with tomato juice, kerosene, turpentine, and pumice stone, and although none of these was wholly effective, by evening I was relatively free of skunk. At least, I could no longer smell myself, and with this false assurance of purity I set out to escort my young lady to the dance.

We had no more than a few hundred yards to walk together, and there was a good evening breeze, so that by dint of remaining downwind from her, I escaped immediate detection. But she was on the alert.

"Hurry up," she said once. "I think there's a skunk somewhere about." There was something close to panic in her voice, and I was surprised by it, for she had always seemed a singularly fearless sort of girl.

The dance was in a barn and it was well attended. Oil lamps supplied the illumination, and boosted the already volcanic temperature to an almost unbearable extreme. I knew before the first dance ended that I would not get away with it. Yet by dint of refusing to sit out any dances, and by moving very quickly through the press, I kept the finger of suspicion from pointing directly at me. I was considerably relieved when, after half an hour of it, my girl clutched me by the arm and in a strangled whisper implored me to take her home at once. She kept peering at the other dancers and there was a stricken look about her.

Once out of door I felt that I should confess my guilt. My lady had a sense of humor, and I was sure that she would be amused by the affair. We paused on the path outside her cottage, and I told her all.

She gasped, turned from me, and ran as if pursued by all the fiends of hell. And never to this day have I looked upon her face again.

It was her older brother who explained. I met him in the local general store one day and insisted that he tell me why his sister would no longer receive me.

He laughed heartily.

"You don't know?" he asked, and it was a stupid question, for how could I have known? "Oh, but this is rich! It's skunk stink," he cried when he could master his mirth. "Jane's allergic to it—it makes her break out in hives—all over—and they last a month!"

Joyce Harrington

DISPATCHING BOOTSIE

It was easy to *think* about killing Bootsie. But doing it, in real life, was a little more difficult. Let me tell you about Bootsie. She was Texas born and bred. Li'l ol' cow patty of a town in West Texas, as she liked to say. Her daddy was a wildcatter, and until she was seven years old, again according to her, they lived on pinto beans and the gusher that was going to come in tomorrow or the next day. All she would ever say about her mother was that she turned sorrowful and died before she had any fun out of life.

Well, gushers sometimes do come in, and Bootsie's daddy hit a whopper. What she remembered about that was first of all eating the first steak of her life and afterward getting sick, and second of all being sent off to boarding school. She learned a lot there. Not really how to read, although she could manage movie magazines if she tried real hard and there happened to be a picture of Burt Reynolds on the page; nothing whatever about math. As she liked to say, "I got so much money, I don't need to count it." No. What Bootsie learned at school was how to dress and what to do with her hair and how to spend all that money.

She also learned to smoke, both plain and funny cigarettes, drink whiskey, and generally behave like a Texas wild woman. Anything she wanted, she only had to ask Daddy.

I met Bootsie about a year after her Daddy had died. Killed in the crash of his private jet on the way to Acapulco. Five of the flower of Texas womanhood went with him. Daddy was evidently making up for all those years of pinto beans and sorrow. Bootsie, as she liked to tell it, cried a whole lot. But after the visit of the lawyers, she perked up. School, by that time, was boring and there was nothing else for her to learn. What she needed, she decided, was a change of scene.

She flipped a coin between New York and Los Angeles—she had learned enough geography to know that one was on the East Coast and the other on the West and both were large and expensive—and it came up in an easterly direction. She rented a suite in the Barclay and moved in with a little Tex-Mex woman named Josefa who washed and ironed her underwear, and a big old hound dog named Bruce. So Bootsie and Bruce and Josefa were set to see New York.

Josefa didn't speak a word of English, but she was quick and intelligent and got along with Bootsie by anticipating her every need. The few times she didn't, Bootsie would yell and scream and throw things at her until she got the drift. Example. "Dammit, Joe! Didn't I tell you yesterday to get rid of those flowers? The damn things remind me of funerals. Out! Out! Out!" And the vase would go sailing across the room, barely missing Josefa where she stood pretending to cower but with her dark eyes flashing malice. "Sí, sí, querida. Hija de puta. Las flores. Pronto. ¡Que tu murieras mil veces con tanto dolor! Gracias a Dios." That's the way it was between them. Screeching abuse on one side, and muttered maledictions of a thousand painful deaths on the other. Bruce terrorized the bellhops and all the other East Side dogs he met on his walks with

Josefa. He adored Bootsie, and even when she kicked him was content to roll over at her feet and grovel abjectly.

I haven't told you what Bootsie looked like. She once showed me a snapshot of herself taken in pre-gusher days back in the cow-patty town. It was straight out of *The Grapes of Wrath,* not that she'd ever read the book or seen the movie, or even heard of the Dust Bowl. She stood, knobby-kneed, staring into the camera in a dress that was a couple of sizes too small and obviously had not been in the vicinity of soap and water for most of its career. Her feet were bare and her toes curled in the dust of the yard of a small shack that was out of focus in the background. Her hair hung lank about her face, chopped off in a homemade Dutch bob. But it was her eyes that dominated the picture. It was a black-and-white print, so you couldn't tell that the eyes were the color of Delft tiles, bright and pitiless blue. What stared at you out of the picture was a hunger so vast it seemed capable of devouring the earth for an appetizer and going on from there. That was then.

When I met her she was nothing short of gorgeous. The hair was a sleek shimmer of white-blonde silk falling straight to her shoulders, and the eyes had learned to sparkle and invite. She was tall, almost as tall as I am, and could have been bony and awkward. But the school had taught her to move gracefully, and nature had endowed her with just enough flesh in all the right places to make her entrances into Regine's the highlight of any evening. If you looked closely at her face, you might have seen the emptiness there, the total void, the hunger that still hadn't been assuaged. But few people ever got past the eyes, the cheekbones, the pale flawless skin, the wide mouth that laughed and chattered and told the grossest kind of jokes with an air of perverse innocence lent her by her West Texas drawl. And, of course, she absolutely reeked of money.

Did I think of playing Pygmalion to her Galatea? There might have been something of that in my attraction to her. I did take her to museums where she sniggered at Matisse and laughed out loud in front of Picasso's Guernica. "I never saw no horse that looked like that," she said. At concerts she fell asleep, and plays bored her into fidgets and twitches unless they were simple-minded musicals that she could leave with a song or two tinkling around inside her skull. What, then, did she like about

New York? Because like it she did. "I purely love this town," she often said.

Well, for one thing, she could, and did, spend more money faster on everything from worthless junk to priceless antiques than she could do in the whole of Texas including Neiman-Marcus. She made a weekly pilgrimage to Cartier's the way ordinary mortals go to the A & P. Gucci's, Saks, Bergdorf's, and a host of snobby little boutiques in between grew to know and love her. She went slumming in Bloomingdale's. When I cautioned her about overspending and tried to lecture her on the wisdom of making sound investments, she quickly put me in my place.

"Don't you fret your li'l ol' head about that, honey. My lawyers take care of all that boring stuff."

And they did. Two of them flew up regularly from Texas, stiff men with bulging briefcases who out-Brooks-Brothered anything seen on Madison Avenue. They didn't like me, and I'm sure that behind closed doors they advised Bootsie to turf me out. By that time I was more or less permanently installed in the hotel suite, although I still kept my tiny one-room walkup in case this one went the way of my not-so-sound investments and the rather large sum of money left me by my dear deceased maternal relative.

And what, you might well ask, did fun-loving Bootsie see in me? I often asked myself whether, in her eyes, I fell into the category of worthless junk or priceless antique. I admit that she was the answer to an aging playboy's prayer. I bear a distinguished name, but the wealth that had made that name a household word had long since vanished. I am handsome, a claim I make with all due modesty, in a civilized kind of way quite different from the rawboned cowboys she must have known back home. No great thinker, but I did offer her a smattering of culture which awed her even as she resisted and mocked. Or was it simply that out of all the men who pursued her, I was the only one who was old enough to be her father?

Whatever the attraction, it was there and real enough for her one day to say to me, while we were sitting around the hotel suite trying to decide what to do for the evening, "Hey, why don't we get married?"

Bootsie was like that. Spur of the moment, and if it seemed like a good idea, we did it. It seemed like a good idea to me.

"Why, indeed, not?" said I, with visions of sugar plums liberally coated with dollar signs dancing in my head.

The wedding took place just as soon as Bootsie had time to go shopping for a whole new wardrobe, and we gave a party that became as legendary as Truman Capote's Black and White Ball. Just three hundred of our closest friends. When the dust settled and we were about to gather up our luggage and Bruce and Josefa for an extended European honeymoon tour, I got the biggest shock of my life. I was looking forward to doing Europe in style. It had been a long time since I had stayed at the Ritz or basked on a Riveria beach. I had promised Bootsie all the great museums and cathedrals; I could almost taste the fabulous food and wine.

She mooched into the hotel suite, scowled at her matched set of Louis Vuitton luggage, kicked the nearest piece, and said, "Get on the phone, honey, and cancel the trip."

"But the reservations are all made," I protested. "The whole tour is planned."

"Who wants to go to boring old Europe?" she said. She pronounced it "Yerp."

She called Josefa out of the tiny room where she spent hours watching soap operas in Spanish and told her to start unpacking.

"What's wrong?" I asked. "If you're tired we can postpone the trip a few days."

"I ain't tired." She pronounced it "tard." The West Texas drawl was beginning to grate on my nerves. I was prepared to overlook certain things in exchange for certain other things, and she was reneging on her side of the bargain. She frowned as if puzzling over a vexing problem in higher math. "It just seems to me that we'd be spending an awful lot of my money to go round seein' a bunch of places that I don't want to see in the first place."

I can't tell you how ominous that sounded to me. And it was merely a foretaste of things to come. I got on the phone and called the travel agent.

The next day the lawyers appeared. I had thought that now, as Bootsie's husband, I would be privileged to sit in on their deliberations, but such was not the case. They invited me to take myself off while they conducted Bootsie's business. Their briefcases seemed exceedingly well stuffed this time. Bootsie merely shrugged and turned her blue eyes helplessly upward. Bootsie was about as helpless as a Sherman tank. I went to the movies.

When I got back, the lawyers had departed and Bootsie was looking thoughtful. That in itself should have warned me, but I was determined to be my usual carefree self.

"Well, my dear," I said, "where shall we dine tonight? Le Veau D'Or? Lutece? Or perhaps a simple meal from room service?"

"I sent Joe out for some Big Macs." She gazed at me, all bright blue enthusiasm. "You were so right, honey. I've been spending way too much. From here on in we're going to economize."

I managed to swallow that one without gagging, but felt entitled to a question or two. "We're . . . you're not broke, are you, my dear?"

She laughed. "Shoot, no! There's still plenty in the old kitty. But I'm a married lady now, and I got to think about the future. I want there to be something left over at the end of the trail."

A horrid suspicion crossed my mind. I was not temperamentally suited to fatherhood nor, although we had never discussed it, did I think that Bootsie was attuned to the patter of tiny feet. But the possibility existed and would account for her strange behavior. There was nothing to do but ask.

"Bootsie, are you, by any chance, pregnant?"

Again she laughed. "Naw. When I get ready to breed, I'll let you know right off. But I do have a little surprise for you. Them lawyers are pretty smart fellows, and they know people all over the place. They been worrying about you, and now that we're married, they feel like they have to look out for you. They found a job for you. Ain't that nice?"

"A job?" I repeated stupidly. "But, Bootsie, dearest, I've never worked at a job. I wouldn't have the foggiest idea what to do."

She came to me then, cuddling into my arms like a little girl and fixing me with her bright blue innocent stare. "That's all right. You'll figger it out. And you'll be making enough money so's I won't have to give you an allowance any more. Think what a saving that'll be. But you won't have to start until we move."

"Move!"

"Oh, yes. Do you realize what this hotel is costing me? I'm going to start looking for an apartment tomorrow. They say that rents are very cheap in Queens."

"Queens!" I was reduced to monosyllables. Marriage had turned my spendthrift Bootsie into a miser. Queens, indeed! I wondered if those smart lawyers could arrange an instant annulment of the marriage, but her next words started me thinking in another direction.

"There's one more thing. They didn't want me to tell you this but you're in it, so I told them you had a right to know. I made my will. It felt real creepy to think about dying, but they said I ought to do it. So I did."

I stroked her silky head and told her not to talk about it if it disturbed her. I told her that the lawyers were absolutely right in advising her to make the will, but that now she should just forget all about it and we'd live a long happy life together. Tears of happiness rose in her blue eyes, and she kissed me while I pondered how and how soon I could arrange to benefit from her arrangements.

Josefa came in carrying a large white sack reeking of onions and greasy meat. Bruce bounded at her heels, as excited by the smell as I was repelled by it. I excused myself from the feast on the grounds of a slight headache and I went to lie down with my thoughts. As I closed the bedroom door, I heard Bootsie say, "I purely love Big Mac's, don't you, Joe?"

I managed to dissuade Bootsie from her plan of settling in Queens by appealing to her newfound parsimony. Every place we looked at involved a double fare, both bus and subway, for me to get to work. Oh, yes. I had decided to go along with the destiny her lawyers had mapped out for me. For the time being. We found a gloomy apartment on the Upper West Side, in what the corner newsstand proprietor assured me was a high-crime district. Josefa was delighted. At the hotel she could only communicate with the occasional Puerto Rican bellhop. Here, she chattered for hours with neighbors and shopkeepers, and even invited some of her new friends in for coffee. I didn't object, although I might have, on the grounds that some of them might have relatives adept in the arcane art of breaking and entering.

Bootsie loved the role she was playing. Happy little housewife with a husband who went off every morning on the subway and returned every evening to a meal that she had prepared with her own hands. Her cooking was dreadful, but I pretended to enjoy it. I encouraged her to take Bruce for long walks in Central Park, both day and night. I told her she'd never be a true New Yorker until she learned to ignore traffic lights and dodge her way across streets in defiance of the speeding taxis and lumbering buses.

I pooh-poohed her concern that the building had no doorman and the elevator was a self-service one. And I told her that the roof was the ideal place for sunbathing. But while all around her, people were being mugged, knifed, shot, strangled in lonely elevators, run over by berserk drivers, pushed off roofs, and otherwise disposed of, Bootsie remained unscathed. I realized that if I expected to benefit from Bootsie's will, I would have to take a more active role. It was not enough to place her in jeopardy and then wait for the action to start.

In the meantime Bootsie's greatest happiness was the receipt of her monthly statement of account. She loved to watch her nest egg grow. She had sold off all her jewelry, returned as many of her expensive clothes as she could and peddled the rest to friends, got rid of the priceless antiques and the worthless junk at a handsome profit, and handed every cent over to the lawyers to reinvest. We lived off her income, but only a small portion of it, and she was constantly looking for new ways to cut corners.

She stopped going to the hairdresser and her dark roots began to show. Her face and body grew pudgy from the starchy meals she prepared. Pinto beans appeared three or four times a week. And the hunger in her blue, blue eyes grew ever more intense and frightening. If I'd had any sense at all, I would have left her then. But there was always the will, the will and the growing nest egg that was achieving the dimensions of something deposited by a dinosaur.

The job that Bootsie's lawyers had found for me was with a brokerage firm in Wall Street. Although I had frittered away some youthful years at Harvard achieving a gentleman's C and so could be considered one of the tribe, I was nothing more in the eyes of the firm than a glorified messenger boy. This suited me fine. While all around me serious younger men pondered portfolios and munched Mylanta tablets, I carried my Mark Cross attaché case (a gift from Bootsie before true parsimony set in) around the city and was reasonably happy in my work. My taxi fares went on the expense account and I had lots of free time.

Free time in which to brood. There had to be some way of dispatching Bootsie and coming into my inheritance. I could poison the pinto beans, but poison, I believed, was easily traced and I would surely be viewed as the most likely Borgia. It had to look like an accident or like one of the many wanton senseless murders that occurred with alarming regularity in our beloved town.

I thought about hiring a dispatcher—one of the small army of gun-toting desperados that the newspapers claimed infested our streets—but how to find one whom I could trust, one who would trust me and do the job on credit until Bootsie's will gave me the resources to pay for her demise? I even considered recruiting Josefa, whose maledictions those days had reached new heights and were conducted in a rapid screeching Spanglish, Josefa having taken the trouble of learning a few pungent items of New York street talk. The burden of Josefa's harangues seemed to be that Bootsie was stingy (agreed), that Bootsie was fat and lazy (becoming more true every day), and that she, Josefa, was homesick and wanted to return to West Texas if only Bootsie would give her the airfare.

Bootsie wouldn't. The terms of Josefa's employment, as far as I could gather, resembled indentured servitude. She received no salary. When times were good and Bootsie was spending freely, Josefa enjoyed the high life and only fulminated to keep in practice. But now that Bootsie was scrimping on everything, even Bruce's dog food, Josefa's curses achieved a kind of desperate poignancy. She might make a good ally.

As a kind of insurance I began smuggling in tidbits for Bruce. Bootsie had cut him off from meat entirely, doling out small portions of a substance that looked like wood chips and smelled like burnt rubber. Bruce grew thin and despondent, and developed a bad case of dandruff. The first time I brought him a snack, half a Sabrett's hot dog with onion sauce, he rewarded me with a limp thud of his tail and a grateful, if weak, bark. After that, I always had something in my attaché case for him when I got home from work, and soon he was my devoted friend. I doubted if I could convince him to rend Bootsie limb from limb, but at least he might not interfere if I had to do a little rending myself.

But still, the appropriate means eluded me and the frugal days stretched into penurious months. I thought often of Bootsie's beautiful money gathering mold and interest when it could be the comfort and solace of my declining years. Something would have to be done. When, on an October evening, I came home to find that she had replaced all the light bulbs with low-wattage numbers which she had no doubt stolen from the subway station, I knew the time had come.

Bruce bounded at me out of the gloom of the shabby flat and I slipped him a chunk of liverwurst that I'd bought at a deli on my way home. Josefa was in the kitchen, stirring the eternal pinto beans and singing dolefully of *amor desleal.*

"Where's Bootsie?" I asked her.

"Gong hout," she told me, adding, "I hope she fall en el río and drowng."

Stifling an urge to shout "Me, too," I reprimanded Josefa for her disloyal sentiments and opened the kitchen window to let out the thick aroma of the beans. The thick aroma of the garbage tossed into the airshaft by our neighbors came in, but I left the window open anyway. By craning outward and upward I could see the purple sky over Manhattan and the hazy reflection of the bright lights that should by rights be mine. I sat on the window sill and dreamed of all the gastronomic delights that were being served reverently by attentive waiters all over town, while a sullen Josefa clunked clumsy crockery onto the rickety table covered with a crumb-laden plastic cloth where we now took our meals. It was too much to be borne.

Bootsie came in while my mind's eye was combing the menu at Le Perigord. She carried a heavy sack which she thumped down onto the drainboard and then came over to me.

"Hi, honey," she cawed, "I just figgered out another way to cut down on our expenses." Beaming with pride, she flung a heavy arm across my shoulder. Her coat gave off the fusty fug of second-hand shops. "You know that vegetable market down the block? Well, they let me pick over all the stuff they were going to throw away. For free."

"Rotten apples?" I protested.

"Just a few spots. Josefa can make applesauce."

Behind her back Josefa made obscene gestures and mouthed indignities.

"And another thing," she rambled on "now that we're living so cheap, it's about time we started living on *your* salary. That way, we can save all *my* money so we'll be in really good shape at the end of the trail."

She bent to kiss me. All I did was flinch. There was something so repellent to me in her greedy blue eyes, her lips which had not seen lipstick these many months, her lank brown hair that smelled of cheap laundry soap, that I couldn't help myself. Where was the slender, sweetly perfumed, exquisitely made-up blonde girl whose money I had fallen in love with less than a year ago? As I say, I flinched, and in so doing overbalanced and felt myself slipping off the window sill on the wrong side of the window. I grabbed. It was only natural. And the nearest thing to grab for was Bootsie's arm. There was some thrashing about. I can't describe it; I was in the midst of it. But when it was over, I was sprawled on the kitchen floor and Bootsie was nowhere in sight.

Until I looked out the window.

"Ooong!" came Josefa's voice over my shoulder, "She gong! You killing her!"

Indeed. She seemed quite dead, lying there among the dented beer cans and defunct perambulators at the bottom of the airshaft. But I would have to make sure before I could allow my fledgling hopes to take flight. Bruce came to the window and whined. I turned to Josefa. "It was an accident. You are a witness to that."

"Sí, sí. Han haccident. La pobrecita. You fight her. She fall hout."

"No. I was falling and she tried to save me. You saw it happen."

She smiled, a dreadful knowing gap-toothed grin. "Oh, sí. I saw. You want to heat now?" She began spooning beans into two of the three bowls.

"God, no! I have to call the police."

She shrugged and sat down at the table. There was no telephone in the apartment—Bootsie had declined to bear the expense—so I had to go down to the corner bodega where the public telephone was strategically positioned adjacent to the crates of dried codfish. I dialed 911 and waited. Nothing. I tried again. Still nothing, not even a crackle on the line to show a sign of life.

"The phone is dead," I said to the shopkeeper, a thin young man standing importantly behind a counter crowded with candy bars, shoelaces, and gum.

"Yess," he said, "two, three months now they don't come to fix him. They say too much breaking the phone, taking the money, no more phone. What can I do? People around here don't have so much phones in the house. They come here to make phone call, buy a beer, buy a soda. buy some candy for the babies. Good for business, no? Now the phone don't work, they don't come. I'm only trying to make a living. Would I break the phone? I got a special on bananas today. Ten cents a pound. Take some home to your kids."

I looked at the special bananas, Bootsie would have loved them, soft and brown-spotted, lying dispiritedly in a cardboard box.

"No, thanks. I need to call the police. My wife is dead."

"¡Ay, Dios!" The young man quickly turned his attention to important business at the back of the store. I could have walked off with all his shoelaces and overripe bananas.

"Where can I find a phone?" I called after him.

He reappeared from behind a stack of six-packs, making shooing motions with his hands. "Closing up now. Go away, please. No phone here."

Back on the street I wondered which way to turn to make my call. The idea of Bootsie dead was still so new to me I needed official confirmation to make it real. And I needed to make sure that the call came from me, establishing her death as an accident. Well, it *was* an accident. Even though I'd been thinking about ways to kill Bootsie, I hadn't thought about this way. It just happened. If it hadn't been Bootsie at the bottom of the airshaft, it would have been me. Not that there'd been any kind of struggle—me trying to push her out, or her trying to push me out—oh, no, officer, just a sad case of a loving wife trying to help a loving husband, and the whole thing ending in tragedy. I put on my tragic face and glanced back up the block.

A squad car was just pulling up in front of the building and Josefa came rushing out to meet it.

I ran. It would never do to let Josefa have the first word. Her command of English was imperfect and she might give the wrong impression.

She saw me coming and screeched, "¡Asesino!"

I peered into the police car. Two faces peered back at me, one black and one unmistakably Irish. With any luck their command of Spanish was imperfect and they wouldn't understand that Josefa had called me a murderer. I grabbed Josefa and clutched her head consolingly to my shoulder. "There, there," I murmured, "everything will be all right. Just shut your mouth and I'll cut you in on the will."

"The will? Ah, el testamento!" Her words were a breathy whisper flavored with pinto beans and onions. "She leave it all to me, you go to jail, you no make trouble. Mi abogado me lo ha dicho."

"Well, your lawyer was wrong." Canny Josefa. Obviously she had gained the impression that she benefited from Bootsie's will, and she wanted to make sure that I would be in no position to contest it. Some ally! I'd have to set her straight, and quickly. "Bootsie made a will when we got married," I whispered into her oiled black hair. "She left all her money to me. She told me so. Behave yourself and I'll take care of you."

Black eyes squinted up at me. "¿Verdad?"

"I swear."

After a flood of Spanish invective Josefa nodded and said, "Hokay." Then she turned on the waterworks.

The two policemen had by this time gotten out of the car and come over to see what the trouble was.

"We got a call about a body at the bottom of an airshaft at this address?"

I glanced at Josefa. She nodded. "I use the telephone of el super." She cried some more.

"My wife," I told them. "It's terrible. She fell out the window. Right before my eyes. There was nothing I could do."

Josefa howled agreement.

We trooped through the building and out the back door. I saw the round pale face of the super staring at us from the grimy window of his basement apartment. From other windows surrounding the airshaft other faces stared down. The night was very quiet and no one threw any garbage. After a while an ambulance came and took Bootsie away.

When it was all over, after all the questions had been asked and poor Bootsie's remains had been shipped back to West Texas for burial next to those of her sorrowful mother and her high-flying daddy, the lawyers came to town. Josefa and I were summoned to their hotel suite for the reading of the will. The suite reminded me poignantly of my early days with Bootsie, days that I would be able to relive, alas, without her at my side.

The lawyers' first words were ominous.

"This is a very odd will," said one.

"Odd, but quite legal," said the other.

"Get on with it," I snapped. If they wanted to continue to administer the estate, they had better get used to treating me as their employer and learn to show respect.

"Well," said Lawyer One, he of the round gold-rimmed spectacles and thinning hair, "she left everything to Bruce."

"Bruce!" My voice, I'm embarrassed to say, emerged in a squeak. "That's impossible! You can't leave money to a dog!"

"Well, you can," said Lawyer Two, long-faced and mournful. "You can and she did. But don't worry. You're both taken care of."

Josefa tugged at my sleeve. "¿Que dice?" she demanded, her dark eyes showing signs of an approaching storm.

"Relax," I told her, and settled back to hear the news.

Lawyer One bent his gold-rimmed spectacles to the blue-backed document and spouted about ten minutes of legalese. For another ten minutes Lawyer Two translated. What it boiled down to was this. Bootsie's fortune, and it was considerable, belonged to Bruce, for his lifetime. Josefa and I were appointed his guardians. We were charged with responsibility for his health and well-being. We were to buy him a ranch in West Texas and anything else his doggy heart desired.

We were to live on the ranch with him, keep him company, find him a suitable lady dog to share his bliss, and in general make his life a canine heaven on earth.

My agile mind instantly perceived that Bruce would require a Rolls-Royce for trips to the vet, a swimming pool to cool off in on hot West Texas afternoons, a tennis court on which to chase balls and a nine-hole golf course in which to bury bones, not to mention a bevy of nubile serving wenches to curry his coat and stuff him with dog biscuits.

If, by chance, Bruce predeceased his guardians, the money was to go to create the Bootsie and Bruce Foundation for Indigent Wildcatters. If either Josefa or I died before Bruce did, the surviving guardian was to have total control of the estate, subject to the advice of Goldrims and Longface. And if we both kicked off before the mutt, the legal beagles took charge.

I looked at Josefa. She looked back murderous questions.

"How old is Bruce?" I asked her.

She shrugged incomprehension.

"¿Cuantos años tiene Bruce?" Out of necessity, I'd picked up a smattering of her lingo. She understood more than she let on and liked to pretend ignorance when it suited her.

"Dos, tres años. Yo no sé," she replied, followed by a muttered stream of abuse a la Zapata.

I nodded my agreement to the lawyers. A two- or three-year-old dog has another ten or twelve years in him. Contesting the will would take up precious time, during which I would be forced to work. Although Bruce was presently enfeebled by city life and poor diet, I would soon get him back in peak condition in the salubrious air of West Texas. And somehow, during his lifetime, I would figure out some way of gaining full control of Bootsie's money, or die trying. It was worth a period of exile.

The ranch is huge, acre upon acre of sagebrush and saguaro, and the ranch house sprawls like an adobe version of Buckingham Palace. Josefa lives in her wing, surrounded by freeloading relatives. I live in mine, solaced by a rotating troop of imported beauties that make the Dallas Cowgirls look like bovine battleaxes. Ever since Josefa sent over her cousin Elizondo and his machete (I bear an interesting scar; Elizondo bears a chastened look at the imprint of my teeth on the remains of his left ear), my wing has been guarded by day and night Pinkertons. Josefa, unaccountably, believes I have attempted to poison her pinto beans and has posted platoons of grinning cousins in the kitchen and outside her quarters.

Bruce lives in oriental splendor in luxurious kennels out back. His every desire is satisfied. He is attended by emissaries of both camps, nymphs and caballeros. Occasionally Josefa and I meet on neutral ground in Bruce's domain, when we both thoughtfully examine his muzzle for the first telltale sign of gray hairs, his joints for arthritis, and his fine brown eyes for the clouding over of cataracts. The years are going by.

It's a dog's life.

Jim Kjelgaard

PAT'TIDGE DOG

As soon as the train lurched to a stop at the little wayside station, Danny Pickett jumped from the express car. He turned to help Red, but almost before he had turned around the big Irish setter had leaped to the cinders beside him. Danny started at once for the beechwoods that began almost where the railroad property ended. The fuss and glamor of the dog show were behind them, Mr. Haggin had the blue ribbon and silver cup that Red had won. But Danny had the dog. And now they were home, here in the Wintapi.

Red paced sedately beside the boy. Nominally the property of Mr. Haggin, a millionaire sportsman who had built an estate in the wild Wintapi, the red dog had attached himself to Danny, son of a hillbilly trapper and farmer. Together, they had trailed and killed an outlaw bear that no hounds had dared follow. Mr. Haggin, an understanding man, had figured out for himself exactly what had happened on that bear hunt, had known that both Danny and the dog had played fair throughout. He had hired Danny to take care of Red, his first duty being to handle him at the New York show. But now that responsibility was ended and Red was Danny's, to do with as he saw fit.

Once in the woods, screened by trees from prying eyes that might see and comment on any letdown in dignity, the boy broke into a wild run. It seemed an eternity since he had seen the rough shanty where he and his father lived, smelled the good scent of streams, forests, and mountains, or had any part at all in the only life he had ever loved. With the dog racing beside him Danny ran over the jutting nose of a mountain, trotted up a long valley, climbed the ridge at its head and descended the other side. He ran in almost a perfectly straight line through the beechwoods to his father's home. Ross Pickett would naturally be out scouting around the ridges on a fine day like this.

But his father's four hounds strained at the ends of their chains and bayed a vociferous welcome. Danny grinned at them and watched Red go up to sniff noses with Old Mike, leader of the hound pack. The three younger dogs sat on their haunches and awaited quizzically their boss's reaction to this dazzling, red-coated invader of their home. But the setter did not falter and Mike knew too much about other animals not to know when one was his superior. The two dogs wagged stiff tails, and Mike sat down to blink indifferently at Danny. Red was accepted.

Danny chuckled and tickled the old hound's tattered ears while the three pups begged for attention. Red sat back with his head cocked to one side and watched jealously. The boy stooped and unsnapped the chains. Wild to be free after a long day's confinement, the four hounds went in a mad race across the field. They came tearing back and were away again. Red raced with them, but wheeled and came back when Danny whistled. The boy tickled his silken ears.

"Leave 'em go," he said. "Leave 'em go, Red. They'll find an' tree somethin' an' Pappy'll get it when he comes in. But you got mo' impawtant work to do, Red. Youah a pat'tidge dog."

The setter walked beside him when Danny went into the house. Outside, everything had been warm sunshine. But inside, where only glancing sunbeams strayed through the single-paned windows that Ross Pickett had set in the walls of his shanty, a definite chill prevailed. Danny stuffed tinder into the stove, lighted it, and added wood when it was blazing. He pulled aside the burlap curtain that hung over the cupboard and took out a pot and skillet. Red trotted beside him when he went out to the springhouse for a piece of pork that Ross had left there to cool and returned to the house to lie in the center of the floor while Danny cooked the meat.

A little before sundown the setter got up and went to sit before the door. Three minutes later there was a heavy tread on the porch and Ross Pickett came in.

"Danny!" he exclaimed. "I knowed you was home on account I heer'd the haouns a 'bayin'. I whistled 'em in an' they come back wi' me. They had a little coon up, an' coons ain't prime yet."

"Hello, Pappy! It shuah is good to be home. You been scoutin' out a trap line?"

"Yup. Stoney Lonesome Ridge fo' foxes. Ought to be a nice take of pelts this yeah; they's lots of rabbits fo' pelt animals to eat off."

But the shine in Ross's eyes belied the workaday talk, and the warm glow inside Danny was far too intense ever to be put into words. He and his father had been so close for so long that they felt and acted and almost thought alike. Each was lost without the other, and now that they were together once more, they could be happy again.

Danny said with affected carelessness that could not hide the enormous pride he felt, "I fetched the Red dog home. Theah he is."

"Well, so you did!" Ross whirled about as though he had just noticed the magnificent setter. "That is a dog, Danny! I reckon you'n him must of cut some swath in Noo Yawk, huh?"

"Red did in the dog ring. He got some prizes fo' Mistah Haggin."

"How'd you like Noo Yawk, Danny?"

"Gosh, I dunno. It's nice but it's awful big. It's a right smart place for them that likes it, but I'd ruther abide in the Wintapi."

Ross Pickett was on the floor beside Red. His expert hands strayed over the dog's back, his legs, his withers, his chest. Danny waited breathlessly until his father finally rose.

"Danny," he said profoundly, "if that Red dog's got a nose, he's got evah'thin' any six dogs should have."

Danny's heart leaped. "He smelt you when you was still three minutes away."

"I should of knowed it," Ross breathed. "He run that big killah heah right into the groun'. Danny, that dog is goin' to be the best vahmint killah we evah had."

Danny turned away. All the joy of homecoming was suddenly gone, and a smothering hand came to still his singing heart. He should have known what his father would say. But until now it had never occurred to him that hunting to Ross meant hunting bears, wildcats, foxes, and raccoons. Every other kind of hunting was only to get meat. Danny gulped. Maybe he could explain but he felt before he started that his father wouldn't understand.

"I—I guess Red ain't goin' to be no vahmint dog."

"Huh! What use would you put such a dog to?"

"Well, he could hunt pat'tidges." Danny continued desperately, "Look, they's some things a man can do an' some he cain't. Makin' Red hunt vahmints would be like makin' one of Mistah Haggin's blooded hosses do a mule's work. It's right in Red's blood to be a pat'tidge dog."

"Oh! Maybe Mistah Haggin tol' you to make him hunt pat'tidges?"

"Mistah Haggin didn' say nothin'," Danny answered miserably. "I jus' know Red's a pat'tidge dog."

"How do you know it?"

Danny tried and failed to put into words some of the things he had learned on his brief visit to New York and in his association with Mr. Haggin. Always before he had accepted his father's notion that a dog was a dog, something to be bent to the will of its master. But that wasn't so. For thousands of years there had been special dogs for special functions— dachshunds for entering badger holes and subduing their occupants, greyhounds for coursing swift game, malemutes for sledge work, and only when you knew something of their blood lines could you really appreciate the fascinating story of dogdom. It was in Red's blood to hunt birds, and partridges were the only game birds in the Wintapi. Making him hunt anything else would verge on the criminal. But how to explain all this to his father?

"I jus' know it," Danny said miserably. "Red on'y hunted the beah on account he thought it was goin' to hurt me."

"Well—if that's the way you feel—" Ross's voice trailed off. He sat down stiffly and ate his supper. After eating, he helped wash the dishes and took his accustomed chair beside the stove. He ignored Red when the big setter tried to thrust his nose into his cupped hand and sensing the rebuff, Red went back to Danny. The boy sat moodily alone. Ross was deeply hurt. He wouldn't have been had his son been able to furnish a good reason why Red should be a partridge dog. But Danny himself knew of no reason save that the setter had been born to hunt partridges. And that sounded silly.

They went silently to bed.

The next morning when Danny got up Ross had already gone. He had taken one of the hounds with him.

But he hadn't asked Danny to go along.

Partridge season was not open yet, but it was legal to have dogs afield for training. Danny's heart was heavy within him while he ate a lonely breakfast. After eating he opened the door and a flood of the sparkling October sunshine came spilling in. Red rushed outside and went over to sniff noses with Mike. He came galloping back to Danny and reared to put both front paws on the boy's chest. Danny pulled his silky ears and stroked his smooth muzzle. If only his father were there to see Red as he saw him! Then the autumn and the sunshine worked their magic. It was enough to be afield with Red. Pappy would understand in time.

Crisp frost-curled leaves crackled underfoot when the pair entered the beechwoods. Red went racing among the trees as a gray squirrel stopped his busy digging for nuts and leaped to a tree trunk. But when Danny whistled he stopped, turned around and came trotting back. For a space he walked beside the boy. Then he leaped a few feet ahead and stopped in his tracks.

He stood with his body rigid and his tail stiff behind him. With a quick little rush he went a dozen feet and stopped again. Then, in a slow, steady stalk, he advanced a hundred feet and stopped on a knoll. He raised one forefoot, stiffened his body and tail.

Danny murmured very softly, "Easy. Easy theah, Red."

The dog trembled, but held his point. Danny leaned over and, as quietly as possible, brushed the leaves from a half-buried limb. He hurled it into the brush at which the setter was pointing and a lone partridge thundered up. The dog took three nervous steps forward, but halted at Danny's, "Back heah, Red."

Danny's knees were suddenly weak and he sat down. Red came over with wagging tail and grinning tongue, and the boy passed both arms about his neck. Starry-eyed he sat still, in his mind living and reliving the scene he had just witnessed. It was a thrill to hear hounds strike a trail, to listen to them baying their quarry and their final frenzy when they cornered it. But this! The hounds were good workmen, but the setter was an artist. And not even Ross had suspected how keen his nose really was.

The early autumn twilight was just dimming out the day when the pair arrived home. A light in the window told that Ross was there before them. Danny opened the door and Red slid unobtrusively in to lie on the floor. Ross, who was standing over the stove, turned and spoke briefly.

"Hi-ya."

"Hi-ya," Danny replied and busied himself setting the table.

From time to time he stole a furtive glance at Red, and once looked with mute appeal at his father's back. But his eyes squinted slightly and the same stubborn mouth that was his father's tightened in grim lines. Once more he looked at Ross's back—and found the determination not to speak until his father did melting away. He tried to make his voice casual.

"Wheah'd you go today, Pappy?"

"Out."

Danny flushed, and his face set in lines ten times more stubborn. Maybe his father thought he couldn't make a pat'tidge dog out of Red. He'd show him! He'd prove such a dog was much more valuable than a hound, and that setters were as practical as hounds. Danny hesitated. Proving to Ross that a partridge dog was worth the food he ate wasn't going to be any harder job than moving Staver Plateau with a tin shovel!

After supper Danny sat by Red for a while, stroking his ears and tickling his chin. But Ross ignored the dog completely. As though he understood, the setter had nothing to do with him.

Partridge season and the first snow came together. Ross as usual was up long before daylight and away on his trap line. When Danny went out with his shotgun and Red he looked longingly at the tracks in the snow. Always before he and his father had gone trapping together. Resolutely he shouldered his gun and walked in an opposite direction, toward the pine and hemlock thickets where the partridges would certainly be seeking a refuge from the storm.

They approached a thick growth of hemlock and Red ranged ahead. He came to a stiff point, and Danny edged up.

A partridge burst out of the hemlocks, showing itself for a split second between the branches, and Danny shot. A ruffled heap of brown feathers, the bird came down in the snow. Red hesitated, turned around to look at Danny as though asking for instructions.

The boy waved a hand forward. "Go on," he said. "Get him."

Red padded forward and stood uncertainly over the fallen partridge. He looked up, then back at the bird.

"Give it to me," Danny said gently.

The setter lowered his head to sniff the partridge and grasped it gently in his mouth. The boy took it in his hand. He threw it down in the snow and Red picked it up again.

They went on, and the setter pointed three more grouse. The last one Danny shot the dog picked up and brought back, though he went about it in an awkward fashion. His tail wagged furiously and his eyes glistened at the lavish praise that the feat called forth from his master. But four birds were the limit.

Danny arrived home first that night, and had supper ready when his father came in. Ross had no furs, as he had set his traps only that day, but he opened his hunting jacket and took out four partridges. He laid them on the table and turned silently away to remove his coat and wash his hands.

Danny's cheeks burned. His father had had no dog. And every one of the partridges had been shot through the head with the little .22 pistol he carried on his trap line.

By the last day of the season Danny knew that his hunch had been the correct one. Red was not only a partridge dog, but he was a great partridge dog, one in a million. He found the birds and pointed them so carefully that only the wildest ones flushed before the gunner could get in his shot. It had taken him only nine trips afield to learn perfectly the art of retrieving, regardless of how thick the brush or brambles in which the bird fell might be. Red paid no attention to the rabbits that scooted before him or the chattering squirrels that frisked through the trees. And when he hunted, no scent save that of partridges drew the slightest interest. Now, on this last day of the season he and Danny were going out for one last hunt.

Ross as usual had already gone, and a few flakes of snow hovered in the air. Little wind stirred and the naked trees were silent. But the blue-black horizon and the clouded sky foretold a heavier storm to come. Danny went back into the shanty and buttoned a woolen jacket over the wool hunting shirt he already wore. He dropped half a dozen twelve-gauge shells into his pocket.

"Goin' be weathah shuah 'nough," he murmured. "Wintah's nigh heah, Red."

The hard little snowflakes rustled against the frozen leaves, and it seemed to Danny that they were falling faster even before he came to the edge of his father's field. But he forgot them then because Red came to a point. Steady as a rock, he stopped just a little way within the woods. Danny flushed the bird. It soared up and out, dodging behind tree trunks and twisting about. But for one split second it showed through the crotch of a big beech and Danny shot. The bird dropped to the ground and Red brought it in.

They went on deeper into the beechwoods where they had found so many partridges before. But Red worked for an hour before he pointed another, and that one flushed so wild that Danny had no shot at it. It was noon before he killed a second bird—and at the same time he awoke to the necessity of getting back to the cabin before he had trouble finding it. The snow was falling so fast now that the trees were only wavering shadows. And there was a rising wind, which meant that the heavy snow would be accompanied by a gale. Danny snapped his fingers.

"Heah, Red."

It was nearly dusk when they reached the cabin. Danny opened the door, stamped the snow from his feet, and sank into a chair. Red crouched full length on the floor, looking at the boy from the corners of his eyes.

Danny cut thick slices from a ham and peeled a great potful of potatoes. His father would be hungry after bucking the storm, would want good things to eat and plenty of them. But the boy worked with deliberate slowness, trying in the accustomed routine of household chores to still the small worried voice that was rising in him. Pappy should have been home before this.

He went to a window and peered into the inky blackness outside. He fought back a rising panic; this was no time for a man to lose his head. He waited another ten minutes.

Then he made up a pack, a thermos of hot coffee, enough food for three days, a knife and ax, plenty of matches, and two woolen blankets. He put on his warmest coat, pulled a felt hat down over his eyes and took his snowshoes from their peg on the wall.

With a happy little whine and a furiously wagging tail, Red sprang up to join him. Danny looked at the setter. The dog could not be of any use. He would hunt only partridges, would pay no attention to Pappy's scent, even though they passed within ten feet of him. Danny shook his head.

"Reckon not, Red. This heah's one hunt I got to run alone. Not even the other dogs are trained for this."

Red flattened his ears and begged mutely. Danny looked away, and back again. The setter wouldn't help any, but he would be company and certainly he could do no harm.

"Aw ri'. Come on."

Red waited impatiently in the snow while Danny took a toboggan from its elevated platform, and when he started off on his snowshoes through the night the dog ran a little ahead. Danny watched him work carefully toward a briar patch and grinned wryly. The setter was still ashamed of his inability to locate more than two partridges, and he was trying to make up for it.

The snow was drifting down in great feathery flakes that dropped softly to earth. The wind had abated and it was not as cold as it had been. But if Pappy were helpless he could freeze. Danny put the thought from his mind and plodded grimly on. Lately he had scarcely spoken to his father, but he still knew where to look for him. Last night Ross had brought in two muskrats and a mink, pelts that could be trapped only along waterways. Therefore he must have run the traps in Brant Marsh and along Elk River. Today he would cover his fox line on Stoney Lonesome Ridge.

But even though he would search until he found his father Danny was aware of the near hopelessness of his mission. If Pappy were lying unconscious after having been caught in a slide or struck down by a falling limb, the snow would cover him and he might not be found until it melted. Danny admitted this. Nobody was too good at anything to guard against unforeseen accidents, not even a skilled woodsman like his father. It was just as well to face possibilities as to close his eyes to them. He must be ready for any emergency.

Red came trotting happily back and was away again. As Danny dragged the toboggan up the long steep trail his father took to Stoney Lonesome, he looked down at his feet. They seemed barely to move. Yet he saw by a dead stub of a tree that stood beside the trail and served as a landmark when they were away from it, that in an hour he had come almost four miles. That was fast travel in deep snow when a man had to drag a toboggan.

It was too fast. A quarter of a mile farther on Danny stopped to rest. He panted heavily, and perspiration streamed down his face and back. He took the felt hat off and opened his jacket. Red returned to stand anxiously beside him.

"If only I'd taught you to hunt men 'stead of pat'tidge," Danny half sobbed. "If only I had!"

He turned to go on. Pappy had to be somewhere, and he was as likely to be near the trail as anywhere else. But if he wasn't, his son would go to all the traps, and from them he would branch out to scour every inch of Stoney Lonesome. Pappy just couldn't die! Why there would be hardly anything worthwhile if it weren't for his father. That foolish quarrel over Red. Danny should have let him hunt varmints or anything else Pappy wanted. If only he could talk to his father once more and tell him how sorry he was!

Danny stumbled and sprawled in the snow. He rose, annoyed and grumbling. He had fallen over Red, who had come to a point in the trail, headed off to the side.

"Go on!" Danny snapped.

Red took three uncertain steps forward beside the trail, then he stopped again. Danny rushed toward him, angry at the dog for the first time. He reached down to grasp his collar, but the toes of his snowshoes crossed and he stumbled sideways. His bare hands plunged deeply into the drifted snow. And they found something soft and yielding, something that gave before them. It was a man's trousered leg. Danny dug frantically and lifted Ross Pickett from his snowy bed. His hand went under his father's shirt.

His body was warm and his heart still beat.

Two days later, back at the cabin, Danny served his father two roasted partridges and a great heap of mashed potatoes. He propped him up on pillows and grinned when his patient began to wolf the food.

"Fo' a man as should of been daid, you shuah hungry," he observed. "How come you can eat so much?"

Ross grinned back. "Cain't kill an old he-bear like me." He tore off a great strip of breast meat and held it up in his fingers, saying, "Come heah an' have some vittles."

Red padded daintily across the floor, and his wagging tail thanked Ross for the offering. Danny's eyes shone, because the two things that he loved best now loved each other.

" 'Twas a mighty lot of foolishment to fight over the dog, wan't it? But even if I hadn't got ovah my mad an' like the mulehaid I am wan't waitin' fo' you to say somethin', I shuah would know what a pointin' dog is now. When the side of that ol' trail give way beneath me, I thought I was a cooked goose fo' certain. How come the dog foun' me, Son?"

Danny answered soberly. "Red foun' you on account he's got a better nose as any houn' dog."

It was the first time he had ever deceived his father—but it was more evasion than lie. Red was a partridge dog through and through. And when he had pointed there in the snow, he had pointed, not Ross, but the two partridges the trapper had shot and put in his pocket.

Saki

LOUIS

"I t would be jolly to spend Easter in Vienna this year," said Strudwarden, "and look up some of my old friends there. It's about the jolliest place I know of to be at for Easter—"

"I thought we had made up our minds to spend Easter at Brighton," interrupted Lena Strudwarden, with an air of aggrieved surprise.

"You mean that you had made up your mind that we should spend Easter there," said her husband; "we spent last Easter there, and Whitsuntide as well, and the year before that we were at Worthing, and Brighton again before that. I think it would be just as well to have a real change of scene while we are about it."

"The journey to Vienna would be very expensive," said Lena.

"You are not often concerned about economy," said Strudwarden, "and in any case the trip to Vienna won't cost a bit more than the rather meaningless luncheon parties we usually give to quite meaningless acquaintances at Brighton. To escape from all that set would be a holiday in itself."

Strudwarden spoke feelingly; Lena Strudwarden maintained an equally feeling silence on that particular subject. The set that she gathered round her at Brighton and other South Coast resorts was composed of individuals who might be dull and meaningless in themselves, but who understood the art of flattering Mrs. Strudwarden. She had no intention of foregoing their society and their homage and flinging herself among unappreciative strangers in a foreign capital.

"You must go to Vienna alone if you are bent on going," she said; "I couldn't leave Louis behind, and a dog is always a fearful nuisance in a foreign hotel, besides all the fuss and separation of the quarantine restrictions when one comes back. Louis would die if he was parted from me for even a week. You don't know what that would mean to me."

Lena stooped down and kissed the nose of the diminutive brown Pomeranian that lay, snug and irresponsive, beneath a shawl on her lap.

"Look here," said Strudwarden, "this eternal Louis business is getting to be a ridiculous nuisance. Nothing can be done, no plans can be made, without some veto connected with that animal's whims or convenience being imposed. If you were a priest in attendance on some African fetish you couldn't set up a more elaborate code of restrictions. I believe you'd ask the Government to put off a General Election if you thought it would interfere with Louis's comfort in any way."

By way of answer to this tirade Mrs. Strudwarden stooped down again and kissed the irresponsive brown nose. It was the action of a woman with a beautifully meek nature, who would, however, send the whole world to the stake sooner than yield an inch where she knew herself to be in the right.

"It isn't as if you were in the least bit fond of animals," went on Strudwarden, with growing irritation; "when we are down at Kerryfield you won't stir a step to take the house dogs out, even if they're dying for a run, and I don't think you've been in the stables twice in your life. You laugh at what you call the fuss that's being made over the extermination of plumage birds, and you are quite indignant with me if I interfere on behalf of an ill-treated, over-driven animal on the road. And yet you insist on every one's plans being made subservient to the convenience of that stupid little morsel of fur and selfishness."

"You are prejudiced against my little Louis," said Lena, with a world of tender regret in her voice.

"I've never had the chance of being anything else but prejudiced against him," said Strudwarden; "I know what a jolly responsive companion a doggie can be, but I've never been allowed to put a finger near Louis. You say he snaps at any one except you and your maid, and you snatched him away from old Lady Peterby the other day, when she wanted to pet him, for fear he would bury his teeth in her. All that I ever see of him is the tip of his unhealthy-looking little nose, peeping out from his basket or from your muff, and I occasionally hear his wheezy little bark when you take him for a walk up and down the corridor. You can't expect one to get extravagantly fond of a dog of that sort. One might as well work up an affection for the cuckoo in a cuckoo-clock."

"He loves me," said Lena, rising from the table, and bearing the shawl-swathed Louis in her arms. "He loves only me, and perhaps that is why I love him so much in return. I don't care what you say against him, I am not going to be separated from him. If you insist on going to Vienna you must go alone, as far as I am concerned. I think it would be much more sensible if you were to come to Brighton with Louis and me, but of course you must please yourself."

"You must get rid of that dog," said Strudwarden's sister when Lena had left the room; "it must be helped to some sudden and merciful end. Lena is merely making use of it as an instrument for getting her own way on dozens of occasions when she would otherwise be obliged to yield gracefully to your wishes or to the general convenience. I am convinced that she doesn't care a brass button about the animal itself. When her friends are buzzing round her at Brighton or anywhere else and the dog would be in the way, it has to spend whole days alone with the maid, but if you want Lena to go with you anywhere where she doesn't want to go instantly she trots out the excuse that she couldn't be separated from her dog. Have you ever come into a room unobserved and heard Lena talking to her beloved pet? I never have. I believe she only fusses over it when there's some one present to notice her."

"I don't mind admitting," said Strudwarden, "that I've dwelt more than once lately on the possibility of some fatal accident putting an end to Louis's existence. It's not very easy, though, to arrange a fatality for a creature that spends most of its time in a muff or asleep in a toy kennel. I don't think poison would be any good; it's obviously horribly over-fed, for I've seen Lena offer it dainties at table sometimes, but it never seems to eat them."

"Lena will be away at church on Wednesday morning," said Elsie Strudwarden reflectively; "she can't take Louis with her there, and she is going on to the Dellings for lunch. That will give you several hours in which to carry out your purpose. The maid will be flirting with the chauffeur most of the time, and, anyhow, I can manage to keep her out of the way on some pretext or other."

"That leaves the field clear," said Strudwarden, "but unfortunately my brain is equally a blank as far as any lethal project is concerned. The little beast is so monstrously inactive; I can't pretend that it leapt into the bath and drowned itself, or that it took on the butcher's mastiff in unequal combat and got chewed up. In what possible guise could death come to a confirmed basket-dweller? It would be too suspicious if we invented a Suffragette raid and pretended that they invaded Lena's boudoir and threw a brick at him. We should have to do a lot of other damage as well, which would be rather a nuisance, and the servants would think it odd that they had seen nothing of the invaders."

"I have an idea," said Elsie; "get a box with an air-tight lid, and bore a small hole in it, just big enough to let in an india-rubber tube. Pop Louis, kennel and all, into the box, shut it down, and put the other end of the tube over the gas-bracket. There you have a perfect lethal chamber. You can stand the kennel at the open window afterwards, to get rid of the smell of the gas, and all that Lena will find when she comes home late in the afternoon will be a placidly defunct Louis."

"Novels have been written about women like you," said Strudwarden; "you have a perfectly criminal mind. Let's come and look for a box."

Two mornings later the conspirators stood gazing guiltily at a stout square box, connected with the gas-bracket by a length of india-rubber tubing.

"Not a sound," said Elsie; "he never stirred; it must have been quite painless. All the same I feel rather horrid now it's done."

"The ghastly part has to come," said Strudwarden, turning off the gas. "We'll lift the lid slowly, and let the gas out by degrees. Swing the door to and fro to send a draught through the room."

Some minutes later, when the fumes had rushed off, he stooped down and lifted out the little kennel with its grim burden. Elsie gave an exclamation of terror. Louis sat at the door of his dwelling, head erect and ears pricked, as coldly and defiantly inert as when they had put him into his execution chamber. Strudwarden dropped the kennel with a jerk, and stared for a long moment at the miracle-dog; then he went into a peal of chattering laughter.

It was certainly a wonderful imitation of a truculent-looking toy Pomeranian, and the apparatus that gave forth a wheezy bark when you pressed it had materially helped the imposition that Lena, and Lena's maid, had foisted on the household. For a woman who disliked animals, but liked getting her own way under a halo of unselfishness, Mrs. Strudwarden had managed rather well.

"Louis is dead," was the curt information that greeted Lena on her return from her luncheon party.

"Louis *dead!*" she exclaimed.

"Yes, he flew at the butcher-boy and bit him, and he bit me too, when I tried to get him off, so I had to have him destroyed. You warned me that he snapped, but you didn't tell me that he was down-right dangerous. I shall have to pay the boy something heavy by way of compensation, so you will have to go without those buckles that you wanted to have for Easter; also I shall have to go to Vienna to consult Dr. Schroeder, who is a specialist on dogbites, and you will have to come too. I have sent what remains of Louis to Rowland Ward to be stuffed; that will be my Easter gift to you instead of the buckles. For Heaven's sake, Lena, weep, if you really feel it so much; anything would be better than standing there staring as if you thought I had lost my reason."

Lena Strudwarden did not weep, but her attempt at laughing was an unmistakable failure.

Alistair Macleod

WINTER DOG

I am writing this in December. In the period close to Christmas, and three days after the first snowfall in this region of southwestern Ontario. The snow came quietly in the night or in the early morning. When we went to bed near midnight, there was none at all. Then early in the morning we heard the children singing Christmas songs from their rooms across the hall. It was very dark and I rolled over to check the time. It was four-thirty A.M. One of them must have awakened and looked out the window to find the snow and then eagerly awakened the others. They are half crazed by the promise of Christmas, and the discovery of the snow is an unexpected giddy surprise. There was no snow promised for this area, not even yesterday.

"What are you doing?" I call, although it is obvious.

"Singing Christmas songs," they shout back with equal obviousness, "because it snowed."

"Try to be quiet," I say, "or you'll wake the baby."

"She's already awake," they say. "She's listening to our singing. She likes it. Can we go out and make a snowman?"

I roll from my bed and go to the window. The neighboring houses are muffled in snow and silence and there are as yet no lights in any of them. The snow has stopped falling and its whitened quietness reflects the shadows of the night.

"This snow is no good for snowmen," I say. "It is too dry."

"How can snow be dry?" asks a young voice. Then an older one says, "Well, then can we go out and make the first tracks?"

They take my silence for consent and there are great sounds of rustling and giggling as they go downstairs to touch the light switches and rummage and jostle for coats and boots.

"What on earth is happening?" asks my wife from her bed. "What are they doing?"

"They are going outside to make the first tracks in the snow," I say. "It snowed quite heavily last night."

"What time is it?"

"Shortly after four-thirty."

"Oh."

We ourselves have been nervous and restless for the past weeks. We have been troubled by illness and uncertainty in those we love far away on Canada's east coast. We have already considered and rejected driving the fifteen hundred miles. Too far, too uncertain, too expensive, fickle weather, the complications of transporting Santa Claus.

Instead, we sleep uncertainly and toss in unbidden dreams. We jump when the phone rings after ten P.M. and are then reassured by the distant voices.

"First of all, there is nothing wrong," they say. "Things are just the same."

Sometimes we make calls ourselves, even to the hospital in Halifax, and are surprised at the voices which answer.

"I just got here this afternoon from Newfoundland. I'm going to try to stay a week. He seems better today. He's sleeping now."

At other times we receive calls from farther west, from Edmonton and Calgary and Vancouver. People hoping to find objectivity in the most subjective of situations. Strung out in uncertainty across the time zones from British Columbia to Newfoundland.

Within our present city, people move and consider possibilities:

If he dies tonight we'll leave right away. Can you come?

We will have to drive as we'll never get air reservations at this time.

I'm not sure if my car is good enough. I'm always afraid of the mountains near Cabano.

If we were stranded in Rivière du Loup we would be worse off than being here. It would be too far for anyone to come and get us.

My car will go but I'm not so sure I can drive it all the way. My eyes are not so good anymore, especially at night in drifting snow.

Perhaps there'll be no drifting snow.

There's always drifting snow.

We'll take my car if you'll drive it. We'll have to drive straight through.

John phoned and said he'll give us his car if we want it or he'll drive—either his own car or someone else's.

He drinks too heavily, especially for long-distance driving, and at this time of year. He's been drinking ever since this news began.

He drinks because he cares. It's just the way he is.

Not everybody drinks.

Not everybody cares, and if he gives you his word, he'll never drink until he gets there. We all know that.

But so far nothing has happened. Things seem to remain the same.

Through the window and out on the white plane of the snow, the silent, laughing children now appear. They move in their muffled clothes like mummers on the whitest of stages. They dance and gesture noiselessly, flopping their arms in parodies of heavy, happy, earthbound birds. They have been warned by the eldest to be aware of the sleeping neighbors so they cavort only in pantomime, sometimes raising mittened hands to their mouths to suppress their joyous laughter. They dance and prance in the moonlight, tossing snow in one another's direction, tracing out various shapes and initials, forming lines which snake across the previously unmarked whiteness. All of it in silence, unknown and unseen and unheard to the neighboring world. They seem unreal even to me, their father, standing at his darkened window. It is almost as if they have danced out of the world of folklore like happy elves who cavort and mimic and caper through the private hours of this whitened dark, only to vanish with the coming of the morning's light and leaving only the signs of their activities behind. I am tempted to check the recently vacated beds to confirm what perhaps I think I know.

Then out of the corner of my eye I see him. The golden collie-like dog. He appears almost as if from the wings of the stage or as a figure newly noticed in the lower corner of a winter painting. He sits quietly and watches the playful scene before him and then, as if responding to a silent invitation, bounds into its midst. The children chase him in frantic circles, falling and rolling as he doubles back and darts and dodges between their legs and through their outstretched arms. He seizes a mitt loosened from its owner's hand, and tosses it happily in the air and then snatches it back into his jaws an instant before it reaches the ground and seconds before the tumbling bodies fall on the emptiness of its expected destination. He races to the edge of the scene and lies facing them, holding the mitt tantalizingly between his paws, and then as they dash towards him, he leaps forward again, tossing and catching it before him and zigzagging through them as the Sunday football player might return the much sought-after ball. After he has gone through and eluded them all, he looks back over his shoulder and again, like an elated athlete, tosses the mitt high in what seems like an imaginary end zone. Then he seizes it once more and lopes in a wide circle around his pursuers, eventually coming closer and closer to them until once more their stretching hands are able to actually touch his shoulders and back and haunches, although he continues always to wriggle free. He is touched but never captured, which is the nature of the game. Then he is gone. As suddenly as he came. I strain my eyes in the direction of the adjoining street, towards the house where I have often seen him, always within a yard enclosed by woven links of chain. I see the flash of his silhouette, outlined perhaps against the snow or the light cast by the street lamps or the moon. It arcs upwards and seems to hang for an instant high above the top of the fence and then it descends on the other side. He lands on his shoulder in a fluff of snow and with a half roll regains his feet and vanishes within the shadow of his owner's house.

"What are you looking at?" asks my wife.

"That golden collie-like dog from the other street was just playing with the children in the snow."

"But he's always in that fenced-in yard."

"I guess not always. He jumped the fence just now and went back in. I guess the owners and the rest of us think he's fenced in but he knows he's not. He probably comes out every night and leads an exciting life. I hope they don't see his tracks or they'll probably begin to chain him."

"What are the children doing?"

"They look tired now from chasing the dog. They'll probably soon be back in. I think I'll go downstairs and wait for them and make myself a cup of coffee."

"Okay."

I look once more towards the fenced-in yard but the dog is nowhere to be seen.

I first saw such a dog when I was twelve and he came as a pup of about two months in a crate to the railroad station which was about eight miles from where we lived. Someone must have phoned or dropped in to say: "Your dog's at the station."

He had come to Cape Breton in response to a letter and a check which my father had sent to Morrisburg, Ontario. We had seen the ads for "cattle collie dogs" in the *Family Herald*, which was the farm newspaper of the time, and we were in need of a good young working dog.

His crate was clean and neat and there was still a supply of dog biscuits with him and a can in the corner to hold water. The baggage handlers had looked after him well on the trip east, and he appeared in good spirits. He had a white collar and chest and four rather large white paws and a small white blaze on his forehead. The rest of him was a fluffy, golden brown, although his eyebrows and the tips of his ears as well as the end of his tail were darker, tingeing almost to black. When he grew to his full size the blackish shadings became really black, and although he had the long, heavy coat of a collie, it was in certain areas more gray than gold. He was also taller than the average collie and with a deeper chest. He seemed to be at least part German shepherd.

It was winter when he came and we kept him in the house where he slept behind the stove in a box lined with an old coat. Our other dogs slept mostly in the stables or outside in the lees of woodpiles or under porches or curled up on the banking of the house. We seemed to care more for him because he was smaller and it was winter and he was somehow like a visitor, and also because more was expected of him and also perhaps because we had paid money for him and thought about his coming for some time—like a "planned" child. Skeptical neighbors and relatives who thought the idea of paying money for a dog was rather exotic or frivolous would ask: "Is that your Ontario dog?" or "Do you think your Ontario dog will be any good?"

He turned out to be no good at all and no one knew why. Perhaps it was because of the suspected German shepherd blood. But he could not "get the hang of it." Although we worked him and trained him as we had other dogs, he seemed always to bring panic instead of order and to make things worse instead of better. He became a "head dog," which meant that instead of working behind the cattle he lunged at their heads, impeding them from any forward motion and causing them to turn in endless, meaningless bewildered circles. On the few occasions when he did go behind them, he was "rough," which meant that instead of being a floating, nipping, suggestive presence, he actually bit them and caused them to gallop, which was another sin. Sometimes in the summer the milk cows suffering from his misunderstood pursuit would jam pell-mell into the stable, tossing their wide horns in fear, and with their great sides heaving and perspiring while down their legs and tails the wasted milk ran in rivulets mingling with the blood caused by his slashing wounds. He was, it was said, "worse than nothing."

Gradually everyone despaired, although he continued to grow gray and golden and was, as everyone agreed, a "beautiful-looking dog."

He was also tremendously strong and in the winter months I would hitch him to a sleigh which he pulled easily and willingly on almost any kind of surface. When he was harnessed I used to put a collar around his neck and attach a light line to it so that I might have some minimum control over him, but it was hardly ever needed. He would pull home the Christmas tree or the bag of flour or the deer which was shot far back in the woods, and when we visited our winter snares he would pull home the gunnysacks which contained the partridges and rabbits which we gathered. He would also pull us, especially on the flat windswept stretches of land beside the sea. There the snow was never really deep and the water that oozed from a series of freshwater springs and ponds contributed to a glaze of ice and crisply crusted snow which the sleigh runners seemed to sing over without ever breaking through. He would begin with an easy lope and then increase his swiftness until both he and the sleigh seemed to touch the surface at only irregular intervals. He would stretch out then with his ears flattened against his head and his shoulders bunching and contracting in the rhythm of his speed. Behind him on the sleigh we would cling tenaciously to the wooden slats as the particles of ice and snow dislodged by his nails hurtled towards our faces. We would avert our heads and close our eyes and the wind stung so sharply that the difference between freezing and burning could not be known. He would do that until late in the afternoon when it was time to return home and begin our chores.

On the sunny winter Sunday that I am thinking of, I planned to visit my snares. There seemed no other children around that afternoon and the adults were expecting relatives. I harnessed the dog to the sleigh, opened the door of the house and shouted that I was going to look at my snares. We began to climb the hill behind the house on our way to the woods when we looked back and out towards the sea. The "big ice," which was what we called the major pack of drift ice, was in solidly against the shore and stretched out beyond the range of vision. It had not been "in" yesterday, although for the past weeks we had seen it moving offshore, sometimes close and sometimes distant, depending on the winds and tides. The coming of the big ice marked the official beginning of the coldest part of winter. It was mostly drift ice from the Arctic and Labrador, although some of it was freshwater ice from the estuary of the St. Lawrence. It drifted down with the dropping temperatures, bringing its own mysterious coldness and stretching for hundreds of miles in craters and pans, sometimes in grotesque shapes and sometimes in dazzling architectural forms. It was blue and white and sometimes gray and at other times a dazzling emerald green.

The dog and I changed our direction towards the sea, to find what the ice might yield. Our land had always been beside the sea and we had always gone towards it to find newness and the extraordinary; and over the years we, as others along the coast, had found quite a lot, although never the pirate chests of gold which were supposed to abound or the reasons for the mysterious lights that our elders still spoke of and persisted in seeing. But kegs of rum had washed up, and sometimes bloated horses and various fishing paraphernalia and valuable timber and furniture from foundered ships. The door of my room was apparently the galley door from a ship called the *Judith Franklin,* which was wrecked during the early winter in which my great-grandfather was building his house. My grandfather told of how they had heard the cries and seen the lights as the ship neared the rocks and of how they had run down in the dark and tossed lines to the people while tying themselves to trees on the shore. All were saved, including women clinging to small children. The next day the builders of the new house went down to the shore and salvaged what they could from the wreckage of the vanquished ship. A sort of symbolic marriage of the new and the old: doors and shelving, stairways, hatches, wooden chests and trunks and various glass figurines and lanterns which were miraculously never broken.

People came too. The dead as well as the living. Bodies of men swept overboard and reported lost at sea and the bodies of men still crouched within the shelter of their boats' broken bows. And sometimes in late winter young sealers who had quit their vessels would walk across the ice and come to our doors. They were usually very young—some still in their teens—and had signed on for jobs they could not or no longer wished to handle. They were often disoriented and did not know where they were, only that they had seen land and had decided to walk towards it. They were often frostbitten and with little money and uncertain as to how they might get to Halifax.

The dog and I walked towards the ice upon the sea. Sometimes it was hard to "get on" the ice, which meant that at the point where the pack met the shore there might be open water or irregularities caused by the indentations of the coastline or the workings of the tides and currents, but for us on that day there was no difficulty at all. We were on easily and effortlessly and enthused in our new adventure. For the first mile there was nothing but the vastness of the white expanse. We came to a clear stretch where the ice was as smooth and unruffled as that of an indoor arena and I knelt on the sleigh while the dog loped easily along. Gradually the ice changed to an uneven terrain of pressure ridges and hummocks, making it impossible to ride farther; and then suddenly, upon rounding a hummock, I saw the perfect seal. At first I thought it was alive, as did the dog who stopped so suddenly in his tracks that the sleigh almost collided with his legs. The hackles on the back of his neck rose and he growled in the dangerous way he was beginning to develop. But the seal was dead, yet facing us in a frozen perfection that was difficult to believe. There was a light powder of snow over its darker coat and a delicate rime of frost still formed the outline of its whiskers. Its eyes were wide open and it stared straight ahead towards the land. Even now in memory it seems more real than reality—as if it were transformed by frozen art into something more arresting than life itself. The way the sudden seal in the museum exhibit freezes your eyes with the touch of truth. Immediately I wanted to take it home.

It was frozen solidly in a base of ice so I began to look for something that might serve as a pry. I let the dog out of his harness and hung the sleigh and harness on top of the hummock to mark the place and began my search. Some distance away I found a pole about twelve feet long. It is always surprising to find such things on the ice field but they are, often amazingly, there, almost in the same way that you might find a pole floating in the summer ocean. Unpredictable but possible. I took the pole back and began my work. The dog went off on explorations of his own.

Although it was firmly frozen, the task did not seem impossible and by inserting the end of the pole under first one side and then the other and working from the front to the back, it was possible to cause a gradual loosening. I remember thinking how very warm it was because I was working hard and perspiring heavily. When the dog came back he was uneasy, and I realized it was starting to snow a bit but I was almost done. He sniffed with disinterest at the seal and began to whine a bit, which was something he did not often do. Finally, after another quarter of an hour, I was able to roll my trophy onto the sleigh and with the dog in harness we set off. We had gone perhaps two hundred yards when the seal slid free. I took the dog and the sleigh back and once again managed to roll the seal on. This time I took the line from the dog's collar and tied the seal to the sleigh, reasoning that the dog would go home anyway and there would be no need to guide him. My fingers were numb as I tried to fasten the awkward knots and the dog began to whine and rear. When I gave the command he bolted forward and I clung at the back of the sleigh to the seal. The snow was heavier now and blowing in my face but we were moving rapidly and when we came to the stretch of arena-like ice we skimmed across it almost like an iceboat, the profile of the frozen seal at the front of the sleigh like those figures at the prows of Viking ships. At the very end of the smooth stretch, we went through. From my position at the end of the sleigh I felt him drop almost before I saw him, and rolled backwards seconds before the sleigh and seal followed him into the blackness of the water. He went under once carried by his own momentum but surfaced almost immediately with his head up and his paws scrambling at the icy, jagged edge of the hole; but when the weight and momentum of the sleigh and its burden struck, he went down again, this time out of sight.

I realized we had struck a "seam" and that the stretch of smooth ice had been deceivingly and temporarily joined to the rougher ice near the shore and now was in the process of breaking away. I saw the widening line before me and jumped to the other side just as his head miraculously came up once more. I lay on my stomach and grabbed his collar in both my hands and then in a moment of panic did not know what to do. I could feel myself sliding towards him and the darkness of the water and was aware of the weight that pulled me forward and down. I was also aware of his razor-sharp claws flailing violently before my face and knew that I might lose my eyes. And I was aware that his own eyes were bulging from their sockets and that he might think I was trying to choke him and might lunge and slash my face with his teeth in desperation. I knew all of this but somehow did nothing about it; it seemed almost simpler to hang on and be drawn into the darkness of the gently slopping water, seeming to slop gently in spite of all the agitation. Then suddenly he was free, scrambling over my shoulder and dragging the sleigh behind him. The seal surfaced again, buoyed up perhaps by the physics of its frozen body or the nature of its fur. Still looking more genuine than it could have in life, its snout and head broke the open water and it seemed to look at us curiously for an instant before it vanished permanently beneath the ice. The loose and badly tied knots had apparently not held when the sleigh was in a near-vertical position and we were saved by the ineptitude of my own numbed fingers. We had been spared for a future time.

He lay gasping and choking for a moment, coughing up the icy salt water, and then almost immediately his coat began to freeze. I realized then how cold I was myself and that even in the moments I had been lying on the ice, my clothes had begun to adhere to it. My earlier heated perspiration was now a cold rime upon my body and I imagined it outlining me there, beneath my clothes, in a sketch of frosty white. I got on the sleigh once more and crouched low as he began to race towards home. His coat was freezing fast, and as he ran the individual ice-coated hairs began to clack together like rhythmical castanets attuned to the motion of his body. It was snowing quite heavily in our faces now and it seemed to be approaching dusk, although I doubted if it were so on the land which I could now no longer see. I realized all the obvious things I should have considered earlier. That if the snow was blowing in our faces, the wind was off the land, and if it was off the land, it was blowing the ice pack back out to sea. That was probably one reason why the seam had opened. And also that the ice had only been in one night and had not had a chance to set. I realized other things as well. That it was the time of the late afternoon when the tide was falling. That no one knew where we were. That I had said we were going to look at snares, which was not where we had gone at all. And I remembered now that I had received no answer even to that misinformation, so perhaps I had not even been heard. And also if there was drifting snow like this on land, our tracks would by now have been obliterated.

We came to a rough section of ice: huge slabs on their sides and others piled one on top of the other as if they were in some strange form of storage. It was no longer possible to ride the sleigh but as I stood up I lifted it and hung on to it as a means of holding on to the dog. The line usually attached to his collar had sunk with the vanished seal. My knees were stiff when I stood up; and deprived of the windbreak effect which the dog had provided, I felt the snow driving full into my face, particularly my eyes. It did not merely impede my vision, the way distant snow flurries might, but actually entered my eyes, causing them to water and freeze nearly shut. I was aware of the weight of ice on my eyelashes and could see them as they gradually lowered and became heavier. I did not remember ice like this when I got on, although I did not find that terribly surprising. I pressed the soles of my numbed feet firmly down upon it to try to feel if it was moving out, but it was impossible to tell because there was no fixed point of reference. Almost the sensation one gets on a conveyor belt at airports or on escalators; although you are standing still you recognize motion, but should you shut your eyes and be deprived of sight, even that recognition may become ambiguously uncertain.

The dog began to whine and to walk around me in circles, binding my legs with the traces of the harness as I continued to grasp the sleigh. Finally I decided to let him go as there seemed no way to hold him and there was nothing else to do. I unhitched the traces and doubled them up as best I could and tucked them under the backpad of his harness so they would not drag behind him and become snagged on any obstacles. I did not take off my mitts to do so as I was afraid I would not be able to get them back on. He vanished into the snow almost immediately.

The sleigh had been a gift from an uncle, so I hung on to it and carried it with both hands before me like an ineffectual shield against the wind and snow. I lowered my head as much as I could and turned it sideways so the wind would beat against my head instead of directly into my face. Sometimes I would turn and walk backwards for a few steps. Although I knew it was not the wisest thing to do, it seemed at times the only way to breathe. And then I began to feel the water sloshing about my feet.

Sometimes when the tides or currents ran heavily and the ice began to separate, the water that was beneath it would well up and wash over it almost as if it were reflooding it. Sometimes you could see the hard ice clearly beneath the water but at other times a sort of floating slush was formed mingling with snow and "slob" ice which was not yet solid. It was thick and dense and soupy and it was impossible to see what lay beneath it. Experienced men on the ice sometimes carried a slender pole so they could test the consistency of the footing which might or might not lie before them, but I was obviously not one of them, although I had a momentary twinge for the pole I had used to dislodge the seal. Still, there was nothing to do but go forward.

When I went through, the first sensation was almost of relief and relaxation for the water initially made me feel much warmer than I had been on the surface. It was the most dangerous of false sensations for I knew my clothes were becoming heavier by the second. I clung to the sleigh somewhat as a raft and lunged forward with it in a kind of up-and-down swimming motion, hoping that it might strike some sort of solidity before my arms became so weighted and sodden that I could no longer lift them. I cried out then for the first time into the driving snow.

He came almost immediately, although I could see he was afraid and the slobbing slush was up to his knees. Still, he seemed to be on some kind of solid footing for he was not swimming. I splashed towards him and when almost there, desperately threw the sleigh before me and lunged for the edge of what seemed like his footing, but it only gave way as if my hands were closing on icy insubstantial porridge. He moved forward then, although I still could not tell if what supported him would be of any use to me. Finally I grasped the breast strap of his harness. He began to back up then, and as I said, he was tremendously strong. The harness began to slide forward on his shoulders but he continued to pull as I continued to grasp and then I could feel my elbows on what seemed like solid ice and I was able to hook them on the edge and draw myself, dripping and soaking, like another seal out of the black water and onto the whiteness of the slushy ice. Almost at once my clothes began to freeze. My elbows and knees began to creak when I bent them as if I were a robot from the realm of science fiction and then I could see myself clothed in transparent ice as if I had been coated with shellac or finished with clear varnish.

As the fall into the winter sea had at first seemed ironically warm, so now my garments of ice seemed a protection against the biting wind, but I knew it was a deceptive sensation and that I did not have much time before me. The dog faced into the wind and I followed him. This time he stayed in sight, and at times even turned back to wait for me. He was cautious but certain and gradually the slush disappeared, and although we were still in water, the ice was hard and clear beneath it. The frozen heaviness of my clothes began to weigh on me and I could feel myself, ironically, perspiring within my suit of icy armor. I was very tired, which I knew was another dangerous sensation. And then I saw the land. It was very close and a sudden surprise. Almost like coming upon a stalled and unexpected automobile in a highway's winter storm. It was only yards away, and although there was no longer any ice actually touching the shore, there were several pans of it floating in the region between. The dog jumped from one to the other and I followed him, still clutching the sleigh, and missing only the last pan which floated close to the rocky shore. The water came only to my waist and I was able to touch the bottom and splash noisily on land. We had been spared again for a future time and I was never to know whether he had reached the shore himself and come back or whether he had heard my call against the wind.

We began to run towards home and the land lightened and there were touches of evening sun. The wind still blew but no snow was falling. Yet when I looked back, the ice and the ocean were invisible in the swirling squalls. It was like looking at another far and distant country on the screen of a snowy television.

I became obsessed, now that I could afford the luxury, with not being found disobedient or considered a fool. The visitors' vehicles were still in the yard so I imagined most of the family to be in the parlor or living room, and I circled the house and entered through the kitchen, taking the dog with me. I was able to get upstairs unnoticed and get my clothes changed and when I came down I mingled with everybody and tried to appear as normal as I could. My own family was caught up with the visitors and only general comments came my way. The dog, who could not change his clothes, lay under the table with his head on his paws and he was also largely unnoticed. Later as the ice melted from his coat, a puddle formed around him, which I casually mopped up. Still later someone said, "I wonder where that dog has been, his coat is soaking wet." I was never to tell anyone of the afternoon's experience or that he had saved my life.

Two winters later I was sitting at a neighbor's kitchen table when I looked out the window and saw the dog as he was shot. He had followed my father and also me and had been sitting rather regally on a little hill beside the house and I suppose had presented an ideal target. But he had moved at just the right or wrong time and instead of killing him the high-powered bullet smashed into his shoulder. He jumped into the air and turned his snapping teeth upon the wound, trying to bite the cause of the pain he could not see. And then he turned towards home, unsteady but still strong on his three remaining legs. No doubt he felt, as we all do, that if he could get home he might be saved, but he did not make it, as we knew he could not, because of the amount of blood on the snow and the wavering pattern of his three-legged tracks. Yet he was, as I said, tremendously strong and he managed almost three quarters of a mile. The house he sought must have been within his vision when he died for we could see it quite clearly when we came to his body by the roadside. His eyes were open and his tongue was clenched between his teeth and the little blood he had left dropped red and black on the winter snow. He was not to be saved for a future time anymore.

I learned later that my father had asked the neighbor to shoot him and that we had led him into a kind of ambush. Perhaps my father did so because the neighbor was younger and had a better gun or was a better shot. Perhaps because my father did not want to be involved. It was obvious he had not planned on things turning out so messy.

The dog had become increasingly powerful and protective, to the extent that people were afraid to come into the yard. And he had also bitten two of the neighbor's children and caused them to be frightened of passing our house on their journeys to and from school. And perhaps there was also the feeling in the community that he was getting more than his share of the breeding: that he traveled farther than other dogs on his nightly forays and that he fought off and injured the other smaller dogs who might compete with him for female favors. Perhaps there was fear that his dominance and undesirable characteristics did not bode well for future generations.

This has been the writing down of a memory triggered by the sight of a golden dog at play in the silent snow with my own excited children. After they came in and had their hot chocolate, the wind began to blow; and by the time I left for work, there was no evidence of their early-morning revels or any dog tracks leading to the chain-link fence. The "enclosed" dog looked impassively at me as I brushed the snow from the buried windshield. What does he know? he seemed to say.

The snow continues to drift and to persist as another uncertainty added to those we already have. Should we be forced to drive tonight, it will be a long, tough journey into the wind and the driving snow which is pounding across Ontario and Quebec and New Brunswick and against the granite coast of Nova Scotia. Should we be drawn by death, we might well meet our own. Still, it is only because I am alive that I can even consider such possibilities. Had I not been saved by the golden dog, I would not have these tight concerns or children playing in the snow or of course these memories. It is because of him that I have been able to come this far in time.

It is too bad that I could not have saved him as well and my feelings did him little good as I looked upon his bloodied body there beside the road. It was too late and out of my control and even if I had known the possibilities of the future it would not have been easy.

He was with us only for a while and brought his own changes, and yet he still persists. He persists in my memory and in my life and he persists physically as well. He is there in this winter storm. There in the golden-gray dogs with their black-tipped ears and tails, sleeping in the stables or in the lees of woodpiles or under porches or curled beside the houses which face towards the sea.

James Herriot

THE GREAT ESCAPE

I poised my knife over a swollen ear. Tristan, one elbow leaning wearily on the table, was holding an anaesthetic mask over the nose of the sleeping dog when Siegfried came into the room.

He glanced briefly at the patient. "Ah yes, that haematoma you were telling me about, James." Then he looked across the table at his brother. "Good God, you're a lovely sight this morning! When did you get in last night?"

Tristan raised a pallid countenance. His eyes were bloodshot slits between puffy lids. "Oh, I don't quite know. Fairly late, I should think."

"Fairly late! I got back from a farrowing at four o'clock and you hadn't arrived then. Where the hell were you, anyway?"

"I was at the Licensed Victuallers' Ball. Very good do, actually."

"I bet it was!" Siegfried snorted. "You don't miss a thing, do you? Darts Team Dinner, Bellringers' Outing, Pigeon Club Dance, and now it's the Licensed Victuallers' Ball. If there's a good booze-up going on anywhere you'll find it."

When under fire Tristan always retained his dignity and he drew it around him now like a threadbare cloak.

"As a matter of fact," he said, "many of the Licensed Victuallers are my friends."

His brother flushed. "I believe you. I should think you're the best bloody customer they've ever had!"

Tristan made no reply but began to make a careful check of the flow of oxygen into the ether bottle.

"And another thing," Siegfried continued. "I keep seeing you slinking around with about a dozen different women. And you're supposed to be studying for an exam."

"That's an exaggeration." The young man gave him a pained look. "I admit I enjoy a little female company now and then—just like yourself."

Tristan believed in attack as the best form of defence, and it was a telling blow, because there was a constant stream of attractive girls laying siege to Siegfried at Skeldale House.

But the elder brother was only temporarily halted. "Never mind me!" he shouted. "I've passed all my exams. I'm talking about you! Didn't I see you with that new barmaid from the Drovers' the other night? You dodged rapidly into a shop doorway but I'm bloody sure it was you."

Tristan cleared his throat. "It quite possibly was. I have recently become friendly with Lydia—she's a very nice girl."

"I'm not saying she isn't. What I am saying is that I want to see you indoors at night with your books instead of boozing and chasing women. Is that clear?"

"Quite." The young man inclined his head gracefully and turned down the knob on the anaesthetic machine.

His brother regarded him balefully for a few moments, breathing deeply. These remonstrations always took it out of him. Then he turned away quickly and left.

Tristan's facade crumbled as soon as the door closed.

"Watch the anaesthetic for a minute, Jim," he croaked. He went over to the basin in the corner, filled a measuring jar with cold water and drank it at a long gulp. Then he soaked some cotton wool under the tap and applied it to his brow.

"I wish he hadn't come in just then. I'm in no mood for the raised voices and angry words." He reached up to a large bottle of aspirins, swallowed a few and washed them down with another gargantuan draught. "All right then, Jim," he murmured as he returned to the table and took over the mask again. "Let's go."

I bent once more over the sleeping dog. He was a Scottie called Hamish and his mistress, Miss Westerman, had brought him in two days ago.

She was a retired schoolteacher and I always used to think she must have had little trouble in keeping her class in order. The chilly pale eyes looking straight into mine reminded me that she was as tall as I was and the square jaw between the muscular shoulders completed a redoubtable presence.

"Mr Herriot," she barked, "I want you to have a look at Hamish. I do hope it's nothing serious but his ear has become very swollen and painful. They don't get—er—cancer there, do they?" For a moment the steady gaze wavered.

"Oh that's most unlikely." I lifted the little animal's chin and looked at the left ear which was drooping over the side of his face. His whole head, in fact, was askew, as though dragged down by pain.

Carefully I lifted the ear and touched the tense swelling with a forefinger. Hamish looked round at me and whimpered.

"Yes, I know, old chap. It's tender, isn't it?" As I turned to Miss Westerman I almost bumped into the close-cropped iron-grey head which was hovering close over the little dog.

"He's got an aural haematoma," I said.

"What on earth is that?"

"It's when the little blood vessels between the skin and cartilage of the ear rupture and the blood flows out and causes this acute distension."

She patted the jet black shaggy coat. "But what causes it?"

"Canker, usually. Has he been shaking his head lately?"

"Yes, now you mention it he has. Just as though he had got something in his ear and was trying to get rid of it."

"Well, that's what bursts the blood vessels. I can see he has a touch of canker, though it isn't common in this breed."

She nodded. "I see. And how can you cure it?"

"Only by an operation, I'm afraid."

"Oh dear!" She put her hand to her mouth. "I'm not keen on that."

"There's nothing to worry about," I said. "It's just a case of letting the blood out and stitching the layers of the ear together. If we don't do this soon he'll suffer a lot of pain and finish up with a cauliflower ear, and we don't want that because he's a bonny little chap."

I meant it, too. Hamish was a proud-strutting, trim little dog. The Scottish Terrier is an attractive creature and I often lament that there are so few around in these modern days.

After some hesitation Miss Westerman agreed and we fixed a date two days from then. When she brought him in for the operation she deposited Hamish in my arms, stroked his head again and again, then looked from Tristan to me and back again.

"You'll take care of him, won't you," she said, and the jaw jutted and the pale blue eyes stabbed. For a moment I felt like a little boy caught in mischief, and I think my colleague felt the same because he blew out his breath as the lady departed.

"By gum, Jim, that's a tough baby," he muttered. "I wouldn't like to get on the wrong side of her."

I nodded. "Yes, and she thinks all the world of this dog, so let's make a good job of him."

After Siegfried's departure I lifted the ear which was now a turgid cone and made an incision along the inner skin. As the pent up blood gushed forth I caught it in an enamel dish, then I squeezed several big clots through the wound.

"No wonder the poor little chap was in pain," I said softly. "He'll feel a lot better when he wakes up."

I filled the cavity between skin and cartilage with sulphanilamide, then began to stitch the layers together, using a row of buttons. You had to do something like this or the thing filled up again within a few days. When I first began to operate on aural haematomata I used to pack the interior with gauze, then bandage the ear to the head. The owners often made little granny-hats to try to keep the bandage in place, but a frisky dog usually had it off very soon.

The buttons were a far better idea and kept the layers in close contact, lessening the chance of distortion.

By lunchtime Hamish had come round from the anaesthetic and though still slightly dopey he already seemed to be relieved that his bulging ear had been deflated. Miss Westerman had gone away for the day and was due to pick him up in the evening. The little dog, curled in his basket, waited philosophically.

At tea-time, Siegfried glanced across the table at his brother. "I'm going off to Brawton for a few hours, Tristan," he said. "I want you to stay in the house and give Miss Westerman her dog when she arrives. I don't know just when she'll come." He scooped out a spoonful of jam. "You can keep an eye on the patient and do a bit of studying, too. It's about time you had a night at home."

Tristan nodded. "Right, I'll do that." But I could see he wasn't enthusiastic.

When Siegfried had driven away Tristan rubbed his chin and gazed reflectively through the french window into the darkening garden. "This is distinctly awkward, Jim."

"Why?"

"Well, Lydia has tonight off and I promised to see her." He whistled a few bars under his breath. "It seems a pity to waste the opportunity just when things are building up nicely. I've got a strong feeling that girl fancies me. In fact she's nearly eating out of my hand."

I looked at him wonderingly. "My God, I thought you'd want a bit of peace and quiet and an early bed after last night!"

"Not me," he said. "I'm raring to go again."

And indeed he looked fresh and fit, eyes sparkling, roses back in his cheeks.

"Look, Jim," he went on, "I don't suppose you could stick around with this dog?"

I shrugged. "Sorry, Triss. I'm going back to see that cow of Ted Binns—right at the top of the Dale. I'll be away for nearly two hours."

For a few moments he was silent, then he raised a finger. "I think I have the solution. It's quite simple, in fact it's perfect. I'll bring Lydia in here."

"What! Into the house?"

"Yes, into this very room. I can put Hamish in his basket by the fire and Lydia and I can occupy the sofa. Marvellous! What could be nicer on a cold winter's night. Cheap, too."

"But Triss! How about Siegfried's lecture this morning? What if he comes home early and catches the two of you here?"

Tristan lit a Woodbine and blew out an expansive cloud. "Not a chance. You worry about such tiny things, Jim. He's always late when he goes to Brawton. There's no problem at all."

"Well, please yourself," I said. "But I think you're asking for trouble. Anyway, shouldn't you be doing a bit of bacteriology? The exams are getting close."

He smiled seraphically through the smoke. "Oh, I'll have a quick read through it all in good time."

I couldn't argue with him there. I always had to go over a thing about six times before it finally sank in, but with his brain the quick read would no doubt suffice. I went out on my call.

I got back about eight o'clock and as I opened the front door my mind was far from Tristan. Ted Binns's cow wasn't responding to my treatment and I was beginning to wonder if I was on the right track. When in doubt I liked to look the subject up, and the books were on the shelves in the sitting room. I hurried along the passage and threw open the door.

For a moment I stood there bewildered, trying to reorientate my thoughts. The sofa was drawn close to the bright fire, the atmosphere was heavy with cigarette smoke and the scent of perfume, but there was nobody to be seen.

The most striking feature was the long curtain over the french window. It was wafting slowly downwards as though some object had just hurtled through it at great speed. I trotted over the carpet and peered out into the dark garden. From somewhere in the gloom I heard a scuffling noise, a thud and a muffled cry, then there was a pitter-patter followed by a shrill yelping. I stood for some time listening, then as my eyes grew accustomed to the darkness I walked down the long path under the high brick wall to the yard at the foot. The yard door was open as were the big double doors into the back lane, but there was no sign of life.

Slowly I retraced my steps to the warm oblong of light at the foot of the tall old house. I was about to close the french window when I heard a stealthy movement and an urgent whisper.

"Is that you, Jim?"

"Triss! Where the hell have you sprung from?"

The young man tiptoed past me into the room and looked around him anxiously. "It was you, then, not Siegfried?"

"Yes, I've just come in."

He flopped on the sofa and sunk his head in his hands. "Oh damn! I was just lying here a few minutes ago with Lydia in my arms. At peace with the world. Everything was wonderful. Then I heard the front door open."

"But you knew I was coming back."

"Yes, and I'd have given you a shout, but for some reason I thought, 'God help us, it's Siegfried!' It sounded like his step in the passage."

"Then what happened?"

He churned his hair around with his fingers. "Oh, I panicked. I was whispering lovely things into Lydia's ear, then the next second I grabbed her, threw her off the couch and out of the french window."

"I heard a thud . . ."

"Yes, that was Lydia falling into the rockery."

"And then some sort of high-pitched cries . . ."

He sighed and closed his eyes. "That was Lydia in the rose bushes. She doesn't know the geography of the place, poor lass."

"Gosh, Triss," I said, "I'm really sorry. I shouldn't have burst in on you like that. I was thinking of something else."

He rose wearily and put a hand on my shoulder. "Not your fault, Jim, not your fault. You did warn me." He reached for his cigarettes. "I don't know how I'm going to face that girl again. I just chucked her out into the lane and told her to beat it home with all speed. She must think I'm stone balmy." He gave a hollow groan.

I tried to be cheerful. "Oh, you'll get round her again. You'll have a laugh about it later."

But he wasn't listening. His eyes, wide with horror, were staring past me. Slowly he raised a trembling finger and pointed towards the fireplace. His mouth worked for a few seconds before he spoke.

"Christ, Jim, it's gone!" he gasped.

For a moment I thought the shock had deranged him. "Gone . . . ? What's gone?"

"The bloody dog! He was there when I dashed outside. Right there!"

I looked down at the empty basket and a cold hand clutched at me. "Oh no! He must have got out through the open window. We're in trouble."

We rushed into the garden and searched in vain. We came back for torches and searched once more, prowling around the yard and back lane, shouting the little dog's name with diminishing hope.

After ten minutes we trailed back to the brightly lit room and stared at each other.

Tristan was the first to voice our thoughts. "What do we tell Miss Westerman when she calls?"

I shook my head. My mind fled from the thought of informing that lady that we had lost her dog.

Just at that moment the front door bell pealed in the passage and Tristan almost leaped in the air.

364

"Oh God!" he quavered. "That'll be her now. Go and see her, Jim. Tell her it was my fault—anything you like—but I daren't face her."

I squared my shoulders, marched over the long stretch of tiles and opened the door. It wasn't Miss Westerman, it was a well-built platinum blonde, and she glared at me angrily.

"Where's Tristan?" she rasped in a voice which told me we had more than one tough female to deal with tonight.

"Well, he's—er—"

"Oh, I know he's in there!" As she brushed past me I noticed she had a smear of soil on her cheek and her hair was sadly disarranged. I followed her into the room where she stalked up to my friend.

"Look at my bloody stockings!" she burst out. "They're ruined!"

Tristan peered nervously at the shapely legs. "I'm sorry, Lydia. I'll get you another pair. Honestly, love, I will."

"You'd better, you bugger!" she replied. "And don't 'love' me—I've never been so insulted in my life. What did you think you were playing at?"

"It was all a misunderstanding. Let me explain . . ." Tristan advanced on her with a brave attempt at a winning smile, but she backed away.

"Keep your distance," she said frigidly. "I've had enough of you for one night."

She swept out and Tristan leaned his head against the mantelpiece. "The end of a lovely friendship, Jim." Then he shook himself. "But we've got to find that dog. Come on."

I set off in one direction and he went in the other. It was a moonless night of impenetrable darkness and we were looking for a jet black dog. I think we both knew it was hopeless but we had to try.

In a little town like Darrowby you are soon out on the country roads where there are no lights, and as I stumbled around peering vainly over invisible fields the utter pointlessness of the activity became more and more obvious.

Occasionally I came within Tristan's orbit and heard his despairing cries echoing over the empty landscape. "Haamiish! Haamiish! Haamiish . . . !"

After half an hour we met at Skeldale House. Tristan faced me and as I shook my head he seemed to shrink within himself. His chest heaved as he fought for breath. Obviously he had been running while I had been walking and I suppose that was natural enough. We were both in an awkward situation but the final devastating blow would inevitably fall on him.

"Well, we'd better get out on the road again," he gasped, and as he spoke the front door bell rang again.

The colour drained rapidly from his face and he clutched my arm. "That must be Miss Westerman this time. God almighty, she's coming in!"

Rapid footseps sounded in the passage and the sitting room door opened. But it wasn't Miss Westerman, it was Lydia again. She strode over to the sofa, reached underneath and extracted her handbag. She didn't say anything but merely shrivelled Tristan with a sidelong glance before leaving.

"What a night!" he moaned, putting a hand to his forehead. "I can't stand much more of this."

Over the next hour we made innumerable sorties but we couldn't find Hamish and nobody else seemed to have seen him. I came in to find Tristan collapsed in an armchair. His mouth hung open and he showed every sign of advanced exhaustion. I shook my head and he shook his, then I heard the telephone.

I lifted the receiver, listened for a minute and turned to the young man. "I've got to go out, Triss. Mr Drew's old pony has colic again."

He reached out a hand from the depths of his chair. "You're not going to leave me, Jim?"

"Sorry, I must. But I won't be long. It's only a mile away."

"But what if Miss Westerman comes?"

I shrugged. "You'll just have to apologise. Hamish is bound to turn up—maybe in the morning."

"You make it sound easy . . ." He ran a hand inside his collar. "And another thing—how about Siegfried? What if he arrives and asks about the dog? What do I tell him?"

"Oh, I shouldn't worry about that," I replied airily. "Just say you were too busy on the sofa with the Drovers' barmaid to bother about such things. He'll understand."

But my attempt at jocularity fell flat. The young man fixed me with a cold eye and ignited a quivering Woodbine. "I believe I've told you this before, Jim, but there's a nasty cruel streak in you."

Mr Drew's pony had almost recovered when I got there but I gave it a mild sedative injection before turning for home. On the way back a thought struck me and I took a road round the edge of the town to the row of modern bungalows where Miss Westerman lived. I parked the car and walked up the path of number ten.

And there was Hamish in the porch, coiled up comfortably on the mat, looking up at me with mild surprise as I hovered over him.

"Come on, lad," I said. "You've got more sense than we had. Why didn't we think of this before?"

I deposited him on the passenger seat and as I drove away he hoisted his paws on to the dash and gazed out interestedly at the road unfolding in the headlights. Truly a phlegmatic little hound.

Outside Skeldale House I tucked him under my arm and was about to turn the handle of the front door when I paused. Tristan had notched up a long succession of successful pranks against me—fake telephone calls, the ghost in my bedroom and many others—and in fact, good friends as we were, he never neglected a chance to take the mickey out of me. In this situation, with the positions reversed, he would be merciless. I put my finger on the bell and leaned on it for several long seconds.

For some time there was neither sound nor movement from within and I pictured the cowering figure mustering his courage before marching to his doom. Then the light came on in the passage and as I peered expectantly through the glass a nose appeared round the far corner followed very gingerly by a wary eye. By degrees the full face inched into view and when Tristan recognised my grinning countenance he unleashed a cry of rage and bounded along the passage with upraised fist.

I really think that in his distraught state he would have attacked me, but the sight of Hamish banished all else. He grabbed the hairy creature and began to fondle him.

"Good little dog, nice little dog," he crooned as he trotted through to the sitting room. "What a beautiful thing you are." He laid him lovingly in the basket, and Hamish, after a "heigh-ho, here we are again" glance around him, put his head along his side and promptly went to sleep.

Tristan fell limply into the armchair and gazed at me with glazed eyes.

"Well, we're saved, Jim," he whispered. "But I'll never be the same after tonight. I've run bloody miles and I've nearly lost my voice with shouting. I tell you I'm about knackered."

I too was vastly relieved, and the nearness of catastrophe was brought home to us when Miss Westerman arrived within ten minutes.

"Oh, my darling!" she cried as Hamish leaped at her, mouth open, short tail wagging furiously. "I've been so worried about you all day."

She looked tentatively at the ear with its rows of buttons. "Oh, it does look a lot better without that horrid swelling—and what a nice neat job you have made. Thank you, Mr Herriot, and thank you, too, young man."

Tristan, who had staggered to his feet, bowed slightly as I showed the lady out.

"Bring him back in six weeks to have the stitches out," I called to her as she left, then I rushed back into the room.

"Siegfried's just pulled up outside! You'd better look as if you've been working."

He rushed to the bookshelves, pulled down Gaiger and Davis's *Bacteriology* and a notebook and dived into a chair. When his brother came in he was utterly engrossed.

Siegfried moved over to the fire and warmed his hands. He looked pink and mellow.

"I've just been speaking to Miss Westerman," he said. "She's really pleased. Well done, both of you."

"Thank you," I said, but Tristan was too busy to reply, scanning the pages anxiously and scribbling repeatedly in the notebook.

Siegfried walked behind the young man's chair and looked down at the open volume.

"Ah yes, Clostridium septique," he murmured, smiling indulgently. "That's a good one to study. Keeps coming up in exams." He rested a hand briefly on his brother's shoulder. "I'm glad to see you at work. You've been raking about too much lately and it's getting you down. A night at your books will have been good for you."

He yawned, stretched, and made for the door. "I'm off to bed. I'm rather sleepy." He paused with his hand on the door. "You know, Tristan, I quite envy you—there's nothing like a nice restful evening at home."

The situation of a patient escaping is by no means unique. It is something which has happened to many vets, particularly in the thirties when small animal work was very much a sideline and there were few organised arrangements for hospitalisation. It was especially traumatic when formidable people like Miss Westerman and Siegfried were involved. It is interesting to record another of the satisfying little operations—the treatment of an aural haematoma. A very quick relief from pain. I also relished the chance to chronicle a typical vignette from Tristan's love life.

Susan Dunlap

A CONTEST FIT
FOR A QUEEN

You can always sunbathe in Berkeley on Washington's birthday, they say. Maybe so. But it was already Valentine's Day and it had been raining since New Year's. I was willing to believe we'd be able to bathe in another week, but odds were it'd be with a cake of Ivory.

Tonight, the thermometer was not ten degrees above freezing (polar by our standards). The rain pounded on the portal like a door-to-door salesman. It was a night made for staying home.

Or it would have been if one of the other tenants in Howard's house hadn't booked the living room for his club meeting. A meeting of the South Campus Respect for Reptiles Committee.

"Do they bring the esteemed with them, Howard?"

"Don't ask. But if you're going through the living room keep your shoes on." Howard shook his head. Clearly this was a topic he didn't dare dip into. The corners of his mouth twitched. He wanted to dip. His mouth opened and shut again. He was dying to dip.

I grinned.

He gave up. "It's an emergency meeting for the Reptilians, Jill. Their status in the animal rights union has been challenged. By the Save the Goldfish Committee."

It took me a moment to recall just what it was snakes ate. "May the better vertebrate win." And thinking of the fish, I added, "I suppose it's too late to make a dinner reservation."

But even before I finished the sentence, I knew the answer. You'll never starve in Berkeley. Even on Valentine's Day there is always a restaurant with an empty table for two. But while Howard insists I am his number-one love, number two (this house in which he dwells as chief tenant and lusts to own) is close behind, and he would never abandon its nurturing nooks and cavelike crannies to the Reptilians.

"Better than that!" he said, running his hand around my back, under my arm till his fingers caressed the side of my breast. "I've got an evening so romantic, a night so exotic, so Continental it should have subtitles. The lover's answer," he said, pulling me closer, "to one-stop shopping."

"Aha. Dinner in bed, you mean."

"And with a new tradition I think you're going to like."

The California-king-sized bed was covered with a spotted madras spread (we'd done dinners here before) and dotted with white cardboard cartons (Styrofoam is outlawed in Berkeley), and plastic plates from freezer dinners. Howard had bought the bed for its mission-style headboard with the four-inch-wide runner at the top—the perfect size for coffee mugs and wineglasses. (By now we had a number of spotted pillowcases.)

"Happy Valentine's Day," Howard said, uncorking the chardonnay. (White goes better with the pillowcases.)

"And to you," I said, saluting him with a spring roll.

From downstairs came a muffled shout. I bit into the spring roll.

"Valentine's Day is a traditional sort of holiday—"

"I thought it had been created by the card companies—"

"So I propose a tradition of our own. A tradition suitable for two esteemed police detectives, like us."

"Here on the bed?"

He leaned forward, puckered his lips, opened his mouth, sucked in the rest of my spring roll. When he'd swallowed, he said, "Valentine's Day collars. Other traditions come later. What's your most memorable Valentine's collar?"

I laughed. Only Howard would come up with a tradition celebrating the best Valentine's Day arrests. I could have negotiated a prize, but as everyone in coupledom knows, no object is to be as cherished as the hard-won right to lord it over one's mate. The Collar Queen, I liked the prospect of that. "In homicide or patrol?"

"Either one. In your entire time on the force." Howard reached for another spring roll.

I could see the lay of the land here. "Oh no! You first."

"Don't you have a collar?"

"Yeah, I've got one, from when I was on patrol. But I'm no fool, Howard, and if I let you sit and listen for twenty minutes, by the time I finish talking there won't be any food left. You start."

From downstairs came a loud hiss. I preferred to think of it as a delegate's indication of dissent. As opposed to his subject's hiss of disgruntlement.

Rain splatted against the window and the wind scraped the glass with a branch of the jacaranda tree. But in here, enclosed by the warm green walls and the crisp white moldings, with the smells of Asian spices mingling with the aroma of wine, the whir of the space heater, it was turning out to be an okay Valentine's. Howard shepherded half the rice onto his plate, added a heaping scoop of vegetable satay, four chicken brochettes, and wad of eggplant with black beans. He crossed his long legs, propped his plate on one knee, and began. "This is from patrol, too. I'd already been working detective detail, but I'd rotated back onto patrol for a while. The call was on a natural death of an LOL. The LOL was in her seventies, but she looked to have been old for that age, not one of the Gray Panthers who'd stomp a mugger into the ground and walk off shaking the dust from her Birkenstocks; no, she was an LOL."

I nodded, leaning against the headboard, balancing my satay on my thigh as I reached for my wineglass.

"She lived in a four-room cottage, west of San Pablo. Hurricane fencing around the perimeter, big dog in the yard. House a square, four identical-size rooms."

"Like a sandwich you cut into quarters?"

"Right. Neighbors heard the dog barking and got concerned that he hadn't been out in that yard all day. Valentine, that was the dog's name, because he had a white heart on his rump."

I smiled. That bit of whimsy made me like the old lady. I could tell it grabbed Howard, too. "How did she die?"

"Heart attack, I think. Certainly natural cause. And fast, I think. The TV was still on. She was sitting in front of it on one of those maroon-flowered antique sofas with the buttons covered in the same material, and all of it looking too hard to sit on. Makes you understand the energy of the Victorian age."

"Had to keep moving, huh?"

"Oh no!" One of the Reptilians shouted downstairs. I glanced at the foot of the door. There wasn't a quarter of an inch between it and the jamb.

Picking up his pace and volume, Howard said, "Not much in her living room—the sofa, one chair, two end tables, a bookcase, a couple pictures on the wall, but no photos or knickknacks strewn around like you find with most LOLs."

"Maybe she didn't have anyone."

"No relatives, right. Nothing unnecessary in the kitchen or the bedroom. Looked like she lived frugally, but not desperately, like a lot of people on Social Security. She was tidy, and she knew what she liked: that Victorian stuff. If someone had told me it was *eighteen* ninety-four instead of nineteen ninety-four there wouldn't have been much to contradict it. Even her books tended to be things like Jane Austen."

I finished my satay and glanced at the carton. Despite his monologue, Howard had managed to down his portion and was eyeing the same carton. I served. "So that's it? *That's* your most interesting case?"

"Wait. I haven't gotten to the interesting part: the fourth room. You've got these three austere, Victorian-lady rooms, then the fourth. It was crammed, floor to ceiling, with the oddest collection of stuff I've come across. Golf clubs, electric trains, stamp collection, a set of something like twenty-seven drill bits, leather suitcases, a black plastic stool in which the middle of the cushion comes out, the scroungiest-looking stuffed pheasant—thing was missing an eye and all its tail feathers—with a Valentine's heart on a ribbon around its neck."

"Must have been easy to shoot."

Ignoring that, Howard went on. "Place was so full you couldn't even see the windows."

"Her late husband's things?"

"Nope, maiden lady. Neighbors said they'd never seen a male visitor. Besides, some of the stuff was almost new, a lot never used. It wasn't like mementos from the love of her life who died in nineteen forty-nine or 'fifty-two."

I put down my second spring roll. "It's all guy stuff, except the stool and that's just weird. Things like the drill bits; you'll find women who've got them, but—"

"Yeah, you can picture the owner: one of those guys who *thinks* he's going to be a handyman and his wife or kids give him the complete deluxe home handyman's set. And in this case I'd bet my last spring roll those bits had never been out of the box."

"Over by the door," a Reptilian shouted downstairs.

Howard tensed, ready to charge downstairs and defend his second love from invasion.

I put a hand on his arm. "Berkeley, the city of diversity, should create a snake run, like the dog park. It'd only take a narrow piece of land. Owners'd put their cobras and pythons on little alligator leashes to exercise them. And the best part for the sedentary snake lover is they wouldn't even have to be in good shape for the walk. Not like our burglar who had to hoist a massage chair, an arched backbend bench the size of a sofa, and enough photography equipment to furnish a studio."

"Jill, how'd you—"

I put up a hand to quiet him. The thought was tiptoeing across the back of my head, just out of reach. Something about his story . . . somethi—"The fucking pheasant!"

"What?"

"That's what his wife called it." I put down my glass. "Howard, I remember that pheasant. I took the call on the burglary it came from. On Linden Terrace. It was just an ordinary case; I wouldn't remember it at all—it must have been six or seven years ago—but the guy insisted on describing his missing pheasant. Seems it was the first thing he ever shot, and in honor of that he gave it to his wife for Valentine's Day back when they were engaged."

"She married him anyway, huh?" He dumped the satay on his rice.

"For better or worse. He even showed me a picture of it, with the red ribbon and the heart. A velvet heart with lace around it like you'd find on a box of candy."

"Probably where it came from. Guy probably gobbled the chocolates while he was waiting for the pheasant to fly." For Howard, the department's sting king, an uneven match like rifle versus wing is certainly not sport.

The warm glow of closed cases beckoned. But it had been years since that burglary. "I suppose there was no reason to confiscate pheasant and company from the old lady's house."

"Hardly. It'd've filled half the evidence room. But the pheasant, I think the neighbor took it, strange as it is to think there could be two human beings who'd want it." Howard fingered the last spring roll and grinned. "So my LOL, Rosamin Minton, was an LOF."

"Little Old Fence?"

"A fence with the worst taste in town. Or a fence who'd moved the electronics and jewelry but couldn't get rid of the rest of the junk." Howard took a bite of satay and nodded. "Still, not a bad Valentine's entry. Not so easy to top. So, Jill, what's your Valentine collar?"

I took a swallow of wine, leaned back against the headboard, adjusted the pillow—that little ledge is great for cups and glasses, but it does nothing for my neck. I picked up my wineglass, looked Howard in the eye, and grinned back at him. "You could have won by a mile, Howard. But not now. Your entry was good, a real competitive racer of a case. I was in bad shape . . . until . . . you reminded me." I lifted my wineglass in salute. I don't often win these contests with Howard—nobody does—but when I do I make the most of it. The robes of the Collar Queen were going to hang quite nicely off my shoulders. "The pheasant burglary took place, Howard, on Valentine's Day!"

Howard gave me a tentative salute. He could see he was being edged out, but he wasn't throwing in the towel yet.

"Howard, the RP, what was his name? I remember thinking it was a funny name for a reporting party—Robert Parton, that's it! He was just outraged that his bird—"

"Flew the coop on Valentine's?"

"Right. His wife did point out that it was on the mantel where he put it for the occasion. A thief could hardly miss it. Then Parton was enraged about the loss of a stained-glass lamp he'd made himself—"

"Lamp with a band of chartreuse hearts at the edge of the shade?"

"Could there be two?" I grinned wider. The lamp had propelled me to neck and neck with Howard. "And Parton was really pissed that the thief had used a couple of his old jackets to wrap the things in. His wife kept reminding him that the stereo and the TV were still there and they were worth plenty more than a bag of used clothes, a lamp, and a moldy bird. But Parton wasn't buying that. He ranted at her, at me, and even at the Chihuahua, for God's sake. Like it should have stood off the thief, single-pawedly!"

"That's it? Your whole Valentine offering? You lose! The answer's obvious. The wife did it?"

"*Au contraire,* my dear Howard. Mrs. Parton was out with Robert at the time of the burglary. And she's hardly the type to hire a few unemployed mafiosi. And more to the point, there were two other burglaries that Valentine's night. And the next year another three with the same

377

MO. And three the following year, when we were half expecting them and still couldn't prevent them. Drove us crazy. And then they stopped."

"And never started again?" He meant did the thief get pulled in for something else or merely move out of town?

"Nope, nothing more. Burglary detail was keeping an eye out. Simpson there really went over those cases, but he couldn't find a link. The Bensquis were in their twenties, the Partons near forty, the Yamamotos in their late sixties. Victims were a bakery chef, an engineer, two artists, one nurse, one doctor, an airline pilot, a copy editor, a short-haul truck driver. There was no connection through their jobs, churches, hobbies, clubs—zilch. They were all in different parts of the city. Some victims had standing Valentine's plans, some went out to dinner on the spur of the moment, one couple just went out for a walk, and bingo! their darkroom was cleaned out! No prints, no suspicious characters, no vans or trucks loitering out front. Stuff never turned up in pawn shops, flea markets, or any of the normal places. Not lead one. And Parton, the doctor . . . well, if he made that number of follow-up calls to any patient, they'd die of shock." I leaned back, took a long swallow of wine, and said, "It was a very frustrating case—nine disparate couples, burgled of stuff of no particular value, and it all ends up with one little old lady who kept it sealed away from her in a back room! But, Howard, reward comes to the worthy. And thanks to your accidental discovery, you have given me an assist in winning the First Annual Valentine's Day Collar Contest. Pay homage to the Collar Queen!"

"No you don't! This is a *collar* contest. There was no collar in your case. You, Jill, got nada!"

"Outside! Look outside!" Downstairs doors banged. Howard hesitated, clearly torn between defending his house and his contest.

"It sounds good," I said. "But I'm not using the bathroom till you make sure everyone's accounted for."

Howard headed downstairs and I cleared off the bed the remnants of the first course, preparatory to the more traditional Valentine's Day tradition.

Tomorrow, I'd track down the department's files on the burglaries. No way was Howard going to win!

* * *

What I did not track down the next morning—Monday—was Simpson of burglary detail. While Howard and I had been making our bet, Simpson had been flying off to the Bahamas.

What was waiting for me at the station was a batch of in-custodys held over the weekend. When you bungle your burgling Friday night, the city gives you free lodging all weekend. By Monday morning you are a sorry, and surly, soul. I didn't finish running the checks on the in-custodys before detective's morning meeting, and afterward ended up transporting one of the surly and sorry to San Mateo County, an hour away. In the afternoon I had a court appearance on an old 217 (assault with intent to murder) and I didn't get around to the late Rosamin Minton's neighbor till after five o'clock.

The Minton house was just as Howard described it: a square clapboard box behind a hurricane fence, in a neighborhood where shabby didn't stand out. Two scraggly trees now stood watch over the walkway, obviously the work of a newer, if not more horticulturally talented, tenant. The present neighbor, the nephew of the pheasant taker, hadn't known Rosamin Minton. He handed over the contraband bird without question. If he could have asked for a sworn statement that I'd tell no one it had nested in his house, he would have. Clearly, he was too embarrassed to ask why, after all these years, it was needed by the officialdom of his city.

I picked up the thing gingerly. Taxidermy, apparently, is not forever. The bird was not just eyeless and sans tail feathers, there were bare spots on its back, and it looked like it had used one wing to fight off its assailant. Even the lace-and-velvet heart looked like it had been slobbered over.

Robert Parton stared at the deceased bird with an expression of horror that matched my own. "It's been chewed! How could anyone—"

"No accounting for taste, Dr. Parton."

He brushed its moldy feathers. "Still, you found it! After all these years! Monica, it's still got the heart I got for you."

Monica Parton looked even more appalled. A woman of some taste, I felt.

Only the Chihuahua found merit in the miserable memento. He was running from one side of the spacious living room to the other, bouncing and lowing like he'd treed the fowl himself.

"Where did you find it?" Parton asked.

"The other side of Berkeley."

"Did you get my lamp? Stained glass; took me six months to make. And my jackets?"

"Robert," Monica said, "the Salvation Army wouldn't even want those clothes. Be glad you've got your bird."

Before they could continue the sartorial debate, I opened my pad and read off a list of the other Valentine's Day victims. "Do you recognize any of these names?"

"No," Robert said, still holding the pheasant overhead, away from its other admirer.

"Mrs. Parton?"

She looked thoughtful, as if giving the list more consideration than had her booty-enthralled husband. But in the end she shook her head.

"Dr. Parton, I know how concerned you were about this burglary. In the five years since then, have you come across anything connected to it? Any motive?"

Both shook their heads. And as I left he was beaming at the bird and she was still shaking her head.

It was the next day before I had time to go over the old Valentine burglary files thoroughly enough to make a list of the losses. The stool with the hole belonged to Jason Peabody.

The Peabody house was one of those two-bedroom stucco jobs with one room over the garage. I'd been in enough of them to know that the living room would be too small for an eight-by-ten rug. The whole Peabody house could have fitted in the Partons' living room. It was just before noon when I rang the Peabody bell. And a minute or two after when the door opened.

"Mrs. Peabody? I'm Detective Smith." I held out my shield.

"Yes?" She had that you've-found-me-out look we on the force see so often that we mistake it for a greeting. "Sorry it took me so long. I needed to put Spot in the back room. Come on in."

A leather couch, matching overstuffed chair, and a coffee table made for a normal-sized room pretty much filled the space. The television sat atop the built-in bookcase, blocking the window. The dining room, too, was a space that could not accommodate one more fork or candlestick, much less a chair. I almost felt guilty as I said, "I have good news. We've found the black plastic stool that was taken in your burglary, the one with the cushion that pulls out to create a hole in the middle."

"Jason's toilet-seat chair." If she was pleased she was hiding it well.

"Your husband is incapacitated?"

She laughed uncomfortably. "No. No. When you take the center out, the chair looks like a toilet seat, a padded black plastic toilet seat."

"But it's not?"

"Oh, no. I should make you guess what it's for." She almost smiled before she recalled to whom she was speaking. I've seen that reaction often enough, too. "Jason kept the stool right there." She pointed to the side of the fireplace, next to the bookcase with the television on it.

The stool was eighteen inches square. With it in place, the Peabodys would have had to inch between it and the coffee table. "What is it?"

"A headstand stool."

Even in Berkeley . . .

"You know, for people who want to do headstands but don't want all their weight on their heads." She was eyeing my reaction, almost smiling. "They stick their heads through the hole, like they're ready to flush them." She swallowed a laugh. "Then they hang onto the legs and kick up. Jason's tall and thin. He always looked kind of like a fern in the wind with his feet waving back and forth by the mantel as he tried to keep his balance." Now she was laughing. "And the TV; it's a miracle it survived."

On duty, we are not encouraged to join in an RP's merriment, lest they later forget, or regret, theirs and become outraged about ours. With some difficulty, I waited for her to stop and said, "One of the other items you lost was a backbend bench."

She glanced at the tiny room. "Oh, jeez, you didn't find that too, did you?"

I was going to give her the standard "Not yet, but we're still looking," but clearly that was not what she wanted to hear. "No."

She brightened. "Nor the massage chair, or the statue of Shiva?"

"Not yet." I would have noticed a leather recliner and a three-foot-tall image of an Indian god of destruction.

"Well, officer, thanks for all your effort. Who would have thought you'd still be working this case after all these years. We appreciate it. But we'll certainly understand if Jason's stuff doesn't turn up. To tell you the truth, he's gone on to other interests. I doubt he'd attempt a headstand now, even if he had the stool."

"And you'd be hard-pressed to make room for the massage chair, or even the Shiva."

It was a moment before she smiled, shrugged and agreed. But that moment said it all.

The next three victims, or wives of the bereft of golf clubs, ratty chairs, garden equipment, books of stamps barely used, aged racing bicycles, aged skis, enough exercise equipment to fill the YMCA, had clearly been warned. Their performances were not worthy of Berkeley Rep., but they'd have made the cut in many little theaters. They were delighted at our discovery, they assured me. Their husbands would be thrilled. They thanked me, thanked the burglary detail, the Berkeley Police Department, and the entire Berkeley criminal community that hadn't gotten around to fencing their conjugal wares.

I didn't believe a word of it.

Esme Olsen, a sturdy gray-haired woman nearer to seventy than sixty, looked as if my knock had jerked her out of another dimension. I found her in her basement folding gold foil carefully along the edges of a piece of teal glass cut in the shape of a tulip leaf. The sketch of the stained-glass panel she was working on was pinned to the wall above the glass cutter and extra foil rolls at the far end of the workbench. Irregularly shaped pieces of glass—red, yellow, green, and three shades of purple—filled the rest of the bench and larger sheets stood in specially made cases behind her. On the top of the cabinet was a photo—probably fifteen years old—of her and a white-haired man as happy-go-lucky as she was intense.

It was almost a formality when I asked, "How would you feel if I told you we're on the trail of your husband's tools: the drill bits, the straight saw, the jigsaw, the shag-toothed saws, the clamps, the hammers, and all?"

"Oh, my God! You're not bringing that junk back here?" No Berkeley Rep. role for her! And from the horror that lined her face as she looked around her stained-glass studio, I could picture the room in its previous incarnation.

"Your husband didn't do much work in this shop, did he?" It was a hunch, but a solid one.

"Work? No. Oh, he had intentions. He'd get on a kick about building bookcases. At one time we had six of them upstairs, more cases than books, I told him. Fortunately, they came apart before he could find things to fill them with. Then he thought he'd build a gazebo. He had wood stacked in the yard for a year, and kindling enough down here to cook the entire house. Then there was the hope chest, or more accurately hope*less* chest. For a while he bought used tables and chairs and thought he was going to refinish them. See, he liked the *idea* of woodworking better than the precision of it."

Some police officers never get suspects so naively open with the police. But I've dealt with enough artists in Berkeley to know that the shift from their total absorption in the visual takes a while, and as they cross the bridge from right brain to left brain, good sense can stumble over the railing. "So you gave yourself a Valentine's Day gift. You arranged for his stuff to be 'stolen.' "

She didn't answer. She'd zoomed to the other end of the bridge. And what she found there horrified her. I wouldn't have been surprised if this was the first time it truly struck her that she'd committed a crime.

The eight coconspirators had warned each other; why hadn't they told Esme Olsen? It made me a whole lot less sympathetic to them. I wanted to reassure Esme Olsen, but I couldn't do that until she answered the questions everyone who'd worked the case had. How did the nine conspirators know each other? We'd been over every possible connection between them. Where did they meet to conspire? Did they get together for afternoon tea and complaints, or drive to bars to map out their burglaries? And Rosamin Minton, how had she come to have the loot stashed at her house? "The police department takes a very dim view of false reporting."

Esme Olsen took a step back and actually looked even smaller than she was. "I didn't mean to get the police involved, honestly, Officer. I thought Harry would have left dealing with the police to me. I thought I'd just *tell* him I reported his stuff missing."

"Give me the names of the other women you planned this with."

She took another step back.

"Mrs. Olsen, you have broken the law. The police department has spent tens of hours investigating. We've had patrol officers, sergeants, and inspectors on this case. This is a serious matter. The names . . . ?"

She looked tinier, paler, older than at any moment since I arrived. In a small voice, she said, "I don't know."

"You planned an elaborate heist that took place over several years, Valentine's Day after Valentine's Day, and you're telling me you don't know the names of your coconspirators?"

"Yes." For an instant I thought she was going to explain that. Then she shut her mouth tight, like a little kid who'd rather be sent to her room than rat on her friends.

Friends who didn't deserve her sacrifice. "I'm afraid I'm going to have to take you to the station."

Her face scrunched in panic, but her question was not what I would have expected. "How long will that take?"

"Till your lawyer bails you out, Mrs. Olsen."

Her face fell. She really did look horrified. I wondered how long she had been hidden away down here, away from the realities of society.

"I've got to be back by quarter to four," she insisted plaintively. "I've got an appointment at the vet at four."

I'd seen everything from Airedales to Chihuahuas today. I realized now that this was the first house I'd visited where I hadn't been greeted by a dog. I hadn't even heard one barking in a back room. "I didn't see a dog?"

"When he's healthy he'll greet you at the gate. He's sick. On antibiotics. Oh, the vet says he'll be fine; and I believe him. I'm probably worrying for nothing, but my old dog died suddenly two years ago and I just don't want to take any chances now."

Now it all fell into place. I loved the idea of nine average Berkeley women who'd taken their spousal clutter into their own hands. A little service for each other. Personalized burglaries—we go to the address provided and steal only what you don't want. No wonder the televisions and compact disks, computers and diamond rings had been untouched while the wily "thieves" made off with aged hacksaws and headstand stools. Now I realized why her friends hadn't warned her. They hadn't seen her today. I smiled. "You weren't lying about not knowing their last names, were you?"

"Oh no. I wouldn't lie to the police."

"You all met at the dog run, right? And your dog was too sick to go out today."

She nodded.

"You could tell me the name of every one of their dogs, right, but you don't know their owners' names?" I knew enough about dog walking to understand that phenomena. By now, after years in the conspiracy, Esme Olsen might be able to call the humans by their first name, but she wouldn't have a clue about last names. "You can skip the women, just tell me what the dogs were called."

She looked puzzled, but so relieved she didn't question my demand. "Let me see, Lucy is the black Lab, and Sacha's the poodle. Then there's Emmet the yellow Lab pup, and Emily, she's mostly Tibetan terrier. And Hannah, the basset, and Sierra, he's a Chihuahua, and—wait a minute— oh, yes, MacTavish, the Scotty."

"And Val is your dog?"

She smiled before she realized she'd exposed her connection to Rosamin Minton.

Then she took me upstairs to see the whiskered brown mongrel with the white heart on his rump. He was a dog definitely on the mend.

"You went to a lot of trouble planning the burglaries. Why didn't you give the stuff to the Salvation Army?"

"Couldn't. That's where Harry shopped for the furniture to refinish. We never thought we'd be endangering Rosamin. She swore she didn't need that extra room. And she *did* need the twenty dollars a month we each gave her. And, Officer, it really did comfort her to know one of us would take Val when she died."

I smiled at her. We were still in the shadow of Valentine's Day, when acts of love are expected. And, I had to admit, there were a few items of Howard's for which I'd have hired Esme and colleagues. For his tenant's snake I'd have given them a bonus. Besides, the city wouldn't want to look ridiculous in court.

There'd be some paperwork and formalities with this case later. And after that I'd accept Howard's concession in the First Annual Collar Contest. But for now, I scratched Val gently behind one floppy ear, said, "Okay, Val, I'll leave you your mistress. Consider this your Valentine's gift," and smiled magnanimously.

Because, after all, magnanimity is a fitting quality for a queen.

Mark Twain

THE PINCHBUG
AND THE POODLE

The minister made a grand and moving picture of the assembling together of the world's hosts at the millennium when the lion and the lamb should lie down together and a little child should lead them. But the pathos, the lesson, the moral of the great spectacle were lost upon the boy; he only thought of the conspicuousness of the principal character before the onlooking nations; his face lit with the thought, and he said to himself that he wished he could be that child, if it was a tame lion.

Now he lapsed into suffering again, as the dry argument was resumed. Presently he bethought him of a treasure he had and got it out. It was a large black beetle with formidable jaws—a "pinchbug," he called it. It was in a percussion-cap box. The first thing the beetle did was to take him by the finger. A natural fillip followed, the beetle went floundering into the aisle and lit on its back, and the hurt finger went into the boy's mouth. The beetle lay there working its helpless legs, unable to turn over. Tom eyed it, and longed for it; but it was safe out of his reach. Other people uninterested in the sermon, found relief in the beetle, and they eyed it too. Presently a vagrant poodle-dog came idling along, sad at heart, lazy with the summer softness and the quiet, weary of captivity, sighing for change. He spied the beetle; the drooping tail lifted and wagged. He surveyed the prize; walked around it; smelt at it from a safe distance; walked around it again; grew bolder, and took a closer smell; then lifted his lip and made a gingerly snatch at it, just missing it; made another, and another; began to enjoy the diversion; subsided to his stomach with the beetle between his paws, and continued his experiments; grew weary at last, and then indifferent and absent-minded. His head nodded, and little by little his chin descended and touched the enemy, who seized it. There was a sharp yelp, a flirt of the poodle's head, and the beetle fell a couple of yards away, and lit on its back once more. The neighboring spectators shook with a gentle inward joy, several faces went behind fans and handkerchiefs, and Tom was entirely happy. The dog looked foolish, and probably felt so; but there was resentment in his heart, too, and a craving for revenge. So he went to the beetle and began a wary attack on it again; jumping at it from every point of a circle, lighting with his fore paws within an inch of the creature, making even closer snatches at it with his teeth, and jerking his head till his ears flapped again. But he grew tired once more, after a while; tried to amuse himself with a fly but found no relief; followed an ant around, with his nose close to the floor, and quickly wearied of that; yawned, sighed, forgot the beetle entirely, and sat down on it. Then there was a wild yelp of agony and the poodle went sailing up the aisle; the yelps continued, and so did the dog; he crossed the house in front of the altar; he flew down the other aisle; he crossed before the doors; he clamored up the homestretch; his anguish grew with his progress, till presently he was but a woolly comet moving in its orbit with the gleam and the speed of light.

At last the frantic sufferer sheered from its course, and sprang into its master's lap; he flung it out of the window, and the voice of distress quickly thinned away and died in the distance.

By this time the whole church was red-faced and suffocating with suppressed laughter, and the sermon had come to a dead standstill.

Orson Scott Card
(with Jay A. Parry)

IN THE DOGHOUSE

As Mklikluln awoke, he felt the same depression that he had felt as he went to sleep ninety-seven years ago. And though he knew it would only make his depression worse, he immediately scanned backward as his ship decelerated, hunting for the star that had been the sun. He couldn't find it. Which meant that even with acceleration and deceleration time, the light from the nova—or supernova—had not yet reached the system he was heading for.

Sentimentality be damned, he thought savagely as he turned his attention to the readouts on the upcoming system. So the ice cliffs will melt, and the sourland will turn to huge, planet-spanning lakes. So the atmosphere will fly away in the intense heat. Who cares? Humanity was safe.

As safe as bodiless minds can be, resting in their own supporting mindfields somewhere in space, waiting for the instantaneous message that *here* is a planet with bodies available, *here* is a home for the millions for whom there had been no spaceships, *here* we can once again—

Once again what?

No matter how far we search, Mklikluln reminded himself, we have no hope of finding those graceful, symmetrical, hexagonally delicate bodies we left behind to burn.

Of course, Mklikluln still had his, but only for a while.

Thirteen true planetary bodies, two of which co-orbited as binaries in the third position. Ignoring the gas giants and the crusty pebbles outside the habitable range, Mklikluln got increasingly more complex readouts on the binary and the single in the fourth orbit, a red midget.

The red was dead, the smaller binary even worse, but the blue-green larger binary was ideal. Not because it matched the conditions on Mklikluln's home world—that would be impossible. But because it had life. And not only life—intelligent life.

Or at least fairly bright life. Energy output in the sub- and supravisible spectra exceeded reflection from the star (No, I must try to think of it as the *sun*) by a significant degree. Energy clearly came from a breakdown of carbon compounds, just what current theory (current? ninety-seven-year-old) had assumed would be the logical energy base of a developing world in this temperature range. The professors would be most gratified.

And after several months of maneuvering his craft, he was in stationary orbit around the larger binary. He began monitoring communications on the supravisible wavelengths. He learned the language quickly, though of course he couldn't have produced it with his own body, and sighed a little when he realized that the aliens, like his own people, called their little star "the sun," their minor binary "the moon," and their own humble, overhot planet "earth" (terra, mund, etc.). The array of languages was impressive—to think that people would go to all the trouble of thinking out hundreds of completely different ways of communicating for the sheer love of the logical exercise was amazing—what minds they must have!

For a moment he fleetingly thought of taking over for his people's use the bipedal bodies of the dominant intelligent race; but law was law, and his people would commit mass suicide if they realized—as they would surely realize—that they had gained their bodies at the expense of another intelligent race. One could think of such bipedals as being almost human, right down to the whimsical sense of humor that so reminded Mklikluln of his wife (Ah, Glundnindn, and you the pilot who volunteered to plunge into the sun, scooping out the sample that killed you, but saved us!); but he refused to mourn.

The dominant race was out. Similar bipedals were too small in population, too feared or misunderstood by the dominant race. Other animals with appropriate populations didn't have body functions that could easily support intelligence without major revisions—and many were too weak to survive unaided, too short of lifespan to allow civilization.

And so he narrowed down the choices to two quadrupeds, of very different sorts of course, but well within the limits of choice: both had full access to the domiciles of the dominant race; both had adequate body structure to support intellect; both had potential means of communicating; both had sufficient population to hold all the encapsulated minds waiting in the space between the stars.

Mklikluln did the mental equivalent of flipping a coin—would have flipped a coin, in fact, except that he had neither hand nor coin nor adequate gravity for flipping.

The choice made—for the noisy one of greater intelligence that already had the love of most members of the master race—he set about making plans on how to introduce the transceivers that would call his people. (The dominant race must not know what is happening; and it can't be done without the cooperation of the dominant race.)

Mklikluln's six points vibrated just a little as he thought.

* * *

Abu was underpaid, underfed, underweight, and within about twelve minutes of the end of his lifespan. He was concentrating on the first problem, however, as the fourth developed.

"Why am I being paid less than Faisel, who sits on his duff by the gate while I walk back and forth in front of the cells all day?" he righteously said—under his breath, of course, in case his supervisor should overhear him. "Am I not as good a Muslim? Am I not as smart? Am I not as loyal to the Party?"

And as he was immersed in righteous indignation at man's inhumanity, not so much to mankind as to Abu ibn Assur, a great roaring sound tore through the desert prison, followed by a terrible, hot, dry, sand-stabbing wind. Abu screamed and covered his eyes—too late, however, and the sand ripped them open, and the hot air dried them out.

That was why he didn't see the hole in the outside wall of cell 23, which held a political prisoner condemned to die the next morning for having murdered his wife—normally not a political crime, except when the wife was also the daughter of somebody who could make phone calls and get people put in prison.

That was why he didn't see his supervisor come in, discover cell 23 empty, and then aim his submachine gun at Abu as the first step to setting up the hapless guard as the official scapegoat for this fiasco. Abu did, however, hear and feel the discharge of the gun, and wondered vaguely what had happened as he died.

Mklikluln stretched the new arms and legs (the fourness of the body, the two-sidedness, the overwhelming sexuality of it—all were amazing, all were delightful) and walked around his little spacecraft. And the fiveness and tenness of the fingers and toes! (What we could have done with fingers and toes! except that we might not have developed thoughttalk, then, and would have been tied to the vibration of air as are these people.) Inside the ship he could see his own body melting as the hot air of the Kansas farmland raised the temperature above the melting point of ice.

He had broken the law himself, but could see no way around it. Necessary as his act had been, and careful as he had been to steal the body of a man doomed anyway to die, he knew that his own people would try him, convict him, and execute him for depriving an intelligent being of life.

But in the meantime, it was a new body and a whole range of sensations. He moved the tongue over the teeth. He made the buzzing in his throat that was used for communication. He tried to speak.

It was impossible. Or so it seemed, as the tongue and lips and jaw tried to make the Arabic sounds the reflex pathways were accustomed to, while Mklikluln tried to speak in the language that had dominated the airwaves.

He kept practicing as he carefully melted down his ship (though it was transparent to most electromagnetic spectra, it might still cause comment if found) and by the time he made his way into the nearby city, he was able to communicate fairly well. Well enough, anyway, to contract with the Kansas City Development Corporation for the manufacture of the machine he had devised; with Farber, Farber, and Maynard to secure patents on every detail of the machinery; and with Sidney's carpentry shop to manufacture the doghouses.

He sold enough diamonds to pay for the first 2,000 finished models. And then he hit the road, humming the language he had learned from the radio. "It's the real thing, Coke is," he sang to himself. "Mr. Transmission will put in commission the worst transmissions in town."

The sun set as he checked into a motel outside Manhattan, Kansas. "How many?" asked the clerk.

"One," said Mklikluln.

"Name?"

"Robert," he said, using a name he had randomly chosen from among the many thousands mentioned on the airwaves. "Robert Redford."

"Ha-ha," said the clerk. "I bet you get teased about that a lot."

"Yeah. But I get in to see a lot of important people."

The clerk laughed. Mklikluln smiled. Speaking was fun. For one thing, you could lie. An art his people had never learned to cultivate.

"Profession?"

"Salesman."

"Really, Mr. Redford? What do you sell?"

Mklikluln shrugged, practicing looking mildly embarrassed. "Doghouses," he said.

Royce Jacobsen pulled open the front door of his swelteringly hot house and sighed. A salesman.

"We don't want any," he said.

"Yes you do," said the man, smiling.

Royce was a little startled. Salesmen usually didn't argue with potential customers—they usually whined. And those that did argue rarely did it with such calm self-assurance. The man was an ass, Royce decided. He looked at the sample case. On the side were the letters spelling out: "Doghouses Unlimited."

"We don't got a dog," Royce said.

"But you *do* have a very warm house, I believe," the salesman said.

"Yeah. Hotter'n Hades, as the preachers say. Ha." The laugh would have been bigger than one *Ha,* but Royce was hot and tired and it was only a salesman.

"But you have an air conditioner."

"Yeah," Royce said. "What I don't have is a permit for more than a hundred bucks worth of power from the damnpowercompany. So if I run the air conditioner more than one day a month, I get the refrigerator shut down, or the stove, or some other such thing."

The salesman looked sympathetic.

"It's guys like me," Royce went on, "who always get the short end of the stick. You can bet your boots that the mayor gets all the air conditioning he wants. You can bet your boots *and* your overalls, as the farmers say, ha ha, that the president of the damnpowercompany takes three hot showers a day and three cold showers a night and leaves his windows open in the winter, too, you can bet on it."

"Right," said the salesman. "The power companies own this whole country. They own the whole world, you know? Think it's any different in England? In Japan? They got the gas, and so they get the gold."

"Yeah," Royce agreed. "You're my kind of guy. You come right in. House is hot as Hades, as the preachers say, ha ha ha, but it sure beats standing in the sun."

They sat on a beat-up looking couch and Royce explained exactly what was wrong with the damnpowercompany and what he thought of the damnpowercompany's executives and in what part of their anatomy they should shove their quotas, bills, rates, and periods of maximum and minimum use. "I'm sick to death of having to take a shower at 2:00 A.M.!" Royce shouted.

"Then do something about it!" the salesman rejoindered.

"Sure. Like what?"

"Like buy a doghouse from me."

Royce thought that was funny. He laughed for a good long while.

But then the salesman started talking very quietly, showing him pictures and diagrams and cost analysis papers that proved—what?

"That the solar energy utilizer built into this doghouse can power your entire house, all day every day, with four times as much power as you could use if you turned on all your home appliances all day every day, for exactly zero once you pay me this simple one-time fee."

Royce shook his head, though he coveted the doghouse. "Can't. Illegal. I think they passed a law against solar energy thingies back in '85 or '86, to protect the power companies."

The salesman laughed. "How much protection do the power companies need?"

"Sure," Royce answered, "it's me that needs protection. But the meter reader—if I stop using power, he'll report me, they'll investigate—"

"That's why we don't put your whole house on it. We just put the big power users on it, and gradually take more off the regular current until you're paying what, maybe fifteen dollars a month. Right? Only instead of fifteen dollars a month and cooking over a fire and sweating to death in a hot house, you've got the air conditioner running all day, the heater running all day in the winter, showers whenever you want them, and you can open the refrigerator as often as you like."

Royce still wasn't sure.

"What've you got to lose?" the salesman asked.

"My sweat," Royce answered. "You hear that? My sweat. Ha ha ha ha."

"That's why we build them into doghouses—so that nobody'll suspect anything."

"Sure, why not?" Royce asked. "Do it. I'm game. I didn't vote for the damncongressman who voted in that stupid law anyway."

The air conditioner hummed as the guests came in. Royce and his wife, Junie, ushered them into the living room. The television was on in the family room and the osterizer was running in the kitchen. Royce carelessly flipped on a light. One of the women gasped. A man whispered to his wife. Royce and Junie carelessly began their conversation—as Royce *left the door open.*

A guest noticed it—Mr. Detweiler from the bowling team. He said, "Hey!" and leaped from the chair toward the door.

Royce stopped him, saying, "Never mind, never mind, I'll get it in a minute. Here, have some peanuts." And the guests all watched the door in agony as Royce passed the peanuts around, then (finally!) went to the door to close it.

"Beautiful day outside," Royce said, holding the door open a few minutes longer.

Somebody in the living room mentioned a name of the deity. Somebody else countered with a one word discussion of defecation. Royce was satisfied that the point had been made. He shut the door.

"Oh, by the way," he said. "I'd like you to meet a friend of mine. His name is Robert Redford."

Gasp, gasp, of course you're joking, Robert Redford, what a laugh, sure.

"Actually, his name *is* Robert Redford, but he isn't, of course, the all time greatest star of stage, screen, and the Friday Night Movie, as the disc jockeys say, ha ha. He is, in short, my friends, a doghouse salesman."

Mklikluln came in then, and shook hands all around.

"He looks like an Arab," a woman whispered.

"Or a Jew," her husband whispered back. "Who can tell?"

Royce beamed at Mklikluln and patted him on the back. "Redford here is the best salesman I ever met."

"Must be, if he sold you a doghouse, and you not even got a dog," said Mr. Detweiler of the bowling league, who could sound patronizing because he was the only one in the bowling league who had ever had a perfect game.

"Nevermore, as the raven said, ha ha ha, I want you all to see my doghouse." And so Royce led the way past a kitchen where all the lights were on, where the refrigerator was standing open ("Royce, the fridge is open!" "Oh, I guess one of the kids left it that way." "I'd kill one of my kids that did something like that!"), where the stove *and* microwave *and* osterizer *and* hot water were all running at once. Some of the women looked faint.

And as the guests tried to rush through the back door all at once, to conserve energy, Royce said, "Slow down, slow down, what's the panic, the house on fire? Ha ha ha." But the guests still hurried through.

On the way out to the doghouse, which was located in the dead center of the backyard, Detweiler took Royce aside.

"Hey, Royce, old buddy. Who's your touch with the damnpower-company? How'd you get your quota upped?"

Royce only smiled, shaking his head. "Quota's the same as ever, Detweiler." And then, raising his voice just a bit so that everybody in the backyard could hear, he said, "I only pay fifteen bucks a month for power as it is."

"Woof woof," said a small dog chained to the hook on the dog-house.

"Where'd the dog come from?" Royce whispered to Mklikluln.

"Neighbor was going to drown 'im," Mklikluln answered. "Besides, if you don't have a dog the power company's going to get suspicious. It's cover."

Royce nodded wisely. "Good idea, Redford. I just hope this party's a good idea. What if somebody talks?"

"Nobody will," Mklikluln said confidently.

And then Mklikluln began showing the guests the finer points of the doghouse.

When they finally left, Mklikluln had twenty-three appointments during the next two weeks, checks made out to Doghouses Unlimited for

$221.23, including taxes, and many new friends. Even Mr. Detweiler left smiling, his check in Mklikluln's hand, even though the puppy had pooped on his shoe.

"Here's your commission," Mklikluln said as he wrote out a check for three hundred dollars to Royce Jacobsen. "It's more than we agreed, but you earned it," he said.

"I feel a little funny about this," Royce said. "Like I'm conspiring to break the law or something."

"Nonsense," Mklikluln said. "Think of it as a Tupperware party."

"Sure," Royce said after a moment's thought. "It's not as if I actually did any selling myself, right?"

Within a week, however, Detweiler, Royce, and four other citizens of Manhattan, Kansas, were on their way to various distant cities of the United States, Doghouses Unlimited briefcases in their hands.

And within a month, Mklikluln had a staff of three hundred in seven cities, building doghouses and installing them. And into every doghouse went a frisky little puppy. Mklikluln did some figuring. In about a year, he decided. One year and I can call my people.

"What's happened to power consumption in Manhattan, Kansas?" asked Bill Wilson, up-and-coming young executive in the statistical analysis section of Central Kansas Power, otherwise known as the damnpower-company.

"It's gotten lower," answered Kay Block, relic of outdated affirmative action programs in Central Kansas Power, who had reached the level of records examiner before the ERA was repealed to make our bathrooms safe for mankind.

Bill Wilson sneered, as if to say, "That much I knew, woman." And Kay Block simpered, as if to say, "Ah, the boy has an IQ after all, eh?"

But they got along well enough, and within an hour they had the alarming statistic that power consumption in the city of Manhattan, Kansas, was down by forty percent.

"What was consumption in the previous trimester?"

Normal. Everything normal.

"Forty percent is ridiculous," Bill fulminated.

"Don't fulminate at me," Kay said, irritated at her boss for raising his voice. "Go yell at the people who unplugged their refrigerators!"

"No," Bill said. "*You* go yell at people who unplugged their refrigerators. Something's gone wrong there, and if it isn't crooked meter readers, it's people who've figured out a way to jimmy the billing system."

After two weeks of investigation, Kay Block sat in the administration building of Kansas State University (9–2 last football season, coming *that* close to copping the Plains Conference pennant for '98) refusing to admit that her investigation had turned up a big fat zero. A random inspection of thirty-eight meters showed no tampering at all. A complete audit of the local branch office's books showed no doctoring at all. And a complete examination of KSU's power consumption figures showed absolutely nothing. No change in consumption—no change in billing system—and yet a sharp drop in electricity use.

"The drop in power use may be localized," Kay suggested to the white-haired woman from the school who was babysitting her through the process. "The stadium surely uses as much light as ever—so the drop must be somewhere else, like in the science labs."

The white-haired woman shook her head. "That may be so but the figures you see are the figures we've got."

Kay sighed and looked out the window. Down from the window was the roof of the new Plant Science Building. She looked at it as her mind struggled vainly to find something meaningful in the data she had. Somebody was cheating—but how?

There was a doghouse on the roof of the Plant Science Building.

"What's a doghouse doing on the roof of that building?" asked Kay.

"I would assume," said the white-haired woman, "for a dog to live in."

"On the roof?"

The white-haired woman smiled. "Fresh air, perhaps," she said.

Kay looked at the doghouse awhile longer, telling herself that the only reason she was suspicious was because she was hunting for *anything* unusual that could explain the anomalies in the Manhattan, Kansas, power usage pattern.

"I want to see that doghouse," she said.

"Why?" asked the white-haired lady. "Surely you don't think a generator could hide in a doghouse! Or solar-power equipment! Why, those things take whole buildings!"

Kay looked carefully at the white-haired woman and decided that she protested a bit too much. "I insist on seeing the doghouse," she said again.

The white-haired woman smiled again. "Whatever you want, Miss Block. Let me call the custodian so he can unlock the door to the roof."

After the phone call they went down the stairs to the main floor of the administration building, across the lawns, and then up the stairs to the roof of the Plant Science Building. "What's the matter, no elevators?" Kay asked sourly as she panted from the exertion of climbing the stairs.

"Sorry," the white-haired woman said. "We don't build elevators into buildings anymore. They use too much power. Only the power company can afford elevators these days."

The custodian was at the door of the roof, looking very apologetic.

"Sorry if old Rover's been causin' trouble ladies. I keep him up on the roof nowadays, ever since the break-in attempt through the roof door last spring. Nobody's tried to jimmy the door since."

"Arf," said a frisky, cheerful looking mix between an elephant and a Labrador retriever (just a quick guess, of course) that bounded up to them.

"Howdy, Rover old boy," said the custodian. "Don't bite nobody."

"Arf," the dog answered, trying to wiggle out of his skin and looking as if he might succeed. "Gurrarf."

Kay examined the roof door from the outside. "I don't see any signs of anyone jimmying at the door," she said.

"Course not," said the custodian. "The burglars was seen from the administration building before they could get to the door."

"Oh," said Kay. "Then why did you need to put a dog up here?"

"Cause what if the burglars hadn't been seen?" the custodian said, his tone implying that only a moron would have asked such a question.

Kay looked at the doghouse. It looked like every other doghouse in the world. It looked like cartoons of doghouses, in fact, it was so ordinary. Simple arched door. Pitched roof with gables and eaves. All it lacked was a water dish and piles of doggy-do and old bones. No doggy-do?

"What a talented dog," Kay commented. "He doesn't even go to the bathroom."

"Uh," answered the custodian, "he's really housebroken. He just won't go until I take him down from here to the lawn, will ya Rover?"

Kay surveyed the wall of the roof-access building they had come through. "Odd. He doesn't even mark the walls."

"I told you. He's really housebroken. He wouldn't think of mucking up the roof here."

"Arf," said the dog as it urinated on the door and then defecated in a neat pile at Kay's feet. "Woof woof woof," he said proudly.

"All that training," Kay said, "and it's all gone to waste."

Whether the custodian's answer was merely describing what the dog had done or had a more emphatic purpose was irrelevant. Obviously the doghouse was not normally used for a dog. And if that was true, what was a doghouse doing on the roof of the Plant Science Building?

The damnpowercompany brought civil actions against the city of Manhattan, Kansas, and a court injunction insisted that all doghouses be disconnected from all electric wiring systems. The city promptly brought countersuit against the damnpowercompany (a very popular move) and appealed the court injunction.

The damnpowercompany shut off all the power in Manhattan, Kansas.

Nobody in Manhattan, Kansas, noticed, except the branch office of the damnpowercompany, which now found itself the only building in the city without electricity.

The "Doghouse War" got quite a bit of notoriety. Feature articles appeared in magazines about Doghouses Unlimited and its elusive founder, Robert Redford, who refused to be interviewed and in fact could not be found. All five networks did specials on the cheap energy source.

Statistics were gathered showing that not only did seven percent of the American public *have* doghouses, but also that 99.8 percent of the American public *wanted* to have doghouses. The 0.2 percent represented, presumably, power company stockholders and executives. Most politicians could add, or had aides who could, and the prospect of elections coming up in less than a year made the result clear.

The antisolar power law was repealed.

The power companies' stock plummeted on the stock market.

The world's most unnoticed depression began.

With alarming rapidity an economy based on expensive energy fell apart. The OPEC monolith immediately broke up, and within five months petroleum had fallen to 38¢ a barrel. Its only value was in plastics and as a lubricant, and the oil producing nations had been overproducing for those needs.

The reason the depression wasn't much noticed was because Doghouses Unlimited easily met the demand for their product. Scenting a chance for profit, the government slapped a huge export tax on the doghouses. Doghouses Unlimited retaliated by publishing the complete plans for the doghouse and declaring that foreign companies would not be used for manufacturing it.

The U.S. government just as quickly removed the huge tax, whereupon Doghouses Unlimited announced that the plans it had published were not complete, and continued to corner the market around the world.

As government after government, through subterfuge, bribery, or, in a few cases, popular revolt, were forced to allow Doghouses Unlimited into their countries, Robert Redford (the doghouse one) became even more of a household word than Robert Redford (the old-time actor). Folk legends which had formerly been ascribed to Kuan Yu, Paul Bunyan, or Gautama Buddha became, gradually, attached to Robert Doghouse Redford.

And, at last, every family in the world that wanted one had a cheap energy source, an unlimited energy source, and everybody was happy. So happy that they shared their newfound plenty with all God's creatures, feeding birds in the winter, leaving bowls of milk for stray cats, and putting dogs in the doghouses.

Mklikluln rested his chin in his hands and reflected on the irony that he had, quite inadvertently, saved the world for the bipedal dominant race, solely as a byproduct of his campaign to get a good home for every dog. But good results are good results, and humanity—either his own or the bipedals—couldn't condemn him completely for his murder of an Arab political prisoner the year before.

"What will happen when you come?" he asked his people, though of course none of them could hear him. "I've saved the world—but when these creatures, bright as they are, come in contact with our infinitely superior intelligence, won't it destroy them? Won't they suffer in humiliation to realize that we are so much more powerful than they; that we can span galactic distances at the speed of light, communicate telepathically, separate our minds and allow our bodies to die while we float in space unscathed, and then, at the beck of a simple machine, come instantaneously and inhabit the bodies of animals completely different from our former bodies?"

He worried—but his responsibility to his own people was clear. If this bipedal race was so proud they could not cope with inferiority, that was not Mklikluln's problem.

He opened the top drawer of his desk in the San Diego headquarters of Doghouses Unlimited, his latest refuge from the interview seekers, and pushed a button on a small box.

From the box, a powerful burst of electromagnetic energy went out to the eighty million doghouses in southern California. Each doghouse relayed the same signal in an unending chain that gradually spread all over the world—wherever doghouses could be found.

When the last doghouse was linked to the network, all the doghouses simultaneously transmitted something else entirely. A signal that only sneered at lightspeed and that crossed light-years almost instantaneously. A signal that called millions of encapsulated minds that slept in their mindfields until they heard the call, woke, and followed the signal back to its source, again at speeds far faster than poor pedestrian light.

They gathered around the larger binary in the third orbit from their new sun, and listened as Mklikluln gave a full report. They were delighted with his work, and commended him highly, before convicting him of murder of an Arabian political prisoner and ordering him to commit suicide. He felt very proud, for the commendation they had given him was rarely awarded, and he smiled as he shot himself.

And then the minds slipped downward toward the doghouses that still called to them.

"Argworfgyardworfl," said Royce's dog as it bounded excitedly through the backyard.

"Dog's gone crazy," Royce said, but his two sons laughed and ran around with the dog as it looped the yard a dozen times, only to fall exhausted in front of the doghouse.

"Griffwigrofrf," the dog said again, panting happily. It trotted up to Royce and nuzzled him.

"Cute little bugger," Royce said.

The dog walked over to a pile of newspapers waiting for a paper drive, pulled the top newspaper off the stack, and began staring at the page.

"I'll be humdingered," said Royce to Junie, who was bringing out the food for their backyard picnic supper. "Dog looks like he's readin' the paper."

"Here, Robby!" shouted Royce's oldest son, Jim. "Here, Robby! Chase a stick."

The dog, having learned how to read and write from the newspaper, chased the stick, brought it back, and instead of surrendering it to Jim's outstretched hand, began to write with it in the dirt.

"Hello, man," wrote the dog. "Perhaps you are surprised to see me writing."

"Well," said Royce, looking at what the dog had written. "Here, Junie, will you look at that. This is some dog, eh?" And he patted the dog's head and sat down to eat. "Now I wonder, is there anybody who'd pay to see a dog do that?"

"We mean no harm to your planet," wrote the dog.

"Jim," said Junie, slapping spoonfuls of potato salad onto paper plates, "you make sure that dog doesn't start scratching around in the petunias."

"C'mere, Robby," said Jim. "Time to tie you up."

"Wrowrf," the dog answered, looking a bit perturbed and backing away from the chain.

"Daddy," said Jim, "the dog won't come when I call anymore."

Impatiently, Royce got up from his chair, his mouth full of chicken salad sandwich. "Doggonit, Jim, if you don't control the dog we'll just have to get rid of it. We only got it for you kids anyway!" And Royce grabbed the dog by the collar and dragged it to where Jimmy held the other end of the chain.

Clip.

"Now you learn to obey, dog, cause if you don't I don't care what tricks you can do, I'll sell ya."

"Owrf."

"Right. Now you remember that."

The dog watched them with sad, almost frightened eyes all through dinner. Royce began to feel a little guilty, and gave the dog a leftover ham.

That night Royce and Junie seriously discussed whether to show off the dog's ability to write, and decided against it, since the kids loved the dog and it was cruel to use animals to perform tricks. They were, after all, very enlightened people.

And the next morning they discovered that it was a good thing they'd decided that way—because all anyone could talk about was their dog's newfound ability to write, or unscrew garden hoses, or lay and start an entire fire from a cold empty fireplace to a bonfire. "I got the most talented dog in the world," crowed Detweiler, only to retire into grim silence as everyone else in the bowling team bragged about his own dog.

"Mine goes to the bathroom in the toilet now, and flushes it, too!" one boasted.

"And mine can fold an entire laundry, after washing her little paws so nothing gets dirty."

The newspapers were full of the story, too, and it became clear that the sudden intelligence of dogs was a nationwide—a worldwide—phenomenon. Aside from a few superstitious New Guineans, who burned their dogs to death as witches, and some Chinese who didn't let their dogs' strange behavior stop them from their scheduled appointment with the dinnerpot, most people were pleased and proud of the change in their pets.

"Worth twice as much to me now," boasted Bill Wilson, formerly an up-and-coming executive with the damnpowercompany. "Not only fetches the birds, but plucks 'em and cleans 'em and puts 'em in the oven."

And Kay Block smiled and went home to her mastiff, which kept her good company and which she loved very, very much.

"In the five years since the sudden rise in dog intelligence," said Dr. Wheelwright to his class of graduate students in animal intelligence, "we have learned a tremendous amount about how intelligence arises in animals. The very suddenness of it has caused us to take a second look at evolution. Apparently mutations can be much more complete than we had supposed, at least in the higher functions. Naturally, we will spend much of this semester studying the research on dog intelligence, but for a brief overview:

"At the present time it is believed that dog intelligence surpasses that of the dolphin, though it still falls far short of man's. However, while the dolphin's intelligence is nearly useless to us, the dog can be trained as a valuable, simple household servant, and at last it seems that man is no longer alone on his planet. To which animal such a rise in intelligence will happen next, we cannot say, any more than we can be certain that such a change *will* happen to any other animal."

Question from the class.

"Oh, well, I'm afraid it's like the big bang theory. We can guess and guess at the cause of certain phenomena, but since we can't repeat the event in a laboratory, we will never be quite sure. However, the best guess at present is that some critical mass of total dog population in a certain ratio to the total mass of dog brain was reached that pushed the entire species over the edge into a higher order of intelligence. This change, however, did not affect *all* dogs equally—primarily it affected dogs in civilized areas, leading many to speculate on the possibility that continued exposure to man was a contributing factor. However, the very fact that many dogs, mostly in uncivilized parts of the world, were *not* affected destroys completely the idea that cosmic radiation or some other influence from outer space was responsible for the change. In the first place, any such influence would have been detected by the astronomers constantly watching every wavelength of the night sky, and in the second place, such an influence would have affected all dogs equally."

Another question from a student.

"Who knows? But I doubt it. Dogs, being incapable of speech, though many have learned to write simple sentences in an apparently mnemonic fashion somewhere between the blind repetition of parrots and the more calculating repetition at high speeds by dolphins—um, how did I get into this sentence? I can't get out!"

Student laughter.

"Dogs, I was saying, are incapable of another advance in intelligence, particularly an advance bringing them to equal intellect with man, because they cannot communicate verbally and because they lack hands. They are undoubtedly at their evolutionary peak. It is only fortunate that so many circumstances combined to place man in the situation he has reached. And we can only suppose that somewhere, on some other planet, some other species might have an even more fortunate combination leading to even higher intelligence. But let us hope not!" said the professor, scratching the ears of his dog, B. F. Skinner. "Right, B. F.? Because man may not be able to cope with the presence of a more intelligent race!"

Student laughter.

"Owrowrf," said B. F. Skinner, who had once been called Hihiwnkn on a planet where white hexagons had telepathically conquered time and space; hexagons who had only been brought to this pass by a solar process they had not quite learned how to control. What he wished he could say was, "Don't worry, professor. Humanity will never be fazed by a higher intelligence. It's too damn proud to notice."

But instead he growled a little, lapped some water from a bowl, and lay down in a corner of the lecture room as the professor droned on.

* * *

It snowed in September in Kansas in the autumn of the year 2000, and Jim (Don't call me Jimmy anymore, I'm grown up) was out playing with his dog Robby as the first flakes fell.

Robby had been uprooting crabgrass with his teeth and paws, a habit much encouraged by Royce and Junie, when Jim yelled, "Snow!" and a flake landed on the grass in front of the dog. The flake melted immediately, but Robby watched for another, and another, and another. And he saw the whiteness of the flakes, and the delicate six-sided figures so spare and strange and familiar and beautiful, and he wept.

"Mommy!" Jim called out. "It looks like Robby's crying!"

"It's just water in his eyes," Junie called back from the kitchen, where she stood washing radishes in front of an open window. "Dogs don't cry."

But the snow fell deep all over the city that night, and many dogs stood in the snow watching it fall, sharing an unspoken reverie.

"Can't we?" again and again the thought came from a hundred, a thousand minds.

"No, no, no," came the despairing answer. For without fingers of *some* kind, how could they ever build the machines that would let them encapsulate again and leave this planet?

And in their despair, they cursed for the millionth time that fool Mklikluln, who had got them into this.

"Death was too good for the bastard," they agreed, and in a world-wide vote they removed the commendation they had voted him. And then they all went back to having puppies and teaching them everything they knew.

The puppies had it easier. They had never known their ancestral home, and to them snowflakes were merely fun, and winter was merely cold. And instead of standing out in the snow, they curled up in the warmth of their doghouses and slept.

Bette Pesetsky

PENNY AND WILLIE

It came to Sylvester one day that his daughter Penny was always home before him when it rained. The realization surprised him. Was he particularly obtuse? He had been to the dentist that afternoon. Perhaps that was it—novocaine made him jumpy. Maybe it sharpened him too.

He was on the bus, the rain beating on the roof, the air warm and damp. At one stop schoolgirls flooded the bus with color, waves of little girls giggling, wearing Day-Glo-colored slickers and backpacks. They were eleven years old. He had a talent, an ability to assess the ages of little girls. He did this by comparing them to Penny. He suspected that this ability would atrophy in time. The girls moved to the back of the bus, shaking the water from their surrealistic backs. Pink, yellow-green, pure red.

Perhaps the sight of the girls triggered something. Some background thought he must have pushed away. The unimportant supplanting the important. He considered that. Wasn't that what he'd heard people did who were faced with terrible problems? This was not like that. This was just life. But still he had seen nothing. He was surprised. Because he loved his daughter. Therefore, why hadn't he noticed that Penny was always home before him when it rained. Penny regularly went to the library after school. Sylvester would be home for at least a half hour before she showed up—unless it was raining. The library wasn't on a bus line. She would have had to walk five blocks coming and going in the rain. Being home alone must have been preferable to that.

If he was right, then she would be waiting for him today. He could hear music coming from the apartment. He rang the bell instead of using his key. The music was loud, and Penny might not hear the door open, and he didn't want to startle her. He waited to see if she would use the peephole. That always worried him, but Penny looked through the hole and then opened the door. "Hi Daddy," she said. A book was draped across her arm—*Life in Ancient Rome*.

"Lower the music, please," Sylvester said. Penny made a face and crossed the room to the phonograph. She had her shoes off and Sylvester could see the blackened pads of her white socks. Her mother would look at them with distress. Joyce disliked dirty clothes. "Pigeon," Sylvester said. "How you doing, pigeon?"

"I turned on the oven already," Penny said, "like the note said. Start oven. Four hundred degrees. Turn on at five o'clock." She pushed back her long, dark hair.

My child, Sylvester thought, is such a thin pale girl. He would have to think through the significance of having realized Penny's unvarying schedule. He went to change his clothes before making the salad.

He always made the salad when Joyce printed *Salad* on the daily kitchen clipboard sheet. She never asked him to, but he did anyway. They ate out twice a week, more often if Joyce called up and said, "I'm bombed, dead, swept away." Then Sylvester would turn off the oven, and if a salad had been cut, he would empty the bowl into a plastic bag for the next day.

He started the salad, ripping up leaves of romaine and bits of chicory. Sylvester liked to put different ingredients in the salad, he experimented. Sometimes unsuccessfully, like the time he combined anchovies with bits of dried fig and scattered them among the greens; and once he had poured on red pepper flakes. No one had been able to eat those salads.

He sliced onions. Stupid, he had been stupid—worse than that. He had been unobservant of what was important. When had it rained last? A week ago—on Tuesday or maybe Wednesday. Penny had been home that afternoon too. Was that indicative of her life? When had the telephone rung for *her*—nor did Penny seem to go out regularly with friends on weekends. What about birthday parties? He was startled at the ache that arose, disturbing what he suspected must be his growing ulcer. He burned and at the same time felt the sensation of descending too quickly in an elevator. He poured a glass of milk and drank it slowly.

Sylvester designed jewelry. He had his own small office, was his own boss. He designed inexpensive, commercial-type jewelry. Once in a while he did something better—a single piece. A gift for someone, a client's wife or the client's girl friend. An artist, they would say, staring at a pin or earrings or a ring. A piece carefully crafted of excellent materials. That, Sylvester realized, was because they did not know any better. He was good—but that was it. He made gifts for Joyce and Penny too. Both had rings and necklaces and bracelets meticulously executed. He had taken particular pleasure in the intricate enamel design on Penny's locket, which she wore all the time. Vines and blue morning glories spelled her name, if you stared long enough at the pattern.

Sylvester always left his office at four to miss the heaviest evening rush. He was home first—unless it rained. Joyce didn't arrive home until after six. He knew that he would speak to Joyce about Penny being alone. But he mustn't mention it to Penny. Did she mind? Of course she must. Was she unpopular? He winced. He envisioned her living a life alone. The music from the living room continued.

*   *   *

He waited after Joyce came home, waited until she had settled down, told the day's anecdotes. They were together in the kitchen. She was adjusting the salad dressing. "Listen," he said softly, "I think Penny is alone too much. Lonely."

Joyce licked the traces of oil from her finger. "Lonely?" she said. "Why do you say that?"

"When it rains," Sylvester said. "She's always home. Like she has no other girls to spend her time with."

Joyce looked at him. "What do you want her to do? Stand outside in the rain?"

Sylvester shook his head. "I'm not joking. I want her to be with other kids."

"Maybe," Joyce said, "she prefers to be alone. Just before you hit the teens, it's funny sometimes. Many girls prefer to be alone. Penny is quiet, shy, maybe a touch bookish."

"Don't analyze her that way," Sylvester said.

"I'm not." Joyce became defensive. "But she seems fine to me. Good grades, good spirits."

Sylvester said no more, feeling moderately intimidated. Joyce, after all, had been an eleven-year-old girl. Joyce also was a clinical psychologist. However, he noticed at dinner that Joyce observed Penny more closely, asking questions about what she had done that day.

Sylvester's parents had both worked, but one or another always seemed to be around when he came home. Then too he had a sister. He had seldom come home to an empty house. When Penny was younger, they had paid a woman to pick her up from school and take her to a special play group. She was too old for that now. He suspected that she would be horrified at any suggestion that she couldn't take care of herself.

The decision to get a dog was impossible. It was impractical. Therefore, he didn't mention it to Joyce. Not that she disliked dogs. No, she always stopped to watch the antics of puppies in pet store windows. But he knew that if he spoke of it, they would discuss the matter and sanely resolve that it was wrong. He would have added to the discussion his own valid reasons why it was impossible.

He began to read the advertisements in newspapers of pets for sale. What he wanted, he realized, was a puppy, but not too young—one past infancy, one trained or almost trained, one not too big. Sylvester himself had never had a dog. Early each morning he began to call likely prospects in Manhattan. It was not easy. He thought he could discern who really wanted to unload an animal, the eagerness, the hard sell, the emphasis on pedigree. It was different with Willie. "I'm getting married," the owner said, "and she, the lady I'm going to marry, has two dogs already. Two old poodles, one is five years old, the other eight. She can't give them up. Willie is young, only six months."

Sylvester made an appointment and went up to the young man's apartment. That was a good sign, he felt, an apartment-raised dog. Willie was a bull terrier, a small white dog with random black spots, spunky, with a mock ferocious manner that ended with his thoroughly licking Sylvester's hand. "He's yours," the man said, "if you can give him a good home. He's a wonderful dog."

Sylvester squatted and petted Willie, and the dog bounced and danced beneath his touch. "I'll take him," Sylvester said. The man nodded, his hands jammed into his pockets. His reluctance reassured Sylvester, the man did not want to part with the animal. "Seventy-five dollars was the advertised price," Sylvester said. He didn't even bargain.

"Yes," the man said. He went to his desk. "Here," he said. "Papers. Willie has papers. I'll get his stuff." The man hooked a slightly nibbled black leash onto the dog's collar, and he gave Sylvester a large grocery bag with an open package of dry dog food inside, a ball with stripes, and a large orange plastic bowl coated around the rim with a crust of dried dog food. Sylvester and the man shook hands. "So long, Willie," the man said.

Willie saw the leash. He trembled in anticipation of a walk. Once on the sidewalk, Sylvester suddenly felt self-conscious. He was a man with a dog. The puppy strained the length of the leash. "No," Sylvester said and tugged back. "This way," he said, and Willie followed. Sylvester waited until he was a block away and then tossed the paper bag into a wire trash basket. It was foolish, he knew, throwing away the food and everything. But he planned to get everything fresh. Everything new for Penny. A red collar and leash, he decided. Would a taxi accept him and the dog? The driver didn't seem to care.

"A damn fool idea," Joyce whispered that evening. "What about our lease?"

"There are a dozen dogs in the building," Sylvester whispered back.

Penny was ecstatic, she was down on her knees as the dog enthusiastically leaped at her. "Mine?" she said. "Honestly, it's mine?"

"You bet," Sylvester said.

"Disease," Joyce said. "Does he have diseases?"

"No," Sylvester said. "Look at him—a perfectly healthy puppy."

"Has he got a name?" Penny asked.

The dog, pleased to be the center of attention, wiggled convulsively and moved from one to the other.

"He was called Willie," Sylvester said. "But he's your dog. We can call him any name you want."

For the next few days Penny tried several names but in exasperation she always ended with Willie. The dog answered to Willie. Joyce liked the dog. "I've nothing against him," she insisted. "He's a sweet dog. But Sylvester, this will prove to be impossible. The logistics of having a dog are impossible."

The trained puppy turned out to be less than half-trained. They put up infant's gates and kept him in the back hall when they were gone. He ate Joyce's plants, leaving only the stubby stalks. Sylvester took over the evening walks, because Penny should not be out wandering about that late. Scheduling became important. But after a month even Joyce admitted that the dog had done something for Penny. It gave her a companion, Sylvester knew. Despite Joyce's objections, Willie abandoned the hall and began to sleep in Penny's room, starting the night on the floor but ending up on the bed. An only child needs a pet, Sylvester said. Sometimes it seemed to Joyce that comment was directed at her.

* * *

Summers they rented a house on the Cape. That very first year they argued over the dog. The man they usually rented from said no animals. No matter how well behaved. No animals. They had to find a new cottage. Joyce blamed Sylvester. By the end of the summer they had accepted the new place, it was farther from the beach, but pets were allowed. Sylvester said that the next summer, if Joyce wanted, they would put Willie in a kennel.

Penny, always an early-to-rise child, became, during her fifteenth year, a late sleeper. It became harder and harder to get her up. Then once up, a quick sip of coffee and she was ready to leave. She had slimmed down considerably. I'll be late! had become the new battle cry of the family. Joyce took over walking Willie in the morning. It was not the dog's fault. The animal should not be made to suffer.

Penny, Sylvester noted, was more and more outgoing. She joined the drama society in high school, and they saw her perform in three plays. In her senior year she had the lead in *The Importance of Being Earnest.* They went to the Russian Tea Room for a celebration dinner, and Sylvester and Joyce gave Penny a strand of cultured pearls. She had become a lovely girl.

Then came the flurry of college catalogues. Penny was going to study drama. At least, Joyce said, she's staying on the East Coast. Sylvester was astonished—college already. Joyce was wholehearted about the preparations. Sylvester was pleased, watching Joyce and Penny giggle together over magazines filled with going-to-college clothes. Willie began to pant, became apprehensive, and if a suitcase was left open or the trunk lid was up, he would immediately climb inside and settle himself on the folded clothes. Baby, Penny would say, and the dog would rush towards her, Penny embracing him.

What you don't realize, Sylvester told clients at lunch, is that the child goes off to college but the dog stays behind. He had a repertoire of Willie stories. He and Joyce felt sorry for the dog. For the first two weeks after Penny left, Willie slept in the hall facing the door. At night he could be heard prowling the apartment, he had never been separated from Penny before for any length of time. "Poor thing," Joyce would murmur. "I wish he could understand that the holidays will be here soon. She'll be back home again."

But not for Thanksgiving, and how they had waited for Thanksgiving. Penny was in the college infirmary with influenza. Sick and lonely, she was crying when Sylvester and Joyce drove up to be with her, boarding the dog with the vet for the weekend. The infirmary served Thanksgiving dinner but Penny couldn't eat. Joyce and Sylvester ate their own dinner at a local coffee shop—the featured Turkey Special.

"There must be somewhere," Sylvester said, "a hugely profitable gravy factory that produces this institutional glue. Smell it! I mean everywhere the odor is the same—not coincidence—a great institutional gravy pot exists."

Joyce wept quietly at the table.

They planned for Christmas then, a feast, presents, tickets to a good show. And Penny came home four days before Christmas. When Willie saw her, his body quivered, and low throaty moans came from his chest. Penny dropped to her knees, and the dog washed her face with his tongue. Joyce and Sylvester just stood there. "Priorities," Sylvester said and smiled, he nudged Joyce.

At dinner Penny told them all about college life. Sylvester was surprised she had cut her hair. Penny hadn't mentioned that when they spoke on the telephone. The short hair made her look older.

The first morning Penny was home, Joyce dragged Sylvester out of bed, she put her finger to her lips to signal that he must be quiet, and led him to Penny's room. She pushed open the partially closed door. Sylvester stared at the bed. Willie was asleep in Penny's arms, his head buried in her shoulder. How young and vulnerable Penny and the dog looked.

There was a month of winter recess before Penny was due back at classes, but at the end of ten days she surprised Sylvester and Joyce by saying that she was going up to Vermont to go skiing with friends. They didn't even know that she knew how to ski. Penny hated sports. Now she laughed. I tried it out a couple of weekends, I seem to have a natural bent for it, she said. Joyce offered to buy her skis—other essentials. Penny said no. Her friend's family had plenty of stuff.

* * *

When Penny abandoned drama, Sylvester was not paying proper attention. There were problems at home. His fault, he knew. He had met the buyer for a small chain of women's specialty stores. She was newly divorced, in her late thirties, pretty, buoyant, witty. He had taken her to dinner several times. He made her a silver bracelet. She admired it extravagantly, but never once said it was an artistic creation. Sylvester respected her for that. It would be an affair soon, he realized. Joyce had begun to notice. It was in the middle of all this that Penny came home, unexpectedly arriving one March afternoon with one small suitcase. Penny had let her hair grow into a wild tangle of curls, she wore dangling gold earrings, long cotton skirts.

"What you look like," Joyce said angrily, "is a cheap imitation of a Gypsy."

"I'm sorry," Penny said, sitting in the living room absently petting Willie, "but your disappointment is not mine. I've got to give life a chance. I have no interest in school."

"Listen," Sylvester said, "you don't know what you're talking about."

Penny stared at him. "My opinions," she said, "are my opinions."

Neither Joyce nor Sylvester was able to dissuade her. It was her junior year—a year and a half to graduation. The young man Ted they met only briefly. The two of them were going to California to build something. The closest Penny came to softening was when she bade Willie good-bye. "I love you, Willie," she said. "I'll send for him when I settle."

Joyce never gave Sylvester an ultimatum. It was never her or me. It was simply that she got up one Saturday morning and said to Sylvester, "I would like you to leave, please." She was wearing a grey quilted robe, looking pale and disheveled.

"The politeness of it all," Sylvester said sarcastically. "We are so polite."

Joyce smiled. "If you prefer," she said. "Get the hell out of here!"

* * *

419

Sylvester moved into the buyer's apartment. The woman's name was Elaine. It was not a splendid affair. It turned out that she traveled most of the time, scurrying up and down the coast from Tampa to Boston. He was a stopover. What he had to do was find his own place, which he located through one of his metal fittings suppliers just at the time he and Joyce decided to file for divorce. He sublet from a man who was going to Japan for two years. The apartment was reasonably close to Sylvester's office, he could stay healthy by walking to work.

He and Joyce had returned to civilized relations. Once in a while he had dinner with her, usually after she had heard from Penny. If he was invited to the apartment, Willie would become tremendously excited. Sylvester was disturbed to notice that the dog seemed to be putting on weight, but he said nothing.

Penny wrote infrequently. It was mostly Joyce who received the postcards with their cryptic mentions of men, always new names; she sent Daddy her love, hugs for Willie.

One day Joyce called Sylvester at his office. Her voice was happy. "I have a letter from Penny—a genuine letter," she said. "Sylvester, she's decided to go back to school—the letter has a return address. She has an apartment! She's enrolled in UCLA. Anthropology, she writes. She's studying anthropology."

They felt relieved, joyous, she wasn't lost, she had come back, it was all worthwhile then. Sylvester knew that he should ask Joyce out, they should celebrate, but he was busy working on his spring line and he had recently met a very attractive young woman.

The year Penny graduated, Sylvester, checking to make certain that Joyce had no similar plans, flew out to L.A., and stayed a week. "Penny looks fine," he told Joyce when he got back. He had invited Joyce for drinks and sushi. She was catching a train, giving a talk in Boston. They had a few hours.

"But how does she *seem?*" Joyce asked. Joyce had gone to see her in L.A. three years before. Penny had said that emotionally she wasn't ready to come back East even for a visit.

"A bit heavier," Sylvester said. "Plans all made, though. Already enrolled in graduate school."

"And a man?" Joyce said. "I presume there's a man."

"Yes," Sylvester said, "a man is living in the apartment—a graduate student."

"You don't approve of this one," Joyce said. "I can hear that in your voice."

"He's all right," Sylvester said. "Nothing wrong with him—about her age I guess. Hard to know. I found him rather self-absorbed, a touch stolid."

Actually, both the man and Penny had bored the hell out of him the entire week.

Sylvester broke up with the girl named Madeleine the very month it became definite that the building where he now lived was going co-op. He didn't want to buy. He wasn't fond of living there. The question was, where to go? He had been toying with the idea of taking a year's sabbatical. Just closing up his business temporarily and going away, but that was fiscally dangerous. Customers were fickle, forgot you instantly.

Joyce called up and invited him to dinner. Come up to the apartment, she said, if you don't mind. Sylvester didn't mind. He selected a bottle of good burgundy and went. Willie barked on seeing him, a nervous sound. The black spots around his muzzle had sprouted grey hairs.

"Hush," Joyce said to the dog. "Hey hush."

"Hi old boy," Sylvester said, patting Willie, scratching him behind the ears. "How you doing, old fellow?"

"Open the wine," Joyce said. "Food's almost ready."

Sylvester waited patiently through the meal, he knew that Joyce must have a reason for inviting him. He listened to her conversation about her work, about her papers, about her successes in her department, she had taken an academic position.

"I have a monstrous request," she said finally, offering espresso in tiny cups with anisette and slivers of orange peel. "I will understand if you refuse, but I felt I had to ask."

"Shoot," Sylvester said.

"I'm going into the hospital," she said.

His heart pounded.

She raised her hand. "Not terrible, not fatal. A hysterectomy but nothing malignant—it just must be. And afterwards, I would like to go down to Fort Lauderdale to my sister's to convalesce, to recoup. With the hospital and the trip—we're talking about six weeks—maybe two months tops. The truth of it is—there's Willie. He's no young pup, you know. I could use the kennel like I do when there's a meeting or something. But two months—at his age—I don't know if he could survive."

Sylvester nodded.

"It's outrageous, I know," she said. "But could you possibly take him?"

The dog, hearing his name, had moved restlessly around the table. Sylvester looked down at him—a sweet, loyal dog. "You know how I feel about Willie. There's my apartment, though." Sylvester said. "No dogs, Joyce. Anyway, I'm planning to leave there. I'm looking right now. Otherwise I'd take him in a minute."

She hesitated. "Here," she said. "You could stay here. I mean if you're looking, I'll be away. I pay the doormen to walk Willie in the middle of the day. I do mornings and evenings—but for a few bucks more I'm certain they'll do the other walks too."

Here? Sylvester thought about it. He could leave his apartment, spend two months looking for a new place. He would certainly be comfortable in this apartment. "If the logistics can be worked out," he said. "I'll do it. And I don't mind the morning and evening walks—probably need the exercise."

They shook hands and agreed to discuss it further.

Sylvester sent over an embarrassing load of boxes. Stacked in Joyce's hall, they looked worse than they had in his apartment. Most of the furniture had been sold, but he was left with this. It's all right, Joyce soothed, anyway I won't be here to look at them. He had arrived the night before she was due to go to the hospital. It was the best he could manage. He slept that night in Penny's old room, on her bed. He was conscious of Joyce sleeping just across the hall, he thought he felt or heard her breathing. He wondered what would happen if he got up and crossed the hall. But he didn't dare, there had been no overtures, no expectations. He fell asleep.

He offered to stay home from the office the next morning and drive Joyce to the hospital. It's not necessary, she said. I'm not feeling like an invalid yet. Sylvester kissed her cheek. He would visit, he said. She nodded. Willie accompanied her to the door, saw that a walk with him wasn't planned, and returned to Sylvester's side.

Penny called during the week Joyce was in the hospital. "It's going just fine," he told her on the telephone, "nothing to worry about. Your mother is doing swimmingly well."

"Thank you, Daddy," Penny said.

Willie, wagging his tail, greeted Sylvester every morning. Sylvester would put on an old sweat shirt and pants and take the dog out for a walk. It was something of a pain, a drag. But Joyce had been doing it all these years, he shouldn't complain. The dog was getting old, he realized. A bit arthritic. He never jumped on Sylvester's bed. Sylvester had abandoned Penny's room for the master bedroom; there was, after all, a television in that room, and the bed was larger. He established a routine, the morning walk, the evening walk, the necessity for always checking to see that there was dog food. Willie was appreciative. Sometimes Sylvester thought he caught him sniffing around the bedroom as if on a hunt. Searching for Joyce, was he? Nevertheless, Willie was a warm companion.

Joyce didn't return to the apartment from the hospital. Sylvester offered his assistance, and this time she accepted. Despite his protests, she asked him to drive her directly to the airport, and she left for Florida.

Sylvester marked it down to curiosity, to concern, but he was ashamed of himself. He looked through the desk drawers, he read Joyce's letters. There was someone named Harold. He sent letters from many different places. There was an extensive correspondence with a Kenneth, but that seemed to be chiefly professional. There were other, more cryptic signs. He was also glad to see that Joyce was doing all right financially, she had never given that enough attention before. She had investments, some stock, and her income was adequate. Although he wasn't legally obligated, there had been no alimony requested—just child support.

Still, he felt responsible—he would never have let Joyce starve. But he needn't worry, he could see that she was all right.

After six weeks Joyce called him. "How's everything?" she said.

"Fine," he said.

"Willie?"

"Fit," he said. "Fine."

She spoke about the weather. "The thing is," she said finally, "would it be possible—would I be a terrible stinker—if I stayed another two weeks?"

"No," he said. He hadn't even started looking for an apartment, but he didn't say that. "The pup and I can easily hold down the fort."

"Thank you, Sylvester," she said. "I really appreciate it."

The woman he had been dating, the sister of one of his clients, found him an apartment in Washington Heights. He paid a premium for it, but it was decent. He had the place painted and then ordered a truck to pick up his boxes. He figured it best that he move out before Joyce arrived. She had his new address, and the superintendent accepted a package from UPS. Joyce had sent him a case of Florida oranges.

He made certain that Joyce's apartment was clean, vacuumed up the dog hair, stocked the refrigerator, checked the dog food supply. Joyce arrived at seven in the evening. She arrived by taxi, and she looked tanned and rested. Sylvester kissed her warmly.

"You look great," he said.

"Thank you," she said.

He saw her quickly examining the apartment. "I'm going to let you get unpacked and settled," he said. "I'll call you later."

"You've been wonderful," Joyce said. "You know I mean that."

"My pleasure," Sylvester said, and waved good-bye.

Willie, a constant of love, accompanied him to the door, and then, becoming aware that Sylvester was not carrying a leash, turned around and, without a backward glance, trotted down the hall to Joyce.

Dave Barry

YELLOW JOURNALISM

If you were to ask me, "Dave, what are the two words that summarize everything that you truly believe in, other than that beer should always be served in a chilled glass?" I would have to respond: "Dog obedience." I own two dogs, and they have both been trained to respond immediately to my voice. For example, when we're outside, all I have to do is issue the following standard dog command: "Here, Earnest! Here, Zippy! C'mon! Here, doggies! Here! I said come HERE! You dogs COME HERE RIGHT NOW!! ARE YOU DOGS LISTENING TO ME?? HEY!!!" And instantly both dogs, in unison, like a precision drill team, will continue trotting in random directions, sniffing the ground.

This is of course exactly what I want them to do. Dogs need to sniff the ground; it's how they keep abreast of current events. The ground is a giant dog newspaper, containing all kinds of late-breaking dog news items, which, if they are especially urgent, are often continued in the next yard. We live next to an aircraft-carrier-sized dog named Bear, who is constantly committing acts of prize-winning journalism around the neighborhood, and my dogs are major fans of his work. Each morning, while I am shouting commands at them, they race around and scrutinize the most recent installments of the ongoing Bear *oeuvre,* vibrating their bodies ecstatically to communicate their critical comments ("Bear has done it AGAIN!" "This is CLASSIC Bear!" etc.).

Of course you cannot achieve this level of obedience overnight. You have to take the time to understand dogs as a species, to realize that they have not always been peaceful domesticated animals who fulfill their nutritional requirements primarily by sidling up to the coffee table when you're not looking and snorking taco chips directly out of the bowl. Millions of years ago dogs were fierce predators who roamed in hungry packs; if some unfortunate primitive man got caught out in the open, the dogs would surround him, knock him to the ground, and, with saliva dripping from their wolflike jaws, lick him to within an inch of his life. "Dammit, Bernice!" he would yell to primitive woman. "We got to get these dogs some professional obedience training!" This is still basically the situation today.

We had our larger dog, Earnest, professionally trained by a very knowledgeable woman who came to our house and spent several hours commanding Earnest to "heel." Wouldn't it be funny if it turned out that animals actually had high IQs and understood English perfectly, and the only reason they act stupid is that we're always giving them unintelligible commands? Like, maybe at night in the stable, the horses stand around asking each other: "What the hell does 'giddyap' mean?"

But the trainer had no trouble getting Earnest to comprehend "heel." Her technique was to give commands in a gentle but firm voice; to consistently praise Earnest for obeying properly; and to every now and then, as a reminder, send 75,000 volts of electricity down the leash. At least that's how I assume she did it, because in no time she had Earnest heeling like Vice President Quayle. Whereas when *I* take Earnest for a "walk" I am frequently yanked horizontal by dog lunges of seminuclear force—Earnest could tow a bulldozer across Nebraska—so that my body, clinging desperately to the leash, winds up bouncing gaily down the street behind Earnest at close to the federal speed limit, like a tin can tied to a newlywed couple's car.

But "heel" is not the only obedience skill our dogs have mastered. They also know:

ANSWER THE DOOR—When a person, real or imagined, comes to our house, both dogs charge violently at the front door barking loudly enough to shatter glass, because they know, through instinct, that there is a bad guy out there and they *must protect the house.* So when we open the door, no matter who is standing there—a neighbor, a delivery person, Charles Manson holding a four-foot machete—the dogs barge *right past him* and race outside, looking for the bad guy, who for some reason is never there, a mystery that always causes the dogs to come to skidding four-legged stops and look around with expressions of extreme puzzlement. Foiled again! He's a clever one, that bad guy!

GO TO SCHOOL—The highlight, the absolute pinnacle, of our dogs' entire existence is riding in the car when we drive our son to school, an activity that gives them the opportunity to provide vital services such as barking at policemen and smearing dog snot all over the rear window. So every morning they monitor us carefully, and the instant we do something that indicates to them that our departure is imminent, such as we wake up, they sprint to the garage door and bark at it, in case we've forgotten where it is, then they spring back to us and bark some more, to let us know they're ready to go, and then they spring back to the garage door, then back to us, and so on, faster and faster, until they become barely visible blurs of negative-IQ canine activity rocketing through the house at several hundred revolutions per minute, and you can just imagine how difficult it can be for us to make them understand the concept of

"Saturday." One nonschool morning my wife felt so sorry for them that she went out in her bathrobe and drove them around the neighborhood for a while, looking for things they could bark at. So don't try to tell me dog training isn't worth it, OK? I can't hear you anyway, because there's a bad guy at the door.

Michael Bishop

DOGS' LIVES

All knowledge, the totality of all questions and all answers, is contained in the dog.

—Franz Kafka, "Investigations of a Dog"

I AM TWENTY-SEVEN: Three weeks ago a black Great Dane stalked into my classroom as I was passing out theme topics. My students turned about to look. One of the freshman wits made an inane remark, which I immediately topped: "That may be the biggest dog I've ever seen." Memorable retort. Two of my students sniggered.

I ushered the Great Dane into the hall. As I held its collar and maneuvered it out of English 102 (surely it was looking for the foreign language department), the dog's power and aloofness somehow coursed up my arm. Nevertheless, it permitted me to release it onto the north campus. Sinews, flanks, head. What a magnificent animal. It loped up the winter hillock outside Park Hall without looking back. Thinking on its beauty and self-possession, I returned to my classroom.

And closed the door.

TWENTY-SEVEN AND HOLDING: All of this is true. The incident of the Great Dane has not been out of my thoughts since it happened. There is no door in my mind to close on the image of that enigmatic animal. It stalks into and out of my head whenever it wishes.

As a result, I have begun to remember some painful things about dogs and my relationships with them. The memories are accompanied by premonitions. In fact, sometimes *I*—my secret self—go inside the Great Dane's head and look through its eyes at tomorrow, or yesterday. Every bit of what I remember, every bit of what I foresee, throws light on my ties with both humankind and dogdom.

Along with my wife, my fifteen-month-old son, and a ragged miniature poodle, I live in Athens, Georgia, in a rented house that was built before World War I. We have lived here seven months. In the summer we had bats. Twice I knocked the invaders out of the air with a broom and bludgeoned them to death against the dining room floor. Now that it is winter the bats hibernate in the eaves, warmer than we are in our beds. The furnace runs all day and all night because, I suppose, no one had heard of insulation in 1910 and our fireplaces are all blocked up to keep out the bats.

At night I dream about flying into the center of the sun on the back of a winged Great Dane.

I AM EIGHT: Van Luna, Kansas. It is winter. At four o'clock in the morning a hand leads me down the cold concrete steps in the darkness of our garage. Against the wall, between a stack of automobile tires and a dismantled Ping-Pong table, a pallet of rags on which the new puppies lie. Everything smells of dog flesh and gasoline. Outside, the wind whips about frenetically, rattling the garage door.

In robe and slippers I bend down to look at the furred-over lumps that huddle against one another on their rag pile. Frisky, their mother, regards me with suspicion. Adult hands have pulled her aside. Adult hands hold her back.

"Pick one up," a disembodied adult voice commands me.

I comply.

The puppy, almost shapeless, shivers in my hands, threatens to slide out of them onto the concrete. I press my cheek against the lump of fur and let its warm, faintly fecal odor slip into my memory. I have smelled this smell before.

"Where are its eyes?"

"Don't worry, punkin," the adult voice says. "It has eyes. They just haven't opened yet."

The voice belongs to my mother. My parents have been divorced for three years.

I AM FIVE: Our ship docks while it is snowing. We live in Tokyo, Japan: Mommy, Daddy, and I.

Daddy comes home in a uniform that scratches my face when I grab his trouser leg. Government housing is where we live. On the lawn in the big yard between the houses I grab Daddy and ride his leg up to our front door. I am wearing a cowboy hat and empty holsters that go *flap flap flap* when I jump down and run inside.

Christmas presents: I am a cowboy.

The inside of the house gathers itself around me. A Japanese maid named Peanuts. (Such a funny name.) Mommy there, too. We have a radio. My pistols are in the toy box. Later, not for Christmas, they give me my first puppy. It is never in the stuffy house, only on the porch. When Daddy and I go inside from playing with it the radio is singing "How Much Is That Doggy in the Window?" Everybody in Tokyo likes that song.

The cowboy hat has a string with a bead to pull tight under my chin. I lose my hat anyway. Blackie runs off with the big dogs from the city. The pistols stay shiny in my toy box.

On the radio, always singing, is Patti Page.

* * *

DOGS I HAVE KNOWN: Blackie, Frisky, Wiggles, Seagull, Mike, Pat, Marc, Boo Boo, Susie, Mandy, Heathcliff, Pepper, Sam, Trixie, Andy, Taffy, Tristram, Squeak, Christy, Fritz, Blue, Tammi, Napoleon, Nickie, B.J., Viking, Tau, and Canicula, whom I sometimes call Threasie (or 3C, short, you see, for Cybernetic Canine Construct).

"Sorry. There are no more class cards for this section of 102."

How the spurned dogs bark, how they howl.

I AM FOURTEEN: Cheyenne Canyon, Colorado. It is August. My father and I are driving up the narrow canyon road toward Helen Hunt Falls. Dad's Labrador retriever, Nick—too conspicuously my namesake—rides with us. The dog balances with his hind legs on the backseat and lolls his massive head out the driver's window, his dark mouth open to catch the wind. Smart, gentle, trained for the keen competition of field trials, Nick is an animal that I can scarcely believe belongs to us—even if he is partially mine only three months out of the year, when I visit my father during the summer.

The radio, turned up loud, tells us that the Russians have brought back to Earth from a historic mission the passengers of Sputnik V, the first two animals to be recovered safely from orbit.

They, of course, are dogs. Their names are Belka and Strelka, the latter of whom will eventually have six puppies as proof of her power to defy time as well as space.

"How 'bout that, Nick?" my father says. "How'd you like to go free-fallin' around the globe with a pretty little bitch?"

Dad is talking to the retriever, not to me. He calls me Nicholas. Nick, however, is not listening. His eyes are half shut against the wind, his ears flowing silkenly in the slipstream behind his aristocratic head.

I laugh in delight. Although puberty has not yet completely caught up with me, my father treats me like an equal. Sometimes on Saturday, when we're watching Dizzy Dean on *The Game of the Week,* he gives me my own can of beer.

We park and climb the stone steps that lead to a little bridge above the falls. Nick runs on ahead of us. Very few tourists are about. Helen

Hunt Falls is more picturesque than imposing; the bridge hangs only a few feet over the mountain stream roaring and plunging beneath it. Hardly a Niagara. Nick looks down without fear, and Dad says, "Come on, Nicholas. There's a better view on up the mountain."

We cross the bridge and struggle up the hillside above the tourist shop, until the pine trunks, which we pull ourselves up by, have finally obscured the shop and the winding canyon road. Nick still scrambles ahead of us, causing small avalanches of sand and loose soil.

Higher up, a path. We can look across the intervening blueness at a series of falls that drop down five or six tiers of sloping granite and disappear in a mist of trees. In only a moment, it seems, we have walked to the highest tier.

My father sits me down with an admonition to stay put. "I'm going down to the next slope, Nicholas, to see if I can see how many falls there are to the bottom. Look out through the trees there. I'll bet you can see Kansas."

"Be careful," I urge him.

The water sliding over the rocks beside me is probably not even an inch deep, but I can easily tell that below the next sloping of granite the entire world falls away into a canyon of blue-green.

Dad goes down the slope. I notice that Nick, as always, is preceding him. On the margin of granite below, the dog stops and waits. My father joins Nick, puts his hands on his hips, bends at the waist, and looks down into an abyss altogether invisible to me. How far down it drops I cannot tell, but the echo of falling water suggests no inconsequential distance.

Nick wades into the silver flashing from the white rocks. Before I can shout warning, he lowers his head to drink. The current is not strong, these falls are not torrents—but wet stone provides no traction and the Lab's feet go slickly out from under him. His body twists about, and he begins to slide inexorably through the slow silver.

"Dad! Dad!" I am standing.

My father belatedly sees what is happening. He reaches out to grab at his dog. He nearly topples. He loses his red golf cap.

433

And then Nick's body drops, his straining head and forepaws are pulled after. The red golf cap follows him down, an ironic afterthought.

I am weeping. My father stands upright and throws his arms above his head. "Oh my dear God!" he cries. "Oh my dear God!" The canyon echoes these words, and suddenly the universe has changed.

Time stops.

Then begins again.

Miraculously, even anticlimatically, Nick comes limping up to us from the hell to which we had both consigned him. He comes limping up through the pines. His legs and flanks tremble violently. His coat is matted and wet, like a newborn puppy's. When he reaches us he seems not even to notice that we are there to care for him, to take him back down the mountain into Colorado Springs.

"He fell at least a hundred yards, Nicholas," my father says. "At least that—onto solid rock."

On the bridge above Helen Hunt Falls we meet a woman with a Dalmatian. Nick growls at the Dalmatian, his hackles in an aggressive fan. But in the car he stretches out on the backseat and ignores my attempts to console him. My father and I do not talk. We are certain that there must be internal injuries. We drive the regal Lab—AKC designation Black Prince Nicholas—almost twenty miles to the veterinarian's at the Air Force Academy.

Like Belka and Strelka, he survives.

SNAPSHOT: Black Prince Nicholas returning to my father through the slate-gray verge of a Wyoming lake, a wounded mallard clutched tenderly in his jaws. The photograph is grainy, but the huge Labrador resembles a panther coming out of creation's first light: he is the purest distillation of power.

ROLL CALL FOR SPRING QUARTER: I walk into the classroom with my new roll sheets and the same well-thumbed textbook. As usual, my new students regard me with a mixture of curiosity and dispassionate calculation. But there is something funny about them this quarter.

Something *not right.*

Uneasily I begin calling the alphabetized list of their names: "Andy
. . . Blackie . . . Blue . . . Boo   Boo . . . Canicula . . . Christy
. . . Frisky . . ."

Each student responds with an inarticulate yelp rather than a
healthy "Here!" As I proceed down the roll, the remainder of the class
dispenses with even this courtesy. I have a surly bunch on my hands. A
few have actually begun to snarl.

". . . Pepper . . . Sam . . . Seagull . . . Squeak . . ."

They do not let me finish. From the front row a collie leaps out of
his seat and crashes against my lectern. I am borne to the floor by his
hurtling body. Desperately I try to protect my throat.

The small classroom shakes with the thunder of my students' barking, and I can tell that all the animals on my roll have fallen upon me
with the urgency of their own peculiar blood lusts.

The fur flies. Me, they viciously devour.

Before the lights go out completely, I tell myself that it is going to
be a very difficult quarter. A very difficult quarter indeed.

I AM FORTY-SIX: Old for an athlete, young for a president, maybe
optimum for an astronaut. I am learning new tricks.

The year is 1992, and it has been a long time since I have taught
freshman English or tried my hand at spinning monstrously improbable
tales. (With the exception, of course, of this one.) I have been to busy.

After suffering a ruptured aneurysm while delivering a lecture in
the spring of 1973, I underwent surgery and resigned from the English
Department faculty. My recovery took eight or nine months.

Outfitted with several vascular prostheses and wired for the utmost
mobility, I returned to the university campus to pursue simultaneous
majors in molecular biology and astrophysics. The GI Bill and my wife
and my parents footed the largest part of our expenses—at the beginning,
at least. Later, when I volunteered for a government program involving
cybernetic experimentation with human beings (reasoning that the tubes
in my brain were a good start on becoming a cyborg, anyway), money
ceased to be a problem.

This confidential program changed me. In addition the synthetic blood vessels in my brain, I picked up three artificial internal organs, a transparent skullcap, an incomplete auxiliary skeletal system consisting of resilient inert plastics, and a pair of removable visual adaptors that plug into a plate behind my brow and so permit me to see expertly in the dark. I can even eat wood if I have to. I can learn the most abstruse technical matters without even blinking my adaptors. I can jump off a three-story building without even jarring my kneecaps. These skills, as you may imagine, come in handy.

With a toupee, a pair of dark glasses, and a little cosmetic surgery, I could leave the government hospitals where I had undergone these changes and take up a seat in any classroom in any university in the nation. I was frequently given leave to do so. Entrance requirements were automatically waived, I never saw a fee card, and not once did my name fail to appear on the rolls of any of the classes I sat in on.

I studied everything. I made A pluses in everything. I could read a textbook from cover to cover in thirty minutes and recall even the footnotes verbatim. I awed professors who had worked for thirty–forty years in chemistry, physics, biology, astronomy. It was the ultimate wish-fulfillment fantasy come true, and not all of it can be attributed to the implanted electrodes, the enzyme inoculations, and the brain meddlings of the government cyberneticists. No, I have always had a talent for doing things thoroughly.

My family suffered.

We moved many, many times, and for days on end I was away from whatever home we had newly made.

My son and daughter were not particularly aware of the physical changes that I had undergone—at least not at first—but Katherine, my wife, had to confront them each time we were alone. Stoically, heroically, she accepted the passion that drove me to alter myself toward the machine, even as she admitted that she did not understand it. She never recoiled from me because of my strangeness, and I was grateful for that. I have always believed that human beings discover a major part of the meaning in their lives from, in Pound's phrase, "the quality of the affections," and Katherine could see through the mechanical artifice surrounding and buttressing Nicholas Parsons to the man himself. And I was grateful for that, too, enormously grateful.

Still, we all have doubts. "Why are you doing this?" Katherine asked me one night. "Why are you letting them change you?"

"*Tempus fugit.* Time's winged chariot. I've got to do everything I can before there's none left. And I'm doing it for all of us—for you, for Peter, for Erin. It'll pay off. I know it will."

"But what started all this? Before the aneurysm—"

"Before the aneurysm I'd begun to wake up at night with a strange new sense of power. I could go inside the heads of dogs and read what their lives were like. I could time-travel in their minds."

"You had insomnia, Nick. You couldn't sleep."

"No, no, it wasn't just that. I was learning about time by riding around inside the head of that Great Dane that came into my classroom. We went everywhere, everywhen. The aneurysm had given me the ability to do that—when it ruptured, my telepathic skill went too."

Katherine smiled. "Do you regret that you can't read dogs' minds anymore?"

"Yes. A little. But this compensates, what I'm doing now. If you can stand it a few more years, if you can tolerate the physical changes in me, it'll pay off. I know it will."

And we talked for a long time that night, in a tiny bedroom in a tiny apartment in a big Texas city many miles from Van Luna, Kansas, or Cheyenne, Wyoming, or Colorado Springs, or Athens, Georgia.

Tonight, nearly seventeen years after that thoughtful conversation, I am free-falling in orbit with my trace-mate Canicula, whom I sometimes call Threasie (or 3C, you see, short for Cybernetic Canine Construct). We have been up here a month now, in preparation for our flight to the star system Sirius eight months hence.

Katherine has found this latest absence of mine particularly hard to bear. Peter is a troubled young man of twenty, and Erin is a restless teenager with many questions about her absent father. Further, Katherine knows that shortly the *Black Retriever* will fling me into the interstellar void with eight other trace-teams. Recent advances in laser-fusion technology, along with the implementation of the Livermore-Parsons Drive, will no doubt get us out to Sirius in no time flat (i.e., less than four years for those of you who remain Earthbound, a mere fraction of that for us aboard the *Black Retriever*), but Katherine does not find this news at all cheering.

"*Tempus fugit,*" she told me somewhat mockingly during a recent laser transmission. "And unless I move to Argentina, God forbid, I won't even be able to see the star you're traveling toward."

In Earth orbit, however, both Canicula and I find that time drags. We are ready to be off to the small Spartan world that no doubt circles our starfall destination in Canis Major. My own minute studies of the "wobble" in Sirius' proper motion have proved that such a planet exists; only once before has anyone else in the scientific community detected a dark companion with a mass less than that of Jupiter, but no one doubts that I know what I am doing.

Hence this expedition.

Hence this rigorous, though wearying, training period in Earth orbit. I do not exempt even myself, but dear God, how time drags.

Canicula is my own dark companion. He rescues me from doubt, ennui, and orbital funk. He used to be a Great Dane. Even now you can see that beneath his streamlined cybernetic exterior a magnificent animal breathes. Besides that, Canicula has wit.

"*Tempus fugit,*" he says during an agonizingly slow period. He rolls his eyes and then permits his body to follow his eyes' motion: an impudent, free-fall somersault.

"Stop that nonsense, Threasie," I command him with mock severity. "See to your duties."

"If you'll remember," he says, "one of my most important ones is, uh, hounding you."

I am forty-six. Canicula-Threasie is seven.

And we're both learning new tricks.

I AM THIRTY-EIGHT: Somewhere, perhaps, Nicholas Parsons is a bona fide astronaut-in-training, but in this tributary of history—the one containing me now—I am nothing but a writer projecting himself into that grandiose wish-fulfillment role. I am an astronaut in the same dubious way that John Glenn or Neil Armstrong is a writer. For nearly eleven years my vision has been on hold. What success I have achieved in this tributary I have fought for with the sometimes despairing tenacity of my talent and a good deal of help from my friends. Still, I cannot keep from wondering how I am to overcome the arrogance of an enemy for whom I am only a name, not a person, and how dangerous any visionary can be with a gag in the mouth to thwart any intelligible recitation of the dream.

Where in my affliction is encouragement or comfort? Well, I can always talk to my dog. Nickie is dead, of course, and so is Pepper, and not too long ago a big yellow school bus struck down the kindly mongrel who succeeded them in our hearts. Now we have B.J., a furrow-browed beagle. To some extent he has taken up the slack. I talk to him while Katherine works and Peter and Erin attend their respective schools. B.J. understands very little of what I tell him—his expression always seems a mixture of dread and sheepishness—but he is a good listener for as long as I care to impose upon him; and maybe when his hind leg thumps in his sleep, he is dreaming not of rabbit hunts but of canine heroics aboard a vessel bound for Sirius. In my capacity as dreamer I can certainly pretend that he is doing so. . . .

A SUMMER'S READING, 1959: *The Call of the Wild* and *White Fang* by Jack London. *Bob, Son of Battle* by Alfred Ollivant. Eric Knight's *Lassie Come-Home*. *Silver Chief, Dog of the North* by someone whose name I cannot recall. *Beautiful Joe* by Marshall Saunders. *Lad, a Dog* and its various sequels by Albert Payson Terhune. And several others.

All of these books are on the upper shelf of a closet in the home of my mother and stepfather in Wichita, Kansas. The books have been collecting dust there since 1964. Before that they had been in my own little gray bookcase in Tulsa, Oklahoma.

From the perspective of my thirty-eighth or forty-sixth year I suppose that it is too late to try to fetch them home for Peter and Erin. They are already too old for such stories. Or maybe not. I am unable to keep track of their ages because I am unable to keep track of mine.

In any event, if Peter and Erin are less than fourteen, there is one book that I do not want either of them to have just yet. It is a collection of Stephen Crane short stories. The same summer that I was blithely reading London and Terhune, I read Crane's story "A Small Brown Dog." I simply did not know what I was doing. The title lured me irresistibly onward. The other books had contained ruthless men and incidents of meaningless cruelty, yes, but all had concluded well: either virtue or romanticism had ultimately triumphed, and I was made glad to have followed Buck, Lassie, and Lad through their doggy odysseys.

The Crane story cut me up. I was not ready for it. I wept openly and could not sleep that night.

And if my children are still small, dear God, I do not want them even to *see* the title "A Small Brown Dog," much less read the text that accompanies it.

"All in good time," I tell myself. "All in good time."

I AM TWELVE: Tulsa, Oklahoma. Coming home from school, I find my grown-and-married stepsister's collie lying against the curbing in front of a neighbor's house. It is almost four in the afternoon, and hot. The neighbor woman comes down her porch when she sees me.

"You're the first one home, Nicholas. It happened only a little while ago. It was a cement truck. It didn't even stop."

I look down the hill toward the grassless building sites where twenty or thirty new houses are going up. Piles of lumber, Sheetrock, and tar paper clutter the cracked, sun-baked yards. But no cement trucks. I do not see a single cement truck.

"I didn't know what to do, Nicholas. I didn't want to leave him—"

We have been in Tulsa a year. We brought the collie with us from Van Luna, Kansas. Rhonda, whose dog he originally was, lives in Wichita now with her new husband.

I look down at the dead collie, remembering the time when Rhonda and I drove to a farm outside Van Luna to pick him out of a litter of six.

"His name will be Marc," Rhonda said, holding him up. "With a *c* instead of a *k*. That's classier." Maybe it was, maybe it wasn't. At the time, though, we both sincerely believed that Marc deserved the best.

Because he was not a registered collie, Rhonda got him for almost nothing.

Now I see him lying dead in the street. The huge tires of a cement truck have crushed his head. The detail that hypnotizes me, however, is the pool of gaudy crimson blood in which Marc lies. And then I understand that I am looking at Marc's life splattered on the concrete.

At supper that evening I break down crying in the middle of the meal, and my mother has to tell my stepfather what has happened. Earlier she had asked me to withhold the news until my father has had a little time to relax. I am sorry that my promise is broken, I am sorry that Marc is dead.

In a week, though, I have nearly forgotten. It is very seldom that I remember the pool of blood in which the collie's body lay on that hot spring afternoon. Only at night do I remember its hypnotizing crimson.

175 YEARS AGO IN RUSSIA: One night before the beginning of spring I go time traveling—spirit faring, if you like—in the mind of the Great Dane who once stalked into my classroom.

I alter his body into that of a hunting hound and drop him into the kennels on the estate of a retired Russian officer. Hundreds of my kind surround me. We bay all night, knowing that in the morning we will be turned loose on an eight-year-old serf boy who yesterday struck the general's favorite hound with a rock.

I jump against the fence of our kennel and outbark dogs even larger than I am. The cold is invigorating. My flanks shudder with expectation, and I know that insomnia is a sickness that afflicts only introspective university instructors and failed astronaut candidates.

In the morning they bring the boy forth. The general orders him stripped naked in front of his mother, and the dog-boys who tend us make the child run. An entire hunting party in full regalia is on hand for the festivities. At last the dog-boys turn us out of the kennels, and we surge across the estate after our prey.

Hundreds of us in pursuit, and I in the lead.

I am the first to sink my teeth into his flesh. I tear away half of one of his emaciated buttocks with a single ripping motion of my jaws. Then we bear the child to the ground and overwhelm his cries with our brutal baying. Feeble prey, this; incredibly feeble. We are done with him in fifteen minutes.

When the dog-boys return us slavering to our kennels, I release my grip on the Great Dane's mind and let him go foraging in the trash cans of Athens, Georgia.

Still shuddering, I lie in my bed and wonder how it must feel to be run down by a pack of predatory animals. I cannot sleep.

APPROACHING SIRIUS: We eight men are physical extensions of the astrogation and life-support components of the *Black Retriever.* We feed on the ship's energy; no one must eat to stay alive, though, of course, we do have delicious food surrogates aboard for the pleasure of our palates. All our five senses have been technologically enhanced so that we see, hear, touch, smell, and taste more vitally than do you, our brethren, back on Earth.

Do not let it be said that a cybernetic organism sacrifices its humanity for a sterile and meaningless immortality. Yes, yes, I know. That's the popular view, but one promulgated by pessimists, cynics, and prophets of doom.

Would that the nay-sayers could wear our synthetic skins for only fifteen minutes. Would that they could look out with new eyes on the fierce cornucopian emptiness of interstellar space. There is beauty here, and we of the *Black Retriever* are a part of it.

Canicula-Threasie and the other Cybernetic Canine Constructs demonstrate daily their devotion to us. It is not a slavish devotion, however. Often they converse for hours among themselves about the likelihood of finding intelligent life on the planet that circles Sirius.

Some of their speculation has proved extremely interesting, and I have begun to work their suggestions into our tentative Advance Stratagem for First Contact. As Threasie himself delights in telling us, "It's good to be ready for any contingency. Do you want the tail to wag the dog or the dog to wag the tail?" Not the finest example of his wit, but he invariably chuckles. His own proposal is that a single trace-team confront the aliens without weapons and offer them our lives. A gamble, he says, but the only way of establishing our credibility from the start.

Late at night—as we judge it by the shipboard clocks—the entire crew gathers around the eerily glowing shield of the Livermore-Parsons Drive Unit, and the dogs tell us stories out of their racial subconscious. Canicula usually takes the lead in these sessions, and my favorite account is his narrative of how dog and man first joined forces against the indifferent arrogance of a bestial environment. That story seems to make the drive shield burn almost incandescently, and man and dog alike—woman and dog alike—can feel their skins humming, prickling, with an unknown but immemorial power.

Not much longer now. Sirius beckons, and the long night of this journey will undoubtedly die in the blaze of our planetfall.

I AM FIFTEEN: When I return to Colorado Springs to visit my father the year after Nick's fall from the rocks, I find the great Labrador strangely changed.

There is a hairless saddle on Nick's back, a dark gray area of scar tissue at least a foot wide. Moreover, he has grown fat. When he greets me, he cannot leap upon me as he has done in past years. In nine months he has dwindled from a panther into a kind of heartbreaking and outsized lapdog.

As we drive home from the airport my father tries to explain. "We had him castrated, Nicholas. We couldn't keep him in the house—not with the doors locked, not with the windows closed, not with rope, not with anything we tried. There's always a female in heat in our neighborhood and he kept getting out. Twice I had to drive to the pound and ransom him. Five bucks a shot.

"Finally some old biddy who had a cocker spaniel or something caught him—you know how gentle he is with people—and tied him to her clothesline. Then she poured a pan of boiling water over his back. That's why he looks like he does now. It's a shame, Nicholas, it really is. A goddamn shame."

The summer lasts an eternity.

* * *

443

TWENTY-SEVEN, AND HOLDING: Behind our house on Virginia Avenue there is a small self-contained apartment that our landlord rents to a young woman who is practice-teaching. This young woman owns a mongrel bitch named Tammi.

For three weeks over the Christmas holidays Tammi was chained to her doghouse in temperatures that occasionally plunged into the teens. Katherine and I had not volunteered to take care of her because we knew that we would be away ourselves for at least a week, and because we hoped that Tammi's owner would make more humane arrangements for the dog's care. She did not. She asked a little girl across the street to feed Tammi once a day and to give her water.

This, of course, meant that Katherine and I took care of the animal for the two weeks that we were home. I went out several times a day to untangle Tammi's chain from the bushes and clothesline poles in the vicinity of her doghouse. Sometimes I fed her, sometimes played with her, sometimes tried to make her stay in her house.

Some days it rained, others it sleeted. And for the second time in her life Tammi came into heat.

One night I awoke to hear her yelping as if in pain. I struggled out of bed, put on a pair of blue jeans and my shoes, and let myself quietly out the back door.

A monstrous silver-black dog—*was it a Great Dane?*—had mounted Tammi. It was raining, but I could see the male's pistoning silhouette in the residual glow of the falling raindrops themselves. Or so it seemed to me. Outraged by the male's brutality, I gathered a handful of stones and approached the two dogs.

Then I threw.

I struck the male in the flank. He lurched away from Tammi and rushed blindly to a fenced-in corner of the yard. I continued to throw, missing every time. The male saw his mistake and came charging out of the cul-de-sac toward me. His feet churned in the gravel as he skidded by me. Then he loped like a jungle cat out our open gate and was gone. I threw eight or nine futile stones into the dark street after him. And stood there bare-chested in the chill December rain.

444

For a week this went on. New dogs appeared on some nights, familiar ones returned on others. And each time, like a knight fighting for his lady's chastity, I struggled out of bed to fling stones at Tammi's bestial wooers.

Today is March the fifth, and this morning Katherine took our little boy out to see Tammi's three-week-old puppies. They have a warm, faintly fecal odor, but their eyes are open and Peter played with them as if they were stuffed stockings come to life. He had never seen anything quite like them before, and Katherine says that he cried when she brought him in.

I AM AGELESS: A beautiful, kind-cruel planet revolves about Sirius. I have given this world the name Elsinore because the name is noble, and because the rugged fairness of her seascapes and islands calls up the image of a more heroic era than any we have known on Earth of late.

Three standard days ago, seven of our trace-teams descended into the atmosphere of Elsinore. One trace-team remains aboard the *Black Retriever* to speed our evangelical message to you, our brethren, back home. Shortly we hope to retrieve many of you to this brave new world in Canis Major.

Thanks to the flight capabilities of our cybernetic dogs, we have explored nearly all of Elsinore in three days' time. We divided the planet into hemispheres and the hemispheres into quadrants, and each trace-team flew cartographic and exploratory missions over its assigned area. Canicula and I took upon ourselves the responsibility of charting two of the quadrants, since only seven teams were available for this work, and as a result he and I first spotted and made contact with the indigenous Elsinorians.

As we skimmed over a group of breaktakingly stark islands in a northern sea, the heat-detecting unit in Canicula's belly gave warning of this life. Incredulous, we made several passes over the islands.

Each time we plummeted, the sea shimmered beneath us like windblown silk. As we searched the islands' coasts and heartlands, up-jutting rocks flashed by us on every side. And each time we plummeted, our heat sensors told us that sentient beings did indeed dwell in this archipelago.

At last we pinpointed their location.

Canicula hovered for a time. "You ready to be wagged?" he asked me.

"Wag away," I replied.

We dropped five hundred meters straight down and then settled gently into the aliens' midst: a natural senate of stone, open to the sky, in which the Elsinorians carry on the simple affairs of their simple state.

The Elsinorians are dogs. Dogs very like Canicula-Threasie. They lack, of course, the instrumentation that so greatly intensifies the experience of the cyborg. They are creatures of nature who have subdued themselves to reason and who have lived out their apparently immortal lives in a spirit of rational expectation. For millennia they have waited, patiently waited.

Upon catching sight of me, every noble animal in their open-air senate began wagging his or her close-cropped tail. All eyes were upon me.

By himself Canicula sought out the Elsinorians' leader and immediately began conversing with him (no doubt implementing our Advance Stratagem for First Contact). You see, Canicula did not require the assistance of our instantaneous translator; he and the alien dog shared a heritage more fundamental than language.

I stood to one side and waited for their conference to conclude.

"His name translates as Prince," Canicula said upon returning to me, "even though their society is democratic. He wishes to address us before all of the assembled senators of his people. Let's take up a seat among them. You can plug into the translator. The Elsinorians, Nicholas, recognize the full historical impact of this occasion, and Prince may have a surprise or two for you, dear Master."

Having said this, 3C grinned. Damned irritating.

We nevertheless took up our seats among the Elsinorian dogs, and Prince strolled with great dignity onto the senate floor. The IT system rendered his remarks as several lines of nearly impeccable blank verse. English blank verse, of course.

PRINCE: Fragmented by the lack of any object
                Beyond ourselves to beat for, our sundered hearts
                Thud in a vacuum not of our making.
                We are piecemeal beasts, supple enough
                To look upon, illusorily whole;
                But all this heartsore time, down the aeons
                Illimitable of our incompleteness,
                We have awaited this, your arrival,
                Men and Dogs of Earth.
                    And you, Canicula,
                We especially thank for bringing to us
                The honeyed prospect of Man's companionship.
                Tell your Master that we hereby invite
                His kinspeople to our stern but unspoiled world
                To be the medicine which heals the lesions
                In our shambled hearts.
                    Together we shall share
                Eternity, deathless on Elsinore!

And so he concluded. The senators, their natural reticence overcome, barked, bayed, and bellowed their approval.

That was earlier this afternoon. Canicula-Threasie and I told the Elsinorians that we would carry their message to the other trace-teams and, eventually, to the people of Earth. Then we rose above their beautifully barbaric island and flew into the eye of Sirius, a ball of sinking fire on the windy sea's westernmost rim.

Tonight we are encamped on the peak of a great mountain on one of the islands of the archipelago. The air is brisk, but not cold. To breathe here is to ingest energy.

Peter, Erin, Katherine—I call you to this place. No one dies on Elsinore, no one suffers more than he can bear, no one suffocates in the pettiness of day-to-day existence. That is what I had hoped for. That is why I came here. That is why I sacrificed, on the altar of this dream, so much of what I was before my aneurysm ruptured. And now the dream has come true, and I call you to Elsinore.

Canicula and I make our beds on a lofty slab of granite above a series of waterfalls tumbling to the sea. The mist from these waterfalls boils up beneath us. We stretch out to sleep.

"No more suffering," I say.

"No more wasted potential," Canicula says.

"No more famine, disease, or death," I say, looking at the cold stars and trying to find the cruel one upon which my beloved family even yet depends.

Canicula then says, *"Tempus?"*

"Yes?" I reply.

"Fug it!" he barks.

And we both go to sleep with laughter on our lips.

TWENTY-SEVEN, AND COUNTING: I have renewed my contract for the coming year. You have to put food on the table. I am three weeks into spring quarter already, and my students are students like other students. I like some of them, dislike others.

I will enjoy teaching them *Othello* once we get to it. Thank God our literature text does not contain *Hamlet:* I would find myself making hideous analogies between the ghost of Hamlet's father and the Great Dane who haunted my thoughts all winter quarter.

I am over that now. Dealing with the jealous Moor again will be, in the terminology of our astronauts, "a piece of cake."

Katherine's pregnancy is in its fourth month now, and Peter has begun to talk a little more fluently. Sort of. The words he knows how to say include *Dada, juice,* and *dog. Dog,* in fact, is the first word that he ever spoken clearly. Appropriate.

In fifteen years—or eleven, or seventeen—I probably will not be able to remember a time when Peter could not talk. Or Erin, either, for that matter, even though she has not been born yet. For now all a father can do is live his life and, loving them, let his children—born and unborn—live their own.

"Dog!" my son emphatically cries. "Dog!"

Margaret Maron

SHAGGY DOG

What you have to understand is just how much Arthur MacHenry and Gillian Greber loved Emily, okay?

And each other, too, of course.

Arthur is the successful, hard-driving owner of an earth-moving company, and I suppose you could say that Gillian is his trophy wife. She is certainly twenty years younger, five shades blonder, and three sizes slimmer than his first wife, who let her hair go gray and started wearing slacks with elasticized waistbands about the time Arthur and Gillian met.

This is not to say that Gillian's a trinket to be dangled from any man's key ring. She's an equally hard-driving stockbroker who ruthlessly fought off several other fast-trackers for the MacHenry account when it was up for grabs, and she didn't permit herself to fall into Arthur's bed until she'd upped the return on his investments by several percentage points, okay?

Arthur as much her trophy as she his—trim, distinguished, and as utterly besotted with her as she with him—a marriage made in heaven and blessed by Wall Street.

But not by children.

On this point they were both clear: no kids. She claimed to have been born without a mommy gene and of his three grown children, one was into drugs, one was into a survivalist cult somewhere in Montana, and the third was convinced that her corporeal body was actually in an alien spacecraft on its way to Alpha Centauri and that what was still walking around on Earth was a telepathic projection.

As for his desire to take another swing at fatherhood, "Three strikes, I'm out," said Arthur.

The first few years of marriage were blissfully carefree. Their life-style was modestly lavish—a large Victorian jewel inside the beltway in the older part of town where hundred-year-old oaks arched above the streets, a weekly cleaning service, a yardman, catered meals that tasted almost homemade, She kept her name and job, his company won a major contract to clear and grade the land for a hundred-acre retirement village, and their combined personal portfolios topped the goal she'd set for them a whole year earlier than she'd planned. They scheduled quality time for each other in their calendars: they traveled when both could get away— Mexico or the Virgin Islands in the winter, wilderness adventures in the summer; they subscribed to the symphony; they attended the Episcopal church every Sunday morning and even based their tithes on actual in-come.

Until Emily showed up on their doorstep one day, they felt no lack in their lives. Once she was there, though, hoo-*boy!*

Overnight, those two objective, articulate, career-oriented adults morphed into baby-talking, overindulgent Mega-Mommy and Doting Daddy.

And for what?

Emily?

Even for a dog, she was a dog.

Beyond ugly.

Picture a thirty-pound cross between a spitz and a spaniel, with an uneven black and tan and yellow coat that had obviously been groomed with hedge trimmers. Picture hind legs slightly longer than the front ones so that she always looked ready to pounce. Picture the raggedy ears of a spaniel, the mouth of a Doberman, the nose of a poodle.

"Ah, but wook at dose big bwown eyes. Her's a shweetie, yes, her is," Gillian cooed, cupping the dog's homely face in her slender hand and kissing its poodle nose.

"Her's Daddy's clever widdle Emily," Arthur beamed as the dog obligingly fetched, shook hands or offered to share a squeaky rubber duck.

Clearly Emily was intelligent. I mean she *did* pick Gillian and Arthur's doorstep, didn't she? And she did know how to ingratiate herself instantly, didn't she?

Gillian and Arthur were smitten from the first, but being the decent, high-principled people they were, they tried not to become too attached too quickly. Such a lovable dog as this, they agreed, must have owners who would be grief-stricken to lose her. She wore no collar, so they notified the local animal shelter, put an ad in the Lost and Found column, and read every homemade LOST DOG sign they passed. They themselves posted a few FOUND signs at strategic crossings.

Nothing.

While they waited, Arthur bought a handsome red leather collar and leash so that they could safely walk her around the neighborhood and ask if anyone recognized her.

Still nothing.

Cautiously, Gillian bought a wicker basket with a goosedown cushion.

"Emily has to sleep somewhere."

"Emily?"

"She was always my favorite poet," Gillian said shyly.

That afternoon, Arthur visited the mall near his office and came home with a pair of beautifully engineered stainless steel food and water bowls and a leather-bound copy of Emily Dickinson's poetry.

"Something for both my girls," he said.

Both smothered him with kisses.

There was an upscale pet boutique near Gillian's office, and when an early frost was predicted the following week, she bought an expensive plaid coat and hat for Emily.

"The clerk said it was the MacHenry tartan," she told Arthur.

By Thanksgiving, it was as if they'd had Emily from puppyhood.

Gillian had never been particularly craftsy, but for Christmas, she knitted matching scarves for Arthur and Emily.

Not a week passed that one of them didn't bring Emily something special: buffalo hide chew bones, a raincoat, neckerchiefs, doggy shampoo, Velcro-tabbed boots to protect her paws from ice and salt, and dozens of toys.

Yellow rubber ducks were her favorite. She would toss them in the air, catch them in her Doberman teeth, and clamp down so quickly that the ducks seemed to give a surprised *quack.* Occasionally a startled Gillian or Arthur would step on one of the squeaky things by mistake, and Emily gave such a wolfish grin when they jumped that all three enjoyed the joke.

After a while they would find the ducks deliberately placed where they'd be sure to step on them. "What a clever girl, her is!" they exclaimed, and laughed together all the more.

Unfortunately, those sharp teeth meant a short life span for the ducks. As soon as the toy had too many tooth holes, Arthur would replace it so that Emily wouldn't choke on pieces of yellow rubber. The pet boutique began giving them discounts on ducks by the dozen.

In the year that followed, Emily's morning and evening walks introduced the MacHenrys to a different side of their neighborhood. There were the pleasures of being outside in all kinds of weather, of greeting the morning when it was dewy and fresh, of peeping through cozy lighted windows on frosty winter evenings or greeting the humans attached to

452

Spike and Goldie, a grumpy English bulldog and a sweet-tempered golden retriever.

(Spike's "daddy" invited Arthur to join his club. Goldie's elderly "mommy" turned out to hold the purse strings of a large cosmetics company that Gillian's company had been wooing. When Gillian walked in with the account, she was promoted to full partner.)

That summer, they took Emily hiking with them in the High Sierra. For walking sticks, they ordered a hand-carved alpenstock for Arthur and a sturdy little shepherd's crook for Gillian. From the same chi-chi outdoors catalog, they ordered a special salve to keep Emily's pads from cracking on the trail, a collapsible/inflatable water bowl and packets of freeze-dried sirloin.

The trip almost ended in disaster, though. On the second day out, Gillian glanced back to speak to Arthur and her foot came down on a twig.

Except that the twig writhed beneath her foot.

She looked down and froze as a young timber rattler gathered itself to coil for a strike.

Emily gave one sharp bark, then moved so rapidly that she was a blur of yellow, black, and tan. They could only watch in amazement as she slung the snake into the air as if it were a rubber duck, caught it by the tail and then slung it again so hard that it cracked like a whip and fell lifeless to the cliff below, broken and bloody.

"My God!" cried Arthur. "Are you all right, sweetheart?"

"She saved my life," said Gillian, throwing her arms around Emily. "Oh, you wonderful, brave baby!"

Since this trip had been planned before they found Emily, the MacHenrys were now firmly convinced that Fate had sent her to them as a guardian angel.

It was a lovely idyllic vacation after that and when the MacHenrys returned refreshed to town, they continued to carry their walking sticks on Emily's daily outings.

Living in one of the oldest, most historical sections of the city meant living not too far from some of the oldest, less desirable sections, and Goldie's owner had been mugged while they were away. She wasn't hurt, merely shaken up a bit, but it was enough to make everyone uneasy. A stout walking stick seemed a sensible precaution.

"Not that anyone would bother me with Emily," Gillian assured Arthur.

Golden retrievers were not much protection, Arthur agreed, and Goldie had lost most of her teeth anyhow; but Emily was young and assertive and her Doberman teeth were a formidable deterrent.

"Look at how she handled that rattler," they told each other. (The length and girth of the rattlesnake had increased with each telling of the story.)

So when Gillian went out that wet autumn night to walk Emily, she was not at first concerned with the man who stopped and stared at them from across the street as they passed beneath a corner light, even though the man's tight jeans and flashy jacket immediately signaled that he was not of this neighborhood.

Nor was she overly apprehensive when he turned and began walking along in the same direction as they, still staring.

When he crossed the street to intercept them, however, she shortened Emily's leash and tightened her grip on her sturdy shepherd's crook.

"Warty?" he said tentatively when he was only a few feet away.

"I beg your pardon?" said Gillian.

"I'll be damned," said the man. "It *is* Warty!"

He patted his thigh, inviting Emily to jump up on him. "Where you been, girl?"

Emily declined to jump, but neither did she growl as she normally would when Gillian drew back from strangers.

"That's my dog," said the man.

"*Your* dog?"

"Yeah. I lost her about a year ago. Right after we moved here." He gestured toward the east, where the large, carefully restored, turn-of-the-century homes gave way to a blue-collar neighborhood of bungalows and tract houses. "I figured Warty tried to get back to the guy up in Pennsylvania that gave her to me, but he said she never turned up. And here she is."

All the while he was talking, Gillian could feel him sizing her up, from her Italian boots to her English slicker.

"Can you prove this is the same dog?" she asked coldly.

The man snorted. "You kidding? You think there's another dog in the world like her, uglier than a warthog? It's Warty, all right. I'll show you. C'mon, Warty, shake hands."

Emily hesitated and then, with something very like a human sigh, she put out her paw.

Gillian felt her heart begin to break. Clearly the man spoke the truth, but just as clearly she knew she could not bear to give Emily up.

"Please," she said. "My husband and I—Could we buy her?"

"Gee, I don't know, lady." Again, that appraising stare.

"Oh, please. Any price. She's like a child to us and if you didn't have her long to begin with—"

"Five grand," the man said flatly.

'Five thousand dollars?" Gillian was taken aback. "But she's not purebred."

He gave a sardonic sneer. "She's one of a kind, lady, and that's the going rate. You give me five thou, I give you a bill of sale."

It was extortion pure and simple, and they both knew it, but then Gillian looked down at Emily, who was looking up at her with such beseeching, humiliated eyes.

"Very well," said Gillian. "If you want to come now, we'll—"

"No checks," the man said sharply. "Cash."

"Then it will have to be tomorrow," Gillian said, just as sharply. "We certainly don't keep that much on hand."

A light mist began to fall as they exchanged names and addresses. He was Mike Phipps and Gillian saw that he lived about six blocks to the east of them.

"My husband and I will be home after six tomorrow," she told him and started to move away, but he grabbed Emily's leash.

"We'll see you at six-thirty, then," he said and, despite her protests and pleas, he hauled Emily away with him.

Emily tried to resist, but Phipps gave the leash a vicious jerk and the dog reluctantly heeled.

* * *

The mist had turned to rain by the time Gillian returned home, but her tears were falling faster. Arthur lowered his newspaper as she came into the den, took one look at her distraught face, and hurried to her.

"Sweetheart, what's wrong? And where's Emily?" Images of wet pavement, bad brakes, and a small shaggy heap of fur lying limply in the gutter flashed through his mind. "She—she isn't hurt, is she?"

"No, she's fine, but oh, Arthur!"

Between her sobs, she told him all that had happened. Arthur was indignant and outraged at the man's effrontery. "But if she *is* his dog—?"

Gillian nodded. "She knew him when he spoke to her."

"Then we shall just have to pay him. Cheer up, sweetheart. It's only money, and if it brings her back to us—"

"But he was so awful. You can't know. Poor Emily. No wonder she ran away from him."

Arthur went to the bank next day, and that evening they both came home early. It had been an unhappy twenty-four hours, but soon it would be behind them.

The doorbell rang promptly at six-thirty. Mike Phipps was on time, but he came alone.

"Where's Emily?" Gillian asked anxiously as Arthur ushered him into the den.

Phipps just stood in the doorway. His hands were thrust into his jacket pockets, but his greedy eyes touched every lovely object in the room with a pawn-broker's cold assessment.

"Well, it's a funny thing. I got her home, and it's like I forgot how much a dog can add to a man's life, you know?"

Bewildered, Gillian could only stare, but construction work had kept Arthur at street level. "How much?" he asked.

Phipps grinned appreciatively. "I like a man that can cut straight through the crap. Ten thousand dollars."

Arthur laid a stack of bills on the polished oak table. "There's the five thousand you and my wife agreed on last night. Either take it and bring the dog back or get out because we won't pay a penny more."

"Oh, I think you will. Look at your wife, man."

Gillian was white-faced, but her sense of right and wrong was just as strong as Arthur's and her chin came up bravely. "We will not be blackmailed, Mr. Phipps. You have our phone number. When you are ready to honor the bargain we made, call us."

Yet thinking of poor Emily alone with this awful man who would probably chain her up outside with nothing but scraps to eat, Gillian gathered up some of the dog's possessions—her wicker basket with the goosedown cushion, a bag of her special food and some of her favorite toys.

Phipps took them with a sardonic sneer. "You don't fool me, lady. You're bluffing, the two of you. You said Warty's like your child? So just think of it as her adoption fee."

"Warty?" asked Arthur when Phipps was gone.

Tears spilled down Gillian's lovely cheeks and she shook her head. It was bad enough that she had to know why Emily's owner had given her that ugly name; she could at least spare Arthur that indignity.

Next evening, there was a message from Phipps on their answering machine when they got home. It was not a message they wanted to hear. The man sounded drunk.

"Somebody here's missing her mom and pop. Say hey to 'em, Warty. Speak . . . come on, dammit, speak!"

There was the sound of something falling, a muffled curse, and then Emily gave a sharp yelp of pain.

"Hear what she's saying? You don't come up with her adoption fees, I might decide to donate her to science. Knew a guy once that washed out of vet school when he operated on a dog and the dog died."

"Sweetheart, please," Arthur said, trying to loosen her hand from his.

Gillian looked down and saw that she'd squeezed his hand so tightly that her nails had left little red half-moons on his palm.

Both of them had read of the experiments done on dogs and cats over the years in the name of science and cosmetics. That Phipps could even consider it—!

"He's just trying to scare us," she said, with a shaky little laugh.

"Of course he is," Arthur agreed briskly. "Pathetic really, trying to make us think he'd pass up our offer and just give her away."

"We were merely firm with him yesterday, weren't we?" she asked, needing reassurance. "He wouldn't feel that we tried to emasculate him, would he?"

"So that he'd give up five thousand on principle? Believe me, love—when it comes to money, men like Phipps have no principles."

He said it with more conviction than he felt.

"Be brave, sweetheart. We cannot give in to extortion. He'll come around. You'll see."

But Phipps's message left them with little small talk, and after dinner Arthur murmured something about contracts that needed his attention in his den.

"Maybe I'll take a walk," said Gillian. "Unwind."

"Shall I come with you?"

She shook her head. "I think I need to be alone."

He nodded so understandingly that she felt like a complete fraud when she stepped out into the autumn night.

A low-pressure system had hung over the city all week, bringing intermittent showers that left the sidewalks adrift in fallen leaves. She had picked up her shepherd's crook by habit and was glad for its support when her feet nearly slipped out from under her on the wet leaves.

The damp night air was chilly, and as she reached into her slicker pocket for gloves, her hand brushed the thick envelope that she'd hidden there. If she went through with this, it would be the first time she'd ever gone behind Arthur's back and the thought of deceiving him pained her intensely.

But what if Arthur's wrong, she thought. What if this Phipps creature *did* mean to carry out his threat? Could she stand idly by and sacrifice Emily for their principles?

It was a simple plan. She would go to Phipps and throw herself on his mercy. "Arthur will never pay you another penny," she would tell him. Then she would give him the five thousand in cash, which she'd drawn out of her personal account this afternoon, and beg him to tell Arthur that he had decided to accept their original offer after all.

Phipps would get his ten thousand, Arthur would retain his principles, and Emily would come safely home.

A simple plan—and yet she couldn't bring herself to do it. Indeed, she spent the first twenty minutes walking in the opposite direction from Phipps's house. Eventually, though, her feet turned eastward and less than an hour after she'd left her home, she found herself staring into the front window of a small bungalow.

The curtain hadn't been drawn, but there was no light in the front room, merely a dim glow from somewhere beyond.

She went up onto the dark porch and pushed the bell button, but it appeared to be broken, so she knocked with more confidence than she actually felt.

Immediately, she saw Emily race into the room. As soon as the dog caught sight of Gillian, she seemed to go mad with joy, leaping up at the window, thrusting her little poodle nose through the mail slot, giving soft little yelps until Gillian slipped her gloved fingers under the brass flap.

But where was Phipps?

Gillian rapped again. With all the noise Emily was making, surely he must hear her?

Emily was whining now, begging Gillian to dissolve the barrier between them.

Helplessly, Gillian touched the old-fashioned latch and, to her surprise, the door swung open. Emily was all over her in an instant, jumping, dancing, racing in circles, tugging at her gloves.

"I know, lovey, I know," she whispered, calming the dog. "It won't be long, I promise."

A cold draft swirled through the house and suddenly, as if she'd forgotten an earlier appointment, Emily trotted across the dark room and into a narrow hall. After a moment of hesitation, Gillian followed, still clutching her shepherd's crook.

The light of the all-white bathroom dazzled her eyes at first. Emily was dancing in excitement again, and Gillian was dumbfounded by the man who crouched in front of the old-fashioned white porcelain sink. She gasped, and he pulled himself erect with the aid of his sturdy Alpenstock.

"Arthur?"

Then her eyes adjusted to the bright lights, and she saw that the dark object on the white-tiled floor beyond him was not a scrunched-up rug but the sprawled figure of Mike Phipps.

He lay face down in a puddle of blood.

Head wound, she thought automatically and looked at Arthur's stick.

"Is he—?"

"Yes."

"Oh, Arthur," she moaned.

For just a moment, his face was reproachful, as if it were her love of Emily and her love alone that had driven him to this.

"It's all right," he said decisively. "No one will think twice about it. They'll think he fell and cracked his skull on the sink or tub. An accident, pure and simple. My car's out back. I'll get Emily's basket, you find her leash and toys."

Quickly, efficiently, they cleared the house of all traces of Emily, then slipped the latch on both the front and the back doors and got in the car unnoticed by any of the neighbors.

Emily sat between them, blissfully happy even though her humans were silent on the circuitous drive home.

Gillian knew she should be shocked and appalled by what Arthur had done, but instead she felt an almost atavistic glow of pride. He was Man, she was Woman, and he had protected the clan of his cave with a primal club.

"Phipps was an evil man," Arthur said at last and reached past Emily to squeeze her hand.

"The world is better off without him," Gillian said, hoping that the squeeze she gave him in return would make it clear that she would never reproach him for this night.

He stopped on a deserted back road where there was a steep drop into a wooded ravine and reached into the back seat. A moment later, she heard the sharp crack of breaking wood, then the clatter of something hitting the rocks below.

But what—?

When Arthur got back into the car, she was touched to realize he was not quite as calm and efficient as he appeared. Somehow he had confused her shepherd's crook with his alpenstock. No matter, she told herself. She would take off early tomorrow evening, chop it into kindling with their camping hatchet and have a cozy fire warming their cave by the time Arthur came home.

Sex had always been good for them, but that night it was sensational.

Afterward, when they had let Emily back into their bedroom and all three were lying cozily in bed, Arthur said, "You didn't leave fingerprints anywhere, did you, sweetheart?"

"I had on gloves the whole time," she reminded him. "What about you?"

"I didn't touch anything except the doorknob and Phipps's neck to see if he was still alive." He pulled her closer with a satisfied sigh. "So we're safe then. Nobody will ever connect your crook to—"

She pulled upright. "My *crook?* But it was *your* alpenstock!"

"You mean you didn't—?"

"No. I thought it was you!"

"You mean it really *was* an accident?"

Curled up at the foot of their bed, Emily, the dog formerly known as Warty, sighed happily at the sound of her humans' laughter.

That last human hadn't laughed when his foot made her duck squeak. He jumped back, lost his balance, and fell heavily, and after that he never moved again. She certainly wouldn't want that to happen to *her* humans.

Something very like a resolution was forming in her homely, shaggy head: Never again would she leave a rubber duck where one of them might step on it.

If you can't be beautiful, then you'd better be smart.

Roger Caras

LIKE CATS
AND DOGS

If the story of the Thistle Hill
Regulars proves nothing else it should finally put to rest the expression
"They fought like cats and dogs." That is one of those concepts based on
partial, ancient truths that gets jammed into a folklore without benefit of
analysis and hangs there resisting all sense and all evidence that might
prove it wrong or at least modify it. By the sheer power of repetition, like
propaganda or a political slogan, it assumes the aura of fact. But aura isn't
evidence and fact requires rather more support than propaganda. Thus, in
time, fiction becomes conventional wisdom, but conventional wisdom is
seldom as wise as its name would seem to imply.

The facts are that the ancestors of our dogs, and our cats, too, were dedicated hunters. They still exist in their original forms, and they are still hunters working their respective habitats over for all they are worth. That means that they were and are as wild species fairly intolerant of each other. They are competitors, frequently after the same prey and the same serendipitous carrion. They also both like the same kind of cover where they can bear and raise their young. But when they are nearly matched in size it probably is a survival advantage for them to leave each other alone. No, not probably; it *is* a survival advantage.

Nature frequently does that, gives animals escape routes, white flags to wave to ward off fang-and-claw encounters. A mountain lion/wolf fight, although some producers might think it would make a terrific scene in a "nature" movie, would profit neither animal nor either species. Numbers can substitute for bulk, as with lions versus African hunting dogs in Africa. No five-hundred-pound lion, powerful as it is—and it *is* powerful—wants to tangle with six or eight sixty-pound African hunting dogs.

In nature the trick is not to win over another animal. That is a last resort when nothing else works. The goal is to survive (which usually means you are made of the right stuff) and reproduce. If that can be done without bloodshed not related to hunting, so much the better. Our own species is so bewilderingly violent that we constantly seek any hint of violence in nature to justify, perhaps, or explain ourselves. It is a fool's errand. We can neither explain nor justify how people who love Mozart can murder or maim, how people who appreciate Monet can rape babies, how people who value fine wine can engage in genocide. It really is a shame that as a footnote we try to protest, *"See, cats and dogs are like that, too."* But there is an enormous difference between getting dinner and having fun.

Dogs—wolves—indeed evolved as chasers with a pursuer's speed and stamina, and when something runs within their sight some dogs can be trigger-happy just as some cats can be. It is natural for dogs to chase, and our dogs are generally larger than our domestic cats. The results can indeed be catastrophic.

All that would seem to support that old conventional wisdom of domestic dogs and cats inevitably being at each other's throats. But that in turn would ignore the undeniable fact of domestication and all it entailed. Both dogs and cats have been changed dramatically by millennia of selective breeding, cats over the last four thousand years and dogs over an incredible time span of between fifteen and twenty thousand years. It is difficult to overstate the changes that much manipulation by purposeful selection can foster. Look at a Great Dane, a Chihuahua, a Bulldog, an Irish Setter, and a Shih Tzu. They are exactly the same species, manipulated into those specialized forms by unrelenting selection. Differences in behavior brought about by the same interferences are hardly less dramatic.

Earlier we discussed how cats have had to surrender that precious solitude built into every feline species except the lion, in order for them to fit into the style of living we have designed for ourselves and all the life forms that we control. I believe a demand has been made on both cats and dogs to coexist for exactly the same reason, to fit in with us. It isn't all that unreasonable a demand if you think about it: *"You guys can live with us and we'll pick up the tab, if you will only stop killing each other. And stop the noise!!"*

Dogs are wonderful hot-water bottles, and cats, once they have gotten the word, love to snuggle up with them. Now that Alice has come around, almost every cat here except Teddy (and he shows no difference at all in his attitude toward dogs and his approach to almost all cats) picks a dog at nap time or for the night and nestles in.

Lilly the Greyhound almost always has a cat and frequently holds it in her front paws as the two friends wash each other's face and ears. It really is lovely to watch, but in at least a couple of ways it represents our domination over both species. We took them from the wild, we molded them by baby-sitting their genes and forced them into entirely new patterns of behavior. That is not a negative statement, but at least let's recognize what is going on under our noses.

There is a chaise lounge in the top-floor sitting room here at the farm, and I have been doing a somewhat casual census of who is sleeping there. Every critter in the place seems to love it. My notes show: *Omari,*

Lilly and Topaz; Lilly and *Alice;* Xyerius, *Alice* and *Mary Todd Lincoln;* Topaz and *Xnard;* Topaz, Xyerius and *Xnard;* and *Omari, Alice* and Reggie. A census in our bedroom shows the same pattern, only there are usually more animals because there is a king-size bed. The average is two cats and two to three dogs. In any room open ad lib to animals it is the same. That is, of course, as long as Teddy, America's favorite male single-parent mother, is not there. The banquettes in the kitchen are usually the same way: dog, cat, person, cat.

We have never had a real cat-and-dog fight, not in thirty-nine years. Considering the number of cats and dogs involved, that must be some kind of record. We did have a catastrophe, though, and a really terrible time was had by all. It was a nightmare we shared in broad daylight. We had a Bulldog named Pudge who loved cats. She was *really* a hot-water bottle and our cats loved her right back. But Pudge, as her name implies (we got her in London where her real name, her kennel name, was Glynis Gay Girl), had a fondness for food that was without boundaries. It was monumental, in fact. For Pudge, insane gluttony was moderation. She was the Henry VIII of the hydrant set. She inhaled food; she worshiped it; her enthusiasm knew absolutely no limits.

On one occasion someone dropped a bit of something edible on the floor. I don't even remember what it was. Pudge and a new kitten arrived at the tidbit at the same time. Pudge snapped her jaws in reflex to assert her prior right to anything that was comestible. Her jaws were like a bear trap. The kitten died, its skull crushed. Clay and Pamela were young then, seven and ten, as I recall, and they both witnessed the whole thing. It was really bad for a while.

It was very difficult to explain to the children why they should not hate Pudge, that she didn't mean to really harm the kitten. How do you explain an animal's reflexive protection of food? The kids loved Pudge and saw the terrible thing they had witnessed as a betrayal. They were ambivalent, confused, and enormously saddened.

Pudge went to live with a lion and tiger trainer in Hollywood, and survived a full ten years, which has to be considered pretty good longevity for that breed. (Bulldogs are dwarfed Mastiffs and although no longer giants themselves, they share the Mastiff's short life span, as do all giant dogs.) She was a fantastic dog, a super, funny personality, but you never know when someone is going to drop a crumb or two. That is not what I would call a cat-and-dog fight. It was an accident. It is somewhat like smoking in bed. It is not arson, but a lot of people have died because someone else did it. What saddens me now is that I can't even remember the kitten's name. She had only been with us a few days, less than a week certainly. And then she died.

We have no misgivings about our cats and dogs together, inside the house or out. Aside from that one ugly incident with Pudge, we have never had anything like an actual fight. Any new dog that even looks inquiringly at a cat gets shouted down immediately. Dickens, the black Greyhound puppy, thought cats would be fun to chase. We didn't even get to complete his correction course. He tried it with Fluffy Louise, who landed a fistful of claws on his nose and made a sharp, explosive sound to go with the corrective gesture. Dickens got the message. He is fine with cats. Even when he had the not terribly bright idea of chasing them, his intention, I am sure wasn't blood, but fun. After all, no puppy or kitten ever stopped to ponder the possible consequence of a good romp. That is, not until they had been imprinted with an unforgettable experience.